THE LIBRARY
ST. MARY'S COLLEGE OF MARYLAND
ST. MARY'S CITY, MARYLAND 20686

Milton's Burden of Interpretation

Milton's Burden of Interpretation

Dayton Haskin

University of Pennsylvania Press
Philadelphia

This publication was assisted by a grant from the Trustees of Boston College.

Copyright © 1994 by the University of Pennsylvania Press
All rights reserved
Printed in the United States of America

Library of Congress Cataloging-in-Publication Data
Haskin, Dayton.
　Milton's burden of interpretation / Dayton Haskin.
　　p.　cm.
　Includes bibliographical references and index.
　ISBN 0-8122-3281-X
　1. Milton, John, 1608–1674—Religion.　2. Books and reading—
England—History—17th century.　3. Bible—Criticism,
interpretation, etc.　4. Bible—In literature.　I. Title.
PR3592.B5H37　1994
821'.4—dc20　　　　　　　　　　　　　　　93-50526
　　　　　　　　　　　　　　　　　　　　　　　　CIP

For my mother and father

Contents

Preface	ix
Texts and Abbreviations	xxi
1. Introduction: Finding a Place	1
2. The Parable of the Talents as Milton's Uneasy Place	29
3. Two Discontinuities in the History of Milton's Thinking About Places	54
4. Standing and Waiting in the Face of Indeterminacy	91
5. Conferring Places with Mary, Seeking Closure with Manoa	118
6. Keeping Secrets, Telling Secrets in *Paradise Regained* and *Samson Agonistes*	147
7. The Bookish Burden Before the Fall	183
Appendix: The Parable of the Talents (Matthew 25:14–30)	239
Notes	241
Bibliography	279
Index of Biblical Places	299
General Index	000

Then he which had receiued the one talent, came and said, Master, I knewe that thou wast an hard man, which reapest where thou sowedst not, and gatherest where thou strawedst not: I was therefore afraide, and went and hid thy talent in the earth. . . .
> —Matthew 25:24–25 (Geneva version)

When I consider how my light is spent,
    E're half my days, in this dark world and wide,
    And that one Talent which is death to hide,
    Lodg'd with me useless. . . .
> —Milton, Sonnet 19

Preface

From its earliest years the movement that we know as Protestantism encouraged an intensely personal way of reading. It took definitive shape in the experience and writings of Martin Luther. The general practice that grew out of this experience was aptly characterized in the advice that William Tyndale offered, out of Luther, to readers of the English Bible: "thinke that every sillable pertayneth to thyne awne silf." This encouragement of introspective reading was amplified by a further claim that "the storyes of the byble" provide "ensamples" of every human "case or state."[1] Tyndale's plan to put the English Bible into the hands of ordinary people proved astonishingly successful: by the time John Milton was born, in 1608, it was widely urged throughout England that the Bible be read "feelingly" and its message applied "experimentally." Reading for "experimental" knowledge was thought to involve testing one's spiritual experience against normative biblical patterns, to find a proper fit between the two. The general assumption was that readers would find precedents that confirmed their faith. This inward-looking reading was understood to be the principal locus of the operation of the Holy Spirit, whose special work was to enlighten the believer in the task of applying the Word of God to the heart.[2] But what if a reader should feel that a biblical "ensample" identifies his or her "case" with a "storie" that ends in "utter darkness"? This book began in a conviction that Milton's well-known sonnet, "When I consider . . . ," explores this question and works against as well as with the tradition of reading for "experimental" knowledge.

A good deal of recent scholarship, seeking to counter popular stereotypes about "puritanism" and Bible-reading, has called attention to the more beneficial consequences (for readers of both the seventeenth and the twentieth centuries) of attending to biblical language and paradigms. It is now common to place religious poetry written in England during the seventeenth century in relation to the broad tradition that descends from the magisterial reformers, and not uncommon to suppose that the doctrines of Luther and Calvin inspired a distinctive "poetics." For the most part critics who, ten and fifteen years ago, were extrapolating a so-called "Protestant poetics" were rather cheerful about it, proposing that it was connected to a general spread of literacy, or that it flourished with the dissemination of the right of individual interpretation, or that it entailed a distinctively literary approach to theology.³ Even oppositional critics intent to avoid reinscribing the poets' ideology have often left unchallenged the idea that Protestant doctrine contributed substantially to the flowering of religious literature.

My project does not call radically into question the existence of this "poetics." In fact, I take the demonstration that religious commitment is not necessarily inimical to poetic practice as a salutary challenge to the prejudice against attending to specifically religious aspects of this literature. My work on Milton has benefited from renewed alertness to features of his achievement that were largely hidden earlier in this century when emphasis on his "humanist" vision served to render his theology irrelevant. Yet, as the word "burden" in my title intimates, I am not entirely sanguine about those aspects of classic Protestant hermeneutics that encouraged introspective reading.

What has been little explored in recent revisionist criticism, from the point of view of its implications for the practice of poets, is the dismay that many readers felt once they opened their Bibles. A sense of intimidation was partly owing to material features of the printed Bible, its size and complexity, its layout and display of learning (more on this momentarily). It was also a function of the fact that the Book was to be "feelingly" read as a guide to salvation or damnation, and that it was thought to define the narrative possibilities for every person's life. It should seem especially curious, I think, that in extrapolating a Reformed poetics so little attention has been accorded to first-person narratives. These offer a good deal of evidence that ordinary readers in the period experienced considerable difficulties when they applied their Bibles "experimentally." Many conversion narratives of the mid-seventeenth century show graphically that particular biblical passages often served, as in the case of the man who feared that his talent had become useless, to predict the writer's damnation. *Grace Abounding to the Chief of Sinners* (1666) offers an extended, well known, and moving example. Like many who followed the popular advice to "thinke that every sillable" of the Bible "pertayneth to thyne awne silf," John Bunyan looked to biblical literature as a unified and coherent field made up of exemplary "places" with which to define his own case and predict his destiny. He tells how he was pinched very sore by one biblical passage, chased down the street by another, clapped on the back by a third. For years, Bunyan claims, he thought of himself as having converted too late, so that his "state" was defined by the "case" of Esau, who had been unable to find a saving "place."⁴

This book explores Milton's work as an interpreter both in relation to learned interpretive practices and in the context of popular reading habits of the sort manifested in *Grace Abounding*. My approach has drawn inspiration from Robert Darnton's proposal that literary theory, while it can uncover "the rhetorical constraints that direct reading without determining it," needs to be complemented by investigating, "within the limits of an imperfect body of evidence," what can be known about how readers read differently in the past. "By paying heed to history," Darnton has urged, "literary critics may avoid the danger of anachronism; for they sometimes seem to assume that 17th-century Englishmen read Milton and Bunyan as if they were 20th-century college professors."⁵ For the purposes of my study, this conjunction of writers is not merely casual: *Paradise Lost* was published in the year following the appearance of Bunyan's autobiography, and its last books offer an alternative interpretation of who the chief sinners were and of how grace abounded to them.

Inevitably, people in seventeenth-century England read in some ways that are no longer available to readers in our time. Yet Milton and Bunyan also read differently from one another; and my study begins by describing some ways of reading that were different from Milton's own. In the period when Milton's major poems appeared, there were widespread claims by readers that they had made a powerful interpretive breakthrough that had transformed their lives forever. By the 1650s such moments of radiant clarity and fullness were called by Quakers and others "openings." In proposing the relevance of this category to *Paradise Lost*, Georgia Christopher has provided, along with an approving estimation, an apt definition: "the 'opening' is a moment when the promise in a passage of scripture that has hitherto seemed dark, puzzling, or merely irrelevant, takes on clarity, certitude and — more important — a liberating application to one's immediate life situation."⁶ Many such experiences are reported in first-person accounts, which therefore show that this way of reading was likely to give rise to writing. One might say that increasingly Bible-readers were becoming, in a phrase used of Adam and Eve in *Paradise Lost* (III, 122), "authors to themselves."

Marshall Grossman has found in this phrase an epitome of the workings of Milton's epic. Extending work by Stephen Greenblatt and Anne Ferry concerning the ways in which some writings from the sixteenth century disclose the birth of a modern conception of selfhood, Grossman has argued that Milton's epic, written in a later period when conceptions of time and history had been significantly altered, shows the poet drawing on a fundamental analogy between "writing a narrative and living a life." Milton thus exploited the metaphorical possibilities of the concept of authorship more thoroughly than any previous writer. Grossman has carefully demonstrated that the narrative sequence of Milton's epic establishes "the temporal unfolding of human events" as a vast "signifying system in which the meaning of any human action is always provisionally anticipated in the act but ultimately deferred until the eschaton." He has also proposed that seventeenth-century English Protestants nonetheless thought that they could have access to the eschatological perspective from which any given action would be evaluated, since in the Bible their God had provided them with a master-text of providential paradigms. The Bible, Grossman asserts, provided a stable frame of reference in relation to which selves could be fashioned and moral actions evaluated.[7]

Widening the focus offered by Grossman and by proponents of a biblical poetics, my introductory chapter takes up the proposal in studies by Owen Watkins and Charles Cohen that "puritan autobiographies" show how individuals used biblical paradigms to fashion a "self."[8] Both the introduction and subsequent chapters consider abundant evidence, including evidence from Milton's own writings, that readers, although they regularly sought to make the Bible serve as a stable frame of reference, experienced substantial difficulties in getting it to do so. In the years when *Paradise Lost* was being composed, a providential interpretation of history had become richly problematic. Far from providing stability, the Bible was the object of repeated and thoroughgoing interpretive controversy. The more that his contemporaries claimed to be able to know and apply its meaning, the more evident it became to Milton that interpretation was an activity fraught with difficulties — and with opportunities. Dark and puzzling places have far greater prominence in *Paradise Lost* than can be accounted for by the category of "openings." Moreover, while "liberating applications" must have seemed to Milton highly desirable, "clarity" and "certitude" cannot be said to be prominent goals of the interpretive activity that informs his mature poems.

Evidence for the habits with which the English Bible was read in Milton's time comes from a range of materials, including poems and political tracts as well as narratives that we now call autobiographical, from "prophesyings" and other scriptural commentaries, and from a variety of devotional books. Biblical language infused all these sorts of writing and others, and its users were profoundly divided by their different readings of this common material. Because readers and hearers understood biblical language so variously, and writers and speakers used it so extensively, the history of interpretation constitutes a rich arena within which to explore the workings of Milton's interpretive energies.[9] To understand with imagination, and a measure of sympathy, Milton's entanglement in his society's habits of borrowing and reinflecting biblical language to define human experience is a challenge of a high order. It cannot be accomplished in any single book.[10]

This book is especially concerned with Milton's thinking about biblical "places," both specific "places" such as the parable of the talents, and biblical "places" generally, taken as a feature of the way in which the Word of God was thought to be mediated to readers. In this respect my project owes something to the revival of interest in the concrete shape and material layout of early modern books. Since the middle of the sixteenth century English Bibles were typically printed in a format that divided the entire collection into verses as well as chapters.[11] While this made for ease of reference, it also had other implications for readers' experiences; and I am especially interested in the spatial metaphor entailed in Bunyan's having identified his "case" with that of Esau, who according to Hebrews 12: 16–17 had been unable to find a "place." While the English "place" translates the Latin *locus* and ultimately the Greek *topos,* there was a slippage among ordinary readers like Bunyan who were looking for a particular "place" for themselves in what they took to be the Book of Life. Another sort of slippage showed up among scholastic divines when they sought to extract and dis-place proof-texts to support particular points of doctrine. At the end of the seventeenth century, attempting to diagnose what had gone wrong in seventeenth-century Bible reading, John Locke described the effects of printing biblical discourses not in flowing paragraphs but "crumbled into Verses, which quickly turn into independent Aphorisms." He pointed out that this visible "partitioning" had so badly "chop'd and minc'd" the Scriptures that both "the Common People" and "even Men of more advanc'd Knowledge" read them "Piece-meal," "by parcels, and in scraps," so that it had become increasingly difficult to discern "the Genuine Sense." "When the Eye is constantly disturb'd in loose sentences," Locke observed, "that by their standing and separation, appear as so many distinct Fragments; the Mind will have much ado to take in, and carry on in its Memory, an uniform Discourse of dependent Reasonings." He went on to locate in childhood the formation of the habit whereby discrete places are abstracted from the contexts that control their meaning: everyone is "from the Cradle . . . used to wrong Impressions concerning them, and constantly accustom'd to hear them quoted" out of context "without any limitation or explication of their precise Meaning, from the Place they stand in, and the Relation they bear to what goes before, or follows."[12]

Milton's Burden of Interpretation proposes that in the critical period 1643–45 Milton began radically to revise the thinking about biblical "places" that he had learned from the cradle. His divorce pamphlets display a new interest in discovering contextual "limitation" for what others took to be "distinct aphorisms" transparently applicable to human life. They evince, moreover, an increasing resistance to the widespread practice of fitting "places" into a standard narrative pattern, according to which one was to pass through a period of sin and guilt as a prelude to receiving abundant grace. In a society populated by large numbers of persons who thought that the Bible contained "places" that defined the "state or case" of every individual person, the New Testament passages condemning divorce were for Milton the opposite of an "opening": they threatened to fix both his eternal and his earthly destiny. When he sought to "open" the potentially damning texts for himself and to set them at a distance from his situation, he allowed himself to see contradictions in the text of the Bible, and he felt the strains of seeking to free himself from facile applications of biblical texts. This fundamentally altered his conception of the interpreter's task to which he had publicly committed himself only a few months earlier when he declared his ambition to be "an interpreter & relater of the best and sagest things" (*CPW,* I, 811).

The startling discontinuity in Milton's thinking about interpretive work is hidden by his own subsequent account, in *Defensio Secunda,* of his writings in the 1640s: giving his work a unified purpose, he characterizes himself as having defended in turn religious, domestic, and civil liberties. Yet the discontinuity was effectively identified by Arthur Barker when he pointed out that in *The Doctrine and Discipline of Divorce* (1643) "the proposed method of exegesis . . . bears a striking resemblance" to methods that in his prolusions and even as recently as *The Reason of Church Government* Milton had rather cavalierly dismissed. Milton himself described his new method when he insisted that "there is scarse any one saying in the Gospel, but must be read with limitations and distinctions to be rightly understood," for "Christ gives no full comments or continu'd discourses, but scatters the heavnly grain of his doctrin like pearle heer and there, which requires a skilful and laborious gatherer; who must compare the words he finds, with other precepts" (*CPW*, II, 338; 1st ed.). Following up on Barker's observation, Stanley Fish has proposed that in the divorce tracts Milton relocated the "plainness" of Scripture, which he had previously taken to be a property of the words themselves, projecting it into the intention of the Author. This, Fish has claimed, amounted to Milton's presuming to know the mind of God and implicated him in the sort of dangerous supplementation against which he had recently been arguing.[13] Be this as may be, Milton's acknowledgment that there are manifold contradictions in biblical literature made for new dispositions in his reading and for new inflections in his poetry; and these are a principal object of my study.

If Milton's own emphasis on continuity in his life served to disguise the momentousness of the change in his way of reading, it should be acknowledged that biographers and critics have also done a good deal to create a picture of Milton's "development." Chapter Two examines the habit, which dates to the seventeenth century, of thinking that the parable of the talents (see Appendix) was Milton's "place," and traces the ways in which Milton's life has been constructed to render it a glorious fulfillment of the parable. Besides proposing ways in which a particular biblical text was, and was not, Milton's "place," this chapter also lays groundwork for other parts of the book. Chapter Three then attempts to isolate two principal discontinuities in Milton's history as an interpreter of biblical "places": not only the glaring discontinuity identified by Barker, but a subtler discontinuity arising out of Milton's rejection of the ways in which his contemporaries routinely appealed to "the analogy of faith" to keep biblical interpretation safely within traditional boundaries. This chapter situates Milton's interpretive work in relation to linguistic, historiographical, and critical developments of the middle decades of the century, a time of many important advances in biblical scholarship. Besides the rabbinical learning made available by John Selden, which Jason Rosenblatt has richly documented in its relation to Milton,[14] the period witnessed the publication of much valuable scholarship, including John Lightfoot's harmonies (1644–57), the *Biblia Polyglotta* (1653–57), and the massive variorum commentary, *Critici sacri* (1660).

The chapters that follow then investigate how Milton's writings involve an engagement with, and revision of, both learned and popular strategies for reading. In Chapter Four I build on research concerning the history of interpreting the parable of the talents to show that it is inaccurate and anachronistic to suppose that Milton readily found in the biblical concept of "talent" a stable frame of reference in relation to which he might define his poetic creativity.¹⁵ This central chapter treats various ways in which the sonnet "When I consider . . ." plays controversial "places" off one another: even more than the early sonnet "How soon hath time . . . ," this crucial poem unsettles conventional ways of thinking about how biblical texts can be "applied" to contemporary life. The final three chapters attempt to work out some implications of the argument that the fictional audiences inscribed in the mature biblical poems were partly made out of the poet's familiarity with real, if limited, readers who were accustomed to thinking of the Bible as a compendium of "places." In describing how Milton's interpretive work informs the poems, these chapters swerve away from the influential theory according to which he is seen as humiliating his readers. In some ways they contribute to the important project, identified by John Peter Rumrich, of "uninventing" a picture of the poet that has influenced the popular idea of "Milton" for a generation.¹⁶ The entrenched practice of framing Milton as "required reading" needs to be replaced by a recognition that his biblical poems invite intelligent scrutiny of the poet's work as an interpreter. In each of these poems, and differently in each, the poet represents himself as interpreting and relating materials to which every reader may have equal and independent access, in fulfillment of Tyndale's goal of making the Bible generally available. The readers addressed by each poem are to observe and evaluate the poet's interpretive performances.

My attempt to identify discontinuities in Milton's own history as a reader necessarily entails a biographical argument, and a further word about the arrangement of materials in Chapters Five, Six, and Seven is therefore in order. The organization of these chapters expresses dissent from a prevailing tendency to induct Milton's *œuvres* into a conventional narrative about the "progress" of intellectual history from his time to our own, and resists the idea that reading the major poems in chronological order from 1667 to 1671 reveals a "progress" in Milton's personal history. It is no part of my purpose to trace a single path through Milton's interpretive practice in the 1660s and 1670s. In particular I do not share the assumptions of critics who wish to make his poetry tell a story that follows from *Paradise Lost* through *Paradise Regained* to a final "statement" in *Samson Agonistes*. I have not sought to claim that Milton's writing illustrates some sort of teleological "development." I see the three major poems on biblical subjects as belonging in interestingly various ways to Milton's interpretive maturity.

There is nonetheless a chronological principle in the organization of the last four chapters of the book. Rather than with putative dates of composition, it has to do with the moments of interpretation that the poems serve to represent. Having treated in Chapter Four two sonnets which, while they are dense with biblical materials, are set in early modern history, Chapters Five and Six each move backward in represented time, first to consider the poem that Milton set at the historical moment when the Old Testament was giving way to the New, then to consider a poem that is set in an earlier historical period, when only a relatively small portion of the Bible had been written. By treating *Paradise Regained* and *Samson Agonistes* as poems that belong to a single volume, these chapters seek to work out some further implications of their joint publication. There is no attempt here to fix the date at which *Samson* was written, but clearly its composition belongs to the period of Milton's history as an interpreter during which he was willing to rest content with the indeterminacies he found in the biblical record.

Following up on Michel Foucault's argument that in the Renaissance writing gained an unprecedented prestige in European epistemology, Chapter Seven pushes still further backward the trajectory through biblical history to examine some features of the ways in which Milton conceives and depicts unfallen "reading." This examination leads ultimately to a rejection of the idea that, when he wrote the major poems of his maturity, Milton thought that verbal complexity was a regrettable result of the Fall. I argue that *Paradise Lost* shows Milton carrying out his interpretive labors with an increasing sense of pleasure in having discovered the necessary endlessness of interpretive activity and that he inscribed his pleasure in the poem by the ways in which he exploited the topos of the world-as-book. This final chapter proposes that a sense of the utter importance of interpretive activities profoundly informs his representation of the original paradise and that the poem redefines the first two commandments in Genesis—"be fruitful and multiply" but "do not eat the fruit"—as powerful hermeneutical criteria. It also discusses some ways in which, working out of his own complex experiences in comparing biblical "places," the poet infused complex interpretive issues into the unfallen world and represented interpretive activity not as a consequence or a symptom of fallenness but as a constituent feature of paradise itself.

* * *

During many years of reading and writing about Milton I have received support from many corners, and it is a pleasure to be able to acknowledge it here. I was fortunate to have been able to study seventeenth-century history with Geoffrey Nuttall at the University of London and to read Milton in the company of Albert Cirillo at Northwestern and of Louis Martz, Leslie Brisman, and John Guillory at Yale. In more recent years Anne Ferry has been a wonderful teacher and colleague; I thank her heartily for the generosity, tact and unfailing intelligence with which she commented on successive drafts of the manuscript.

While working at Boston College, I have received both institutional and personal support. A Faculty Fellowship gave me freedom from teaching duties and enabled me to complete a first draft. Fellow members of the Seminar on Culture and the Economy, chaired by Paul Schervish, helped me to think through many implications of the materials I was gathering. Pheme Perkins, Cheryl Exum, and Anthony Saldarini provided learned counsel on the Hebrew and Greek versions of the Bible, David Gill equally expert knowledge about classical literature. Colleagues in the English Department made the workplace hospitable. I am grateful in particular to Rosemarie Bodenheimer, Amy Boesky, Robert Chibka, Paul Doherty, Andrew Von Hendy, and Judith Wilt for their interest in the book and to many students for questions that kept it developing. Mary Thomas Crane gave timely advice that qualifies her as a kind of midwife. Amy Stackhouse and Scott Cullen helped with many practical details.

I am indebted as well to other colleagues who have contributed to this project. In the early stages Christopher Hill and Gary Stringer suggested valuable leads, and Robert Collmer and Albert Labriola lent encouragement. John O'Malley helped me read commentary on the parable of the talents written in Italian. Ilona Bell, Karen Edwards, Robert Greene, Edward Jones, and Amy McCready made available copies of their own writing in advance of its appearing in print. I am also grateful for the steady professional dedication shown by librarians at the Houghton Library through many years. After I began writing, David Ferry, Jonathan Post, and Keith Stavely offered good advice on sections that they read. Marshall Grossman and another reader for the Press provided intelligent commentary on the whole manuscript and helped me to decide upon the shape that I have finally given to my argument. For the deficiencies that remain I alone am responsible. Among these I acknowledge that, due to considerations of length, my bibliography has been limited to enumerating books and articles actually cited in the book. I should have liked also to list many other fine works from which I have learned a great deal.

Much of the writing about Bunyan in Chapter One and some of that about *De Doctrina Christiana* in Chapter Three draws upon "The Burden of Interpretation in *The Pilgrim's Progress*," which originally appeared in *Studies in Philology*, vol. 79, no. 3 (Summer, 1982), pp. 256–78. Some paragraphs in Chapters Three and Four have been drawn from a history of interpreting the parable of the talents which I contributed to *Wealth in Western Thought: The Case For and Against Wealth*, ed. Paul G. Schervish (1994), an imprint of Greenwood Publishing Group, Inc., Westport, CT. Parts of Chapter Five first appeared in *Milton and the Idea of Woman*, ed. Julia M. Walker (1988), pp. 169–84, and the *Proceedings of the Patristic, Medieval, and Renaissance Conference,* in Vol. 10 (1985), pp. 75–86. A few sentences in Chapter Seven previously proved of use in a piece I wrote on Milton's sonnet, "Ladie that in the prime of earliest youth"; that article is part of P. G. Stanwood's collection, *Of Poetry and Politics: New Essays on Milton and His World* (1994). I gratefully acknowledge permissions to incorporate my earlier work into this book and thank, respectively, the University of North Carolina Press, Greenwood Press, the University of Illinois Press, the Augustinian Historical Institute at Villanova University, and Medieval and Renaissance Texts and Studies at SUNY Binghampton.

Above all I thank my wife and fellow-laborer, Margaret Thomas. Her intelligence, imagination, and companionship have sustained this project, and her daily life has repeatedly renewed its inspiration.

Texts and Abbreviations

Sixteenth- and seventeenth-century spelling is often startling to eyes trained to correct "errors." Its eccentricities help to remind us of some differences between Milton's era and our own. Much of this book concerns such matters, and in quoting from early printed sources I have retained the original spelling and punctuation to highlight some material differences. (Abbreviations have generally been expanded, however.) By the same token, I have sometimes cited sixteenth- and seventeenth-century editions when modernized editions are available. In the case of quotations from the Bible, for ease of reference and unless otherwise noted, I have cited the American Bible Society edition of the Authorized (King James) Version of 1611. I have respected the practice found in the Geneva Bible and the Authorized Version where words with no equivalents in the original text are set in italic type. Not only was this familiar to readers in Milton's time, it often helped to alert them to interpretive issues.

In quoting from Milton's poems, I have used *The Works of John Milton*, gen. ed. Frank Allen Patterson (New York: Columbia University Press, 1931–38), which preserves seventeenth-century orthography.

In reproducing original titles from early printed works, I have given longer titles when these have seemed revealing of the nature and scope of their contents. Upper-case and lower-case usages have been retained when this was feasible; where preserving the original would seem unduly distracting, however, I have normalized them. Roman and italic type titles are rendered throughout in italic.

Abbreviations of Frequently Cited Works

CPW   *Complete Prose Works of John Milton*. Ed. Don M. Wolfe et al. 8 vols. New Haven, CT.: Yale University Press, 1953–82.

GA   John Bunyan. *Grace Abounding to the Chief of Sinners*. Ed. Roger Sharrock. Oxford: Clarendon Press, 1962.

OED   *The Oxford English Dictionary.* 2d ed. Oxford: Clarendon Press, 1989.

PMLA *Publications of the Modern Language Association.*

PP   John Bunyan. *The Pilgrim's Progress from This World to That Which Is to Come.* Ed. James Blanton Wharey. Revised by Roger Sharrock. Oxford: Clarendon Press, 1960.

Works *The Works of John Milton.* Gen. ed. Frank Allen Patterson. 18 vols. New York: Columbia University Press, 1931–38.

1. Introduction: Finding a Place

> Worldly-Wiseman]. *How camest thou by thy burden at first?*
> Christian]. By reading this Book in my hand.
> — Bunyan, *The Pilgrim's Progress* (p. 18)

In the year 1545, shortly before his death and long after the event in question, Martin Luther wrote an account of what he took to be the turning point in his life. He connected it with an interpretive insight into a "place," as he called it, a particular biblical text. The dread phrase "the righteousness of God" in Romans 1: 17 had long been a plague to him, he explained, so that he "raged with a fierce and troubled conscience." Yet he had kept "beat[ing] importunately upon Paul at that place [Latin, *eo loco*], most ardently desiring to know what St. Paul wanted" when he spoke in these terms. The insight, when it came, involved making a connection between two "places," Paul's own words about "the righteousness of God" and his quotation from the prophet Habakkuk, "He who through faith is righteous shall live." Here, according to Luther, was the beginning of a whole new life for him. His account does not proceed to describe that new life in relation to the public forum, where for more than twenty-five years he had been a powerful force. Rather it emphasizes the private pleasure that he experienced in discovering analogies as he continued to read: "There a totally other face of the entire Scripture showed itself to me. Thereupon I ran through the Scriptures from memory. I also found in other terms an analogy [*analogiam*], as, the work of God, that is, what God does in us." Luther goes on to list other phrases that made exhilarating sense to him once he had seen that they implied God's agency and human receptivity. Then he makes a powerful identification of his reading with the regaining of Eden: "Thus that place [*iste locus*] in Paul was for me truly the gate to paradise."[1]

The interpretive discovery, we should notice, is presented in a topographical language that suggests a conception of the Book as a vast field, or set of fields, filled with "places" (Greek, *topoi*) that bear potential relations to one another. The liberating discovery had occurred where two "places" were made to interpret one another: Paul had applied an old text to a new situation, covering over the temporal (and quasi-spatial) gap. At the "place" in Romans Luther had been knocking as it were at Paul's door, but it was Paul, he says, who "wanted" something. The reversal of expectations helps to convey the basic insight. Luther had discovered a passive righteousness: it posits a meaning that he insisted was decidedly not of his own making. His anxious activity of searching seemed to fade into utter insignificance as he felt himself being acted upon by something that had been waiting for him all along. This he summed up in the image of a text that spoke to him immediately, as if he were suddenly in the same "place" that Paul had occupied many centuries earlier and had access thereby to a genuine assurance that he was loved unconditionally.

Luther's experience of an insight into his reading did not induce complacency. It prompted him to study linguistic usage, comparing text with text, concentrating on how biblical language conveys meaning. Like the turn to questions of theory among literary critics in our period, elegantly described by Paul de Man as a "return to philology,"[2] classic Protestant hermeneutics came to involve an intense self-consciousness about the workings of language. At its best it promoted a religious devotion that celebrated the pleasures of the text as the means to recovering Eden.

In associating so crucial a moment in his life with a particular verse, Luther, although it was not his interest to draw attention to this, located his story in a long tradition of narratives that connected personal conversions with particular biblical "places." Although he knew a good bit of patristic literature and continued to refer to it at times, his principal strategies for breaking from the authority of the papal church were to appeal to "the Bible only" and to use St. Paul's strictures against "mere human traditions" to discredit the whole idea that previous interpreters provided a source of authority. When these strategies were turned into foundational principles, although it might have been a kind of heresy to say so, they coalesced into a set of conventions that constituted Protestant tradition. There was no better way to claim authenticity for one's position than by submitting to the conventional idea that one was following "the Bible only" as the unique source of authority in all religious matters. This helps to explain a feature of Luther's account that has received relatively little attention. In the sentence that follows the assertion that the Pauline place was for him "truly the gate to paradise," Luther acknowledged the tradition in which he was placing his experience when he tried to claim independence from its most famous exponent: "Later I read Augustine's *The Spirit and the Letter*, where contrary to hope I found that he, too, interpreted God's righteousness in a similar way, . . . though . . . imperfectly."

Augustine had written a personal narrative that was similar to Luther's story in a number of ways that Luther, although a member of the Augustinian religious order, was not eager to acknowledge. Both Augustine and Luther were deeply introspective, and both were plagued by intense feelings of guilt. Both connected a decisive moment in their lives with a particular biblical place, and in each case it was a passage from Paul's Epistle to the Romans. In fact, each thought of Paul as his model. This offered Luther a justification for suppressing his recognition of some ways in which his story resembled Augustine's. Just as Augustine's insight into the righteousness of God was but an imperfect anticipation of his own interpretation, developed independently, so the turning point in Augustine's life happened to be like the one in his because both were modeled after the authentic experience of Paul recorded in the Scriptures.

When Luther suppressed his indebtedness to Augustine, he diverted attention from a key link in the chain of mediation by which his Christian faith had reached him. Instead he sought to associate his personal story with one that was safe from the charge that it entailed mere human tradition. The story of Saul's conversion into St. Paul, whether one appealed to the autobiographical section in the Epistle to the Galatians or to the various accounts in the Acts of the Apostles, was inscribed in biblical "places" and was therefore eminently authentic. Luther, himself a *Paulus redivivus*, made it the decisive paradigm, and in early Protestantism the medieval *imitatio Christi* increasingly gave way to an *imitatio Pauli*, on which conversion narratives in the Reformed tradition were then frequently modeled.[3]

The Place of Augustine

In seventeenth-century England, as a matter of convention, spiritual autobiographies included a prominent linkage of many experiences, and especially of conversion, to Bible-reading. Where the voice of God had addressed Saul on the road to Damascus, passages excerpted from what was called the Word of God might, analogously, be heard as directly addressed to one's personal situation. Knowledge of this convention had been disseminated not only in the anecdote about Luther's conversion but also through the *Confessions*, where the first great autobiographer depicted the moment of his conversion as an encounter with a biblical place. Unlike Luther, however, Augustine called attention to how traditional it was to be converted by hearing a text. He referred his experience directly to an earlier story about St. Anthony, who, "by hearing a sentence of the Gospel" and "taking [it] as spoken to him in particular," had undertaken to lead a monastic life.[4]

It is a matter of some curiosity that Augustine's *Confessions* were rendered into English rather late, the first translation appearing in 1620. In some measure this may have been due to the difficulty of finding an adequate English vocabulary for expressing the astonishingly introspective detail of the original. A language of inwardness, as Anne Ferry has shown, was developed in English only in the later sixteenth century.[5] The hypothesis that the *Confessions* contained material that proved especially difficult to translate receives some confirmation in the prefatory matter in William Watts's version of 1631, where he reports that translating Augustine's book turned out to be the most difficult task he had ever undertaken in his life. Watts had been motivated in his work, however, by the fact that the first English translation of the full *Confessions* had been made by a Catholic, Sir Tobie Matthew, who among other alleged failings had been "spitefull to the Holy Scriptures; which he neuer honors with quoting in his margent." In Watts's version the frontispiece illustrates the famous episode from Book VIII in which Augustine tells of having been converted at the moment when he took up and read a passage from Romans (13: 13). Yet Watts suppresses mention of the fact that the earliest English rendering of that episode, which had appeared nearly forty years before Matthew's translation and was also by a Catholic, had prominently displayed the relevant biblical references.[6] Although there was no complete translation of the *Confessions* until 1620, the story of Augustine's having found an apt biblical place was already well known in England in Elizabethan times, when lines between Catholic and Protestant spirituality were sometimes fruitfully blurred. The episode from Book VIII had been translated into English in Robert Parsons's *Booke of the Christian Exercise* (1582), an adaptation for English readers of a Jesuit devotional book that had been popular on the continent.[7] In 1584, Edmund Bunny brought out his modified version of the book, adapted for Protestant devotion. "Bunny's Resolution" enjoyed extraordinary popularity well into the seventeenth century. The importance of the section on Augustine's conversion to writers of spiritual autobiographies is well attested in a number of works, including the *Confessions* of Richard Norwood and the *Reliquiae Baxterianae*.[8] The passage (quoted here from "Bunny's Resolution") calls attention to how conventional it had already been by Augustine's time to associate a turning point in one's life with the discovery of a biblical place tailored to one's personal situation:

> I did . . . weep most bitterly, wyth a deep contrition of my heart, & behold, I heard a voyce as if it had been of a boy or maid singing from some house by, & often repeating: Take vp and reade, take vp and read. And straight way I changed my countenance, & began to think most earnestly with my self, whether children were wont to sing any such thing, in any kinde of game that they vsed: but I neuer remember, that I had heard any such thing before. Whefore [sic] repressing the force of my teares, I rose, interpreting no other thing, but that this voice came from heauen, to bid me open the book that I had with me (which was S. Paules Epistles) and to read the first chapter that I should finde. For I had heard afore of S. Antonie, how he was admonished to his conuersion, by hearing a sentence of the Gospel, which was read, when by occasion he came in to the church: and the sentence was: *Goe and sell all that thou hast, and giue to the poore: and thou shalt haue a treasure in heauen: and come and folow me.* Which saying S. Anthonie taking as spoken to him in particular, was presently conuerted to thee (O Lord). Wherefore I went in haste to the place wher Alipius sate, for that I had lefte my booke there when I departed: I snatched it vp, and opened it, and read in silence the first chapter that offered it selfe vnto mine eyes: and therein were these wordes, *Not in bankettings or in drunkennes: not in wantonnesse & chamber-workes, not in contention & emulation: but doe you put on the Lord Iesus Christe: and do you not perfourme the prouidence of the flesh in concupiscence.* Further then this sentence, I would not reade, neither was it needful. For presently with the end of this sentence, as if the light of securitie had been poured into my heart, all the darkenesse of my doubt-fulnesse fled away.[9]

Augustine's account of the similarity between his experience and that of "S. Anthonie," who took a passage "as spoken to him in particular," is a masterpiece of literary self-consciousness. Upon hearing the voice, Augustine explains, he did not immediately follow its instructions but first reflected on its likely origin. He *chose* to interpret the voice as a set of instructions from God. By virtue of his familiarity with the anecdote about Anthony, of his having been reading from St. Paul, and of his having been crying out to God for deliverance, he had done all he could to place himself in a framework where reading the Bible might become equivalent to hearing a divine message. What should be particularly striking in the account is that he mentions that he read in silence: striking not simply because silent reading was unusual in antiquity, but because this detail links this critical moment to an earlier episode in the *Confessions* where Augustine had reported on his fascination in watching Ambrose read silently, presumably so that he (Ambrose) might have his thoughts to himself while he read Scripture and be able to hear the interior teacher.[10] Far from being anxious about acknowledging his indebtedness to Anthony and Ambrose, Augustine delighted in making their "places" as integral a part of his story as the biblical place that he chose to take "as spoken to him in particular."

In "Bunny's Resolution" we find less of a sense of participation in a historic tradition than we do in Augustine, and less acknowledgment of a need for cooperation between readers of different eras. It is true that Bunny recognized that this recent work of Catholic devotion could be useful also for English Protestants. Nonetheless, it is instructive to attend to the points at which he sought to "correct" his Jesuit predecessors' work. For the purposes of understanding the seventeenth-century convention whereby a proper Protestant's calling was thought to be articulated in a biblical place, there are two features of Bunny's corrective activities that deserve attention: one is suggested in the change he wrought in the Catholic subtitle for the book, the other in the marginal annotations he added to the story of Augustine's conversion.

According to Parsons's subtitle, the "resolution" toward which the book was aimed was "the seruice of God": *The First Booke of the Christian Exercise, appertayning to resolution. VVherein are layed downe the causes & reasons that should moue a man to resolue hym selfe to the seruice of God: And all the impedimentes remoued, which may lett the same.* Bunny's first correction was to change the title of the book to suggest a different use: it was to be a guidebook to salvation. Suppressing Parsons's subtitle altogether, Bunny called his version *A Booke of Christian exercise appertaining to Resolution, that is, shewing how that vve should resolue our selues to become Christians indeede.* Bunny's new title suggests that English Protestants were already thinking in terms of what would be called the "greatest case of conscience that ever was," whether one is a "child of God or no." With the wide dissemination of William Perkins's casuistical writings, after 1590 language about being "Christians indeed" became the register within which discussions were carried on about whether one was truly elect or reprobate. The reprobate was one whose faith, if it ever came into being, was only temporary and would wither away. The Protestant use to which *A Booke of the Christian Exercise* was to be put is further clarified in the 1619 edition of *The Second Part:* here the emenders bestowed on the book an alternative title that Baxter seems to have had in mind when, in 1673, he named his own cases of conscience manual: "A Christian Directory, guiding all Men to their saluation." In short, the revised subtitles point to the importance that seeking assurance had taken on in English Protestant culture, and they confirm that along with this pursuit went a redefinition of the Christian life that gave considerably more scope to interpretive tasks than the general Catholic approach did.

Bunny's other significant correction of Parsons (for our purposes here) was one that involved directions for reading the Bible. Bunny feared that readers might appeal to biblical places to justify actions that compromised the meaning of Scripture as defined in basic Protestant doctrines: "no generall rule [can be] drawen vnto others" from the example of Anthony. Such a way of life requires "some special calling besides" the general call issued in Scripture to all true Christians; and it may

> well be doubted, whether S. Anthonie had on that place sufficient groundworke of those doings, vnlesse he had some speciall motion besides. It was otherwise with S. Austen, whose conuersion was not, but to such things as we are al bounden vnto, and vpon such a place as speaketh to all.[11]

To rule out appeals to traditional "doctrines deliuered from hand to hand, either by word of mouth, or by writing, beside the Canonicall Scriptures," Elizabethan Protestants increasingly urged the centrality of "the analogy of faith" in interpreting biblical places. This concept, which referred to a body of truth which Scripture was supposed to provide, was a powerful hermeneutical criterion capable, as Chapter Three will show in detail, of exercising controls on virtually every aspect of interpretive practice. Here, it will be sufficient to explain that the "analogy of faith" was defined by Perkins as "the summe of religion gathered out of the clearest places of Scripture" and to point out that, before it became a site of considerable controversy among seventeenth-century Protestants, it was simply invoked to discredit such post-biblical traditions such as the monastic way of life.[12]

Predestined Endings, Seeking Assurance, Temporary Faith

In the stories of Luther and Augustine a particular biblical verse, written long before the birth of each of these historical figures and taken as a divine message, was said to have brought great comfort to a person who was deeply troubled. The *Booke of the Christian Exercise* made plain to English readers that Augustine had tied the place in Romans closely to another biblical place, about the "light burden" or "easie yoke" promised by Christ to all who labor (Matt. 11: 28–30). Luther, for his part, revived procedures for reading that might make any words from the Bible seem suddenly full of consoling meaning, as if newly spoken for the first time precisely to bring comfort in a situation far removed from that in which it was "originally" spoken or written. It was essential in Luther's view that every reader feel in immediate contact with the biblical Word itself.

The reading practices inspired by the experience of Luther were aptly characterized in the advice that Tyndale offered, out of Luther's early writings, to readers of the English Bible. Encouragement to read with an introspective eye and to find nourishment is amplified in the 1534 Bristol copy of Tyndale's Bible:

> Then go to & reade the storyes of the byble for thy lerninge & comforte, & se euery thinge practysed before thyne eyes: for accordinge to those ensamples shall it goo with the & all men vntill the worldes end. So that into whatsoever case or state a man may be brought, accordinge to whatsoever ensample of the bible it be, his ende shalbe accordinge as he there seith and readeth.[13]

When Luther and Tyndale encouraged readers to "sucke out the pithe of the scripture," their guiding assumption was that people would find a gracious word of mercy to apply to their own situations. Tyndale was quite explicit about the "comfort" that he expected readers to "finde in the playne texte and literall sense."

This sort of advice was newly inflected, and rendered more urgent, as the doctrine of double predestination took hold in the popular imagination and the Bible became a guidebook to salvation. If God had chosen a select few for salvation and had consigned the rest to damnation, and if the Bible alone mediated God's saving grace, then it seemed logical that one would be saved by finding assurance of one's salvation in comfortable biblical "places." The obligation to find assurance began to be widely publicized in the 1590s, especially by Perkins, who tied to it the idea that even a reprobate could have temporary faith. Divines in the tradition that descends from Perkins, presupposing that everyone had been predestined either to salvation or damnation, insisted that the truly elect would make their calling and election sure.

For Luther and for Calvin, the biblical notion of predestination had been an aspect of the great doctrine of grace freely given: it offered consolation because it illustrated that salvation was in no way dependent upon human effort. In the English Calvinist tradition, the doctrine of predestination, far from being a subtopic within the discussion of the workings of faith as it is in Calvin's *Institutes,* was brought dramatically to the fore and came increasingly to determine what readers were to look for in the Bible. Perkins and William Ames (both of whom had been at Christ's College, Cambridge, in the generation before Milton arrived there) developed their systematic theologies within a framework that emphasized predestinarian doctrine. The structure of their theological treatises is quite different from Calvin's *Institutes* in this respect: the leading interest was no longer the knowledge of God but rather the order in which salvation is effected. The full title of Perkins's doctrinal treatise points to the decisive change in focus: *A Golden Chaine, or the Description of Theologie, Containing the Order of the causes of Saluation and Damnation, according to Gods word.* The new focus represents a significant adaptation of Calvin, since the question of salvation or damnation displaced questions about God as the central concern. What was implicit in Perkins became explicit in Ames: that faith was no longer conceived as a mode of knowledge and that it was becoming in large part a function of the will. In the treatises and sermons of seventeenth-century English Calvinists, faith came to be treated as a developmental process. It was described as passing through recognizable stages, the *ordo salutis*. The work of practical divinity was therefore to offer believers advice on how to bring their faith to maturity. When divines in the line that descends from Perkins treated "the causes of Saluation and Damnation," they came almost routinely to make of predestination a philosophical first principle. The prominence that they accorded this doctrine raised questions of cause and effect, the theoretical question how God could fore-ordain someone to damnation and the practical one how a person could be assured of salvation. This had important effects upon Bible-reading, as attested especially in the growing number of conversion narratives.

Of course many (including John Milton, who came flatly to reject *double* predestination) sought to moderate the harsh doctrine that descended through the line of Perkins. There is a rich practical instance of this in the *Confessions* written by Richard Norwood about 1640. Norwood's autobiographical narrative tells of his having been intrigued for a time with the prospect that there must be some "middle estate" between election and reprobation, because he seemed not to belong to either. His experience of the world (he had traveled widely and lived in Italy and in Bermuda, as well as England) and his familiarity with pagan philosophers "and other eminent persons who by their virtues and endowments . . . seemed not to be inferior to the better sort of Christians" (p. 65) gave him hope that a middle category might exist. From this "imaginary" longing he was delivered, he explained, by reading Perkins, who put the fear of God in him. What is most significant in Norwood's account, just because he takes it for granted, is that being religious meant accepting the assumptions on which "experimentalist" advice was administered. He had read Augustine, and he read often in his Latin Bible. He also read Perkins. Yet far from feeling an affinity for the advice that Perkins offered, he had to struggle to get his experience to fit its prescriptions for the godly. As he followed the instructions to attend to "sundry places of Scripture," that his calling and election might be made sure, he developed a "harsh conceit of God and of his ways." Writing his spiritual autobiography more than twenty years after this, Norwood acknowledged that he could "hardly shake off" the view of God he had learned from Perkins, although he knew it was "heathenish" (p. 75).

The course that Norwood took, both before his conversion and after, was typical and representative. It served to illustrate the workings of a peculiarly English synthesis of materials drawn from the continental reformers. The authorized paradigm enshrined in Luther's life-story had been accommodated, among English "Calvinist" divines familiar with the writings of Zwingli and Beza, to illustrate the *ordo salutis* described in their theological manuals. To answer the question how one was to be assured of salvation, these divines had driven a wedge between faith, which they still regarded as a free gift of God, and assurance, which was thought to be a necessary component of "saving" faith to be achieved by legitimate human effort. Some proposed that assurance was a rare blessing and not necessary for salvation. What they required (and Milton concurred with them when he treated the subject in Book I, chapter XXV of *De Doctrina Christiana*) was that the believer *seek* assurance, which was increasingly thought to be the reward of godly conduct. According to Richard Sibbes, one is saved by grace, but assured by works. It was Ames, however, who explained most clearly that "the heart or will . . . bears the whole burthen of assurance." That practising such a faith had become onerous was the interpretation frequently placed on their experience by converts who, as Augustine had, appealed to the saying of Jesus recorded in Matthew 11: 28–30: "Come unto me, all ye that labour and are heavy laden, and I will give you rest. . . . For my yoke is easy, and my burden light."[14] Assurance, it should be added, was not simply a moment of recognition. In practice, as dozens of personal narratives show, assurance was achieved only in a continuing struggle which could know no permanent resting place on this side of death.[15]

The theory that separated faith and assurance at once created spiritual problems and suggested how they might be answered. The problems began showing up regularly in the 1590s in books ostensibly dedicated to cases of conscience. This new devotional literature bears little resemblance to Catholic casuistry. For English Protestants, there was ultimately only one question of conscience in the framework of which all others were treated: am I saved or damned? The nature of the case is summed up in the title of Perkins's enormously popular treatise of 1589, which went through numerous reprintings by the early seventeenth century: *A Treatise tending vnto a Declaration, whether a man be in the estate of damnation, or in the estate of grace: and if he be in the first, how he may in time come out of it: if in the second, how he may discerne it, and perseuere in the same to the end.* Starting with the assumption of an inalterable decree of reprobation, a central idea in Perkins's treatise is that even a reprobate, though doomed eventually to fall away, may for a time have faith. Until the fall takes place such a person's life may suggest evidence of election. Numerous seventeenth-century divines pressed home the theory. "*There bee many who are the children of God by a generall profession,*" Samuel Hieron wrote, "*and doe make a full account to be saued, which notwithstanding shall bee shut out.*" Therefore, he advised, the "*task worthy of a Christian*" is "with all diligence, to proue himselfe, and to cause his spirit to search, within, *what certaine euidences he can there find, that he* is an heire indeed." The danger of self-deception is so great that this task is "*to bee performed* euery day."[16]

An inauthentic or "temporary" faith was easy to confuse with an authentic and "saving" one,[17] for both could issue into those good works which might indicate that a person was using the talents of the Lord and that the sower's seed had not fallen on thorny ground. What separated the truly elect from the mere temporizer therefore was a willingness to keep searching the Scriptures and to persevere to the end. The motivation for such endurance might be based upon a personally appropriate and assuring text, or group of texts, garnered from the Scriptures. There were problems, however, even with this procedure. Robert Blair tells, for instance, how once he had made his collection of assuring texts and felt he had a "stock of grace in [his] keeping that would suffice to carry [him] through all difficulties," he nonetheless encountered many new puzzles. He noticed, in fact, that "many gracious sound believers" were "much puzzled," whereas "many secure, unhumbled misbelievers, . . . without the warrant of the Word, conceit themselves to be beloved of God."[18] In view of the criteria spread abroad by divines, one wonders how Blair knew which group was which. Still, his observations serve to illustrate the sorts of concerns that the theory about temporary faith was meant to allay.

The doctrine of temporary faith, which presupposed the doctrine of double predestination, was also a function of the separation of assurance from faith. Whereas for Calvin faith was a firm persuasion in the mind and therefore a mode of knowledge that already entailed assurance, for Perkins and the experimental divines, faith was not truly saving faith unless it would ultimately issue into assurance. A person might have either "historical" or "temporary" faith but nonetheless lack "saving" faith. Key biblical places for proving the doctrine were Matt. 7: 21–23 ("Not every one that saith unto me Lord, Lord..."), Heb. 6: 4–6 ("*it is* impossible... if they shall fall away, to renew them again"), and the parable of the sower. Like the seeds that "fell upon stony places, where they had not much earth" and took "no root," people with temporary faith "withered away" (Matt. 13: 5–6). Reprobates who seemed for a time to have faith ultimately revealed that they had been predestined to revert to the state of damnation.

Against the possibility that one might fail to persevere, Perkins, in the whole range of his writings — exegetical, doctrinal, and practical — returned again and again to that "case of conscience" that he called "the greatest that ever was: how a man may know whether he be the child of God or no." He repeatedly encouraged his readers to assure themselves that they were the children of God, invoking Paul's advice to the Corinthians — "Examine yourselves, whether ye be in the faith" (2 Cor. 13: 5) — as an injunction not only to scrutinize one's interior life but to read the Bible with an introspective earnestness. The watchword for this kind of reading was a verse excerpted from the Second Epistle of Peter and re-addressed to contemporary readers: "Give diligence to make your calling and election sure: for if ye do these things, ye shall never fall" (1: 10).[19] This verse pointed to the basic task for Bible-readers, to discover apt scriptural "places" or "ensamples" which would assure them that their story was going to have a happy outcome. Bible-reading became a practical expedient while one waited for assurance, and Bible-searching was thought to be the proper activity for making one's calling "effectual." The certitude to be attained in this process was the only sure hedge against apostasy, the "horror of horrors" in the Perkins tradition.[20]

The idea of reprobation continued to occupy a position of prominence in practical divinity all through and long after the seventeenth century. There is no reason to think that people forgot that it was possible to abandon the faith. On the contrary, the 1640s and 1650s were marked by all sorts of anxieties, despairs, and apostasies. After the rise of the sects, the sheer diversity of religious opinions proved a scandal, and many were tempted to abandon a faith that suddenly seemed a human invention.

"How can you tell but that the Turks had as good Scriptures to prove their *Mahomet* the Saviour, as we have to prove our *Jesus* is," Bunyan asked. "Everyone doth think his own Religion rightest, both *Jews,* and *Moors,* and *Pagans;* and how if all our Faith, and Christ, and Scriptures, should be but a think-so too?"[21]

Among people who had previously considered themselves religious, there were many who reported having become altogether unsettled. Elizabeth Chambers told how, having examined the Bible and being unable any longer to find there anything good, she felt she must be a reprobate, "undone," damned and "lost forever." A woman whose initials were E. C. suddenly discovered an enormous "burthen" when her child was born, and found that her guilt was intensified two years later when the child died: "I could read the Promises," she said, "but found none of them to me." In an account not marked for the author's gender, one D. R. told of becoming convinced (s)he was "a child of wrath," and though (s)he knew that Paul counseled the Corinthians to examine themselves to see whether they were "of the faith," (s)he "could not other wise judge, but that I was a Reprobate, and this condition was very burthensome to my spirit, and neither in hearing or reading, could I for the time finde any ease of this my trouble." Many writers of conversion narratives tell how they feared that they had fallen away irrevocably. From early in his writing career Bunyan insisted that some "portions of holy Scripture belong" to the damned. He took the idea of temporary faith so seriously that, in *The Pilgrim's Progress,* he dramatized in the case of Ignorance the possibility that a self-deceiving person might fall away even in the last moments of life.[22]

"Experimental" Reading Practices

A century and more after Tyndale's instructions for finding comforting biblical "places" were first propagated, they were said to be yielding spectacular results. In 1649, Francis Roberts, giving directions for how to read the Bible, told how Augustine had found great "comfort" and "delight" when he responded to the *tolle, lege.* Roberts went on to enumerate a number of more recent examples. Each suggested a different way in which "places" might be found. A Mr. Midgely from Yorkshire was on the point of drowning himself when he decided to look one last time into his pocket New Testament. He immediately chanced upon no less a text than "*Come unto me all ye that labour and are heavy laden*" and was saved from both death and despair. Mrs. Katherine Brettergh of Lancashire, although she read at least eight chapters per day, often feared the Bible "*was become to her the Book of death.*" Yet having asked her husband to read to her, and hearing the seventeenth chapter of John, she kept interrupting him to explain how particular passages applied to her case and brought her comfort. Whereas, according to Roberts's account, Midgely had merely chanced upon an appropriate text and it was not clear whether Mrs. Brettergh had chosen the passage that her husband was reading to her, John Holland was shown to have been quite decisive about his choice of a "place." On the day before he died, he called for a Bible, and "turning with his own hands to the 8. chap. of *Pauls* Epistle to the Romans," he gave the book to a friend to read aloud and at the end of every verse asked for a pause, during which he expressed his sense of comfort. This went on "for the space of two houres or more." Whatever the accuracy of Roberts's particular claims here, there is no mistaking that many readers found great pleasure in their Bibles. Read as "*Letters* or *Epistles* sent downe from God out of *heauen*," the Scriptures brought "unspeakable comfort" to thousands of earnest readers.[23]

While those who linked their callings to biblical places made the most spectacular responses to Tyndale's advice, many readers sought biblical words of comfort and assurance for other moments in life as well. George Herbert's second sonnet on "The H. Scriptures" conveys a sense of the rich interpretive possibilities attendant upon the quest for assurance. The poet addresses a Book that he thinks of as a compendium of various texts that illuminate one another:

> OH that I knew how all thy lights combine,
>   And the configurations of their glorie!
>   Seeing not onely how each verse doth shine,
> But all the constellations of the storie.
> This verse marks that, and both do make a motion
>   Unto a third, that ten leaves off doth lie:
>   Then as dispersed herbs do watch a potion,
> These three make up some Christians destinie:
> Such are thy secrets, which my life makes good,
>   And comments on thee: for in ev'ry thing
>   Thy words do finde me out, & parallels bring,
> And in another make me understood.
>   Starres are poore books, & oftentimes do misse:
>   This book of starres lights to eternall blisse.[24]

That Herbert should have thought to contrast Bible-reading and astrology here is suggestive, and a later section in the chapter will take up some instances of superstitious Bible-reading. At this point, it should be noted that the poem acknowledges that discovering affinities between one's own experience and a biblical paradigm could induce feelings of surprise and delight. It also harks back to the way of reading celebrated by Luther in the account of the turning point in his life: "combin[ing]" one text with another "that ten leaves off doth lie," seeing one's own life as anticipated by and offering commentary on "configurations" of passages, feeling that the "parallels" promise a "destinie" of "eternal blisse." Elsewhere, speaking of the country parson's reading habits, Herbert characterizes the interpretive procedures that infuse his own biblical poetics: "the chief and top of his knowledge consists in the book of books, the storehouse and magazene of life and comfort, the holy Scriptures. There he sucks, and lives." The good reader makes "a diligent Collation of Scripture with Scripture. For all Truth being consonant to it self and all being penn'd by one and the self-same Spirit, it cannot be, but that an industrious and judicious comparing of place with place must be a singular help for the right understanding of the Scriptures."[25]

The interpretive procedures to which Herbert was referring were common but by no means universal in seventeenth-century England. Here, what requires acknowledgment is that the Bible could be and was read in different ways: as an account of historical deeds, as a handbook of moral precepts, as a collection of promises and threats, as a book of consolation. Different people read it looking for different things, and the same person sometimes read it primarily in one framework for one set of circumstances, and in a different framework for another. Herbert's poem recognizes that readers were accustomed to thinking of the Bible as a source not only of knowledge but of experience. For many people, reading the Word seems to have been like going to the theatre, witnessing a spectacle, or hearing a lecture. It involved a significant non-rational component.[26] Bible-readers often spoke of "feeling faith" or of the "experimental" knowledge they got from the Book. In fact, the phrases "experimental religion" and "experimental divinity" came widely to be used a generation or two before it was common to speak of "experimental science." The phrases had become current with the rise of a literature about afflicted consciences, and they remained in use as long as that sort of literature was popular, that is, through the middle decades of the seventeenth century.[27] Associating their religious experience with a dynamic sense that their lives involved recurring tests, people used the word "experimental" to characterize the sincerity and intensity of their devotion. They spoke about the emotional impact of the "experimental" knowledge they got from the Bible and opposed this to a knowledge (sometimes called "historical" knowledge) derived from "mere testimony or conjecture." Roberts proposed that even people who have the "accomplishments of Art" and "know much of Scripture theoretically" cannot successfully read the Author's mind in the Bible if they do not apply the text to their own lives. The "gracious person," he claimed, "understands the Scriptures, experimentally, feelingly, as a Traveller knows remote countries in which he hath actually been," and not just by maps.[28]

A representative instance of the way in which "experimental" knowledge was connected with this way of reading comes from John Preston (1587–1628). He instructed people to read the Bible as if listening for a living voice addressed directly to them: "those that heare the voyce of the Sonne of God, have experimentall knowledge, the other is but speculative." He admonished readers to examine themselves, moreover, to discern "whether [they] have heard the voyce of the Sonne of God, or no." When we consider that the Scriptures were often read orally, not only in public worship but in more private contexts as well, Preston's language suggests that to a notable extent the practice of the devotional life was conceived as a literary activity: "Know yee the passages and working of regeneration and repentance? finde yee the Word as fire, and as a hammer? . . . Have ye an experimentall knowledge? . . . are your hearts opened at the hearing of the Word?"[29]

Ideally, of course, a reader's search was meant to turn up gospel-promises, invitations to put one's trust in God to effect a happy closure to one's life. Often, as personal narratives report it, it worked: various "lights" were "combined" into an assuring promise that motivated perseverance. Two similar instances may be made to stand for many: the *Memoirs* of John Shawe, who had been Milton's fellow student under William Chappell at Christ's College, and the personal narrative of Anne Venn. Enlisting a common formula, Shawe closed his narrative with a series of references to biblical places (e.g., Rom. 8: 28: "all things shal work together for good . . .") designed to predict that whatever "passages" may yet be written in his life by his divine Author, a happy end was in store for him. Anne Venn used the same place in October of 1652 when she was "writing a letter unto a dear kinswoman" who was in distress. As she wrote out the passage, she reports, "the Lord was pleased to cause it to fall with power upon my heart"; and she recognized how true the words were to her own "experience."[30]

The practices associated with gaining "experimental" knowledge from the Bible included, and were not exhausted by, what we now routinely designate as typological reading. We know that the Reformers, although in theory they rejected allegory and the fourfold interpretive system of the Middle Ages, retained typology. (It is worth remembering, however, that seventeenth-century readers and writers did not have to conform their practices to the maps provided by twentieth-century theorists, many of whom have sought to set up sharp distinctions between typological and allegorical modes of symbolism.) Typology became a rubric under which widely varying applications of biblical texts were made by people who claimed to credit only the literal historical sense. Readers used the conventions of typological reading to identify themselves with the divine purposes they found sketched out in "the Bible only." They readily assimilated the events and circumstances of contemporary life, both private and public, with those found in biblical stories, often speaking about biblical events as if they were recapitulated in their own hearts and in contemporary history.[31] The extreme examples — Lodowick Muggleton and John Reeve commissioned by God in 1652 as the Two Last Witnesses foretold in Revelation, James Naylor riding into Bristol in 1656 on an ass amidst shouts of "Hosanna to the Son of David" — are only the most well known. Many other readers invoked typology to establish disjunctions as well as similarities between themselves and their biblical predecessors. In any event, even if there was skepticism about whether the Bible had predicted the course of public events in seventeenth-century England, many were accustomed to thinking that it offered normative paradigms in relation to which they could chart their spiritual "progress." Sometimes the Holy Spirit was said to be the author both of the Bible and of the individual's life. Experience, as "one of the chiefest" ways in which God teaches, could be understood as "the inward sense and feeling, of what is outwardly read and heard" from the Scriptures. "*Experience*," according to Vavasor Powell, "is a Copy written by the Spirit of God upon the hearts of beleevers." The idea that God's Spirit was thus continuing to write had important implications for interpretive practice. On the one hand, as William Bridge formulated the general principle, "whatever your Condition be, study those Scriptures which do concern your Condition, and this wil help you to understand rhe [sic] Scriptures." On the other hand, however, as Bridge went on to warn, it was therefore necessary to "[t]ake heed that you be not too indulgent of your Condition, Disposition, or Opinion." For concentration on one's own case was likely to give rise to damaging interpretations.[32]

Some Ill Effects of Reading for "Experimental" Knowledge

Like the doctrine of predestination, the practice of plotting one's spiritual life by way of biblical paradigms had a double edge. A few lines from another poem by Herbert indicate that the fit between the biblical precedent and the contemporary situation was not always comfortable. In "The Bunch of Grapes," the speaker presents the course of his life in images drawn from the Exodus tradition:

> I did towards Canaan draw; but now I am
> Brought back to the Red sea, the sea of shame.
>
> For as the Jews of old by Gods command,
>   Travell'd, and saw no town;
> So each Christian hath his journeys spann'd:
>   Their storie pennes and sets us down.

These lines train the whole system of typological interpretation upon the heart of the individual believer. By identifying his "Condition" with a story that has already been written, the speaker implies that his course has been plotted and that he knows how his personal story is to come out. He also attests to how oppressive this introspective interpretive practice could be when, for instance, one of the numerous biblical "ensamples" of backsliding would turn up. Herbert's lines here suggest, by way of the word-play in the last line quoted, that readers sometimes felt "penne[d]" in and "set down" when they recognized that their own stories had been written in advance for them. The idea (expressed elsewhere in the poem) that "Gods works are wide, and let in future times" could cut two ways, since the Bible provides "ensamples" of unhappy "endes" as well as happy ones. There is a straining in the rest of Herbert's poem, as the speaker tries to convince himself that "our murmurings" are only a prelude to a surpassing experience of joy.

The division of experience between joy and comfort on the one hand and melancholy and affliction on the other runs all through the enormous body of evidence that seventeenth-century readers have left us about how they read their Bibles. Robert Burton's *Anatomy of Melancholy* provides an early and acute account of the deleterious effects that reading for experimental knowledge could have. While the author is approving of the Reformed religion in general and of Bible-reading in particular, he acknowledges that those who follow St. Paul's advice to *"pray continually"* and

David's encouragement to *"meditate on [God's] Law day and night"* risk serious disorders when they fix on particular "places" as definitive representations of their own "estates":

> Yea, but this meditation is that that mars all, and mistaken, makes many men far worse, misconceiving all they read or hear, to their own overthrow; the more they search and read Scriptures, or divine Treatises, the more they puzzle themselves, as a bird in a net, the more they are intangled and precipitated into this preposterous gulf. *Many are called, but few are chosen Mat.* 20.16 and 22.14, with such like places of Scripture misinterpreted, strike them with horror, they doubt presently whether they be of this number or no: God's eternal decree of predestination, absolute reprobation, and such fatal tables [decrees] they form to their own ruin, and impinge upon this rock of despair. How shall they be assured of their salvation, by what signs? . . . how shall they discern they are not reprobates?[33]

It bears noting that Burton, who anticipated the great heresy-mongers of mid-century in his cataloguing of deviations, nowhere urges that looking for personal texts was itself problematic.

Burton's account of the quest for assurance attests that "experimental" Bible-reading was in large measure a function of the prominence of predestinarian doctrine. The idea that the Bible contained promises and threats and provided a variety of "ensamples," one of which might accurately describe each reader's own spiritual "estate," made it an especially valuable resource for those curious about their eternal destinies. While such curiosity was said to be itself a sign of reprobation and was officially discouraged, it is clear that readers often sought to find a personally appropriate place or network of places that would provide "discoveries" that they were among those who "savingly believe the Scriptures."[34]

In discriminating between a saving faith and a merely temporary one and in requiring that readers search their consciences as well as their Bibles, divines in the Perkins tradition defined the contours of the classic problem of achieving certitude. Finding a place was of particular importance to all who accepted the idea that they needed to make their calling and election sure. If a text was the right sort of place, that is, if it associated the reader with a biblical character who was saved, it offered "experimental" assurance of election. If it was not, its effects could induce despair. A generation before spiritual autobiographies proliferated and left extensive evidence about how particular readers thought of their lives as summed up by specific verses, Burton, who was fascinated by deviations from the pattern, was already enumerating frequently "misapplied" places:

> *Many are called, few are chosen. Not every one that saith Lord. Fear not, little flock. He that stands, let him take heed lest he fall. Work out your salvation with fear and trembling. That night two shall be in a bed, one received, the other left. Straight is the way leads to Heaven, and few there are that enter therein.* The parable of the seed, and of the sower, *some fell on barren ground, some was choked. Whom he hath predestinated, he hath chosen. He will have mercy on whom he will have mercy.*

The fact that Burton was able to list these places by a kind of shorthand shows how well known they were. The list is clearly not exhaustive: "These and the like places," he continues,

> terrify the souls of many; election, predestination, reprobation, preposterously conceived, offend divers, with a deal of foolish presumption, curiosity, needless speculation, contemplation, solicitude, wherein they trouble and puzzle themselves about those questions of grace, free-will, perseverance, God's secrets.... [What] the Casuists discuss, and the School-men broach, ... divers mistake, misconstrue, misapply to themselves, to their own undoing, and so fall into this gulf. They doubt of their Election, how they shall know it, by what signs.

The experiences reported half a century later by Bunyan in *Grace Abounding* are but conspicuous examples of the extremes to which the demand for introspective reading might drive the conscientious, who were to be "killed stark dead by the law of works contained in the Scriptures."[35]

While the practice of speculating about one's eternal destiny was subject to critical scrutiny, what seems to have gone largely unremarked was the practice, so prominent in Bunyan's speaking about being chased and pinched and clapped on the back by texts, of disclaiming responsibility for the choice of one's biblical place. Peter Carlton has analyzed this feature of *Grace Abounding,* denominating as "disclaiming locutions" those instances where the speaker represents himself as being acted upon rather than as acting. The convention was already well established when Norwood, imitating Augustine, recounted how he achieved assurance. Perkins happened to speak to him in memory at a moment of crisis, counseling him to read. Thus he found his place in Colossians "by accident" (Norwood, pp. 81–83).

Such locutions are a practical consequence of the credit that Bible-readers gave to the doctrine of passive righteousness, whereby God alone is responsible for one's salvation, including those mental (and we should also say "experimental") events where the drama of one's pilgrimage is played out. "Disclaiming locutions," according to Carlton, "filled the void left" when the reformers cast out the idea that there was an authoritative body of interpreters in the church. "By constituting certain thoughts and feelings as happenings, such statements transformed mental events into direct communications from God, making them implicitly authoritative." One need not go so far as Carlton, who calls it "self-deception," to agree that Bunyan, while he reports on voices that spoke within him, was "busily arranging a happy ending in the midst of despair."[36] Disclaiming locutions served as the grammar by which one attributed saving activity to God. Bible-reading (and sometimes writing about the Bible as well) became a special case, something spoken of as an action by God, not by the reader. It was, in other words, the privileged locus for reintroducing into Protestantism, even among those who like Ames denounced Arminianism, the importance of the will and of human effort. In the face of a forbidding notion of what predestination might entail, people needed something to do. Reading became the prescribed activity. For many, given the stakes, it turned out to be an onerous and perilous one.

If the doctrine of passive righteousness helped to generate the convention of disclaiming responsibility, it may also have given renewed impetus to the ancient practice of divination by books. The practice of consulting *sortes* had been prevalent in later paganism, and several fourth-century councils of the church condemned it. One way the divination proceeded was for a person to take a book in hand — it might be a copy of Homer or Virgil or the Bible — open it at random, allow an eye or perhaps a finger to fall upon some place on the page, and then interpret the passage found there as a divine message specially addressed to the business at hand. In the *Confessions* Augustine reports that he had once made a habit of this practice. He was weaned from it, he says, by a kindly physician, who simply observed that "if any man should, by chance consult some one of the *Poets*, amongst the *Pagans*; and his verse should happen to be strangely consonant to the present busines, . . . it was not to be wondred at" if it seemed to have "reference to the condition and affaries of him, that askt the question." Such incidents occurred "rather by chance than good cunning," for "that which the Poet both deuised, and thought was very different."[37] Yet in his subsequent account of his conversion, at the point where he reported that he opened his codex to whatever place appeared, there might seem to be a suggestion that he had reverted to divination.

In early modern England, *sortes* seem to have provoked divergent reactions. According to *The discouerie of witchcraft* (1584), some people were seeking their fortune by turning suddenly to a verse of Homer or Virgil, but the practice was too ludicrous to warrant the author's sustained attention.[38] On the other hand, in the *Apologie for Poetrie,* Sidney referred to them as part of his testimony to the esteem in which poets have been held, as if *sortes* had a certain prestige. As for biblical *sortes,* Burton and other divines, although they deplored the "wresting" of places by persons who used the Bible to assign themselves a damned "estate," were inhibited by their culture's commitment to the Bible from naming as superstition the idea that a biblical place could predict one's eternal destiny.

It is difficult to say just how widespread bibliomancy was in the seventeenth century.[39] In the face of anxieties about their eternal destinies, however, it seems plausible that many people who had been encouraged to look to "the Bible only" as the authoritative source of God's saving word were sometimes tempted to divine their fates by a kind of fortune-telling. Certainly there is a evidence that seventeenth-century English people, from ordinary folk and country parsons to Archbishop Laud and Charles I, took up the practice of turning to the Bible to find a timely place. Amidst the new "liberty of prophesying" in the 1640s and 1650s, the practice of opening the Bible at random may have been widespread. The parliamentary general, Sir William Waller, turned to biblical *sortes* to divine whether his wife would make it safely through labor. There was a tale that circulated about Mrs. Joan Drake of Emersham, who "had a custom of turning over the *Bible,* to put her Finger suddenly upon some Verse, saying, *Now whatsoever my Finger is upon, is just my Case, (whatsoever it be) and my Doom.*"[40] She was not unique in her practice. In the event, the places that Mrs. Drake encountered always proved "encouraging and comfortable." She seems to have become almost addicted to the practice, so that she could not be persuaded to leave it. But what if she had chanced upon a place that doomed her? Others did, though not necessarily by opening their Bibles at random.

In *A Few Sighs from Hell* (1658) Bunyan described in detail the plight of one who did "but suppose that any one place of the Scripture doth exclude him, and shut him out of, and from a share in the promises":

> O it will trouble him, grieve him, perplex him, yea he will not be satisfied until he be resolved, and the contrary sealed to his soul, for he knows that the Scriptures are the word of God, all truth; and therefore he knows that if any one sentence doth exclude or bar out him, for want of this or the other qualification; he knows also that not the word alone shuts him out but he that speaks it, even God himself and therefore he cannot, will not, dare not be contented untill he find his soul and Scripture together (with the thing contained therein) to embrace each other, and a sweet correspondency and agreement be between them.[41]

Introduction: Finding a Place   23

Dozens of ordinary Bible-readers have left abundant signs that introspective Bible-reading did not always yield "sweet correspondency" but rather damaging results. Here is a representative testimony written about 1653 by someone identified only as A. O. The writer had been familiar with the Bible since childhood, and the crisis occurred in adult life:

> when I read the Scriptures, I found e-every [sic] threatning and judgement therin, that I fixed my thoughts upon, to speak terror to my soul; and my distraction was so great, that my friends said that I was mad, and kept the Bible from me.

The experience must have been fairly widespread. Bunyan made it the starting point for *The Pilgrim's Progress,* where Christian's family think him mad and try to keep him from reading in his book. A few years later Bunyan's Mr. Badman was echoing a common charge that the Scriptures "were as a Nose of Wax, and a man may turn them withersoever he lists: . . . they are the cause of all dissensions and discords that are in the Land."[42]

What became public dissension after 1640 had been anticipated by private discord, the afflicted consciences which were the subject of the final section of Burton's *Anatomy*. Even before the proliferation of dissonant interpretations during the freedom of the Interregnum, there were satires like George Wither's that emphasized a connection between despair and faulty interpretation:

> This is that *Passion* giueth man instruction
> To wrest the *Scripture* to his own destruction:
> And makes him thinke, while he on earth doth dwell
> He feeles the tortures and the plagues of Hell.[43]

It is not easy to say how widespread were experiences of despair. One index of a fascination with the subject was the popularity — before, during, and after the civil wars — of the story of Francis Spira, a sixteenth-century Italian Protestant who seems to have died convinced that he had sinned irrevocably. The *Relation* of his story went through numerous editions. It inspired a play on the Elizabethan stage, and all through the seventeenth century preachers in England and New England retold the tale. Both Burton and Bunyan referred to it. While it seems not to have been the purpose of the compilers to attack the idea that each Bible-reader has a right to an independent interpretation, the book makes a clear connection between Spira's insistence on that right and his despairing identification of himself with Judas and Cain. "You may interpret the matter as you will," Spira is quoted as saying,

> but I am sure, I am not onely the Actor, but the argument, and matter of the Tragedy; I would it were frenzie, either fained or true; for if it were fained, I could put it off at pleasure; if it were a reall frenzie, yet there were some hope left of Gods mercie, whereas now there is none. . . . I am a cast-away.[44]

What seems to have been almost unique among English Protestants, however, was widespread fear about committing the so-called sin against the Holy Ghost. Baird Tipson has called attention to the concern among English preachers and eventually among ordinary people with the sin referred to in Matthew 12: 31–32. The concern was unprecedented in Christian history. Tipson's study of a "dark side" of seventeenth-century Protestantism shows that many Bible-readers associated their experience with damning places and that the fear of committing this unpardonable sin "lay close to the heart of English Calvinist experience." Many candidates for admission to gathered churches have left evidence that they feared having committed it. While the particular identity of this sin was widely contested, virtually all accounts seem to have taken it for granted that everyone knew what it was. Spira had accused himself of being guilty of this sin, which precluded his ever receiving God's mercy. Yet the most common source of the almost morbid fascination with this sin seems to have been Perkins's *Golden Chaine*. Perkins's works disseminated the idea that blaspheming against the Holy Ghost was a sure sign of reprobation. In the seventeenth century the biblical places referring to this sin became increasingly popular among people who thought that particular texts defined their spiritual experiences.[45] John Hales, even before he made his famous bid good-night to John Calvin, felt free to criticize the more dangerous absurdities entailed in urging the rights of private interpretation. He sought to dissuade the appliers of damning texts by appealing to them in their own terms. His sermon on "Abvses of obscure and difficult places of holy Scripture" (1617) pointed out that some of the ancients had defined the sin against the Holy Ghost as the wresting of Scripture passages to one's own destruction. He argued specifically that the Holy Ghost does not enlighten individual Bible-readers with "particular information for resolution in any doubtfull case [of conscience]." In the course of recommending that really difficult interpretive questions be deferred indefinitely, Hales linked the desire for knowledge about predestination to "the same disease that my first parents in Paradise had, a desire to knowe more then I need."[46]

Burdens of Guilt and of Interpretation

The tangles in which many earnest Bible-readers of Milton's era lost themselves are seen most clearly in a case which seems to have been atypical only in its extremity. As a young married man with some experience in the army Bunyan embraced the task of searching the Scriptures for evidences that would make his calling and election sure and thus justify his perseverance. So deeply did he descend into the despair bred by introspective concentration on the dread text about Esau from Hebrews 12 that he became, he says, a "burthen" to himself (*GA*, p. 45). *The Pilgrim's Progress,* a work of his maturity, represents a further stage in its author's journey: it incorporates the anxious searching reported in the conversion narrative and represents it graphically in the figure of the burden borne on Christian's back. Yet it dispenses with this burden rather early in the story. The narrative then invites us to take an interest in a different sort of interpretive onus, that which in the Apology and the Conclusion the author explicitly assigns to the reader of his book.

These two burdens, although they are distinct and of different natures, are related. Both the burden on Christian's back and that which the allegory imposes upon the reader can be understood with reference to developments within the piety that descends from Perkins. Already in Richard Kilby's popular books, which were forerunners of spiritual autobiographies, the word "burden" stood prominently in the titles. *The Burthen of a Loaden Conscience* was first published about 1608 and went through numerous editions. It was followed by a work that completed the pattern which would be followed by Bunyan and others a generation later: *Hallelv-iah: Praise yee the Lord, for the vnbvrthening of a Loaden Conscience: by His grace in Iesus Christ vouchsafed vnto the worst sinner of all the whole world.* Bunyan, who knew the trials of an afflicted conscience first hand, took the image of the burdened, troubled Christian reader as the starting point for his imaginative reconstruction of the biblical story:

> I looked, and saw him open the Book, and Read therein; and as he read, he wept and trembled: and not being able longer to contain, he brake out with a lamentable cry; saying, *what shall I do?* (*PP,* p. 8)

It is clear from the outset of *The Pilgrim's Progress* that, whatever else it suggests, Christian's burden represents the guilt of man's first disobedience, a guilt that is no doubt compounded by personal sins, on which the narrator does not dwell. The image of guilt as a burden was thoroughly traditional. Comparing Christian's burden with precedents in the medieval sermon tradition, however, points up how thoroughly the Reformers' emphasis on the Bible had connected guilt and the burden not only with one another but also, more especially, with the experience of reading. As the opening paragraph of *The Pilgrim's Progress* unfolds, we learn of the intimate connection between the burden and the Book. Bunyan's alliteration underlines it:

> I dreamed, and behold *I saw a Man cloathed with Raggs, standing in a certain place, with his face from his own House, a Book in his hand, and a great burden upon his Back.*

Christian himself recognizes, as he owns first to Evangelist and then to Mr. Worldly Wiseman, that he got his burden "[b]y reading this Book" (*PP,* p. 18). A marginal gloss confirms our suspicion that the book is the Bible. That it is only an incomplete — or an imperfectly understood — version, however, will be evident after Christian loses his burden. Then he will receive a roll, given him by one of the Shining Ones. Unlike his book it will bring him comfort and refreshment when he reads.

Another marginal gloss, next to the first paragraph, reminds us that the image of guilt as a burden is biblical. The image comes from Luther's favorite book in the Old Testament, where the Psalmist complains that "mine iniquities are gone over mine head: as an heavy burden they are too heavy for me" (Ps. 38: 4). Christian's interpretation of his plight also owes a great deal to Luther's favorite books in the New Testament, Paul's letters to the Galatians and the Romans. Paul had argued that the Scripture — what, by synecdoche and according to standard Jewish usage, he called "the Law" — serves to accuse and condemn the sinner. This intimate connection between guilt and interpretation, for which the burden on Christian's back is so powerful a figure, came to the forefront in Christian piety only at the Reformation. It was Luther who rescued the connection between the burden and the Book, and he made it a cardinal notion that the true Christian is to live by "the Bible only," and not by "mere human traditions." Bunyan's Christian is singled out by the fact that the book awakens in his sensitive conscience the oppressive feeling of guilt. None of his neighbors, he explains, has made a similar interpretation; none "saw their danger as I saw mine" (*PP,* p. 26). It is significant then that Christian loses his burden just after he has visited the House of the Interpreter and made "progress" in learning to interpret for himself.[47]

With its conception of a burden that is discovered by reading and is lost just after acquiring interpretive skills, *The Pilgrim's Progress* offers a working definition of "faith in Christ" that links belief closely to reading. It is a linkage that Bunyan likely learned about at a particularly formative time, in the months after his first marriage, when he says that his wife had brought him a dowry of two popular devotional books: Arthur Dent's *Plaine Mans Path-way to Heauen. Wherin euery man may cleerly see whether he shall be saued or damned* and Lewis Bayly's *Practise of Pietie: Directing a Christian how to walke*. Both books taught a doctrine that associates feelings of guilt with illiteracy. Their teaching that a deficiency of scriptural knowledge is a sign of reprobation sent Bunyan on a quest for book-learning, along with religion, and Bunyan made the language of the Perkins tradition his own. *Grace Abounding* shows that he fully accepted an idea about faith that implied the need to develop it into a saving faith that included assurance. The story of his quest for a place shows, moreover, that he also accepted the notion that the authorized means for performing this work was to read the Scriptures experimentally. In this tradition the difficulties that he had in understanding the Bible could be understood both as a sign of his sinfulness and as blessed "afflictions" through which it was necessary to pass before achieving assurance.

Read in tandem with *Grace Abounding*, *The Pilgrim's Progress* shows that its author, who had felt an enormous interpretive burden in the face of "the Bible only," came to terms with his problem by continuing to read and by writing out his interpretations. His experience took its origins in the standard Lutheran reading of Galatians and Romans, reinforced by the popular insistence that the Scriptures be searched diligently and applied to oneself introspectively. These Scriptures—understood as "the Law"—accuse and condemn the sinner. They were commonly understood also to send a reader who is truly elect on an imaginary pilgrimage through the pages of the book. In *The Pilgrim's Progress*, Bunyan made of this an interpretive journey, designed to encourage the elect reader to the Celestial City of assurance, by means of right interpretation. In this regard it is of note that just as "burden" (or "burthen") was a common term not only for a "load of labour, duty, responsibility, blame, sin, sorrow, etc." (*OED*, I, 2) but also for "That which is borne in the womb" (*OED*, I, 4), so "travel" (or "travail") was a usual word not only for "bodily or mental.... toil" (*OED*, sb. 1), but also for "the labour and pain of child-birth" (*OED*, sb. 4).

Bunyan's experience, it should be added, was unlike that of Paul and Augustine and Luther in one important respect. He did not begin his journey as a well-educated man, and reading and interpreting were likely for him (and for many of his readers) burdensome in a more elementary sense. His books witness to the fact that as he was learning to read the Bible in the period after his first marriage, Bunyan was learning as well to make virtue of the labors involved in overcoming biblical illiteracy. The following chapters trace something of the history of his much more learned contemporary's progress, by diligence and ceaseless study, through the pages of this Book. For John Milton, the Bible became burdensome *after* he had rather than *while* he first learned to read, and after he had, in various and complicated ways, come to think of Matthew 25: 14–30 as a personally appropriate "place."

2. The Parable of the Talents as Milton's Uneasy Place

> ". . . the holy Ghost never intended that men who have Gifts and Abilities should bury them in the earth, but rather did command and stir up such to the exercise of their gift, and also did commend those that were apt and ready so to do, *they have addicted themselves to the ministery. . . .*"
> —John Bunyan, *Grace Abounding to the Chief of Sinners* (p. 84)

Since late in the seventeenth century, when an early anonymous biography of John Milton appeared, the parable of the talents (Matthew 25: 14–30; see Appendix) has often been pressed into service as if this biblical place above all others defined his "calling." Since late in the nineteenth century, critics and biographers, undaunted by the fact that Milton never wrote a spiritual autobiography, have often enlisted a familiar plot to supply what seems to them an unaccountable lack in the record: Milton's individual life is assumed to recapitulate a larger cultural "progress" towards an enlightened secularism. In this plot the concept of "talent" is made the hinge on which Milton turned from his youthful expectation that he would be a churchman to his mature identity as a political writer and a poet. It is now quite generally supposed that the parable influenced in a decisive way the choice of a poetic vocation in which Milton, after having been "Church-outed by the Prelats" (*CPW*, I, 823), could use his uncommon gifts to fulfill his natural abilities. Particularly indicative of the construction of an edifying biographical narrative is the proposal, put forward by William Haller in the 1930s, that Milton left behind the virtual equivalent of a spiritual autobiography, "singularly complete," although it requires "to be pieced together from various sources in his writings of different dates." Haller had to admit that Milton never revealed a "precise moment when he first felt the conviction of grace," but he nonetheless managed to create the impression that Milton had had the requisite conversion. According to Haller, Milton voiced in "Lycidas" a "personal confession of his effectual calling from God to be a poet," which he then answered "by the dedication of his talents to service prompted by faith." Milton, claimed Haller, found that the "gifts that made him fit for the church made him fit to serve God as a poet." For "the talent Milton discovered within himself was [the] same power to use words. This discovery and the shaping into act of the resolution to render back his talent enriched by great accomplishment was the decisive experience of his youth."[1]

Such claims for the applicability of the parable of the talents to Milton's life are much too facile. Nonetheless, there are some grounds for thinking that this "place" was particularly important to Milton in constructing his own sense of his life and work. As early as 1633 he referred to the parable in a letter to an unknown friend in which he included Sonnet 7 and defended his life of diligent study. In *An Apology Against a Pamphlet* (1642), without using the word "talent" as such, he referred to "guifts of Gods imparting" for which he would have to render a "certaine account" (*CPW*, I, 869). His best known reference to the parable appears in Sonnet 19, but his most extensive reference to it comes in the autobiographical preface to the Second Book of *The Reason of Church Government* (1642), where he invoked it to stress a sense of personal responsibility for which he wished to become known. In annotating the passage the editors of the magisterial Yale edition of the prose have given wide dissemination to the idea that this was "Milton's favorite parable" (I, 801n.).

There are also grounds for recognizing, however, that Milton's thinking about the parable in relation to his "Condition" was much more complicated than the standard biographical construction would have us suppose. For one thing, the parable did not always teach that every person is required to cultivate "natural abilities." In fact, in verse 15 the parable puts an explicit difference between "talents" and "abilities," and the long tradition of interpreting the "talents" dating to the church fathers referred them to the Scriptures themselves. Thus the association, as late as the passage from Bunyan, of multiplying talents specifically with a preaching "ministery." In fact, "talent," which was originally a unit of weight and then a unit of money, has through the centuries been taken to refer to Christian doctrine, to the Bible, to opportunities for service, and only relatively belatedly to natural abilities. Moreover, in Milton's childhood, even before Bunyan was born (in 1628), the parable was already being inducted into the sort of spiritual life in which one was expected to discover and acknowledge one's inherent sinfulness. In a sermon of 19 April 1618 preached not far from Milton's home, John Donne urged the importance of fulfilling the injunction in the parable to be productive, and he did this in a manner that tied the parable to the biblical place (I Tim. 1: 14–15) from which the title *Grace Abounding to the Chief of Sinners* would be taken nearly fifty years later. Donne proposed that using one's talents was the appropriate way to get beyond a feeling of utter unworthiness. "This is the conclusion for every humble christian," he urged, "no man is a greater sinner then I was, and I am not sure but that I may fall to be worse then ever I was, except I husband and imploy the Talents of Gods Graces better then I have done."[2]

The conjunction of the parable with the place to which both Donne and Bunyan joined it offered, early and late in Milton's life, a possible model, and it should be striking that he did not make use of it. The optimistic tones in which Milton's appropriation of the parable is generally treated seem to be inspired by the fact that in the long course of his writing career, both in prose and verse, Milton rarely accused himself of any wrongdoing. He left a more ample written record of his personal development than any major English writer who preceded him. Yet the rich autobiographical passages in *The Reason of Church Government* and *Defensio Secunda* (1654) offer nothing reminiscent of Augustine's wonderful account in the *Confessions* of his adolescent participation in the destruction of a pear orchard. Far from being repentant for his quarrels with his tutors, or for anything that may have happened with Mary Powell, Milton shows no impulse to present himself as a chief of sinners to whom, after a personal conversion, grace abounds. Defending himself from the charge that his blindness was a punishment, like Job he cries out as if in direct address to God, and appropriates the language of experimental religion to protest his innocence rather than to confess his guilt:

> And with respect to myself, though I have accurately examined my conduct, and scrutinized my soul, I call thee, O God, that searcher of hearts, to witness, that I am not conscious, either in the more early or in the later periods of my life, of having committed any enormity which might deservedly have marked me out as a fit object for such a calamitous visitation. But since my enemies boast that this affliction is only a retribution for the transgressions of my pen, I again invoke the Almighty to witness, that I never, at any time, wrote anything which I did not think agreeable to truth, to justice, and to piety. This was my persuasion then, and I feel the same persuasion now.[3]

Consistently Milton charted his course as an unbroken development, with interruptions to be sure, but without any dramatic reversal. Not only did he not leave behind a "singularly complete" conversion narrative to be "pieced together," but he did not display the anguished conscience that according to the conventions of spiritual autobiographies was a prerequisite for passing beyond hypocrisy to assurance of one's salvation.

Still, as Milton's insistence on self-scrutiny suggests, there were ways in which his conception of his life's story was continuous with popular ideas and practices that inform seventeenth-century conversion narratives. We know that there were occasions in his life when Milton did cite biblical passages to voice his experience. In the first years of his blindness, for instance, he had written into the autograph albums of two foreign visitors the phrase "for my strength is made perfect in weakness" (2 Cor. 12: 9) and signed his name to it. He also made prominent use of the same passage in *Defensio Secunda*. In these years, the passage was part of a standard repertoire. The preceding part of the verse — "My grace is sufficient for thee" — was the passage that, in the struggle for assurance that was waging in Bunyan's consciousness, rivalled the threatening passage about Esau (Heb. 12: 16–17). Other devotional literature of the period shows that this verse, along with Matthew 11: 28–30 (about the "light burden" borne by those who are "weary and heavy laden"), was regularly invoked as a source of surpassing consolation. The verse had been serving this purpose for well over a hundred years. It was regularly printed as the epigraph for Luther's oft reissued *Commentarie vpon the Galathians*.[4]

Given Milton's persistent emphasis on personal accountability throughout his writing career, it would be surprising to find him joining the ranks of writers who disclaimed responsibility for biblical passages that flashed upon their consciousness and fixed their eternal destinies. Nevertheless, it seems that Marshall Grossman is right when he proposes that Milton was intent on using the Bible as a "master text": the Scriptures were thought to make available a final perspective in relation to which any particular life's story might be understood as headed towards one of "two contrastive endings," a final reward or punishment.[5] Clearly, Milton was fascinated with the idea that every person is accountable and every life recountable, and to illustrate the biblical basis for this idea, when he put together his own account of his faith, he cited "Matt. xii. 36, 37: *every idle word that men speak, they will be called to account for it on the day of judgment: for according to your words you will be justified, and according to your words you will be condemned*" (*CPW*, VI, 622). In this regard it is of interest that the one sort of disobedience to which Milton publicly acknowledged he had ever been tempted was the abuse of his natural gifts, and in particular, his gift for language.

The Reason of Church Government was the first of Milton's antiprelatical tracts to be published with his name on the title-page; and in it he defended his intervention in the controversy as an exercise of "those few talents which God . . . had lent" him (*CPW*, I, 804). The autobiographical digression records his imaginings of an accusing voice with which he would have to contend if he did not use his ability and his learning for public service.[6] Engaging the popular idea that each person's life-narrative is to be rehearsed at a final reckoning before God's throne, Milton projects a future moment that his present intervention now insures will never come about, when he would have come before the judgment seat to hear a voice like the one in Matthew 25: 26–30, which condemns the man who hid his talent:

> Timorous and ingratefull, the Church of God is now again at the foot of her insulting enemies. . . . [W]hen time was, thou couldst not find a syllable of all that thou hadst read, or studied, to utter in her behalfe. Yet ease and leasure was given thee for thy retired thoughts out of the sweat of other men. Thou hadst the diligence, the parts, the language of a man. . . . God listen'd if he could heare thy voice among his zealous servants, but thou wert domb as a beast; from hence forward be that which thine own brutish silence hath made thee. (*CPW*, I, 804–5)

If we listen to Milton's various allusions to the parable — "that one Talent which is death to hide," "that comand in the gospell set out by the terrible seasing of him that hid the talent," "remembring . . . that God even to a strictnesse requires the improvment of . . . his entrusted gifts" (*CPW*, I, 320; 801) — it seems as if this may have been Milton's least favorite parable. He writes as if the dreadful voice that doomed the man who buried his talent was for him the functional equivalent of the passage from Hebrews that made Bunyan feel that he was excluded from the kingdom. "[T]he terrible seasing of him who hid the talent," like the case of Esau who had sold his birthright and could find no place of repentance, was a text that threatened to define the experience of one of the damned. Milton's fascination with this aspect of the parable has not received much attention.[7] Concentrating on the significance of his allusions for his vocational decisions, critics who have been busy constructing an optimistic account of the relevance of the parable to Milton's dedicated pursuit of a poetic career have allowed small scope to the decidedly negative tones of these allusions. Nor have they taken much account of Milton's apparent tendency to think of himself as a version of the third figure in the parable.

Working with the Conventions of Experimental Divinity

As the quotations from Donne and Bunyan at the start of this chapter suggest, the negative tones in Milton's allusions to the parable were typical. The sort of fear of the master voiced by the third figure in the parable had a distinctive resonance in a culture that accorded prominence to doctrines about reprobation and insisted that the elect were required to make their "calling and election sure." In the theological treatise that he compiled over many years and continued working on through the 1650s,[8] Milton voiced his dissent from the doctrine of double predestination, and in particular from the doctrine of predestined reprobation. Already in *The Reason of Church Government* he had been insisting, obliquely but unmistakably, that he himself would not be passively numbered among the reprobate.

Ever since the discovery of *De Doctrina Christiana* early in the nineteenth century, readers have been fascinated with its points of dissent from so-called orthodox doctrines. While some have been shocked or saddened, and others have devised strategies to induct the author into the ranks of the orthodox,[9] the category of "heresy" has served to endear Milton to another group of readers, whose perspective has been more or less enshrined in the magisterial Yale edition. The introductory apparatus in that volume, aside from providing the obligatory account of the composition and transmission of the document, concentrates exclusively on its doctrinal eccentricities. Those who emphasize Milton's "heresies," and invite others to admire his courageous defiance of religious authority, sometimes proceed as if his dissent implies that he treated the Bible as "a Nose of wax." Yet from the start of the treatise Milton emphatically denies that "heresy" aptly denominates any of his views. Some readers make a great deal of a single reference to the superiority of an inward Scripture over the written Bible (VI, 587), thereby saving Milton from the folly of his own insistence upon "the Bible only." What has been lost, what wranglers over questions about whether Milton was a heretic or not distract us from seeing, is what should seem most astonishing about this quotation-filled treatise: that is, it is a purposefully grotesque and monstrous (my invocation of Rabelais here is admiring not derogatory) image of the one Book which Milton and his imagined readers claimed to be the sole religious authority available.

By deciding to compile this treatise and by the ways in which he organized it, Milton implicated himself deeply in a Calvinist framework. He was seeking not to demolish or neglect it but to revise and transform it. He spoke in the idiom of the divines, and he made it his own: "God has revealed the way of eternal salvation only to the individual faith of each man, and demands of us that any man who wishes to be saved should work out his beliefs for himself" (VI, 118). His espousal of Arminian positions involved a recognition that the most serious dangers to religious freedom in his time lay neither in popery, which he held nearly beneath contempt, nor in a spiritualist dismissal of the Scriptures, but in a perversely urged interpretive disposition that placed intolerable burdens on the consciences of earnest readers. Instead of proposing either a deistical or a spiritualist alternative to Calvinism, Milton's theological treatise offered a more thoroughgoing engagement with biblical literature. The so-called "heresies" which have elicited praise or condemnation depending upon the predilections of modern critics are first and last a function of a serious attempt to adhere to "the Bible only."

Briefly to review, then, the well-known features of Milton's treatise that bear most directly on his relation to the program according to which one was required to make one's calling and election sure: far from rejecting the idea of an *ordo salutis,* Milton retains it and reshapes it. Even before he takes up Predestination (early, in chapter 4 of Book I), he treats at length God's Decrees (chapter 3). He stresses that predestination is conditional, looking to one's future belief and continued faith (*CPW,* VI, 168; 174). When he comes (in chapters 17–20) to discuss the standard topics of Renovation, Vocation, Regeneration, Repentance, and Saving Faith, his choice of categories accords well enough with systematic theologies in the Perkins tradition, and he proves willing explicitly to draw out implications about which others had been hesitant. In the discussion of saving faith, he deduces that "the seat of faith is not really the intellect but the will" and boldly insists that "our own effort is always required" (476; 480). In the chapter on Justification, he risks entertaining the idea that faith could be said to be a kind of "work": "if to believe is to act then faith is an action, or rather a habit acquired by frequent actions, not merely infused" (489). When he treats Assurance of Salvation and the Perseverance of the Saints (chapter 25), he quotes 2 Peter 1: 9–11. Yet he omits the verse (10) that had been the very watchword among experimentalist divines: "give diligence to make your calling and election sure: for if ye do these things, ye shall never fall." Milton insists that assurance "must be in our power, since it is our responsibility" (504). By comparison with other reformed treatises and with the practical divinity of his time, he lays great stress on the importance of the human will to persevere: "those who persevere, not those who are elect, are said to attain salvation" (509). This issue is made to provide the framework for the second book of the treatise, where Milton begins by defining "the true worship of God" as "eagerness to do good works" and invokes, instead of 2 Peter 1: 10, the passage which immediately precedes it (1: 5–8). This biblical place — *"try your hardest, all of you, to add virtue to your faith . . . for if you have these things, and to an abundant degree, they will ensure that you are not inert or unfruitful"* (*CPW,* VI, 637) — stands behind Michael's final advice to Adam in *Paradise Lost* (XII, 581–87). Milton's dissent from the prevailing Calvinist reading of 2 Peter 1: 10 involved a recognition that interminable wranglings about predestination were wasteful, even harmful. Catholics had identified the quest for certitude about one's personal salvation as the Achilles' heel of Calvinism, and this likely kept many other Protestants from explicitly acknowledging that seeking a biblical place to make one's calling and election sure often had deleterious effects.[10]

Already in Sonnet 7 and in its accompanying letter of 1633, Milton had been thinking and writing in the context of the growing literature on cases of conscience, where Conscience was said to be "Mans Over-Seer" and introspective readers drew on biblical texts for a language to define their personal "conditions."[11] After the publication of *Poems of Mr. John Milton* in 1645, he wrote poetry with increasing attunement to the despairs felt by people who had been accustomed to looking for their case defined in Scripture. He was decidedly unlike Bunyan and other writers of spiritual autobiographies in the way he dealt with the practices of reading for experimental knowledge. Milton developed early a considerable facility operating within — and with — this tradition of Bible-reading in which texts intruded into people's consciousness as voices addressed to their situations. This facility is clearly evinced in his deft handling of dreadful threatening voices that he quotes, as it were, in *The Reason of Church Government*. Like this first voice quoted above, Milton projects a second imagined voice, one that suggests that divine retribution will assume the form that in Dante is called the *contrapasso*, that is, that the punishment will fit the crime. This passage parallels the biblical original in its contrast between the slothful servant who is finally excluded and the worthy servants who are rewarded:

> Or else I should have heard on the other eare, slothfull, and ever to be set light by, the Church hath now overcom her late distresses after the unwearied labours of many her true servants that stood up in her defence; thou also wouldst take upon thee to share amongst them of their joy: but wherefore thou? where canst thou shew any word or deed of thine which might have hasten'd her peace; . . . what before was thy sin, is now thy duty to be, abject, and worthlesse. (*CPW,* I, 805)

The recording of the dreadful threatening voices makes explicit what Milton meant when he referred in the letter to an unknown friend to "that comand in the gospell set out by the terrible seasing of him that hid the talent." With its concern to explain away that "certaine belatednesse" which he acknowledged to be within him, the letter also helps to clarify Milton's distinctive and personal way of understanding the parable of the talents at this time, that is, as a text that gave voice to some expectations which he had begun to internalize. Defending himself against the possible charge that his life of study was slothful, he was interested in urging precisely the irrelevance of the place about the unprofitable servant to his current situation. The letter shows that, if the parable were to be applied to him, it was imperative to attend to the limits of the analogy, and the parable was to be interpreted by way of another text, a place within the parable of the laborers in the vineyard (Matt. 20: 1–16), in which he heard a promise:

> [T]his very consideration of that great comandment [about using one's talents] does not presse forward as soone as may be to underg[o], but keeps off wth a sacred reverence & religious advisement how best to undergoe[,] not taking thought of beeing late so it give advantage to be more fit, for those that were latest lost nothing when the maister of the vinyard came to give each one his hire. (*CPW*, I, 320)

In this way Milton seems to have found it useful to have someone else attempt to impose a biblical place upon his situation. Arguing that the text about the unprofitable servant did not fit him, he appealed instead and indirectly to the activity of the first servant, who, in the Geneva version, was said to have "occupied" with his talents (25: 16); the Authorized Version rendered this "traded." Milton, when he interpreted the parable by way of the other parable about labor, was relying more directly on the Greek, *ergasato*, literally "worked," rendered *operatus est* in the Vulgate. That is, using his philological training and the method of "conferring places," he conceived the process of laboring to understand and apply the Scriptures as imitating the action of the servant who multiplied his talents. In accord with a standard patristic interpretation of the parable, to which we will return below, Milton interpreted the initial talents, which were weighty and valuable and were bestowed on each person "according to his several ability" (25: 15), to be the Scriptures themselves. He understood himself to be working with them, multiplying them, as he reinterpreted a place that threatened him by way of a different place that promised a full reward to those who begin to labor even at the eleventh hour.[12] In this way he argued that the judgment pronounced against the man with a single talent would, in his case, be premature. By a discreet choice of biblical places with which to work, Milton thus offered something of a model of how reading for experimental knowledge might be responsibly carried out. It was not by magically hearing a single text and supposing that one had merely happened upon it that one was to be saved. Rather one was to work out one's salvation, as if in fear and trembling, by "an industrious and judicious comparing of place with place."[13]

"That precious Talent" in the Earliest Life of Milton

While Milton himself alluded to the parable of the talents in ways that complicate the idea that it was for him a definitive "place," whoever wrote the early "Life of Mr. John Milton"[14] thought it likely that readers were already familiar with the idea that his subject had had a special affinity for the parable. Curiously, this biographer connected the exercise of "that precious Talent" with the expeditiousness of Milton's choice of a bride. Although this suggested indirectly that the marriage marked a point at which Milton's fulfillment of the injunctions of the parable had been at risk, the potential conflict remains beneath the surface of the narrative. In this matter, as in most others, the writer follows Milton's own lead and provides no details about domestic troubles.

When the biographer first speaks of Milton's "Talent," he couples with it the demonstrative adjective in a manner reminiscent of the poet's own reference to "that one Talent" in Sonnet 19. Whereas in the sonnet Milton's "that" points the reader to the "one talent" which the biblical parable shows it was "death to hide," here "that" refers to Milton's own "talent," which is said to have involved the ability to make good use of his time. The telling allusion comes in the course of a treatment of the period when Milton was writing the anti-prelatical tracts:

> his manner of Settlement fitting him for the reception of a Wife, hee in a moneths time (according to his practice of not wasting that precious Talent) courted, marryed, and brought home . . . a Daughter of Mr Powell.[15]

Despite the fact that in the letter of 1633 and in Sonnet 19 Milton had alluded to the parable in contexts where he was urging the importance of waiting for a propitious moment still to come, it is characteristic of the biographer's perspective to associate fulfilling the parable with making the most of one's time. In this sense the biography presents itself as the "true account" that Milton had himself projected into the distant future. Milton was now dead, his life completed, so that a shapely narrative was possible. This sort of theory about the biographer's work is provided by Charles Cotton, in commendatory verses written in 1672/3, and printed in the fourth edition of Izaak Walton's *Lives* in the year after Milton's death. The writings of Donne, Wotton, Hooker, and Herbert are acknowledged in these verses to have inspired Walton to write their lives; only a reader of the completed record was able to show "how th'Almighties grace, / By various, and, more admirable ways, / Brought them to be the Organs of his praise." Walton had been able to write the definitive account of Donne's life in ways that Donne himself could not, because the ultimate meaning of all his actions could not be fixed until his death. Walton enjoyed an ultimate providential perspective from which even the sins of youth could be finally evaluated.[16]

Similarly, the survivor who wrote the first biography of Milton thought he had license for casting Milton's writings into a frame that had necessarily remained unavailable while the poet lived. The completion of the life made timely the idea that Milton's writings, passed on now to aftertimes, proved that his "talents" had been employed. The thesis of the biography—that Milton's life is to be celebrated because he provided an exemplary model of how to use his natural endowments for the service of others—is already implicit in the first two paragraphs. There the writer presents his conception of a biographer's task in terms parallel to those adduced by spiritual autobiographers of Milton's era, who routinely referred to the idea that their stories might prove religiously useful for others:

> To write the Lives of Single Persons is then a commendable Undertaking, when by it some Moral benefit is design'd to Mankind. Hee who has that in aim, will not imploy his time or Pen, to record the history of bad men, how sucessful or great soever they may have bin. . . .
> But to celebrate, whether the Guifts or Graces, the natural Endowments, or acquir'd laudable Habitts of Persons eminent in thir Generations, while it gives glory to God, the bestower of all good things, and (by furnishing a Modell) tends to the edification of our Brethren, is little less then the duty of every Christian. (p. 17)

In the pages that follow the writer frequently praises Milton for having acted in accord with the principle that gifts, graces, natural endowments, and acquired habits, which come ultimately from "the bestower of all good things," are to employed for the edification of others. This application of the parable was wholly in keeping with the dominant interpretation of the sixteenth and seventeenth centuries, spread abroad when the Geneva Bible proclaimed that the parable forbids "idleness" and commands that one use one's talents "to Gods glorie and his neighbours profite."[17] There was "no ill management of his time" in Milton's Italian journey (p. 21). His private studies were aimed at laying in "a large stock of knowlege, which as design'd not for the purchase of Wealth, so neither intended hee it, as a Misers hoard, to ly useless" (p. 21). When Milton set up a household of his own, "his first labours were very happily dedicated to, what had chiefest place in his affections, and had bin no small part of his Study, the service of Religion" (p. 21). After he went blind, "hee began that laborious work of amassing out of all the Classic Authors, both in Prose and Verse, a *Latin Thesaurus* . . . ; Also the composing *Paradise Lost* And the framing a *Body of Divinity* out of the Bible" (p. 29). His labors, "notwithstanding the several Calamities befalling him in his fortunes" (p. 29), were prodigious. The biographer adds a list of the works of Milton's later years, from *Paradise Regained* and *Samson Agonistes* to the *Accedence*, the *Logica,* and the Greek Thesaurus he had begun, concluding that Milton "scarce left any part of learning unimprov'd" (p. 29). Summing up his subject's character, the writer slides over from remarks that sound like the testimony of an intimate into the sort of language with which the author of *The Reason of Church Government* might have hoped to render his account before the divine judgment seat:

> He had naturally a Sharp Witt, and steddy Judgment; which helps toward attaining Learning hee improv'd by an indefatigable attention to his Study. . . . Yet did hee not reckon this Talent but as intrusted with him; and therefore dedicated all his labours to the glory of God, & some public Good; Neither binding himselfe to any of the gainfull Professions, nor having any worldly Interest for aim in what he taught. (p. 29)

In short, the earliest biography drew together two related features of autobiographical passages in Milton's writing, the association of his life with the parable of the talents and the emphasis on his "indefatigable attention to his Study." It served to consolidate a view that Milton himself had sought to project but over which he could not exercise ultimate control. In the effort to create a unified impression of a life headed toward a satisfying closure, the early anonymous biographer, who ignored all controversy about the meaning and implications of the parable, appealed to it as a transparent, normative, and sufficient framework for understanding the whole of his subject's life.

Milton's *ingenium*

Although Milton provided in the written record the materials with which to see in his life a fulfillment of the parable, he was not so explicit about this as his biographers and translators have been. Nor did he (any more than Luther or the mature Bunyan or hundreds of other Bible-readers) think that there was a single biblical place that epitomized his case for life. There are actually rather few references to his "talents" in Milton's prose, and "talent" is a *hapax legomenon* in his poetry, appearing only in Sonnet 19. The idea that the parable was important to Milton has, however, influenced the practice of translators, who sometimes use the word "talent" to render the Latin word *ingenium*. The translations, in their turn, then color our idea of Milton's biography, perhaps nowhere more conspicuously and influentially than in the famous autobiographical passage from the *Defensio Secunda* of 1654, where Milton begins the survey of his participation in the controversy about church government by telling how determined he was to be "of use" to his country, his church, and his fellow Christians. He declares that he had resolved to suspend his other interests and "*huc omne ingenium, omnes industriæ vires transferre*" (*Works*, VIII, 128). Already in Fellowes's translation in the early nineteenth century, *ingenium* was rendered as "talents." In the Yale edition Helen North has followed suit: he resolved ". . . to devote to this conflict all [his] talents and all [his] active powers" (*CPW*, IV, 622).

In its modern secular sense "talent" is an apt enough rendering of the Latin here. The problem is that in the mid-seventeenth-century "talent" had not been thoroughly disconnected from the biblical parable and did not refer unequivocally, as *ingenium* does, to natural ability. In his universal dictionary of 1658, Milton's nephew, Edward Phillips, glossed "talent" only as a sum of money.[18] For most people, the word still had a decidedly biblical resonance; and the idea that the "talents" in the parable were natural abilities, far from being established, was an object of controversy. For the parable explicitly distinguishes between talents and "abilities" (Matt. 25: 15). It is anachronistic to render *ingenium* as "talent," and it pre-judges the sorts of questions about the relations between nature and grace in which Milton and his contemporaries took so active an interest. More important still, it disguises the fact that when Milton alluded to the parable before 1642, he prescinded from much that was controversial about it, and he invoked it as if its meaning and application were evident. Nonetheless, these habits of translation, which call attention to Milton's fascination with his *ingenium*, help to show one way in which the parable was attractive to him.

In his Latin poetry Milton several times employed the word *ingenium* with reference to his natural disposition, and increasingly he used it to refer specifically to his poetical abilities. In *Elegia prima,* speaking of the circumstances surrounding his rustication, he tells Diodati that the threats of a stern tutor and other indignities have been intolerable to his *ingenium.* Here he seems to have been referring to his "nature" (Shawcross), or "spirit" (Carey). In retrospect we can see that he may have been thinking that scholastic training was inimical to the poetical spirit.[19] Elsewhere, in *Elegia tertia,* the connection with poetical power is clearer: his *ingenium* (translated by Carey as "talent") is said not to be up to the task of relating what he has seen in a dream-vision. In *Elegia quinta,* he avails himself of the word twice, first as he wonders whether the coming of spring will affect his *ingenium,* that is, whether it will renew his inspiration. The second appearance of the word brings his conception of his *ingenium* into a context analogous with the biblical parable, where the bestower of talents expects a return:

> Quid tam grande sonat distento spiritus ore?
>   Quid parit haec rabies, quid sacer iste furor?
> Ver mihi, quod dedit ingenium, cantabitur illo;
>   Profuerint isto reddita dona modo.[20]

Here Milton locates his *ingenium* in the context of a network of transactions, revealing an awareness of the duties attendant upon receiving personal gifts. Although Carey renders the last line "her gifts will be repaid with interest," there is no reference to the biblical parable in the poem. The poet's insight seems to be rooted rather in etymology. *Ingenium,* what we would in current English denominate "in-born" talent, or skill, is intimately related to what is "borne," that is what is "produced" or "brought forth" (*in* + *geno,* or *gigno*). In this respect it is worth recalling not only that the word "burden" could refer to what is borne in the womb, but that the Greek word *tokos,* usually translated "interest" in English versions of the parable of the talents, also signifies "offspring."

Some Are Born Great, Some Achieve Greatness

"Ingenuity" is not a poetical word, and it is not surprising that Milton nowhere in his English poetry uses it. Nor does he use the word "ingenuous," although he did employ this adjectival form, which in the seventeenth century was frequently confused with "ingenious," several times in his prose. Robert A. Greene has traced the emergence of the usage whereby, before it came to refer to inventive skill and scientific insight (cf. ingenious), "ingenuity" was used in the mid-seventeenth century to refer to a kind of moral rationalism that involved qualities of candor, liberal-mindedness, and openness to learning.[21] Milton regularly used the word in this sense, referring in the *Animadversions* both to "the ingenious Reader" (*CPW*, I, 693) and "*the ingenuous Reader*" (I, 664). It was common to join the adjective to this noun in the 1640s, when amidst the increasing freedom to publish, writers often addressed themselves to "ingenuous" readers on whom they claimed to count for an open-minded hearing. Milton elsewhere joined "ingenuous" with the adjectives "noble" (I, 841), "honest" (I, 854), "friendly" (I, 884), and "wise" (II, 286) and in *Areopagitica* spoke of "the free and ingenuous sort" who "evidently were born to study, and love lerning for it self" (II, 531). In *Tetrachordon* he virtually identified ingenuity with "*cleer conscience, willingnesse to avouch what might be question'd, or to be better instructed*" (II, 581). Some years later, in *A Treatise of Civil Power*, he connected "Christian ingenuitie" specifically with the practice whereby readers "examin seriously" in order to find what is "cleerly . . . true" (VII, 271).

This idea of Christian ingenuity as a characteristic of wise, noble, honest, and friendly persons who were "born to study" was regularly associated with a specific biblical place, a text that from early in the Reformation had been invoked to prove the Christian's right and obligation to search the Scriptures and to try every doctrine. Protestants routinely charged papists with requiring of the common people an unthinking "implicit faith." To illustrate that the Bible itself taught that every believer needed to have an "experimental" knowledge, they appealed to Acts 17: 11, where the Jews of Berea are said to have been "more noble [*eugenesteroi*] than those in Thessalonica, in that they received the word with all readiness of mind, and searched the Scriptures daily, whether those things [that Paul had taught them] were so."[22]

Biblical commentators differed on the meaning of the adjective *eugenesteroi*. Calvin was in the minority when he proposed that it was to be taken literally, meaning well-born, and that it referred to the "nobilitie" that consists in "excellencie of byrth." He claimed that the Bereans provided a rare instance where "those who are great in the world . . . undertake the reproach of the crosse." The Geneva Bible, by contrast, explained that the word meant, "Not more excellent of birth, but more prompt, and couragious in receiuing the worde of God."²³ This was the view developed by Thomas Jackson, who interpreted *eugenesteroi* as "of a more ingenuous disposition" and praised the Bereans for believing not on the basis of Paul's personal authority but because they had tested his doctrine by searching the Scriptures for themselves. Greene has shown that other seventeenth-century commentators elaborated this idea into high praise for the Bereans' exercise of reason, as free men, and for the intelligence, modesty, and humility with which they examined the evidence of the Scriptures, comparing texts of the sacred writings without the "Puritan anguish over assurance of salvation." Matthew Poole's variorum Bible commentary glossed *eugenesteroi* with *ingenuus* and *ingenium liberale*.²⁴

It was for this sort of nobility, partly derived from birth and breeding, but chiefly a function of the disposition to search the Scriptures, that his first biographer introduced Milton as descended from the "true Nobility" that characterized the Bereans:

> The learned Mr. John Milton, born about the yeer sixteen hundred and eight, is said to bee descended from an antient Knightly Family in Buckinghamshire, that gave name to the chief place of thir abode. . . . However that bee, his Father was entitled to a true Nobility in the Apostle Pauls Heraldry; having bin disinherited about ye beginning of Queen Elizabeths reign by his Father a Romanist . . . [for] reading the Bible. (p. 18)

That Milton likely took pride and delight in making known the cause of his father's disinheritance is suggested by the fact that all the early biographers, whatever sources they consulted, included this incident.

The first biographer's interest in his subject's Berean lineage is of a piece with his concern to present Milton's true account. Already in Calvin's commentary on the passage in Acts there was a tendency to think of the Bereans as people who had multiplied their talents in their master's absence. Calvin emphasizes that their faith shows "howe effectuall and fruitfull [Paul's] preaching had beene. For those who had onely tasted of the first principles of godlinesse, doe neuerthelesse profit and goe forward though hee be absent, and exercise themselues in the continuall reading of the Scripture." He contrasts them with those who rest in "idlenes," having "no care to profite," so that they "loose that small seed, which they had at the first."²⁵ Other writers were even more direct in connecting the place in Acts with the parable of the talents. John Preston listed diligent listening as the first remedy for difficulty in hearing Christ's voice speaking in the Scripture, in fulfillment of the injunction to use one's talents. He went on then to recommend a whole process to follow:

> lay up what you heare: let it abide and continew with you . . . you must *doe as Mary did; she layed up all the sayings that shee heard of Christ, and pondered them in her heart, Luke* 2. 51. The Disciples often questioned of Christ: which proves, that they pondered his Words in their hearts: So the Nobles of *Berea, they searched the Scripture*.[26]

Other commentators also associated the activities of the Bereans with Matthew's parables of watchfulness. On the one hand the Bereans were likened to the five wise virgins of Matthew 25: 1–13:

> The *Jews* of *Berea* did excel . . . not so much in birth as in disposition: . . . they seriously thought upon what [Paul] had said, and compared it with the Scriptures. And thus God gave them the preparation of the heart; and they brought their empty Vessels. No wonder then that the Oyl of Grace ran into them, and filled them. The *Jews* do call their Learned men, the sons of Nobles; and according to that expression, these *Bereans* that had acted so ingenuously and wisely, were said to be more Noble.

On the other hand, they were compared to those who multiplied their talents. One gloss on Acts 17: 12 (the verse after the one about searching the Scriptures concerns the multiplication of believers) quotes Matthew 25: 28 to establish a virtual equation between diligent searching and using one's talents: "God blessing his own gifts, giving still *unto them that had,* and made use of them."[27] This equation aptly sums up Milton's characteristic understanding of the meaning of multiplying talents. It was, however, an understanding to which he was not always and everywhere slavishly devoted.

Spending a "talent of sport"

For his part, Milton rarely referred to the Bereans as such, although (as Chapter Three will show) he invoked their precedent at a telling moment in the *Treatise of Civil Power*.[28] In *Colasterion,* however, he spent a good deal of ink attacking the ignoble "nameless" writer of the answer to his *Doctrine and Discipline of Divorce*. Consistently, he cast his antagonist into the station of an impudent workingman, whose "*genuine* [i.e., in-born] basenes" (*CPW*, II, 751) ill equipped him for what the author of *Tetrachordon* had come to regard as the noble mental labor of biblical interpretation. At several points Milton defends the crudeness of his own satirical language by proposing that it befits his adversary. In the penultimate paragraph, claiming that the whole work of refutation is beneath him, he makes his most casual and curious allusion to the parable of the talents.

The simultaneous publication of *Tetrachordon* and *Colasterion* represents an unusual moment in Milton's career as a biblical interpreter, a point at which his writing bifurcated into two distinct veins. Disdaining the close biblical interpretation that he pored into the scriptural commentary, in *Colasterion* Milton began to heap scorn on ordinary Bible-readers who lacked the proper birth and breeding for scriptural interpretation, much as a wife might lack "fitness" for "spiritual conversation." The nameless answerer is said to be a "Pork," unworthy of philosophical refutation, since he "never read any" philosophy (737). Milton chastises him for "presuming out of his utter ignorance in the Ebrew, to interpret" the language of Deut. 24: 1 (744). In fact, Milton's whole tract is meant to assign his critic, as its Greek name indicates, "a place of punishment" for his foolish intervention in the dispute. As a "Servingman both by nature and by function, an Idiot by breeding, and a Solliciter by presumption," he is incapable, according to Milton, of appreciating "the gentlest ends of Mariage," even of understanding "what the meaning is of gentle" (741). The principal evidence of the critic's ignorance and his lack of gentle breeding, which come to the same thing, is precisely his inability to "bee satisfy'd" with the noble argument of *The Doctrine and Discipline of Divorce*. Milton compares him to "a Boar in a Vinyard, . . . champing and chewing over, what I could mean by this *Chimera* of a fit conversing Soul, notions and words never made for those chopps." Like the Lady scorning to "go on" with Comus, Milton declares in exasperation, "But what should a man say more to a snout in this pickle, what language can be low and degenerat anough?" (747).

What seems to have touched Milton closely was the charge that, by virtue of his birth and breeding and especially his learning, he was the one unfit for "meet conversation." "It is true," his critic had written,

> if every man were of your breeding and capacitie, there were some colour for this plea [about the need for "meet conversation"]; for we believe you count no woman to due conversation accessible, as to you, except she can speak Hebrew, Greek, Latine, & French, and dispute against the Canon law as well as you, or at least be able to hold discourse with you. But other Gentlemen of good qualitie are content with meaner and fewer endowments, as you know well enough. (*CPW*, II, 742n.)

When he had answered all his antagonist's other charges point by point, though omitting to answer this one, Milton concluded *Colasterion* by heaping on further abuse, insisting that his "ridiculous adversary" (757) had hardly elicited from him the noble effort of which he was capable. Comparing himself to Hercules, the cleaner of the Augean stable, he refers to his refutation as an "under-work of scowring and unrubbishing the low and sordid ignorance of such a presumptuous lozel" (756).

It was in this context of emphasizing that momentous labors had been imposed upon him that Milton drew upon the text which so many of his admirers have thought to be his special biblical place, only to use it with an air of casualness and even mockery. Although he might have wished a worthier adversary, his "fate," remarks Milton with mock-disappointment, "extorts from mee a talent of sport, which I had thought to hide in a napkin" (757). Milton did not deign here to make the careful comparison of place with place that characterized *Tetrachordon* and that became the basic method in the *De Doctrina Christiana*. Instead he merely conflated Matthew's parable of the talents with Luke's parable of the pounds, where the third servant, rather than burying his talent, "kept [a pound] laid up in a napkin," because he feared his master was "an austere man, taking up that [he] laid not down, and reaping that [he] did not sow" (19: 20, 22). In 1645, exasperated by the ignorance of his opponents, Milton seems to have had less reason than he had in 1633 to be threatened by the parable of the talents. He now had plenty to show for himself, a substantial body of prose works already in print and a book of poems soon to make their appearance. Yet the continuing insistence on his strenuous labors suggests a certain uneasiness with the biblical place that, like the charge that he had made himself unfit for marital conversation, seemed to touch his own case rather closely.

Mental Labor as Milton's "portion"

In his years at university, when he was already discovering his considerable poetical ability, Milton had routinely dismissed scholastic exercises as inimical to his *ingenium*. Yet in the written record of his life, he never ceased to emphasize that he understood "labour and intent study" to be his "portion in... life" (*CPW*, I, 810). Unlike the "portion" of marital happiness which the first divorce tract shows he had also anticipated (II, 256), this "portion" was native, an inheritance from his father, through whose "ceaselesse diligence and care" (I, 808) he had been educated, and it was congruent with his poetical abilities, what he came to call "natures part" (I, 889). Paradoxically, and felicitously, this was an inheritance that did not preclude the need for effort; rather it embodied and justified that necessity. To be destined from childhood for a preaching ministry was to have a calling in which one was permitted and obliged, more than in any other station within Protestantism, to work.[29] Hence, the attraction of the parable of the talents.

This feature of his self-understanding was in no way compromised when Milton declined to take orders in the church. By the time he wrote *Areopagitica* he had made a cardinal principle out of the idea that every man is his own priest, urging the utter necessity of each person thinking through his position for himself, as truth cannot be possessed apart from the process by which it is sought: "A man may be a heretick in the truth; and if he beleeve things only because his Pastor sayes so, or the Assembly so determins, without knowing other reason, though his belief be true, yet the very truth he holds, becomes his heresie." The sentence that follows announces the crucial metaphor: "There is not any burden that som would gladlier post off to another, then the charge and care of their Religion" (*CPW*, II, 543). To Milton, this insistence on the personal responsibility of each believer was the logical extension of the original genius of the Reformation. The "reforming of reformation itself" was dependent upon responsible personal interpretation, the taking up of one's burden to interpret the Scriptures for oneself.

The Epistle at the head of the *De Doctrina Christiana* introduces Milton's mature theological views in a manner continuous with this emphasis on mental work. He had labored, Milton explains, "with all possible diligence, never sparing [himself] in any way" (VI, 118). In fact, he presents the treatise as the result of a series of Herculean efforts:

> I began by devoting myself when I was a boy to an earnest study of the Old and New Testaments in their original languages, and then proceeded to go carefully through some of the shorter systems of theologians. I also started, following the example of these writers, to list under general headings all passages from the scriptures which suggested themselves for quotation, so that I might have them ready to hand when necessary. At length, gaining confidence, I transferred my attention to more diffuse volumes of divinity, and to the conflicting arguments in controversies over certain heads of faith. (VI, 119)

Dissatisfied with the controversial writings of Protestant scholastics, he made "a fresh start," he says, and compiled "by my own exertion and long hours of study" a treatise based on the Scriptures alone (120).

This insistence on the difficult mental labors he had performed ties the mature work to the early autobiographical writings. Already in the letter of 1633, defending himself against the charge that his continuing private studies amounted to committing an "unprofitable sin of curiosity," Milton had cited the passage in which Christ commands all "to labour while there is light" (John 9: 4). He asked sympathy from his correspondent, moreover, by suggesting that, without sufficient learning, he would be left as "the most helplesse, pusilanimous & unweapon'd creature in the word" (I, 319). As Christopher Grose has shown with respect to this passage,[30] Milton was already associating himself here with those who "labour in the word," especially with the Apostles, whom he would later praise as eminent "in their powerfull preaching, their unwearied labouring in the Word, their unquenchable charity" (I, 715). When Milton referred elsewhere in the letter to the parable of the talents, he interpreted it, as we have seen, by way of a parable about laboring, and he spoke of a "due & tymely obedience to that comand in the gospell set out by the terrible seasing of him that hid the talent" (I, 320). The paternal legacy, as William Kerrigan has amply proposed, was duty, a strong sense of what was commanded, especially by the gospel. The son would please his father by working long and hard, at a young age already sitting up late to read, risking his allotted share of oil in his midnight watches.[31]

It was especially in the tracts of 1642, written in the months before he married, that Milton most extensively and adamantly stressed "the wearisome labours and studious watchings, wherein [he had] spent and tir'd out almost a whole youth" (I, 869). Characteristically, he depicted these studious labors as a use of the talent which God had lent him. Just as characteristically, he took this line of interpreting the parable for granted, as if the meaning of this place were utterly plain and he needed to say nothing about what was traditional and what was innovative about the ways in which he applied it. Yet interpretations of the parable which suppressed the monetary sense of "talent" and proceeded as if Jesus had been talking literally about natural abilities were common chiefly among readers who, unlike Milton, did not know Latin and Greek. Readers who were familiar only with the vernacular Bible easily overlooked the fact that the parable itself does not equate talents and abilities.

Milton's Burden and the Parable of the Talents

In 1643, Milton's attitudes about the nature of Scriptural plainness changed radically. Yet he continued to emphasize his conscientious intellectual labors, even as he directed them increasingly to interpreting biblical places. It will be the work of Chapter Three to begin documenting some manifestations, in the years that followed Milton's first marriage, of his having embraced a new burden of interpretation. Chapter Four will then explore some uses to which Milton put the parable, and some biblical places that he associated with it, in two well-known sonnets. Here, however, I want to consider the ways in which, before the Scriptures themselves began to seem burdensome to him, Milton made an older, traditional understanding of "talent" serve his purposes in the debate about church government. Three of the five instances of the word "talent" in the corpus of Milton's prose come from the anti-episcopal tracts. In each instance Milton connects talents, as the Church Fathers and many medieval commentators had done, specifically with the obligation of prelates to read and interpret the Scriptures. As Haller understood when he associated this biblical place with the poet's "calling," Milton relies on this traditional understanding of the parable to justify his intervention in the controversy and to validate a displacement of authority to a learned layman.

Given his resolve to stand on the plain truth of "the Bible only" as the sole source of authority in religion, and given his complaints against his adversaries for smothering that truth with a "hors load of citations and fathers" (I, 822), it was not in Milton's interest to point out ways in which his interpretation of the parable accorded with that of several Church Fathers, including Origen, Athanasius, and Augustine, who took the parable as specially addressed to prelates. (Just as Luther had depicted Augustine's ideas on justification as an imperfect anticipation of his own insight into the plain meaning of Pauline "righteousness," so Milton, had it been called to his attention that he was following a traditional line of interpretation, might have claimed that his predecessors had simply perceived the plain truth which God had made available to all.) Among those who saw in the parable a prelate's obligation to preach the gospel was Clement of Alexandria, who, in the introduction to his miscellanies, equated proclaiming the Word, whether by preaching or by writing, with the multiplying of talents. Similarly, Caesarius of Arles, speaking at an episcopal consecration, urged that the bishop was to fulfill the injunction of the parable by reading Scripture, by preaching, and by teaching. Origen made just this sort of use of the parable. Encountering a text that he found puzzling, he took occasion to remark that preachers are to go to work interpreting such places in order to earn interest on the Word of God.[32]

In the early church it was characteristic to appeal to the parable against deficient church leaders. Athanasius invoked the parable to chide a bishop for negligence of his duties. Augustine ended a sermon on the Good Shepherd by insisting that presbyters and bishops have an obligation to speak up in the face of evil. Alluding to a prelate's duties as a watchman over God's people, he pointed out that the overseer will have to give an accounting: if he fails to speak up, his fate may be likened to that of the servant in the parable who hid his talent. Elsewhere, in another sermon, Augustine recommended that one way to use the talents was to "answer murmurers." He chided bishops who fail to superintend, and he encouraged heads of households to look "with all vigilance" to the salvation of those in their charge.[33]

All these interpretations took the talents of the parable to refer not to natural abilities (the modern "talent") but to Christian doctrine, and often to the Scriptures themselves. It is true that presbyters and bishops were expected to have the requisite natural abilities for their vocations, but the chiders of bishops blamed them for failing to use talents, not for failing to have them. Other interpreters, especially after the patristic period, did associate talents more closely with natural abilities. Both the pseudo-Bede and Hugh of St. Victor, in fact, used the word *ingenium* with reference to the talents in their commentaries.[34] It was Chrysostom, however, who among the Fathers most closely anticipated the tendency that can be seen in Milton's practice to understand the talents both as the Word of God itself *and* as the natural abilities of those to whom the Word had been entrusted. Chrysostom's Homily LXXVIII (on Matt. 25: 1–30) offered an extraordinarily rich interpretation of the adjacent parables of the ten virgins and the talents, in which he proposed that God has endowed humans with language and entrusted the Word to us that we might speak up "both for our own salvation, and for our neighbor's advantage." In another homily, he asserted that the preacher is required to share the spiritual wealth he has stored in his mind. He cited the parable of the talents to illustrate that shared knowledge enriches both the hearers and the speaker, whereas hoarding is misanthropic and leads to the isolation threatened in the example of the figure who hid his talent.[35]

There were of course more extravagantly allegorical interpretations of the parable that would have been less congenial to Milton. Gregory the Great gave the definitive formulation to an interpretation that enjoyed wide popularity through the Middle Ages.[36] He interpreted the various talents in Matthew's parable as features of human capacities for knowledge: the five talents were said to refer to the five senses, the two to *intellectus* and *operatio* (spiritual understanding and good works, or theory and practice), and the one talent to *intellectus* alone. Curiously, this made the second figure in the parable the recipient of the greatest gifts. It helped, however, to explain why the master ordered that the single talent be given to the one who already had ten: lacking theory, he was in greater need. Only with *intellectus* would he be able to follow Gregory's advice to "Make connections between one thing and another, and so learn for yourselves how to do other things than those you have already learned from the preacher's words." Although Gregory retained the traditional interpretation whereby multiplying talents meant teaching effectively from the Scriptures and insisted that "the one with understanding must take care not to remain silent," he made two important changes: he brought to the fore the concern with the varying abilities of the three figures and, in accord with the new pastoral situation in a world where most of the people of whom he knew were at least nominal Christians, he altered what had been a concern with conversion to the faith into a concern for moral conversion.[37] In the Reformation period, those who associated moral conversion with works-righteousness sought to restore the idea that conversion to faith, that is, to "saving" faith, is required.

For his part, Milton was interested in invoking the parable against his adversaries, both against the bishops themselves and against hirelings who had neglected to acquire the necessary learning for the ministry and failed to provide good preaching. Arguing in the *Animadversions* against Bishop Hall's insistence upon set prayers in liturgy, he spoke of the ministers' capacity spontaneously to pray in the congregation as "their noblest talent" (*CPW*, I, 685). Later, in *An Apology*, he attacked ignorant ministers, ill equipped to exercise their callings. He compared them to bungling "mechanicks" unskilled in their trades, negligent of their "talents," and forgetful of their art: "How few among them that know to write, or speak in a pure stile, much lesse to distinguish the *idea's,* and various kinds of stile: in Latine barbarous . . ." (I, 934).

It is against the background of the church Fathers' idea of talents as the Scriptures with which churchmen have been entrusted, the medieval notion that the talents refer to natural abilities, the Reformers' assumption that "Christians indeed" are those who have been converted to evangelic faith, and his own attacks on prelates for forbidding the spontaneous use of talent in prayer and on the ignorant clergy for their barbarous style that Milton's other, more personal allusions to the parable are best understood. In *The Reason of Church Government,* he not only alludes to it when he projects those dreadful threatening voices against which he means to defend himself in advance, but also as he declares how burdensome he finds it to remember "that God even to a strictnesse requires the improvment of these his entrusted gifts" (I, 801). All through the preface to Book II Milton attempts to explain how the vast knowledge that he has stored up, which should be "the best and lightsomest possession of the mind," could be experienced as such a "burden" and "waight" as he felt he could scarcely bear (801). Associating himself with prophetic figures, who had been favored by God with "pretious truths" and "treasure inestimable without price" (801, 802), he was seeking to define his burden of interpretation as a function of resistance on the part of a hard-hearted audience, who would not see and hear the simple truth plainly revealed in the Scriptures. These readers of the Scriptures were mystified under "this impertinent yoke of prelaty" (820). They did not appreciate the distinction between his "learned pains," which were meant "to help ease and lighten the difficult labours of the Church," and the "unlearned drudgery" of those whose idea of knowledge was "to club quotations" and to lay down a "hors load of citations and fathers" (822).

When he set out this distinction Milton, although he had already been busy collecting materials for his Theological Index, could not have foreseen his *De Doctrina Christiana*, its pages "cram[med] . . . even to overflowing, with quotations" (VI, 122). His idea of scriptural truth was that it was plain; and his understanding of the importance of the parable of the talents was that, in virtue of his natural abilities (*ingenium*) and his studious and diligent labors (his "portion"), he was required to speak up, even in the face of resistance from those in power. What he was not prepared to see was that his intervention in disputes with other interpreters already implied that the relevant places in Scripture might be at least partly obscure. Supremely confident as he was that a true Christian is not influenced by mere human traditions, Milton disguised, even from himself, the decisive change in his thinking about the nature of the Christian's burden. That change involved his imagining that interpretive difficulties were not merely a function of a hard-hearted lack of charity on the part of readers. Gradually he came to think that they were also to a great extent a matter of inherent contradictions in the biblical record itself.

3. Two Discontinuities in the History of Milton's Thinking About Places

> "... not to make verbal curiosities the end, that were a toylsom vanity, but to be an interpreter & relater of the best and sagest things among mine own Citizens throughout this Iland in the mother dialect...."
> — *The Reason of Church Government* (*CPW*, I, 811–12)

When early in 1642 Milton declared his ambition to become "an interpreter & relater of the best and sagest things," he likely could not have foreseen how soon he would effect the most significant discontinuity of his interpretive career. The change by which a totally other face of the entire Scripture showed itself to Milton did not take place as a spiritual conversion on the model of Paul and Augustine and Luther. It did involve, however, contemplation of his life in relation to specific biblical places. In time this gave rise to a radical rethinking of the interpretive criterion known as "the analogy of faith" and to an extraordinarily elaborate account of his personal faith on a scale unequaled in the spiritual autobiographies of the era. That his account appeared in a *De Doctrina Christiana* rather than a *Confessiones* is an indication of a quiet violence to the existing order wrought by an individual talent. As he immersed himself in layer upon layer of received texts, Milton came to deal with the inevitable ambivalence of his stance by conceiving himself as a grateful beneficiary of the rich poetic store contained in the Bible and as an inspired iconoclast in the face of the interpretive tradition.[1]

While Milton's mature writings suggest that this understanding of himself endured through the rest of his life, it is nonetheless possible to define two telling discontinuities in his adult thinking about biblical places and thus to isolate three principal phases in the history of his work as an interpreter. Until 1642 there seems to have been nothing especially problematic for Milton in the standard practice whereby any obscure place in Scripture was to be explained by reference to what were commonly considered plainer places. He was accustomed to accepting the familiar doctrine that the plain words of the Bible provide the ultimate criterion for judgment in spiritual matters. For all his differences with the prelates, he had reason to hope that further Reformation would clear away their sloth and prejudice and make what was clear to him clear to all. In this period he was already collecting passages from the Scriptures that would be potentially useful for quotation in his own writing,[2] and he was accustomed to thinking about his life in relation to the parable of the talents. He had been considering with some care how that place did — and did not — apply to his "condition."

Some time not long after his marriage to Mary Powell in 1643, Milton began to regard the New Testament texts forbidding divorce as hard sayings, and thereafter he took a much more active interest in the process by which the Scriptures are interpreted. In this second phase of his interpretive career, he turned to other principles as his chief criteria for interpretation: the diligent "conference of place with place," whereby difficult texts were to be restored to their original meanings and harmonized according to a sense of the overall drift and scope of the whole Bible. This phase is differentiated from the earlier one by a growing conviction that difficult texts are numerous and that legitimate biblical interpretation requires the sort of consideration that he had given to the parable of the talents; in short, that intellectual labors which he had been expending upon the reading and writing of non-biblical works were equally necessary for dealing with biblical texts.

In this transitional phase Milton had ready to hand what Mary Thomas Crane has described in *Framing Authority* as "the humanist logic of gathering and framing." He transferred the sorts of interpretive techniques that he had learned in a humanist education to the reading of the Bible. One important aspect of this transfer was that Milton came increasingly to treat biblical "places" in terms that humanist readers derived from the Aristotelian and Ciceronian systems of *topoi:* the "commonplaces" provided a means for the systematic classification of ideas. In the early modern period such "places" were regarded by humanist educators and logicians as "fragments" of text ready to be "gathered." Typically, in sixteenth- and seventeenth-century England such "gathering" was conceived as merely preliminary to the more important task of "framing" the fragments into a synthesis that would cover over the historical gap between ancient texts and modern experience. Framing included the selection, rearrangement, and assimilation of texts. It often served to demonstrate the gatherer's ability to tame what was threatening in an alien literature and thereby to confirm the prevailing cultural code. The chief criterion for gathering texts was their potential compatibility with contemporary *doxa*, the common beliefs already established in the culture. Often, as in Thomas Wilson's *Rule of Reason* (1551) and Dudley Fenner's *The Artes of Logike and Rhetorike* (1584), these beliefs were specifically the leading doctrines of Protestant religion.[3] In light of Crane's study it is of considerable interest that in the second phase of his interpretive career, Milton ascribed unusual prominence to the task of "gathering," and that, moreover, the texts that he gathered often rubbed against the grain of received doctrine and current opinion.

In time the new reading habits that Milton began to cultivate in the 1640s issued into a disciplined, imaginative way of writing that is nonetheless incompatible with the view that he gradually "freed" himself from scriptural authority. His convictions about interpretive labors deepened over time and remained sufficiently constant that he expressed them as follows in *De Doctrina Christiana*, the major interpretive work of his maturity:

> The requisites [for proper interpreting] are linguistic ability, knowledge of the original sources, consideration of the overall intent, distinction between literal and figurative language, examination of the causes and circumstances, and of what comes before and after the passage in question, and comparison of one text with another. It must always be asked, too, how far the interpretation is in agreement with faith. (*CPW*, VI, 582)

The last phrase in the passage, *fidei quoque analogia ubique spectanda est*, involves a technical term (*analogia fidei*) and a biblical allusion (to Rom. 12: 6) that this rendering by John Carey obscures.[4] The "analogy of faith" was a biblical phrase that had become, in the course of Christian history, a technical term for the community's overall sense of the meaning of the Scriptures. As such it served as a powerful interpretive criterion potentially affecting the understanding of any given biblical place, and it was readily available to any interpreter who sought to demonstrate the compatibility of any given biblical place with the prevailing *doxa*. In seventeenth-century England the scope and meaning of the phrase, and the implications of the interpretive criterion associated with it, became an object of dispute. While the requirements for interpretation presented in *De Doctrina* sound conventional enough, then, it is of considerable importance for appreciating Milton's mature writing to recognize signs that, by the way in which he handled the analogy of faith, he contributed to creating a new hermeneutic. His redefinition of this concept, which was subtle and gradual, had far-reaching implications for his interpretation of biblical literature, and this redefinition, which was effected practically rather than asserted theoretically, marks Milton's turn into a third phase of his interpretive career. As a mature interpreter he urged that a constituent feature of saving "faith" was a willingness to rest content with what is plainly revealed, without raising questions for which there are no clear answers.[5]

It is not possible, or necessary, to identify a particular moment when the second interpretive phase gave way to the third, for Milton continued gathering and comparing places, as the many revisions in the manuscript of *De Doctrina* illustrate. What requires attention is the fact that Milton's functional redefinition of the analogy of faith not only made possible his confident exposition of his views on the relations between the Father and the Son and on other controversial points of theology, but also opened up for his practice as a poet a considerable space for imaginative activities. The interpretive stances from which *Paradise Regained, Samson Agonistes,* and *Paradise Lost* were written all owe a good deal to a quiet but profound dissent from the dominant understanding of the analogy of faith. It will be the work of the latter part of this chapter to document this dissent and to begin to explore some of its implications.

The more startling change in Milton's career as an interpreter, from the first phase to the second, was effectively identified by Arthur Barker in his treatment of the divorce tracts.[6] Although critics have explored some aspects of this change, its far-reaching importance has been generally hidden from view. There are at least three reasons for this: the assumption (which Milton continued to share with a large portion of his contemporaries) that the Bible provides precepts by which Christians are expected to live, Milton's own frequent insistence (both before and after 1642) on his unremitting mental labors and on his duty to speak publicly, and the fact that since the late seventeenth century Milton's readers have frequently thought of his life in the sorts of terms offered by the parable of the talents.[7] Milton himself, both by his allusions to the parable in accounts of his life and by repeated references to his diligent mental labors, promoted the idea that his career was marked by unbroken development in response to the duties attendant on God's gifts to him. The disruptive experience that Milton had in the months after he first married precipitated, however, the one really glaring discontinuity in his career as an interpreter. In a society where many people found paradigms in biblical places for defining whether they were among the elect or the reprobate, Milton recognized that a facile application of the New Testament places about divorce threatened to fix him in lasting misery. Already convinced that his eternal destiny had not been determined in advance, and having thought through, as early as 1633, some ways in which the parable of the talents was not precisely applicable to his current situation, he argued in *The Doctrine and Discipline of Divorce* that continuing in a bad marriage was not a sign of reprobation but rather an occasion for being "over-tempted." This sort of temptation, far from being imposed by God, was socially constructed. In making out this argument, when he might have appealed to other sources of authority, Milton did not abandon his potentially disastrous commitment to live by "the Bible only." Rather he pursued a more thoroughgoing resolve to become an interpreter of biblical literature, arguing out of a conviction that God's revelation in the Bible could not have been given for the purpose of frustrating a natural desire for love and companionship. In this conviction Milton's sense of the overall meaning of the Scriptures was evinced, and in it were the roots of a redefinition of the analogy of faith.

Changes in Milton's Conception of His Burden

In the antiprelatical tracts of 1641–42, for all his emphasis on his tireless intellectual labor, Milton made relatively little use of particular texts to advance his argument, and he wrote almost nothing about the process of interpreting the Bible. In *Of Reformation* (1641) he anticipated the objection that "the Scriptures are difficult to be understood, and therfore require the explanation of the Fathers," by acknowledging that "some places . . . remain clouded" and observing that they therefore could have little to do with "*saving knowledge.*" Instead of seeking to refute his opponents' views, he simply assumed that, because the Scriptures plainly taught a position contrary to theirs, his task was to persuade them of the simple truth.[8] "The very essence of Truth," he urged, "is plainnesse, and brightnes," and the truth of the Bible is manifest to people of every station unless they themselves obscure it by their own "darknes and crookednesse." The Scriptures are said to "protest . . . their own plainnes, and perspicuity, calling to them to be instructed, not only the *wise,* and *learned,* but the *simple,* the *poor,* the *babes,* foretelling an extraordinary effusion of *Gods* Spirit upon every age, and sexe, attributing to all men, and requiring from them the ability of searching, trying, examining all things, and by the Spirit discerning that which is good" (*CPW,* I, 566).

Already in *The Reason of Church Government* (1642), however, there was the hint of a change when Milton implied that the simple clarity of biblical truth is a belief, an object of a personal choice. He rededicated himself to a view that, within a few months, he would modify substantially:

> Let others therefore dread and shun the Scriptures for their darknesse, I shall wish I may deserve to be reckon'd among those who admire and dwell upon them for their clearnesse. And this seemes to be the cause why in those places of holy writ, wherein is treated of Church-government, the reasons thereof are not formally, and profestly set downe, because to him that heeds attentively the drift and scope of Christian profession, they easily imply themselves. (I, 750)

Milton's understanding of "the drift and scope of Christian profession" and of the way in which the Scriptures can be said to be plainly true changed dramatically soon after he married. Amidst what we assume to have been pain and disappointment,[9] he was obliged to question whether "that which is most necessary to be known is most easie" (*CPW*, I, 566) and to acknowledge that the Scriptures are not always immediately plain and clearly applicable: the biblical places forbidding divorce, which might seem to others so clearly and plainly to pertain to his situation, he now experienced as highly problematic. Soon he was arguing that these passages could be applied to Christians' lives only after diligent interpretive scrutiny. There is no need to be cynical about this change. For Milton, the "case of conscience" was not whether to remain in an unsatisfying marriage or to seek divorce. (Much less was it "whether [he was] a child of God or no.") The problem was that the laws of the land made it virtually impossible for him to act according to his conscience.[10] In an attempt to persuade those in power to change the law, Milton abandoned the idea that all applicable Scripture passages are transparent and began to demonstrate difficulties that are inherent in passages that most members of his society were accustomed to assuming were immediately applicable to contemporary life. From this point onward Milton came increasingly to write in ways that raised interpretive questions.

Already in the prefatory material for the second edition of *The Doctrine and Discipline of Divorce* Milton was promoting a new openness on the part of "ingenuous" readers. He urged it on the Parliament and the Assembly:

> Let this therefore be new examin'd.... Let the statutes of God be turn'd over, be scann'd a new, and consider'd; not altogether by the narrow intellectuals of quotationists and common placers, but (as was the ancient right of Counsels) by men of what liberall profession soever, of eminent spirit and breeding joyn'd with a diffuse and various knowledge of divine and human things; able

> to ballance and define good and evil, right and wrong, throughout every state of life; able to shew us the waies of the Lord, strait and faithfull as they are, not full of cranks and contradictions, and pit falling dispenses, but with divine insight and benignity measur'd out to the proportion of each mind and spirit, each temper and disposition, created so different each from other, and yet by the skill of wise conducting, all to become uniform in vertue. (II, 230)

Having discovered that even the idea that the Scriptures are plain requires interpretation, that the Scriptures become plain (cf. II, 282) to those who labor diligently to examine and consider them, Milton was able to draw on his previous experience with the parable of the talents to effect a transition into a new phase of his interpretive practice. At this point the details in the parable that concern "various knowledge," differences of "temper and disposition," and the "proportion" in which various abilities are "measur'd" out took on unprecedented importance. They are related quietly but profoundly, on the one hand, to the sort of "liberall profession" and "benignity" for which the Bereans had been praised in Acts 17, and on the other with the task of demonstrating that the "waies of the Lord" are "strait." Along with his new perspective on interpretive work Milton began to draw on the language and categories of experimental religion the better to recommend his arguments. Even in *The Judgement of Martin Bucer*, which gives more scope to other authorities than any of the other divorce pamphlets, Milton insists that "only the infallible grounds of Scripture" had been his "guide" in constructing his argument; and he calls upon the God "who tries the inmost heart, and saw with what severe industry and examination of my self, I set down every period" to be his "witnes" (*CPW*, II, 433; italics have been removed).

In his controversial writings of the 1640s Milton did not use the word "burden" in the sense that was common in experimental religion, referring to the guilt from which those who were "Christians indeed" would be delivered by the Redeemer. In the anti-prelatical tracts he used the word "burden" in older senses, to refer both to what the prelates imposed from without ("ceremonies"; I, 975) and to what he experienced within (prophetic knowledge; I, 801–4) when he contemplated calling his audience's attention to the plain meaning of the Scriptures. In the first of his divorce tracts he also deployed the word to refer both to what was imposed and to what he experienced within himself, still making no confession of personal sinfulness: "The greatest burden in the world is superstition; not onely of Ceremonies in the Church, but of imaginary and scarcrow sins at home" (II, 228). Here, however, there was a closer relation between the internal and external burdens. Appropriately enough, since his own experience of marriage seems to have made the issue urgent for him, Milton used the language of experimental religion to make the connection come clear. The "burden" seen by others as the apt image of guilt is displaced by Milton to characterize the results of oppressive interpretive dispositions: in forbidding divorce the "Canon Courts in *England*" are said to have placed a "burden" on marriage that runs counter to laws "writt'n by *Moses* [and] character'd in us by nature" (*CPW,* II, 237).

Yet the rhetorical argument in *The Doctrine and Discipline of Divorce* depends profoundly upon the distinction between the general and particular callings of Christians. On several occasions Milton cites Perkins, in particular the *Treatise of Conscience,* and argues that in relation to "the higher calling of . . . Christianitie," the "inferior calling of marriage" must give way if the two are in conflict (II, 268). The whole argument for permitting divorce is premised, in fact, on the idea that one's spiritual welfare is the overriding consideration. What is most burdensome about a bad marriage is that, by subjecting a Christian to continued cohabitation with someone whose company does not conduce to making the calling and election sure, it inhibits and disenables the service of God. It may even "drive him at last through murmuring and despair to thoughts of Atheism" (260), leaving "him in a dispairing plight of abject and hard'n'd thoughts" (339). The association between living in a badly married state and reprobation is quite explicit: "the continuall sight of his deluded thoughts without cure, must needs be to" the man who has made a faulty choice of a bride, "if especially his complexion incline him to melancholy, a daily trouble and paine of losse in some degree like that which Reprobates feel" (247). At the base of Milton's plea for liberty to divorce is the idea that the doctrine of predestined reprobation silently supports the requirement that the party who has made a mistaken marriage choice remain "yoked" (both wedded and burdened). Milton argues (from a characteristically masculinist viewpoint) that a marriage in which the woman proves "an unmeet help" is precisely an "unpredestin'd misery" (346), and in the second edition he added that predestination wrongly understood "*makes God the author of sin*" (287; cf. 293–94). Not God but the upholders of the canon law are guilty of "tyrannizing the blessed ordinance of mariage into . . . a most unnatural and unchristianly yoke" (341).

Milton also draws upon the language and categories of experimental divinity to insist that a bad marriage is not a punishment but an affliction. He argues that the affliction of a bad marriage is constructed by human society. It is not imposed by some supernatural power, and since socially constructed afflictions are within the power of men to remove, men have an obligation to do so.[11] Milton insists that God instituted marriage precisely "as a cordial and exhilarating cup of solace the better to beare our other crosses and afflictions" (311; cf. 277, 234). Both at the beginning and again near the end of the treatise he alludes to the favorite text of converts who have passed through a period of affliction (Matt. 11: 28–30) when he argues that "the waies of God . . . are equal, easy, and not burdensome." In the second instance, however, he makes a telling addition: "nor do they [the waies of God] ever crosse the just and reasonable desires of men" (342). This last point has contributed to the widely held idea that in the divorce tracts Milton's appeals to the Bible are aimed at getting it to say just what he wants to say, as if biblical categories (as they were understood in his culture) had not already informed his desires.[12] What Milton's addition signals, however, was his growing conviction that "the drift and scope" of biblical literature, which constitutes the analogy of faith and provides the ultimate criterion for interpretation, itself precludes invoking the Bible for purposes of oppression.

While Milton sometimes uses the metaphor of the burden, along with the related metaphors of the yoke and bondage and affliction, to characterize the plight of the badly married Christian, the principal way in which he uses the word "burden" implicitly casts the upholders of the current law into the role of the scribes and Pharisees: "they bind heavy burdens and grievous to be born, and lay them on men's shoulders" (Matt. 23: 4; cf. *CPW*, II, 233). Milton associates himself with Christ as a liberator of the text and the deliverer of Christians from the enforcers of an "obstinate *literality*," the textual policemen who will themselves be called to account "at the last day" (279). The specific problem, especially as it is depicted in chapter XX of Book II (1644 ed.), is with legislators who uphold the prohibition against divorce. Insofar as the legislators profess to live by "the Bible only," this problem is precisely a function of mis-interpreting Scripture, "laying on [more] excessive burdens" than the Law did, thus putting Christian souls in danger of being "cast away" (279). Milton charges that the Scriptures have been overlaid with "burdensom & remorsles obscurity" and are "tangl'd with manifold repugnances" (340), "to the over-burdning, if not the over-whelming of many Christians better worth then to be so deserted of the Churches considerate care" (242). The terms "burden" and "tangles" here suggest how closely associated misinterpretation and mismatching were in Milton's imagination.

As in the anti-prelatical tracts, so in this chapter Milton presents himself as engaged in a kind of contest with others who, like him, have been entrusted with the Word. The parable of the talents, as he had been thinking about it at least since 1633, is just beneath the surface. The enforcers of the current law are depicted as representatives of the "austere" taskmaster imagined by the man who hid his pound in a napkin (Luke 19: 20–22). Milton insists that "neither Scripture nor reason hath laid this unjust austerity upon divorce." It is the work of canon lawyers, who "lay unnecessary burdens upon all men" (342), themselves "delighting . . . to make men the day-labourers of their own afflictions." By contrast, Milton presents his tract as the product of "no every daies work" (340) and counters that "God loves not to plow out the heart of our endeavours with over-hard and sad tasks. God," he says, "delights not to make a drudge of vertue" (342).

In the course of arguing that afflictions are not always to be imputed to "Gods sending," Milton writes a commentary on the situation of the man who hid his talent. Those "whose Creed is custom," he observes, "will be still endeavouring to hide the sloth of thir own timorous capacities with this pretext, that for all this tis better to endure with patience and silence this affliction which God hath sent." Against this Milton argues in the manner of those who deplored the wresting of texts by readers convinced of their own reprobation: when a person fails to use lawful means to rid himself of evil, he "is accessory to his own ruin: nor will it excuse him, though he suffer, through a sluggish fearfulnes to search throughly what is lawfull, for feare of disquieting the secure falsity of an old opinion" (341). In short, Milton implies that those who silently support the status quo are kin to the pharisees who enforce the current laws against divorce. Both groups think of the works of the moral law in the terms illustrated by the man who hid his talent, that is, as a "matter of compulsion" (cf. *CPW*, VI, 536).[13]

The Writer's Bias

Although in *The Doctrine and Discipline of Divorce* Milton still writes as if the sense of the Scriptures is transparent and requires only a perceptive liberator to bring out the meaning, there are unmistakable signs that he has crossed a border and glimpsed a new prospect. He acknowledges that there are "places of Scripture wherin just reason of doubt arises from the letter." These passages are not insignificant, touching only matters of indifference. Rather they are places that require attention to their historical and intertextual positioning, "considering upon what occasion [they were] set down" and "comparing other Texts" (II, 282). Even the "words of Christ" often need to be recovered "from manifold contradictions" (355). The really striking assertion, however, is that "there is scarse any one saying in the Gospel, but must be read with limitations and distinctions, to be rightly understood." This opinion is tied to a new self-consciousness about the process of interpreting and to a new theory about the process by which scriptural truth is discovered:

> Christ gives no full comments or continu'd discourses, but scatters the heavnly grain of his doctrin like pearle heer and there, which requires a skilfull and laborious gatherer; who must compare the words he finds, with other precepts, with the end of every ordinance, and with the general *analogy* of Evangelick doctrine: otherwise many particular sayings would be but strange repugnant riddles. (338; quoted from the 1643 ed.)

Milton's interest here in the process by which biblical truth comes to be known, an interest that would give rise in *Areopagitica* to something like a general theory,[14] marks a discontinuity with the views expressed in the tracts of 1641–42. The emphasis on his own "labour and faithfull diligence" (226) serves, however, to mask the change. So does the continuing emphasis on the right and duty to speak, which in *The Reason of Church Government* he had presented as his way of fulfilling the parable of the talents. In *The Doctrine and Discipline of Divorce,* an author who claims to be "gifted with abilities of mind that may raise him to so high an undertaking" (224) insists on his rights: "Let not other men thinke their conscience bound to search continually after truth, to pray for enlightning from above, to publish what they think they have so obtaind, & debarr me from conceiving my self ty'd by the same duties" (226).

In recent years it has become increasingly common to dwell on the contradictions in Milton's position. Yet instead of exploring them as an index of cultural tensions in which Milton was embroiled, critics have often been proceeding as if the contradictions merely reveal mystifications self-servingly wrought by an autonomous author. One recent critic has charged the author of the divorce tracts with hypocrisy, proposing that Milton deliberately suppressed what he knew to be ambiguous in the Hebrew of Deuteronomy 24: 1 and that this was a "flagrant violation" of the very principles of interpretation to which he was committed.[15] This charge culminates in the conclusion that Milton makes "the Scripture say what[ever] his reason tells him it should say," and it promotes the notion that Milton used sleight of hand to bring the Bible into line with his "just and reasonable desires."

In the dispute over divorce, however, Milton showed himself to be increasingly less confident about the power of reason and more committed to biblical authority. *Tetrachordon,* which addresses the four principal places where divorce is treated in the Bible, shows that he took more seriously than ever the idea that the debate needed to be conducted in relation to scriptural precepts. *The Judgement of Martin Bucer* shows that, despite his official commitment to "the Bible only," Milton understood that an appeal to human authority (the work begins, it will be recalled, with a series of testimonies to Bucer's learning and virtue) might prove useful, and *Colasterion,* so far from demonstrating reliance upon reason, is chiefly marked by invective.[16] Even *The Doctrine and Discipline,* which gives more scope to arguments based on reason than any of the succeeding tracts, does not so much aim to convince its readers by reason. Ultimately it proposes the highest of moral standards, in keeping with the ideals of the Sermon on the Mount (where Christ first proposed his teaching about divorce), whereby readers define their "selves" by the spirit in which they apply the law to their own cases. The enthusiasm with which Milton's work was received by some antinomians and other radicals suggests that reason conceived as operating independently of the Scriptures had little to do with the cogency of the argument.[17]

Milton's arguments in the divorce controversy do not show that he was attempting to make Scripture say what reason told him to be true. They reveal rather that he was not a wholly disinterested interpreter. Already in the seventeenth century some biblical scholars recognized that both Moses, as he is represented in Deuteronomy providing for a bill of divorce, and Jesus, in prohibiting divorce, were chiefly concerned with the situation of women, who had few legal rights in Jewish society.[18] As the notorious gender bias of his arguments makes plain, Milton ignored the theory that Moses and Jesus sought to condemn abusive behavior towards women by men. Considering himself the injured party, he was hardly prepared to think in those terms. Nonetheless, as some of his contemporaries recognized, he made out an argument that might apply equally to an injured woman. (That is, Milton's intuition about the sense of the biblical texts was more disinterested than the discursive argument he framed.) In any event, Milton's imperfect exegesis is evidence of how bias interferes with clarity of thought and reasonable argumentation. Personally interested as he was in the matter in 1644, he was no more or less qualified to argue for the legalization of divorce on the grounds of reason than he was on the grounds of scriptural doctrine. What warrants much more attention than is generally accorded it is the writer's indirect acknowledgement of his own interest in the matter. In the prefatory address to Parliament and the Assembly added to the second edition of *The Doctrine and Discipline of Divorce,* the author asked sympathy for the sort of burden-bearer he himself might have ignored until recently:

> Indeed mans disposition though prone to search after vain curiosities, yet when points of difficulty are to be discusst, appertaining to the removall of unreasonable wrong and burden from the perplext life of our brother, it is incredible how cold, how dull, and farre from all fellow feeling we are, without the spurre of self-concernment. (II, 226)

The "spurre of self-concernment" had prompted Milton to "turn over" and "scan a new" and "consider" what society took to be "the statutes of God," and he asked those in power now to do likewise. His personal interest in the matter points up a need that he was nonetheless increasingly unwilling to acknowledge: the need for a community of interpretation made up of persons from different times and places and personal situations, who could provide something of a consensus about the "faith" in relation to which individual interpreters may operate. In the fissiparous climate of the 1640s, the possibility of achieving such a community was rapidly receding. Milton's increasingly isolated situation was (to a degree that he was not prepared to recognize) a cost of the now traditional and self-contradictory insistence on the right and duty of individual interpretation. It is no surprise therefore that Milton, who went on to write the work called *De Doctrina Christiana,* seems never to have thought of the parable of the talents in the terms provided by Augustine in his *De Doctrina Christiana.*

In the course of developing an argument that, had Milton not been intent on asserting his independence of tradition, could have been of considerable interest to him, Augustine had proposed that the parable of the talents has significant implications for biblical hermeneutics. Arguing that even places that seem plain may be obscure and using a measure of sarcasm, Augustine made the parable teach the lesson that anyone who seeks to read off the plain sense of Scripture without the aid of other human interpreters is the equivalent of the man who buried his talent:

> reading and understanding, as he does, without the aid of any human interpreter, why does he himself undertake to interpret for others? Why does he not rather send them direct to God, that they too may learn by the inward teaching

of the Spirit without the help of man? The truth is, he fears to incur the reproach: "Thou wicked and slothful servant, thou oughtest to have put my money to the exchangers." Seeing, then, that these men teach others, either through speech or writing, what they understand, surely they cannot blame me if I likewise teach not only what they understand, but also the rules of interpretation they follow. For no one ought to consider anything as his own, except perhaps what is false. All truth is of Him who says, "I am the truth." For what have we that we did not receive? and if we have received it, why do we glory, as if we had not received it?[19]

Whether Milton ever read this particular passage or not, he assiduously resisted this sort of perspective, repeatedly emphasizing instead of any indebtedness to predecessors his independent mental labors. In middle age, amidst developments in politics and in hermeneutics during the 1640s and 1650s, he found himself progressively more alienated from interpretive communities, even as he pleaded for "the removall of unreasonable wrong and burden from the perplext life of our brother." He also found himself increasingly engaged in philological disputes.

The Return to Philology

According to his nephew, during the period when Mary Powell was separated from him, Milton considered marrying "a very Handsome and Witty Gentlewoman" named Miss Davis.[20] This suggests either that he was contemplating a form of disobedience to the law or that he was unduly optimistic about how quickly his arguments in favor of divorce would yield a legal remedy. In any event, by writing the divorce tracts Milton was acknowledging that Parliament and the Assembly had legal power over him. He was also attempting to engage them in a dialogue that required shared principles, on the basis of which the argument might proceed. While there was scope for a certain amount of rational argumentation, these principles included some potent assumptions that were not so much irrational as non-rational. The most prominent of these was the religious belief that the Bible provides both knowledge of all that is necessary for salvation and precepts for living a godly life. To this belief another was joined: that the Bible is its own best interpreter and that through the work of the Holy Spirit its meaning may be clearly discerned. Milton's new consciousness that even passages in the gospel may be "obscure" did not necessarily call into question these principles. Yet his new understanding of the nature of the Bible's clearness and plainness necessitated a return to philology on his part and a radical revaluation of fundamental interpretive principles. With his natural gift for languages and having been trained to some extent in Hebrew as well as Greek and Latin, in the 1640s Milton proved a worthy heir of the sixteenth-century revolution in biblical hermeneutics. He lived in what is rightly considered a great age of sacred philology, and in some philological disputes that touched his own case he was able to hold his own.[21]

Milton did not return to the philological methods acquired in his youthful study of non-biblical literature in order to establish a more strict linguistic usage. Rather, convinced by his religious beliefs that the Bible was meant to promote liberty,[22] he drew on the resources of the philological tradition to raise hermeneutical questions and to document the complexity with which interpretive tasks are performed, in accord with the principle that *"continual searching [is] requir'd of us by* Solomon *to the attainment of understanding"* (*CPW,* II, 584; cf. Prov. 2). His attention to the minute workings of biblical language led him to theoretical questions of the first order of importance.

In the 1640s, the proposal that the sayings of Jesus concerning divorce were "hard places" warranted philological demonstration. In *Tetrachordon* he provided a good deal of it, and one example will serve the purposes of illustrating what he took to be at stake. Glossing the exception clause in Matthew's version — no divorce *"Saving for the cause of fornication"* — Milton argued against the plain sense as it appears in English Bibles by pointing out that not only was this a translation but that New Testament Greek is itself filled with *"Hebraisms* & *Syriacisms."* Denigrating the Greek language and exalting the Hebrew, he proposed that the frequent non-Greek usage in the sacred texts reminds Gentiles that God's majestic language is as foreign to their ears as His "grace and mercy" are to their fallen natures and that the "forein stile" serves to "induce them to the fountaines" of scriptural truth (II, 671). He proceeded then to consider the words and usage behind both "cause" and "fornication," arguing that "the Evangelist heer *Hebraizes*" according to a "common eastern phrase" that also appears in Exodus, chapter 5, where it signifies *"Proportion."* There "the Israelites are commanded to doe their tasks, *The matter of each day in his day."* Glossing the biblical place that stands behind the allusion in the final line of his own Sonnet 7 ("How soon hath Time . . ."), Milton observes, "A task we know is a proportion of work, not doing the same thing absolutely every day, but so much." This gives him a basis for shaking his imagined reader's confident understanding of the New Testament place about the "cause" or "proportion" of fornication, and he seizes the opportunity by going on sarcastically to propose that if one followed the strict philological sense of the words one would have to say that Christ permitted divorce only for one peculiarly perverse form of adultery:

> Whereby it may be doubtfull yet, whether heer be not excepted not only fornication it self, but other causes equipollent, and proportional to fornication. Which very word also to understand rightly, wee must of necessity, have recours again to the Ebrew. For in the Greek and Latin sense by fornication is meant the common prostitution of body for sale. So that they who are so exact for the letter, shall be dealt with by the *Lexicon,* and the *Etymologicon* too if they please, and must be bound to forbidd divorce for adultery also, untill it come to open whoredom. . . . (II, 672)

Rather than seeking to police the boundaries around the word "fornication," Milton attempts to get his reader to accept a more fluid interpretation that includes figurative senses as part of the divine speaker's intention.[23] He implies, moreover, that he thinks Christ's saying was heuristic rather than prescriptive, and that Christ's intention was precisely that one have to labor with the senses of the word, to ascertain the full scope of its applicability, its "proportion" to a particular situation:

> we may reason with as good leav, and as little straining to the text, that our Saviour on set purpose chose this word *Fornication,* improperly appli'd to the lapse of adultery, that we might not think our selvs bound from all divorce, except when that fault hath bin actually committed. For the language of Scripture signifies by fornication (and others beside St. *Austin* so expound it) not only the trespas of body . . . but signifies also any notable disobedience, or intractable cariage of the wife to the husband, as Judg. the 19. 2. Whereof at large in *the Doctrin of Divorce, 1. 2. c.* 18. (II, 672)

Citing his own writings alongside Scripture here, although it does not imply a parity of authority, is of a piece with the reference to Augustine and others: it shows that Milton was not about to abandon the idea that the Scriptures are plain. It suggests that he would argue, as Luther had argued when he grudgingly acknowledged that Augustine had anticipated his understanding of justification by faith,[24] that the similarity of interpretation between himself and Augustine was a function of that plainness, and of their respective interpretive labors, rather than being a case of his having been influenced by, or of his appealing to, a mere human authority. Still, as the publication of *Martin Bucer* had already shown, Milton was having to struggle with the status of others' interpretations. He did not yet have a criterion other than the "plainness" of scriptural teaching for judging the validity of a given interpretation. He was, moreover, well on his way to abandoning the criterion on which most of his fellow Protestants characteristically relied in difficult cases.

In composing *Tetrachordon* Milton made a far more extensive and thoroughgoing comparison of particular biblical places than he had in *The Doctrine and Discipline of Divorce*. Significantly, he said nothing, however, about "the analogy of faith." In this respect he was already entering what I have called the third stage of his career as a biblical interpreter, in which he was increasingly isolated from other interpreters and most likely to produce interpretations that were idiosyncratic. This movement away from the larger community of interpreters largely corresponds to Milton's political and religious disillusionment with the Presbyterians at this time, and another feature of the gloss in *Tetrachordon* that we have been considering provides as explicit an indication as we have that Milton was beginning to associate faulty interpretation with the historical process by which the Scriptures had come to be interpreted in the terms of Greek philosophy.

In the course of developing the idea that its frequent "Hebraisms" confer upon New Testament Greek "a forein stile," Milton parodies the Greek language and comes close to pronouncing "the analogy of faith" an illegitimate interpretive procedure. By coining an English verb on a Greek model (Milton's "scholiaze" in the sole instance cited in the *OED*), he suggests that the translation of Jesus's own language into Greek already marked the beginning of the process (cf. also "*Analogies*" and "*Analysis*") by which the pristine plainness of the gospel was corrupted:

> He . . . who thinks to *Scholiaze* upon the Gospel, though Greek, according to his Greek *Analogies,* and hath not bin Auditor to the oriental dialects, shall want in the heat of his *Analysis* no accomodation to stumble. (II, 671)

Before considering in detail what was involved in Milton's silent suppression of appeals to the analogy of faith as an interpretive criterion we should linger a bit longer in the transitional second stage of his interpretive career, when he was still invoking "the *analogy* of Evangelick doctrin" and appealing to a principle called on the title-page of the first edition of *The Doctrine and Discipline of Divorce* "the Rule of Charity." It is an index of Milton's profound implication in a tradition which professes to scorn "tradition" that, although he used the definite article in the phrase "the Rule of Charity," he made no mention of its most famous proponent, Augustine, like Milton long after him, had discovered only belatedly that the Scriptures were difficult and that the resources of grammar and rhetoric were required for interpreting them.[25]

Two Title-Pages and the Analogy of Faith

The changes in Milton's views about interpretation were not merely a function of his personal problems, and they did not arise because he thought the texts prohibiting divorce were themselves a threat to his freedom and happiness. The changes were profoundly related to general developments in Protestant interpretive procedures and especially to issues that were being hotly contested, amidst the greater "liberty of prophesying," in the 1640s. The close argument to which we have been attending took up a controversial issue in comparative linguistics. *Tetrachordon* anticipated by three years the brilliant demonstration by Thomas Gataker that the New Testament abounds in Hebraisms. The title page of *The Doctrine and Discipline of Divorce* suggests a good deal about Milton's point of insertion into other debates over interpretive method. The changes in the title-page for the second edition are an index of the need to accommodate his argument to the contours of those debates.[26]

In the first edition of his first divorce tract Milton attempted to convince those who were, as he imagined, accustomed to thinking that the scriptural teaching on the subject was plainly formulated in the two passages in Matthew's gospel. He sought to move them, as he had moved, beyond thinking that in this matter the ultimate interpretive principle was an appeal to the *ipsissima verba* of the Savior. To this end he proposed that, given the context in which those words were placed in Matthew's gospel, the saying required close scrutiny and consideration, especially in relation to the other biblical places which Jesus and the Pharisees were then controverting. In this way Milton sought to show the necessity for a "conference of place with place" in a matter customarily thought too plain to warrant it, and he asked his readers to make "the *analogy* of Evangelick doctrine" their ultimate interpretive principle, in light of which the comparison of places would be carried out. What is called on the title-page of the volume "the Rule of Charity" becomes in the body of the argument a more particular name for what is gathered from "the *analogy* of Evangelick doctrine." It serves as the functional equivalent of what Tertullian had called the *regula fidei* and what Protestants, using a biblical phrase that had also circulated widely in the patristic era, routinely called the *analogia fidei*. Each of these phrases has its own history and connotations, but they all refer more or less to an overall sense of "the consistent body of truth that Scripture affords,"[27] or, to cite Milton's own terms, to "the drift and scope of Christian profession" (*CPW*, I, 750). Milton was already interpreting Scripture in a rather personal way when he argued that the essence of the gospel is a divine charity that promotes responsible human freedom. If we consider for a moment his appeal to charity in relation to condemnations from earlier periods of the intolerable burdens that are created by excessive legislation, by the Apostle Paul, by Augustine, Thomas Aquinas, and John Hus, what situates Milton in a particular time and place is his contention that legislation about the *adiaphora* is positively precluded. In the post-Reformation debate about "things indifferent," Milton espoused the position that what is not specifically required by Scripture, no one may legislate. Moreover, no biblical precept may be applied apart from considering the overall "drift and scope" of Scripture, which, Milton insists, promotes freedom and love. Defining faith against those who would reify it, insisting that it is a process (active trust shown through love), citing Paul's "*Charity beleeveth all things*" and still making no reference to Augustine, Milton proclaimed that "wee cannot safely assent to any precept writt'n in the Bible, but as charity commends it to us" (II, 340). Theodore Huguelet, gathering up Milton's language out of the divorce tracts the way Milton might have gathered up biblical places, has proclaimed "the all-interpreting voice of Charity" Milton's "loadstarre" of exegesis and "high governesse of our belief," the "supreme decider of all controversie, and supreme resolver of all Scripture," "the summe of all commands" (II, 309, 340, 637, 678). Huguelet, although he lists precedents for such a "rule" from Augustine to Erasmus, maintains that Milton discovered this hermeneutical axiom for himself, when, working on the anti-prelatical tracts, he applied Ramistic method to the reading of Scripture.[28]

Be this as it may, Milton's substitution of charity for faith as the ultimate interpretive criterion was not unique. The way in which he understood this substitution, however, enabled him to argue that a particular action that was customarily regarded as uncharitable, even sinful, was under certain circumstances both charitable and absolutely necessary. The salient features of Milton's attempt to reverse conventional ideas about divorce are epitomized in the language of the elaborate subtitle of the 1643 *Doctrine and Discipline of Divorce:*

> RESTOR'D TO THE GOOD OF BOTH SEXES, From the bondage of Canon Law, and other mistakes, to Christian freedom, guided by the Rule of

Charity. Wherein also many places of Scripture, have recover'd their long-lost meaning: Seasonable to be now thought on in the Reformation intended.

To this title was added an epigraph that might serve to reinforce the idea that the seemingly new doctrine which the volume was introducing was no more than a recovery of "long-lost meaning":

MATTH. 13. 52. *Every Scribe instructed to the Kingdome of Heav'n, is like the Maister of a house which bringeth out of his treasurie things old and new.*

Milton himself was likely responsible for this epigraph. The same biblical place reappears prominently in the first chapter of *De Doctrina Christiana* (*CPW*, VI, 127–28), where Milton takes it as a divine command in response to which he has compiled his treatise. In the chapter devoted to the Holy Scriptures the verse appears again in the paragraph where he argues that every believer is "entitled to interpret" Scripture "for himself" (VI, 583–84). Whether Huguelet is correct or not about Milton's having applied Ramistic method to reading Scripture, it is clear that the traditional idea that every interpreter has the right to interpret "for himself" offered Milton the possibility of silently importing into his interpretation powerful assumptions that predetermine to a great extent what will be found in "the Bible only." Even if there were important senses in which the Bible might be said to be "the best interpreter" of itself, it could not be the "only" interpreter of itself. It did not provide, for instance, the historically conditioned criterion that Milton and others invoked when they claimed that there could be no legislation about "indifferent" matters.

Many features of the title-page of *The Doctrine and Discipline* were altered for the second edition. Presumably, since the changes generally accord with the claims of the new prefatory material and with alterations in the body of the tract, Milton himself was responsible for them. This is not to claim, however, that the differences between the two title-pages represent profound changes in Milton's own opinions between the two editions. Probably they reflect increased sensitivity to the rhetorical situation. The language of the first title-page made *The Doctrine and Discipline,* which had sold out by the end of 1643, sound like the sort of grist for a Ranter or Familist mill that Mrs. Attaway took it to be when she left her husband and eloped with William Jenny.[29] This helps explain the addition of a second epigraph, aimed at undermining both the customary supposition that Christ's plain teaching precluded all discussion and his "ingenuous" readers' tendency to assume that "the Rule of Charity" was an antinomian principle. The new title-page made no mention of "Christian freedom," or "the Rule of Charity." It said nothing about "recover[ing] the long-lost meaning" of "many places," and it did not recommend the present as a "Seasonable" moment for further reformation. Instead, it identified the author as "*J. M.*" (Milton's full name appeared at the end of the new introductory address), and suggested that the author was as concerned as his godly readers to ward off "bad consequences." It also made new claims about the methods and contents of the volume:

> Restor'd to the good of both SEXES, From the bondage of CANON LAW, and other mistakes, to the true meaning of Scripture in the Law and Gospel compar'd. Wherin also are set down the bad consequences of abolishing or condemning of Sin, that which the Law of God allowes, and Christ abolisht not. Now the second time revis'd and much augmented, In Two BOOKS: To the Parliament of *England* with the Assembly.

These changes on the title-page were a function, then, of a concern to overcome prejudice and to get his argument a hearing among those in power. Milton envisages achieving this by inviting his readers to participate in the same interpretive process he has been going through: finding "the true meaning of Scripture" by comparing the Law and Gospel and by contemplating the "consequences" of mis-interpretation. This sounds conventional and innocuous (which was the point), until we attend to the disputes about hermeneutics that were taking place in the 1640s.

Two of Milton's known antagonists in the controversy about divorce were deeply implicated in disputes about the grounds of biblical interpretation. It is well known that, in August, 1644, Herbert Palmer, in a sermon before Parliament, made reference to "a *wicked booke* . . . abroad and *uncensured,* though *deserving to be burnt,* whose *Author* hath been so *impudent* as to *set his Name* to it, and *dedicate it to your selves.*"[30] Palmer himself was just then emerging as an exponent of the idea that revelation is to be equated with the written Scriptures themselves, that is, that the Bible is not the mere record of revelation but itself constitutes revelation. This was the prevailing view and had already been developed by the end of the sixteenth century, when Whitaker set out the classic Protestant arguments for the divinity and sufficiency of Scripture in his debates against Cardinal Bellarmine. In the seventeenth century it came to be associated with an idea of verbal dictation by the Holy Spirit to the scriptural "penmen," "so that," as one expositor put it, "the very words of Scripture are to be accounted the words of the Holy Ghost." The view espoused by Milton in the divorce tracts and developed in the *De Doctrina* was closer to the minority position classically formulated in John Goodwin's book of 1648, *The Divine Authority of the Scripture Asserted*.[31] Goodwin distinguished between the authentic Word of God, which could not be wholly reduced to ink and paper, and the written Scriptures, which are the vessels that provide access to revelation but do not exhaust its riches. The minority theory allowed for more interpretive space in which to operate than did the dominant theory that accorded priority to the written word.

Another of Milton's antagonists in the divorce controversy was Joseph Caryl, who was at the time he licensed the "Nameles Answer" against *The Doctrine and Discipline of Divorce* already at work on his massive commentary on the Book of Job. Caryl had added what Milton calls "his censure" (II, 727) to the "Nameles Answer," charging that the marriage bond required to be upheld against "dangerous abuses" urged by "unstaied mindes and men given to change" (see *CPW*, II, 727n.). Milton's reply in *Colasterion* emphasized how insensitive Caryl was to honest "discontents," men of sound mind who (like Job) found a bad marriage "difficult to endure." He taunted that Caryl was unfit to write about Job, since he seemed to "have no more true sense of a good man in his afflictions, then those *Edomitish* Freinds had, of whom *Job* complains, and against whom God testifies his anger" (II, 728). He might have added that Caryl, for all his own learning and industry, was an opponent of the methods of comparative philology in biblical interpretation. The Bible, Caryl insisted, is unique among all the books in the world and "disdaines the very mention of *comparison,* with any other humane Author whatsoever." Moreover, each part of the Bible is unique and authoritative in its own right, so that it is important to take into account the differences among its human authors and the circumstances in which they wrote and to be able to distinguish prose from verse and "Historicall" from "Propheticall" writing. Although such a position sounded like the common argument proposed by Catholic scholars, and rubbed against the grain for those who thought that the Holy Spirit had verbally dictated timeless truths to the "penmen," it was nonetheless potentially acceptable to learned Protestants, including Milton. Caryl, however, took a decidedly contrary viewpoint when he argued, as Catholics often did,[32] against the conference of places. It is "dangerous," he asserted, to compare "Booke with Booke, Chapter with Chapter." He continued:

> There is not in this great volume of holy counsell, any one Book orChapter [sic], Verse or Section, of greater power or authoritie than other. *Moses* and *Samuel,* the writings of *Amos* the Shepherd, and of *Isaiah* a Descendant of the blood Royall; the writings of the Prophets and Evangelists, the Epistles of

Paul, and this historie of *Iob,* must be received (to use the words of the *Trent Councell* in the fifth Session, but to far better purpose) *Pari pietatis affectu, with the same holy reverence and affection.* They use it about Traditions, matching Traditions with the Scriptures; but we may fully match all Scripture together, and say, all must be received with the same devotion and affection.[33]

Recognizing that all sectaries had a text, or for that matter that they might have ten texts, to sponsor their positions, Caryl was forbidding the use of the sort of "dangerous" procedures that Milton employed in *The Doctrine and Discipline of Divorce.* Milton compared the biblical places about divorce with one another and argued not that they "all must be received with the same devotion and affection," but that they all needed to be interpreted in light of "the Rule of Charity," which summed up the whole message of the Scriptures and provided the standard against which any particular command is to be measured. Caryl no doubt had his own idea of what the general tenor of Scripture teaches, and even if he might have agreed that it taught a "rule of charity," he certainly did not agree that a divorce could be a loving action. To neutralize the interpretive conclusions that Milton had drawn from a conference of places, Caryl joined an agreed upon interpretive principle (readers need to attend carefully to the circumstances in which any given passage was written) to a more controversial one (every passage has equal authority). In this way he set up a stand-off between the apparently contradictory teachings of Moses and Jesus on divorce, the better to preserve the legal status quo.

For his part, Milton went on to build *De Doctrina Christiana* on interpretive principles that attended to the circumstances in which any given place had been written. He also compared various places, in an attempt to deduce a coherent doctrine on issues that were variously treated in the Bible. His painstaking conference of places was carried out in light of his own sense of the general tenor of the whole scriptural message, which emphasized charity and liberty and required him radically to redefine, in decidedly personal terms, "the analogy of faith."

The Analogy of Faith as the Ultimate Criterion of Interpretation

By the mid-seventeenth century in England, some general lines of Protestant hermeneutics, which had been worked out in polemics against Catholics, were well established. As the controversies about church government and divorce illustrate, however, there was considerable disagreement about the scope and application of principles and about what was to be concluded by using them, even among those ostensibly committed to "the Bible only." Given the importance of "the analogy of faith" as the rule invoked in attempts to close many discussions, it is surprising how little attention modern students of the literature and thought of this period have given to this principle of last resort.[34]

In the context of anti-papist polemics in the sixteenth century, Protestant appeals to the analogy of faith had proved dramatically successful. Luther, in his Lectures on Romans, explaining that at 12: 6 Paul had meant that "prophecy must be in harmony with faith," had himself harmonized the idea of analogical predication in matters of faith with his cardinal doctrine of passive righteousness. He insisted that a legitimate "analogy" is not actively created by the intellect but passively received without going "beyond the bounds of faith." The doctrine is intimately connected with the biblical places that Luther, upon attaining his insight into Romans 1: 17, understood analogously with "the righteousness of God": "I ran through the Scriptures from memory. I also found in other terms an analogy, as, the work of God, that is, what God does in us."[35] As long as it was invoked to uphold doctrines that had been defined over against "papistical" works-righteousness, "the analogy of faith" proved useful. Its transformation into a virtual principle of exegesis, however, gave it a double edge, and it became a site of contention.

Seventeenth-century English Protestants looked back to William Whitaker's *Disputation on Holy Scripture, Against the Papists* (1588) as a *locus classicus* enunciating their interpretive principles. Whitaker had set out in order rules for biblical interpretation, referring often to Augustine's *De Doctrina Christiana*. He urged that inasmuch as "the end of all Scripture is, as Augustine observes, the love of God and of our neighbour, he . . . determines that without any doubt that is no true interpretation which does not serve to build up the edifice of this genuine charity." One of Augustine's best-known rules was that "one place must be compared and collated with another; the obscurer places with the plainer." Unlike Augustine, Whitaker illustrated it by declaring that James 2: 21, which affirms that Abraham was justified by works, was an obscure place, and he went on to explain it by way of Romans 4: 2, where "Paul . . . expressly says, that Abraham was not justified by works." Having encountered two places that seem to contradict one another, Whitaker knew which one is plain and which obscure not on some basis of language but in light of a general principle, in this case the cardinal Protestant doctrine of justification by faith alone. Another of his rules, that "all our expositions should accord with the analogy of faith, which we read of, Rom. xii. 6," evinces even more clearly that his ultimate interpretive principle was conformity to a doctrinal commitment.[36] Luther had found in Romans a canon of interpretation which he used to establish a new hierarchy within the canon of biblical books. In the doctrine of salvation by grace alone he had seen the epitome of "the gospel." By the late sixteenth century living by "the Bible only" meant accepting this doctrine as a fundamental in relation to which all credal statements were to be judged. The analogy of faith, Whitaker wrote,

> is nothing else but the constant sense of the general tenour of scripture in those clear passages of scripture, where the meaning labours under no obscurity; such as the articles of faith in the Creed, and the contents of the Lord's Prayer, the Decalogue, and the whole Catechism.[37]

On the basis of this principle, he went on to rule out transubstantiation and justification by works as "popish doctrine" that is "repugnant to the analogy of faith." Elsewhere in the *Disputation* Whitaker defended the Protestant analogy of faith against the papist idea that "the rule of faith is more extensive than the Creed, and denotes that doctrine which the apostles delivered to the churches, and which was publicly received by all, that is to say, all tradition written or unwritten." He proposed an alternative view of tradition, one that became common among those who would later be called "Anglicans," claiming that the example of Augustine and the Fathers shows both the necessity and the limitations of consulting learned commentaries.

In the generations after Whitaker many churchmen, seeking to hold back what their opponents were calling a "further reformation," appealed to the analogy of faith in ways that made it function as an essentially conservative principle. Perhaps no one more eloquently availed himself of the analogy of faith as a dogmatic shibboleth than John Donne, who in one sermon compared it to a "lock" on the mysterious Book of Psalms, so that "no *Heretique*, no *Schismatique,* shall get in." In another sermon Donne treated it as a principle of community between authorized ecclesiastical interpreters of various ages and associated it with the Christian duty to "search the Scriptures." In this context he proposed that ordinary Christians, when they encounter a dark place in Scripture, should conduct their searches by consulting authorized interpreters. Elsewhere Donne urged that the analogy of faith provides the stopping point in matters of interpretation: it is the measure in which to judge "fundamentall things, *Sine hæsitatione credantur,* They must be beleeved without disputing; there is no more to be done for them, but beleeving."[38]

Instead of settling issues, however, the analogy of faith often turned out to be so imprecise an interpretive principle that, as different persons and groups developed and articulated varying senses of "the general tenour of the scripture," it proved the Achilles's heel of Protestant hermeneutics. What seemed to be an intrinsic criterion of interpretation, according with the idea that the Scripture is the best interpreter of itself, became in the systematic treatises of Protestant scholasticism the sort of external criterion that it already was for Donne when he counseled his hearers to conduct their searching by consulting those who "have a warrant to search." As each theologian put together his own comprehensive account of divinity, it became increasingly apparent that every preacher, indeed every reader, has a personal idea of what "the general tenour of the scripture" is. What one person thinks may be extracted from the "plain places" in "the Bible only" may seem to another to involve an imposition of alien doctrines and categories. In the 1640s, to get round this, the framers of the *Westminster Confession* attempted quietly to substitute for the analogy of faith as the ultimate interpretive principle "no other but the Holy Spirit speaking in Scripture." This criterion temporarily shifted the locus of dispute. The urge to hold off the "Pretension" of sectaries and other enthusiasts to "new lights" is well illustrated in a list of interpretive criteria enumerated by the philologist Henry Hammond. They included, along with several other "ordinary means" available to interpreters such as "rational inference, collation of places, [and] consulting of the Original languages," what Hammond called simply the "analogy of received doctrine."[39]

After the Restoration, the "analogy of faith" was invoked with renewed vigor by those seeking religious uniformity and comprehension. Jeremy Taylor, in his *Dissuasive from Popery* (1664), an attempt to rally all Protestants against their old common enemy, formulated a representative and especially clear restatement of the analogy of faith. What is most striking about Taylor's discussion of the term is that he now proposes it as an interpretive canon to be invoked not as a last resort but from the start of one's interpretive work. As such, it would exercise a sharp control on what issues would ever come up for consideration, and it would define in advance much of the shape that interpretive questions could take. Discussing the training and requisites for preachers, Taylor asserted that what should be taught from the Word of God was twofold: "all that God spake expressly, and all that by certain consequence can be deduced from it." He then went on to insist of the latter instances "that your deduction be evident":

> In the making deductions, the first great measure to direct our reason and our inquiries is the analogy of faith; that is, let the fundamentals of faith be your cynosura, your great light to walk by, and whatever you derive from thence, let it be agreeable to the principles from whence they come. It is the rule of St. Paul, Προφητεύων κατ' ἀναλογίαν πίστεως, "Let him that prophesies, do it according to the proportion of faith;" that is, let him teach nothing but what is revealed, or agreeable to the αὐτόπιστα, "the prime credibilities" of Christianity; that is, by the plain words of Scripture let him expound the less plain, and the superstructure by the measures of the foundation, and doctrines be answerable to faith, and speculations relating to practice, and nothing taught, as simply necessary to be believed, but what is evidently and plainly set down in the holy Scriptures; for he that calls a proposition necessary, which the apostles did not declare to be so, or which they did not teach to all Christians, learned and unlearned, he is gone beyond his proportions; for every thing is to be kept in that order where God hath placed it. There is a "classis" of necessary articles, and that is the apostles' creed, which Tertullian calls "regulam fidei," "the rule of faith."[40]

Taylor's exposition calls for several observations. First, when he speaks of a "measure," he is obliquely recalling that *analogia* was (like the Latin *proportio* and *ratio*, which sometimes served to translate it) a mathematical term used to express numerical likeness. (It was taken over by Plato, who borrowed it to discuss proportionality among the four elements and between different kinds of knowledge; as a philosophical term it was developed further by Aristotle. Among the medieval schoolmen it was used chiefly in the phrase *analogia entis*, where it served as a principle in natural theology whereby things predicated of creatures might be predicated, analogously, of God.) Taylor goes on virtually to equate the *analogia fidei* with Tertullian's *regula fidei*, thus evincing the fact that the principle had come to be used as a canon of interpretation, a kind of boundary line beyond which exegesis was not to go.

Second, Taylor grounds the rule not in the philosophical tradition but squarely in biblical usage. He thus makes it to cohere with the general doctrinal principles whereby grace and nature are set at odds with one another and all supernatural knowledge is derived solely from Scripture. Medieval philosophers had used the "analogy of being" as a cornerstone in their pursuit of a natural knowledge of God. Protestants typically rejected the *analogia entis* on the grounds that fallen nature can know nothing about God and that it is presumptuous to impose mere human concepts onto the

Divine Being, who has in any event revealed what needs to be known about Him in the Scriptures. The *analogia fidei* presupposes the workings of regenerate reason on the materials that God Himself has provided in the Scriptures. It is on the basis of biblical revelation, not natural reason, that one may legitimately call God Father or think of Him as a providing shepherd.

When Taylor actually cites the passage from Romans, where Paul exhorts his readers to use their gifts according to the proportion of their allotment, he suggests how readily his interpretive principle could be correlated with a crucial detail in the parable of the talents.[41] Like the parable, Romans 12: 6 confirms the idea that each person is allotted gifts in proportion to "his several ability" and is responsible for using these gifts accordingly:

> Seing then that we haue giftes that are diuers, according to the grace that is giuen vnto vs, whether *we haue* prophecie, *let vs prophecie* according to the proportion of faith: Or an office, *let vs waite* on the office: or he that teacheth, on teaching.[42]

The Geneva Bible (which is quoted here, with its abbreviations expanded) had glossed "prophecie" as "preaching & teaching" and "office" as "ministerie, all suche offices, as apperteine to the Church, as Elders, Deacons, &c." The usefulness of the phrase "proportion" or "analogy" of faith for interpreters lay not simply in its being biblical but also in its linguistic reference (whether via *logos* or *ratio*) to the Word, which was commonly said to be self-interpreting and to provide the sole norm by which to judge all doctrine. In other words, by virtue of the presence of the phrase in Romans "the analogy of faith" could be considered an intrinsically biblical rule, not some external norm in relation to which the Bible was to be interpreted. Sometimes this was referred to as *analogia scripturae*. As such it served as a nearly perfect disguise under which, consciously or unconsciously, tacit presuppositions might be imported into one's interpretive work.

The principle that Taylor enunciates was meant to prevent disputes, or to settle them once they arose; no doubt it sometimes worked this way. Yet scarcely anything was so controversial among seventeenth-century English Protestants as questions about what constituted the "fundamentals," and which things were only *adiaphora*. This dispute issued into questions about what was to be binding in matters "indifferent," as when Milton proposed that England's legislators ought not to presume to determine whether a particular man had grounds for divorcing his wife. After the Restoration, there continued to be widespread disagreement about the status of the various early Christian creeds and about the authority of the Church Fathers as interpreters. At one end of the spectrum were those who were optimistic that the creeds and patristic theology provided normative indices of what was in "the Bible only." At the other were those, including Milton, who were suspicious that the early Christians, especially insofar as they introduced the Greek language and the metaphysical categories of Greek philosophy into Christian theology, had corrupted the pristine truth, simplicity, and plainness of "the Bible only." Taylor inclined toward the more optimistic position, elsewhere glossing Paul's "analogy of faith" by way of Clement of Alexandria, who had claimed that it involved knowing what may decently be predicated of God, and by way of Augustine, who had used it as a principle for explaining the hard places in Scripture by way of the plain.[43]

Amidst the "liberty of prophesying," the analogy of faith had emerged as a means by which, without using the dread word "tradition," many Protestants sought to retain a basic credal core of Christianity. Taylor proposed that the analogy of faith be joined to "the consent of the Catholic church," to insure that every doctrine conform to what "all Christians always have consented," the practice of the church being "the best commentary" on obscure passages from Scripture. Thomas Edwards, in the controversy over church government, charged that the authors of *The Apologeticall Narration* had relied too narrowly on only part of the Scriptures, the Epistles and the Book of Acts. He appealed to Tertullian and Whitaker as spokesmen for a "supreme rule" that looked to the whole of scriptural doctrine. More conspicuously conservative an invocation of the principle came from John Owen, who complained that the pride and vain curiosity of learned interpreters often led them into heresy. Against this prospect, Owen insisted on a "reverential subjection of mind, and diligent attendance unto the *analogy of faith*" as the "best perservative" against "*singular*" expositions of the Scripture. Owen sought, moreover, to restore the analogy of faith to its status as an intrinsic interpretive principle. On the matter of consulting the Church Fathers as a "rule of Scripture," he remarked, "No man of ingenuity who hath ever read or considered them . . . with attention and judgment, can abide by this pretense."[44]

Owen's reference to "men of ingenuity" rightly suggests that, amidst debates about proper interpretive principles, the passage about the Bereans (Acts 17: 11) was also contested. In fact, before the end of the century this biblical place became the favorite text of anti-Trinitarian writers, who found in its praise of those who "search the Scriptures" with open minds the warrant for the sorts of re-examination of biblical doctrine that issued into Unitarianism. Many of these writers came to their conclusions by adhering closely to "the Bible only." Logically enough, they proposed that Trinitarian doctrine, which is not explicitly formulated in the Scriptures, is a strained extrapolation that cannot be sufficiently verified on textual grounds. It is therefore not part of the rule of Scripture to which all true Protestants are obligated. The very fact that, after diligent searching of the Scriptures, they could dispute this doctrine was said to be proof that it could not constitute a "fundamental" of Protestant belief. One of their antagonists, William Sherlock, appealed to "the Analogie of Faith" as a means for ruling out such "Arian" doctrines, and invoked the Bereans as models for the interpretive procedures used by the early church when it devised the basic Christian creeds.[45]

Appeals to the analogy of faith on the one hand and to the interpretive model set by the Bereans on the other were not confined to abstract theological disputes. At times they also showed up in debates about gender relations. Arguing for the right of women to speak up in religious matters, the Quaker Anne Docwra reveals another way in which, especially after the Restoration, the traditional principle known as "the analogy of faith" was enlisted by those who sought to curb innovations. She observed that the "Twentieth Article" of the Church of England "forbids expounding one place of Scripture to make it repugnant to another," and she urged that an important implication of this principle was that Scripture passages which allow that women have acted as prophets cannot be canceled out by the invocation of other passages that enjoin women to silence. "All you that are like the *Noble Bereans*," she wrote to her readers, "that are diligent Inquirers of this Age, I shall leave you to search the Scriptures, and see if these things be not true." With the Bereans she contrasted those that make "a Money-Trade of Religion" and persecute "such as do not conform to it."[46] By the late seventeenth century, appeals to an ultimate interpretive principle that would prevent disputes about the meaning and application of Scripture were made chiefly by those in power. From Milton's point of view such appeals served to impose a premature unity onto the diverse strands of biblical literature, and thus to curtail legitimate imaginative freedom.

Milton's Interpretive Work and the Bereans

The theory that all saving truth was already contained in the Bible, to which nothing could be added, did not keep seventeenth-century Protestants from greatly multiplying the number of religious books.[47] Not intimidated from writing by their theory, English Protestants of various hues searched the Scriptures for themselves, often associating their interpretive activity with the Bereans of Acts 17; and they wrote out their interpretations in vigorous contests with one another. In the divorce tracts Milton denominated as "the method of religion" a process whereby Bible-readers were obliged to "gather up" for themselves, by comparing various places, "a generall and religious command" out of the Scriptures; he deplored the "*Papistical way of a literal apprehension against the direct* analogy *of sense, reason, law and Gospel*" (II, 264, 431). In *Areopagitica,* he endorsed the idea that a good reader develops, equivalently, a personal analogy of faith:

> To be still searching what we know not, by what we know, still closing up truth to truth as we find it (for all her body is *homogeneal,* and proportionall) this is the golden rule in *Theology* as well as in Arithmetick, and makes the best harmony in a Church. (II, 551)

By the time he was writing the *De Doctrina,* Milton was proclaiming that the conscientious believer is almost obliged to write a book. To take seriously his use of the rhetoric of individual responsibility, however, is to glimpse a curious heaven peopled only by those who have the learning and the leisure to perform Herculean labors. Balancing this forbidding prospect was Milton's awareness that he had been given "many rather then few" talents (*CPW,* I, 869), and that not everyone was capable of compiling a personal synthesis of divinity. In any event, the main point of his treatise was not the doctrines that its author framed but the model for interpreting Scripture that it embodies:

> I do not teach anything new in this work. I aim only to assist the reader's memory by collecting together, as it were, into a single book [*in unum corpus*] texts which are scattered here and there throughout the Bible, and by systematizing them under definite headings, in order to make reference easy. (VI, 127)

All this sounds a modest enough presentation of the work. Yet, as readers of *Areopagitica* well appreciate, the process of closing up truth with truth implies that the written Scriptures are like the body of Osiris, needing to be reassembled into a lost original, the Word of God that transcends the words of the scriptural penmen. Milton's idea of reading here is, as William Shullenberger has demonstrated, "a binding or collecting, a project of imaginative unification" to result in a corpus. By concentrating on the words of the Bible only, Milton aims to discover in the general tenor of the Scriptures the deep structure of God's language, which generates all the various particular texts.[48] *De Doctrina Christiana* is his attempt to collate texts *in unum corpus,* a textual body of the Word of God that will not be complete short of the Second Coming. That the Bible is seen to require collecting and reassembling testifies to its not having already fixed meaning permanently. Milton stresses that God's decrees (what Shullenberger aptly denominates "the deep structure of the lexicon of being") are conditional. History is an unfinished process of speech, and no human life is fated (that is, already completely "spoken") in advance of its being freely lived out.[49] Hence, the possibility of, indeed the need for, the labor of an imaginative reconstruction of scriptural truth on the part of believers, each "according to his several ability."

In this regard Milton might have pointed out some important presuppositions on which he based his dismantling of the Bible verse by verse and reassembling it anew in a theological treatise of Gargantuan proportions. Reading Scripture according to the humanist logic of gathering and framing meant that increasingly Milton valued the Scriptures as a diverse collection of "places," that is, of textual fragments suitable for gathering. The Bible was a storehouse in which earnest searching would less often yield a "place" that defined one's "condition" than a range of potentially relevant and potentially contradictory places requiring comparison and responsible application. By understanding the process of gathering (rather than framing) to be the reader's chief responsibility, Milton greatly reduced the nervousness that one might have felt in the face of the cornucopian wealth of places. Questioning the assumption that copious diversity was to be controlled by relying on predetermined aspects of common Protestant beliefs, he provoked readers to see that post-apostolic readers actually have decided advantages over the biblical writers: they know the issues of later times for the resolution of which God was thought to have given a lasting revelation, and they know the works of the whole canon, with which to work towards a higher synthesis than was available to any particular biblical writer. In accord with the humanist recognition that different people possess the "gift" for framing authentic discourse "in sundry measure,"[50] Milton understood these advantages to be especially available to those "men of rare abilities, and more then common industry" who, as he had proclaimed in *Areopagitica,* "God . . . raises to his own work . . . not only to look back and revise what hath bin taught heretofore, but to gain furder and goe on, some new enlightn'd steps in the discovery of truth" (II, 566). For such reasons, among others, Milton declared in *De Doctrina* that "it is in the interests of the Christian religion that men should be free not only to sift and winnow any doctrine, but also openly to give their opinions of it and even to write about it, according to what each believes" (VI, 122).

The notion that one should express one's opinions "according to what [one] believes" involved for Milton a different "proportion" than that commonly known as the analogy of faith. In the parable of the talents, Milton had a model for understanding that to each person the burden of interpreting the Scriptures fell in proportion to "his several ability." The Latin of the passage that follows the one quoted just above entails the metaphor of proportion (in the words *pro* and *prout*) in ways that are obscured by John Carey's translation. Moreover, it shows that Milton enlists the metaphor of the heavy weight (*pondere*), which was part of the relevant background of the Greek "talent." (In the ancient Mediterranean world "talent" had been both a heavy unit of weight and the largest of monetary denominations.)

> Id denique ago, ut ex iis quæ sive vetera sive nova atulisse censebor, pro eorum pondere ac momento, imo pro scripturam potius auctoritate quarum nituntur creberrimis testimoniis, intelligere omnes possint, quanti intersit religionis Christianæ, concedi libertatem non excutiendæ solum cuiuscunque doctrinæ, palamque ventilandæ, sed etiam de ea, prout cuique fide persuasum est, sentiendi atque etiam scribendi. (*Works*, XIV, 10–12)

This declaration of Milton's "aim" (Carey) involves the drawing of inferences from a mass of biblical data. Milton does not claim to make inferences by way of the traditional *analogia fidei*. Rather, as Sumner's translation brings out, "an inference . . . will be stronger in proportion to the weight and importance of those opinions, or rather in proportion to the authority of Scripture, on the abundant testimony of which they rest." (Milton's word *nituntur* implies *resting upon, being supported by*, scriptural places. It carries the connotation that this support is the result of having made a considerable effort; one sense of *nitor* is "to exert oneself," or "to strive.") Conversely, doctrines like that of the Trinity, which have the support of the analogy of faith and of "custom," are not countenanced in the body of the treatise when Milton judges there to be a lack of scriptural weight. Anticipating the likelihood that his opinions will sound like heresy, Milton deploys the categories of experimental religion and recommends the "conference of places" in an attempt to ward off the same sort of prejudice that he had encountered in the 1640s when he openly presented his interpretation of the biblical places concerning divorce. Sumner's translation makes this clearer than Carey's does: "I do not expect from candid [*ingeniis*] and judicious readers a conduct so unworthy of them, that like certain unjust and foolish men, they should stamp [*damnent*] with the invidious name of heretic or heresy whatever appears to them to differ from the received opinions, without trying the doctrine by comparison with Scripture testimonies [*non scripturæ testimoniis collatis*]" (*Works*, XIV, 10–13).

This plea was of course not published, as it happened, until the nineteenth century. In his own lifetime, Milton limited himself, or was limited, to publishing only a rather general statement of interpretive principles. In *A Treatise of Civil Power* (1659), he expressed his mature conception of the nature of the individual interpreter's rights, putting it at the service of an argument that no external authority may impose an interpretation of Scripture on the individual's conscience. "He then who to his best apprehension follows the scripture, though against any point of doctrine by the whole church receivd, is not the heretic; but he who follows the church against his conscience and perswasion grounded on the scripture" (*CPW*, VII, 248). Equating "religion" and "conscience," Milton defines them in terms reminiscent of the devotional tradition in which it is incumbent on every believer to make his calling and election sure. The equation effects a redefinition of the practice of the Christian life and thereby introduces a rather different context in which to understand the obligation to search the Scriptures. "I . . . mean by conscience or religion, that full perswasion whereby we are assur'd that our beleef and practise, as far as we are able to apprehend and probably make appeer, is according to the will of God & his Holy Spirit within us" (242).

In order to secure this perspective, which sounds conventional enough at first, Milton goes on to appeal to even more hallowed principles: that "the main foundation of our protestant religion [is] . . . the holy scripture," and that readers require "the illumination of the Holy Spirit" to make knowledge of the Bible "warrantable." In the course of this rehearsal of pieties, as he insists that Protestants have "no other divine rule or autoritie from without us warrantable to one another as a common ground but the holy scripture," he quietly establishes a basis for ruling out the creeds and foundational doctrines which were commonly supposed to be the basis of the analogy of faith. An emphasis on the need for "experimental" knowledge of the Scriptures then feeds Milton's principal argument in the treatise: by its very nature such knowledge cannot be transferred from one person to another; everyone must attain it personally, under the guidance of the Spirit, so that "it follows cleerly, that no man or body of men in these times can be the infallible judges or determiners in matters of religion to any other mens consciences but thir own" (242–43). Milton then seeks to clinch the point by joining two biblical places:

> And therfore those Beroeans are commended, *Act.* 17.11, who after the preaching even of S. *Paul, searchd the scriptures daily, whether those things were so.* Nor did they more then what God himself in many places commands us by the same apostle, to search, to try, to judge of these things our selves: And gives us reason also, *Gal.* 6. 4, 5. *let every man prove his own work, and then shall he have rejoicing in himself alone, and not in another: for every man shall bear his own burden.* (VII, 243)

Having thus defined the "burden" borne by Christians as the practice of searching the Scriptures to test their knowledge, the passage proceeds then to provide confirmation by returning to foundational principles of the Reformation. These include the deploring of popery and of mere human traditions, the assertion of Scripture-sufficiency, and even an appeal to the etymology of the term *Protestant*. In this way Milton seeks to equate those whom he presently fears with the external authorities whom the first Reformers rejected. Writing before most of the early Unitarians and, as he insisted, independently of them, Milton thus made prominent use of Acts 17: 11 as a plea for free and responsible examination of Scriptural doctrine. What was most characteristic of his mature interpretive practice, however, was his shrewd combination of this hallowed place with Galatians 6: 4–5, interpreted as an injunction to mental work. This particular conjunction of places defined the burden of individual interpretation to which the *De Doctrina Christiana* represented his response.

The massive *De Doctrina Christiana* was not a mere extension of the Theological Index in Milton's *Commonplace Book*. It was a book of another order altogether. It could not have been conceived in the period when Milton's idea of Scriptural plainness virtually insured that whatever was gathered from the Bible would reinforce some antecedent doctrinal commitment and when he was accustomed to scorning the "almost monstrous [*prope monstrosa*] tomes" of the "subtle" scholastics and to dismissing the "wranglings of crabbed old men."[51] The reasons that Milton ultimately gave for compiling his theological treatise, and the urgency he assigned to the project, were a function of a specific set of experiences that he had in the early 1640s, when he developed what was for him a radically new way of understanding the relation of biblical places to Christian life, that is, when he accepted as his "portion" in life the burden of interpreting the particular words of the Bible so as to reconstruct a Word of God different from and sometimes less than the sum of the Bible's parts.

Milton's new understanding of the nature of biblical places made the parable of the talents more pertinent, and differently pertinent, to his life and work than it had seemed before 1642. When, many years later, he came to present the process by which he had compiled the *De Doctrina*, his language was deeply informed by a sense that his work of scriptural interpretation was the multiplying of talents prior to an accounting: "God offers all his rewards not to those who are thoughtless and credulous, but to those who labor constantly and seek tirelessly after truth" (*CPW,* VI, 120); "I . . . laid up provision for the future in that I should not thenceforth be unprepared or hesitant when I needed to give an account of my beliefs" (121); "I shall mention those methods that proved profitable for me, in case desire for similar profit should, perhaps, lead someone else to start out upon the same path" (118–19).

With its radical ill-sortment of biblical places, the *De Doctrina* is of considerable interest when seen as an account of what a diligent laborer has done with his master's investment. The treatise makes the component parts of Protestant Christianity stand out. It wrests hundreds of biblical places from their scriptural contexts, and yet brings those contexts, and Milton's overall sense of Scripture, to bear on their interpretation. Its idiosyncratic and eccentric doctrines encourage reflection, even with respect to its more orthodox doctrines; and the arguments presented for the unconventional opinions provide the materials and principles with which each reader is encouraged to work out a personal religious synthesis. Ultimately, the treatise dramatizes the workings of an interpretive process that locates both current pleasures and eventual salvation in a continuing dialogue with the Word of God. That Word is understood not as what was dictated to the sacred penmen and has been reduced to ink and paper, but as an authorized language in which each believer needs to become fluent by personal labor and intense study experienced not as "toylsom vanity," but as an encounter with "the best and sagest things." Milton's commitment to interpreting according to such a process made the parable of the talents serviceable in new ways. His use of it as a framework within which he understood his interpretive labors became increasingly subtle, and the ramifications of the parable for defining those labors was thoroughgoing. For he found in the injunction to multiply talents a dynamic model for understanding the complex relations between the authorized source and the new texts which that source enabled. His restrained allusions also constitute therefore a powerful intervention in the long history of interpreting the parable. Seen in relation to previous interpretations, according to which the principal referent for the "talents" in the parable was this Word itself apportioned to each person "according to his several ability," Milton's understanding of this biblical place as an epitome of intertextuality was at once more traditional and more utterly transforming of the tradition than has been commonly appreciated.

4. Standing and Waiting in the Face of Indeterminacy

> "He speaks with great modesty of himself, as if he had not five, or two, but only one talent."
> —Thomas Newton, *The Poetical Works of John Milton* (1761)

In setting forth the argument of this book it has been no part of my purpose to propose a new theory about the dates at which Milton was at work on *De Doctrina Christiana*. I have only urged that his conception of this project postdates the period in which he had first been gathering biblical places, as any young scholar might, into a commonplace book. For it was not until Milton admitted to himself that "there is scarse any one saying in the Gospel, but must be read with limitations and distinctions," that he conceived the need for a massive personal synthesis. In turning now to the poem that begins with the line "When I consider how my light is spent" (Sonnet 19), which contains Milton's best known allusion to the parable of the talents, I should say from the outset that I will make no attempt here to settle the longstanding controversy about the date at which Milton wrote the poem, which first appeared in print only in 1673. For the purposes of my argument the important point is that, whenever the poet was at work on it, "When I consider . . ." epitomizes the views embraced by Milton in the third principal phase of his career as an interpreter. The poem belongs to and perhaps heralds Milton's hermeneutical maturity, during which he was achieving greater certitude about the sense of some biblical places and at the same time coming increasingly to appreciate that both the sense and the "experimental" application of many places had yet to be determined. But if a precise date of composition cannot be fixed (and probably ought not to be), nonetheless a good deal can be ascertained about the historical specificity of this sonnet as a piece of discourse from the 1640s and 1650s.

As the notion of a "real life" author "behind" a text has in recent years been called radically into question, there have emerged especially good reasons for questioning assumptions on which some of Milton's sonnets have been turned into transparently autobiographical poems.¹ One cost of persistent attempts to induct Sonnet 19 into a narrative that focuses on moments of crisis in the poet's career is that they have obscured the ways in which the poem works against specific conventions of reading for experimental knowledge.² Critics have gone to an altogether disproportionate amount of trouble trying to explain the temporal phrases "E're half my days" from Sonnet 19 and "my three and twentieth yeer" from Sonnet 7 ("How soon hath time . . . ?") in relation to Milton's life. This approach distracts us from noticing the uses that such phrases have in their respective sonnets, both of which concern the difficulties encountered by young persons who have set out early on a path of virtuous conduct. It also obscures the brilliance with which Milton brought together two sets of conventions in these poems: the auditing motif from Renaissance lyrics and the tradition of experimental reading. In previous chapters I have begun to question familiar ways of thinking about Milton's "talent," ways that tame the biblical parable and make it available for constructing an optimistic account of the growth of a poet's mind. Here, in proposing some ways for getting beyond the predominantly biographical concerns that have similarly domesticated Milton's interest in the parable, I will relate the initial speaker in Milton's "talent" sonnet to other readers who were accustomed to looking for a personally appropriate scriptural "place." Ultimately, I want to explore various ways in which Sonnet 19 and Sonnet 7 engage the biblical parable and to show that it is unwarranted to suppose that Milton was offering in these poems definitive representations of himself. What Sonnets 7 and 19 tell us, finally, about Milton's biography is that he knew very well the language and procedures of the cases of conscience tradition,³ that he recognized its deep affinities with prominent features of the English sonnet tradition, and that he was expert at fusing these traditions to make poems at once beautiful and deeply moving. Milton is separated from his contemporaries in that he showed infinitely more skill in refashioning biblical language to make it represent experiences that were widely shared but not elsewhere so artfully recreated.

Responsibly Redefining Temporary Faith

In the years after he developed a sense of the burden of interpretation, Milton worked in both poetry and prose towards radical redefinitions of many features of experimental predestinarianism. In particular he rejected an interpretation imposed on the parable of the talents by those who wished to see in it a model for understanding a predestined temporary faith. In the hands of Perkins, who conflated the multiplying of talents with doing what Jesus had called "the one thing necessarie" (Luke 10: 42), the parable had been turned into an injunction to find assurance of one's elect status by reading the Bible experimentally.

The distinction between faith and assurance appeared regularly in Perkins's writings. In *The Combat betweene Christ and the Deuill displayed*,[4] Perkins aimed his exegesis at demonstrating that the Savior set an example in making his own calling and election sure. Having just received his calling at the baptism, Jesus resists the temptations in the wilderness, and this is said to produce for him the requisite assurance. In *A Treatise of Callings*, Perkins's whole argument built to a lengthy discussion of the final account that every person will have to make before the divine Judge. Perkins warned that "he that hath been vnfaithfull, or vnjust in the workes of his calling, shall heare the same voice of Christ, saying; *Take him, binde him hand and foote, and cast him into vtter darknesse.*" Lest this happen to his reader, the author recommended a proleptic and imaginary rehearsal for a final accounting of the sort that, as we have seen, Milton projects in *The Reason of Church Government*: "wee must consider," wrote Perkins, "what gifts we haue receiued for the discharge of our callings . . . for they are the talents of our Lord, and he lookes for a reckoning."[5] Perkins imagined the final judgment as a great public reading, for which each person's private self-examination should be a preparation. The implications of Perkins's judgment scene are nothing short of horrifying. "[A]ll men and Angells," he explained, will be

> set before the presence of Christ, then shall euerie worke that they haue done, be made manifest, euen the most secret workes of all, as Ecclesiasties saith; *God will bring euery secret thing to light.* And if any thinke it strange, we must know, that God hath bookes of record, wherein all mens thoughts, and words, and deedes, good, or bad, secret, or open, are inrolled. . . . We may not imagine that these be materiall bookes like to the registers of men. . . . But by these bookes wee must vnderstand: first of all the infinite knowledge and prouidence of God: secondly, the co[n]sciences of men, to testifie of our doings, and be as a thousand witnesses.[6]

This powerful imaginative picture of social control provided the "practical" impetus for acting in accord with the repeated advice to make one's calling and election sure. Milton, in the course of his treatment of predestination in *De Doctrina Christiana*, examined and criticized the metaphor that Perkins had exploited, insisting that the Bible mentions only "the book of life" and never a "book of death" (*CPW*, VI, 169–70).

While it is sometimes said that the doctrine of temporary faith faded in the seventeenth century, there is plenty of evidence that in the 1640s and 1650s fears about a merely temporary faith revived. The doctrine figures prominently in English translations of continental works of divinity, such as the *Abridgment* of Wollebius's *Compendium Theologiæ Christianæ*. Grotius, in *His Most Choice Discovrses,* traced it back to Augustine, who taught that "faith joyned with charity, and regeneration, are not certain tokens of Predestination, because many that had that faith, and were regenerated, not only fail, but eternally perish." "*No man can be secure,*" Grotius concluded from Augustine's teaching, "*until this life, which is a temptation upon earth, be consummate.*" In a more popular vein, John Gardner, introducing Jane Turner's *Choice Experiences* (1653), urged that the account would "provoke self-examination" on the part of readers. What it meant for them to be "watchfull, lest [they] fall" was to "[r]ead with diligence [and] consider with patience." Even well after the Restoration the doctrine was remembered by some with fear and trembling. Although she does not use the term "temporary faith," Mary Mersen distinguished three sorts of election, one of which was addressed to persons who demonstrated their unworthiness by being unwilling to "wrestle," as Jacob had, "for the blessing" of assurance.[7]

In *De Doctrina Christiana,* Milton treated the doctrine of temporary faith at considerable length and quite differently from ways in which Perkins had handled it. In chapter xxv of Book I, he accepted the division between faith and assurance and proposed that assurance is not a necessary component of "saving" faith. He defined assurance not as certitude that one had been predestined to salvation but as a persuasion that *if* one persists in faith and charity, one will undoubtedly attain eternal life. He thus took occasion to emphasize that perseverance, while it was a gift from God, was the responsibility of believers themselves. Similarly, in the chapter devoted to Predestination (I, iv), he appealed to the parable of the sower to argue that, while there are different human dispositions even before the Word is preached, all persons have a sufficient ability to resist evil (*CPW*, VI, 186). Milton's mature dissent from the sorts of views about reprobation and temporary faith that had descended from Perkins is well known, and this has obscured the fact that in "When I consider . . ." the initial speaker is familiar with the sorts of warnings that predestinarian divines had been spreading abroad. Instead of acknowledging that the speaker fears that, since his "light is spent," he has been accorded the punishment of the man who hid the one talent, "utter darkness," readers have grown accustomed to reading the opening line as a transparent reference to Milton's blindness.

The Fashioning of Milton's Poetic "Vocation"

If in the Renaissance period in England writers learned to fashion a "self," the authorized version of Milton's "self" has nonetheless been fashioned belatedly, by isolating and combining various passages from his writings to construct the autobiography that Milton never wrote. In this process the idea that the parable of the talents was important to Milton's conception of his poetic vocation was already put forward at the end of the seventeenth century, as Chapter Two has shown. Since the eighteenth century the idea that Sonnet 19 is an autobiographical poem has taken on increasing prominence. Newton's influential title, "On His Blindness," invites readers to make a simple equation identifying the speaker of the poem with the poet who went on to write *Paradise Lost*. In his notes Newton joined to this biographical reading the idea that Milton was alluding to the parable, although this identification created a new interpretive problem. For it is odd that Milton, who elsewhere intimated that he knew he had been given "many rather than few" gifts (*CPW*, I, 869) should identify himself with the figure who had received but a single talent. Newton sought to explain away one oddity by proposing another: Milton, he claimed, "speaks with great modesty of himself, as if he had not five, or two, but only one talent."[8] The oddity is compounded when we note that Milton thus seems to identify himself with the failure, who was punished for his sloth.

Readers in our time have not been much troubled by these oddities. Like the biblical parable to which it alludes, the poem has been domesticated, made familiar, so that it seems "natural" to assume that it records the temporary doubts of a great poet who feared for a time that his blindness would preclude his fulfilling his "long-felt, God-given capacity for composing a truly great poem."[9] The history sketched out in the preceding chapters suggests, however, an alternate way of understanding Milton's "talent." In view of that history it is not surprising that Robert Herrick, for instance, used the word to refer to a poetic legacy left by Ben Jonson:

> My *Ben*
> Or come agen:
> Or send to us,
> Thy wits great over-plus;

> But teach us yet
> > Wisely to husband it;
> > Lest we that Tallent spend:
> And having once brought to an end
> > That precious stock; the store
> Of such a wit the world sho'd have no more.[10]

The idea that Jonson's poetry passed on his "Tallent" to his successors was in keeping with the principal way in which the biblical parable had been read since patristic times: in scriptural commentary "talents" were understood to be apportioned to people in proportion to their natural abilities, and "talent" was often made to refer to the Scriptures themselves, taken as a sort of poetic capital with which Christians were to trade in order to make converts. Yet it was inevitable that "talent" should come also to refer to a poet's native wit. Milton's use of the word in Sonnet 19 suggests that he recognized that both senses of the word are congruent with the idea that a reader might feel an anxious burden in the face of the scriptural past.

Milton's use of the word "talent" was in any event unusual, and this was attested by Dr. Johnson. Curiously, despite his own interest in the parable and in Milton's poetic career, Johnson's *Dictionary* does not cite the sonnet to illustrate any of the senses of "talent." The citations do illustrate, however, that by the later seventeenth century the meaning of the word "talent" was in flux. Johnson had decided views on how it ought, and ought not, to be employed. He himself used the word only once in his poetry, and the appearance of the word in his poem in praise of Dr. Robert Levet neatly accords with the *Dictionary* entry for what he calls the proper metaphorical usage, "borrowed from the talents mentioned in the holy writ." A "talent" in this sense is a "Faculty; power," or "gift of nature." "It is used," Johnson adds, "sometimes seriously, sometimes lightly." In the Levet poem the use is "serious," and the sense is "modest" in a manner decidedly reminiscent of Milton's poem as glossed by Newton:

> His virtues walk'd their narrow round,
> > Nor made a pause, nor left a void;
> And sure th' Eternal Master found
> > The single talent well employ'd.[11]

In addition to the senses of a monetary denomination and a natural power, Johnson's *Dictionary* also provided a third definition for "talent," one which he regarded as involving an "improper and mistaken" use of the word. Citing an example from Swift, in which "talent" means "Quality," or "disposition," Johnson might have had recourse to the distinction between a "talent" and a "bent" in Milton's sonnet. "Bent" was used especially to refer to a "Mental inclination or tendency; disposition" (*OED* sb.² 6b.), and had been, in Milton's time, the standard religious term for what the Holy Spirit altered in regeneration.¹² This concept appears in Sonnet 19 in the adjectival form:

> And that one Talent which is death to hide,
> Lodg'd with me useless, though my Soul more bent
> To serve therewith my Maker. . . .

Milton's sonnet makes sense of, rather than erases, the distinction implied in the parable when it is said that talents were given "to every man according to his several ability." Worried about what to do with the talent which has been given him, the speaker insists that his inclination is to use it for service. His puzzlement and frustration are a function, then, of two contradictory impositions: a talent to be used and no light in which to use it. At this point he seems to be thinking in terms more characteristic of the classical tradition than the biblical: in Homer *phaos* ("light") refers to the arena in which one conducts the business of life, and it can take on a sense that means something like "the opportunity and determination to act for personal benefit and advantage." In the fifteenth book of the *Iliad* Ajax uses the word in a way that indicates "that the possibilities for success live within human powers to act, and one cannot simply wait passively for circumstances to change."¹³ In short, Milton's considerer is thinking of his "talent" in ways from which the Christian idea of grace is meant to free him.

The sedimentation in the history of the word "talent" has likely blinded us to what goes against the grain in the sonnet. We have difficulty seeing how alien a thing the talent is. For not only has the origin of the word as a balance or unit of weight been forgotten, but the previously separate senses of natural *power* and natural *disposition* have been conflated in popular usage. This slippage has had important implications for interpreting both the biblical parable and Milton's sonnet. The *otherness* of the talent, emphasized by the demonstrative pronoun "that" in the sonnet, is elided when "talent" is considered a personal quality, one's natural bent. The resources of the philological tradition can help readers recover this older sense and open them to seeing what is problematic. Nonetheless, it was futile for Dr. Johnson to attempt to establish controls on how "talent" was properly to be used. What proved decisive in the history of the word "talent" was the joining of the senses of having power and of having a personal disposition to use that power. This virtually guaranteed that the idea of having talent would be connected to ideas about achieving personal fulfillment. "Talent" came to be seen as a God-given or natural "gift," and the proper use of one's "talent" to be life's proper task. This idea seemed compatible with a religious interpretation of the parable. Once it had become conventional to speak of writers as having talent, this generated a moralistic way of auditing their performance. Coleridge, for instance, judged himself harshly for having failed to produce in accord with his "Talents."[14] He may well have been contrasting himself with the sage and serious Milton, who ultimately fulfilled what his "talent" had promised.

Today readers of Sonnet 19, encouraged by Newton's title, commonly think of "light" as the poet's eyesight and identify "that one Talent" with a "poetic faculty" by which Milton thought he would serve God in his particular calling. Having gone blind, so this simply autobiographical way of reading goes, Milton was in peril of not fulfilling his promise: he might never achieve that for which he had been so aptly equipped by his natural bent for languages, by the extraordinary education his family had provided him, and more recently by the wide public experience he had had in the revolutionary government. From this perspective the dilemma faced by the poet in what Newton entitled "On His Blindness" seems merely temporary, and his having gone blind is treated as something which, although it was no doubt painful to him, proved ultimately rather trivial, since the same poet nonetheless went on to write *Paradise Lost*.

Undoing Newton's Wresting of the Sonnet on the "one talent"

While it makes for a certain poignancy to think of Sonnet 19 as the poet's meditation on his blindness at a moment of intense personal crisis, it is also possible, and enriching in other ways, to see the sonnet as transcending the private and lyrical modes into which customary readings have fitted it. Even William Riley Parker has acknowledged that the poem "might have been written, with no alterations, by a poet in full possession of his eyesight but with some awareness of the Scriptural (and poetic) meanings of the terms 'light' and 'dark.'" Ultimately, the sonnet is more about the problem of being of service than about blindness. Since the service of others (rather than the cultivation of one's natural abilities) was what many interpreters in the seventeenth century were earnestly seeking to get the parable of the talents to teach, it makes sense to think that the poem grapples with the implications of the parable. It does not reject "the point" of the parable *tout à fait*.[15]

The justice of Parker's observation is better appreciated if we attend to the meditative practices of religious people on both sides during the period of the civil wars. Amidst the disorientations of the middle decades of the century, literature for afflicted consciences, which had been popular around the end of the sixteenth century, became newly relevant and was revived. What Christopher Hill, writing of people on Milton's side in the early 1650s, has denominated "the experience of defeat" had its analogies among royalists in the 1640s.[16] Consider the case of Francis Quarles, who seems to have experienced a severe testing of his faith in the mid-1640s. According to the address to the "Courteous Reader" at the start of the second part of Quarles's *Judgement and Mercie for Afflicted Soules* (1646), the author's experience was not unusual: "*Now when the theme of every man's discourse is his sad losses in these times, your Authour bids me tell you, that in these he had not the least share: for from him his very* Religion *was stolne away; nay, yet more cruell, even then when he had the most need of it; in the time of his sicknesse.*" The next sentence goes on to identify Quarles's "Religion" with "*this small Essay (the Epitome of his ejaculatory soul)*," which was allegedly pirated and "printed without his knowledge," so that (according to the convention) the present edition can be offered to the world without taint to the author's modesty.[17] Given the ecclesiastical upheavals that had taken place between Quarles's death in 1644 and the printing of his work in 1646, royalist sympathizers would see a good deal more in the phrase "*from him his very* Religion *was stolne away*" and thus amidst their increasing afflictions have an added reason for finding Quarles's meditations useful.

The second part of Quarles's treatise anticipates Milton's "talent" sonnet and shows that specific language as well as common meditative practices were shared by religious people on both sides of the conflict. In the structure of each of its twenty meditations, in the prominence it gives to certain themes, and in its diction, *Judgement and Mercie for Afflicted Souls* by its parallels makes Milton's sonnet look less like an autobiographical portrayal of *his* ejaculatory soul than an epitome of mid-seventeenth-century devotional literature. Each of Quarles's twenty meditations begins, as sonnets generally do, with some complication. Any number of these problems might be used to designate the situation of the speaker at the start of Milton's sonnet, a figure who has been "consider[ing]" his current situation: "The weary man's Burthen," "The deserted man's misery," "The Humble Man's Depression," "The fearfull man's Conflict," "The sinner's accompt," "The good man's Distrust." In each meditation the statement of the problem is followed by a number of other steps: a brief version of a potential resolution is given (under the heading, e.g., "His Rest," "His Supply," or "Her Relief"). This is followed by the enumeration of a number of Scripture texts, "Proofs," meant to offer consolation. Then follows a "Soliloquie" spoken by the meditator and providing a sort of locus of the combat, and often a clarification of what is at issue, formulated from a point of view that assumes that faith is preferable to unbelief. Finally, the meditation ends with a prayer, spoken in more confident tones than the introductory complication.

The first of Quarles's meditations begins where sonnets apparently written by Anne Locke had begun a hundred years earlier and where Bunyan's *Pilgrim's Progress* would begin thirty years later, with "The weary man's Burthen."[18] In the introductory section the meditator exclaims

> How intolerable is the *Burthen* of this sinne! how insufferable is the weight of my offences! . . . I have lost the *favour* of my God, I have frustrated the end of my *creation*. . . . What shall I do? . . . who shall deliver me from this Burthen? Poore miserable man that I am, who shall release me from this Bondage?

It will come as no surprise to readers of Milton's sonnet, or of the conversion narratives of this era, that the first text used to answer the speaker's dilemma is Matthew 11:28, "*Come unto me all you that are heavy laden, and I will give you rest.*" But, just as we see in the repeated anxieties afflicting the author of *Grace Abounding,* or even in the afflictions depicted by the poet in *The Temple,* troubles keep recurring, so that there is no permanent "rest-[ing]" place but only a series of experiences which keep playing out the problem in various forms. It is the instance that Quarles places last in this series that most thoroughly anticipates Milton's sonnet in its themes and diction.

Headed "The good man's Distrust," Meditation 20 begins with the phrase "WHen I consider. . . ." What the meditator considers this time is not in the first instance his own wretched situation. It is almost as if he has been reminded once too often that "God doth not need / Either man's work or his own gifts." For he is considering "the *All-sufficiencie* of my God," which makes it seem unlikely to him that God will make good on his promise: "He invites my laden soul to come, and offers *rest*. Alas, I come, and yet my laden soul can find no *ease*" (1: 129). The meditation proceeds by enumerating a whole series of instances in which there is an evident gap between the promises he has heard and what the meditator actually experiences. In this way, the standard procedure of all the preceding meditations is called into question. Then the meditator concludes this section with an allusion to the parable of the talents which associates his experience of this gap with that of the third figure in the parable. Interestingly, the problem shifts from what God has failed to do to what the meditator now feels he himself is unable to do: "My soul, what are his promises to thee, that art not able to perform those hard conditions that gives thee *interest* to those promises?" Here, when the meditator interprets the "talents," which he does not explicitly name, as God's "promises," he identifies them not simply with the Scriptures but with a certain way of reading the Scriptures, one which seems no longer possible for him.

As the introductory meditation gives way to the next steps in the pattern, the meditator is challenged, among other things, to believe in a God who "accepts the *will* for the *deed*," and to believe of this God that "*both from his absence and his presence thou gainest light.*" In his soliloquy the meditator associates his complaining with that of the Israelites in the desert: "How often," he tells himself, "hast thou murmured for that, which if enjoyed had been thy ruin! God hath promised, but hath delayed performance, to exercise thy *patience*. . . . Endure, hope, believe. . . ." Unlike Milton's sonnet, the meditation does not end on this note of expectation; it ends with the meditator's prayer, addressing God and including his own promise to "sing the wonder of thy goodnesse, and praise thy Name for ever" (1: 130).

In the context of seventeenth-century devotional literature, then, the considerer in Milton's Sonnet 19 can be seen as a representative figure.[19] He is worried about the permanent implications of acting or not acting under vastly changed circumstances, after an experience of defeat. Assuming that his eternal destiny is at stake, the considerer is worried about his ability to do good works now that (as he thinks) "the hour has come when no man can work," or at least he cannot work. Milton's sonnet thus takes seriously the anxiety of many conscientious readers of his era who thought about their personal situations in the language and categories of particular biblical passages. In this respect the poem differs remarkably from the one with which the denomination Milton's "First Sonnet on His Blindness" groups it. In the sonnet addressed to Cyriak Skinner, Milton claims that he is consoled by his conscience for having lost his sight in an act of self-sacrifice.

By contrast, the speaker at the beginning of "When I consider . . ." has a troubled conscience. He feels guilty and thinks he is being punished. He is like Milton's Samson in taking his physical condition to be am emblem of his moral and religious plight. He associates himself with the figure in the biblical parable who was cast into "outer" or "utter" darkness for not having doubled his master's original investment, as the men with five and two talents each did.[20] In short, the introductory complication in the sonnet presents a speaker whose frame of mind is like one that Bunyan's pilgrim observes in the House of the Interpreter: this is a Man of Despair who thinks that his life's story is over and that it is too late for change. He hears "nothing but threatnings, dreadful threatnings, fearful threatnings of certain Judgement and firy Indignation" (*PP,* p. 35), until the voice of patience intervenes "to prevent / That murmur."

This way of thinking owes something to the sort of advice offered in the popular literature about cases of conscience. Henry Jessey's book of 1650, for instance, encourages readers "not [to] sit still, and doe nothing, to meet the Lord, but *Vp and be doing,*" according to the message of the parable: "Having received any Talent of light, or gift, wee must improve it." Such advice might seem to imply a theology of works-righteousness that would drive someone to protest against the unfairness of God's requiring "day-labor" when "light" has been denied.[21] Like the poet who wrote Sonnet 19, preachers sometimes anticipated the danger that such an inference might be drawn. In a Candlemas sermon on Matthew 5: 16, for instance, Donne assimilated the light which is to "shine before men" with the talents of the parable, and explained that light is a "treasure deposited" with the disciples who heard the Sermon on the Mount. The first disciples were "depositaries for us," and multiplying talents is, by implication, multiplying disciples through the ages. Donne even spells out the lesson that patience would deliver in Milton's sonnet: "Every good work hath faith for the roote; but every faith hath not good works for the fruit thereof." In fact, Donne thought it far more often necessary to ward off despair than to tame the presumptuous. Milton, if he regularly heard in the talents parable a burdensome threat, was just the sort of case of conscience that Donne liked to handle.[22]

That the burden is deeply connected with what was commonly termed the general calling becomes clearer as further biblical allusions are introduced into Milton's poem.[23] In line 8, the considerer labels the worries that he has been voicing "That murmur." The demonstrative pronoun serves to distance the thoughts that he has been expressing even before we reach the usual moment for the turn in line 9. The word "murmur" is still more revealing, because it was virtually a technical term in devotional literature for naming the complaints lodged by people with afflicted consciences. Here it suggests that the New Testament talent is the equivalent of the paradigmatic calling that the Israelites had received in the desert. In the tradition of the chosen people who resented their calling, murmured against God, and longed for the fleshpots in Egypt, the third figure in the parable assumes that the master is a mean taskmaster and buries his talent in hopes of not having to be bothered about it.

The speaker at the outset of the poem knows only too well that the parable of the talents, like the Israelite belief in election, was commonly interpreted as teaching a doctrine of social responsibility. The question that he is about to propose — "Doth God exact day-labour, light deny'd"? — is "fondly" or foolishly asked because, having adopted the view that the denial of light is a punishment, he can only hear an answer such as "Yes, of course God exacts day-labor: *Thou* wicked and slothful servant, thou knewest that I reap where I sowed not . . .?" (Matt. 25: 26). On the other hand, from the perspective of one who would call that worry a "murmur," the question may be considered foolish for quite a different reason: the God who "doth not need / Either man's work or his own gifts" is utterly different from the exacting taskmaster created in the imagination of the slothful (out of his memory of service in Egypt?); it is foolish to think that He would be so unjust as not to look into a person's heart to take a "true account."

At the start of Milton's sonnet, then, we are admitted to the mind of someone who has been wrestling with a fundamental problem that faced ordinary people in the 1640s and 1650s. The poet, like many writers of conversion narratives in these years, shows how one may get beyond an overwhelming and despairing sense that it is too late. He presents his individual experience in a manner that is at once shaped to fit and validated by a typical pattern which it serves to illustrate. This pattern derives from the tradition of religious psychology and of reading for "experimental" knowledge, which affords large scope to introspection. In "When I consider . . ." Milton accommodates to this tradition the sonnet form. He does it in a manner that calls into question some aspects of introspective reading and points up their dangers.

Hearing the Parable as a Threat

The lonely figure in Milton's sonnet who thinks at first that his loss of light is evidence of his having been cast into utter darkness was not alone. There were many like him. The tendency of Bible-readers to find in the parable a threat rather than a promise is well illustrated in the quotation from Donne at the beginning of Chapter Two. More explicitly, the personal narrative of a woman identified only as "M. K." illustrates the likelihood that readers in the 1650s would hear a threat. Her story appears in a collection of conversion narratives compiled within a few years of the time that Milton's sonnet seems to have been written. In the course of this autobiographical account, M. K. tells of having married a minister's son and of taking a house with him in Westminster, where they betrayed their religious upbringing, fell in with idle company, and spent almost all their means. Unlike her husband, M. K. resolved to repent. But when her husband refused to quit the company of a man who drank and practiced various vices, she decided to murder him. Having thus run away from her true "Captain," Christ, she nonetheless remembered God's favors on her behalf and seems not to have carried out the murder. But she was haunted thereafter by a particular text.

M. K. was obsessed, she says, with the idea that God was coming "to see what use *I had* made of the talent that he had given me." She feared that God would find that it had been "not only wrapt up in a napkin, but exceedingly abused." And from here M. K. goes on to describe in terms well known to readers of narratives like *Grace Abounding to the Chief of Sinners* what God would find in her heart: "a sinke of sinne, a Cage of uncleane Birds, a Den of Theeves, a place for Dragons." The result, she says, was that Satan then tempted her to believe that *"thou shalt never be called to an account for any thing,"* so that she should take her fill of sinning.[24] As we might expect from the fact that the story was included in the volume of which it is now a part, M. K. was at last assured of divine love. The story of M. K. shows that, for some readers at least, the urgency of the parable lay not so much in the possibility that the text could be made to turn up a safe way to salvation, but was more a function of the fact that the stakes were high and the parable warned against a sure path to hell.

The speaker in Milton's sonnet and M. K. — admittedly an odd couple — had something striking in common. They had found a scriptural "place" that seemed to resonate with their experience and to define their condition. Not only did they (at times at least) incline to think of the parable of the talents as their particular text, but they tended to see themselves as the third character, the one who was condemned. The reason that the parable of the talents was not consoling but proved useful as a deterrent against sinful behavior is well summed up by Jeremy Taylor when, in his treatment of cases of conscience, he speaks of the relevance of texts that contain both promises and threats: "a threatning in all laws," he explains, "is of more force and efficacy then a promise; and therefore when under a threatning more is requir'd, . . . because one thing is enough to destroy us, but one thing is not enough to preserve us."[25] This principle provides relevant background to the use that Milton makes of the parable in the sonnet. In the tradition of searching the Scriptures for a personally appropriate text, the speaker who "consider[s] how [his] light is spent" confesses his inclination to interpret his loss of light as the equivalent of the punishment (being cast into "utter darkness") meted out to the man who had hidden his talent. Like the author of *Grace Abounding* who was haunted by the passage about the belated Esau, he needs to learn that this text has not fixed his eternal place.

The case of the figure whom we encounter at the start of Milton's sonnet is presented then in typical terms, its language characteristic of the tradition and woven by the poet into a striking instance. The nature of the religious and interpretive problem is aptly summed up by Milton's Quaker friend, Isaac Pennington, in his response to the question, "How may a man make his calling and election sure?" and to a concern about "the Ground of Men's misunderstanding and wresting of Scriptures." Pennington compares anyone who "hugs and receives every [scripture text] that riseth in him" to people blindly seeking a mountain or hill as a "resting place" when they are in the dark. When God's Spirit comes and tries to disabuse them of their faulty interpretation, "they cannot hear" because they are already fixed in their thinking. The remedy that he prescribes is that "a man must watch and wait" and learn to "distinguish between the nature and voices of spirits in himself, that so he may know . . . when the Lord speaks, and also when the mysterious spirit of deceit strives to speak like the Lord."[26] The roots of the problem lie in the inference, drawn by those familiar with the doctrine of double predestination, that one's eternal destiny has been fixed ahead of time by God and that it may be discovered by assiduous searching of the Scriptures.

Calvin had warned against just this faulty inference, and in the biblical language that Milton would also rework in his sonnet. Calvin forbade seeking to pry into "the hidden secrets of the wisedome of God . . . to vnderstand what is determined . . . at the iudgement seate of God." One who does this is said thereby to damn himself: he "throweth himselfe headlong to be swallowed vp into the depth of the vnmeasurable deuouring pit: he wrappeth himself with innumerable snares and such as he cannot winde out of: then he ouerwhelmeth himselfe with the bottomlesse depth of blinde darknesse." Whereas the figure in the parable represents himself as a victim, Calvin, who assigns active doing to the one who pries into the mysteries of election and reprobation, makes it clear that faith requires that one "stand and waite."[27] Like the biblical parable itself, Milton's sonnet offers the reader an interpretive option, the implications of which are a matter of eternal life or death. If you can free yourself from an intense consciousness of the demands inherent in having "talents," there is space within which to risk a creative response to what has been given; whereas, if you choose to see yourself as a victim, and to assign responsibility for the injustice of your situation to a despot, you cannot move towards a comic ending. Living in a world where everything has been predetermined, there would be no possibility of receiving, or of responding decisively to, a free gift.

The drama in Milton's sonnet springs from the conflict between the speaker's fixation on the parable and the attempt by patience to anticipate and ward off (both available senses of "prevent") his assuming so deadly a "resting place":

> But patience to prevent
> That murmur, soon replies, God doth not need
>   Either man's work or his own gifts, who best
>   Bear his milde yoak, they serve him best, his State
> Is Kingly. Thousands at his bidding speed
>   And post o're Land and Ocean without rest. . . .

From the perspective of patience, the speaker's question about God's expectations of him is "fond" because its self-centered introspective premises, evident in the contorted syntax, the resentful past participles ("spent," "Lodg'd," "deny'd"), and heavy reliance on first-person pronouns in the octave, are wrong; even he knows that his "true account" lies in the future, and therefore he should see that the verses about "the terrible seasing of him that hid his talent" do not constitute his place. This does not mean that the poem flatly rejects "the point" of the parable. Rather it rejects a harmful way of reading the parable. One way that it does this is by hedging round the allusion with subtle reminders of the larger context in Matthew's gospel. The "light" that is "spent" in the opening line picks up the parable of the ten virgins (25: 1–13), and the "standing" in the final line makes an *inclusio*, indicating that attentive servants are not going to fall asleep. The reference to God as "Kingly" suggests the final judgment by the heavenly King (25:

31–46), who also oversees the work of traders "post[ing] o're Land and Ocean without rest" in conspicuous fulfillment of the injunction to "occupy till I come" (Luke 19: 13).

Readers have not failed to recognize that it falls to the voice of patience to take the pressure off the speaker who has heard dreadful threatening voices.[28] In fact, the general structure of the sonnet, with the complication giving way to another voice that offers a resolution, is typical enough of the form, as attested by the first sonnet of *Astrophil and Stella*. From Sidney, George Herbert borrowed a similar device in other sorts of lyrics, including the second "Jordan" poem and "The Collar." What is not widely agreed upon with respect to "When I consider . . ." is the tone of patience's speech and the precise nature of the resolution. The issue, aptly summed up in the *Variorum Commentary,* is whether the last three lines of the poem merely reinforce patience's counsel to submission, or whether they extend that message. The interpretive problem is the more acute for there being no quotation marks in the 1673 edition. It is possible, though not necessary, that the voice of patience speaks only until the full stop after "Kingly" and that the final sentence belongs to another voice, perhaps one more closely identified with the initial speaker, who by voicing the sentiments contained in the final lines attests to his liberation. In any event, it has proved difficult to discern the tone of the sestet. Is the effect of the intervention to silence the "domb . . . beast" in Milton and to root out his pride by insisting on submission to a powerful King who does not need this "abject" and "worth-lesse" servant, or is it to encourage the speaker to associate himself with a community of servants all of whom have a place in a larger divine scheme of things? While it may be that "Thousands at his bidding speed . . . ," it is not clear that the one to whom the final line is addressed will ever get a bidding. What may be said with a measure of confidence, however, is that "They also serve who only stand and waite," especially in view of its "also" and "only," is addressed precisely to one who, like the third figure in the parable, has been thinking of himself as having a relatively lesser place, or fewer opportunities than those ambassadors and soldiers and merchants who "post o're Land and Ocean without rest." In this sense, the resolution has been carefully tailored to the complication.[29]

The issue, then, is whether the resolution is a counsel of submission, inducing only resignation or whether, in the final lines, that counsel is extended into something further. Milton's handling in *De Doctrina Christiana* of the course through which saving faith passes suggests that we might look for separable stages in the sestet. He explains that a faith which entails only submission is insufficient. It must be complemented by assurance, which is a further degree of faith (*CPW*, VI, 502–5). This does not mean that the sestet, which quotes the voice of patience as it humbles the speaker with the chastening reminder that "God doth not need" his talents or good works, provides the requisite assurance. The voice of patience weaves a "text" of its own devising, a tissue of allusions,[30] including Matthew 11: 28–30, where Jesus says,

> Come unto me, all *ye* that labour and are heavy laden, and I will give you rest. Take my yoke upon you, and learn of me; for I am meek and lowly in heart; and ye shall find rest unto your souls. For my yoke *is* easy, and my burden light.

As Chapter One has illustrated, in the 1640s and 1650s, this was a favorite text for those who sought to reinterpret affliction as an educative blessing—both for divines who wished to console people with troubled consciences, and for ordinary people who were suffering through the monumental changes in politics and religion during the Interregnum. In addition to the example we have seen in Quarles's *Judgement and Mercie*, there are many more from spiritual autobiographies. If the voice of patience in Milton's poem does not offer full assurance but only invites an active waiting upon the Lord's bidding as the appropriate action to be taken in its absence, this is consistent with the standard observation of divines that a premature consolation only worsens the malady. It also allows scope for Milton's insistence in *De Doctrina Christiana* that each person take responsibility for achieving his own assurance.[31]

In Sonnet 19 Milton has imagined a movement towards a reassuring moment that still lies in the future. The poem takes seriously the most perplexing problem of introspective Bible-readers, the possibility that one's faith is merely temporary and would be "spent" before one had persevered to the end. But it does not solve or dissolve the problem. Instead it offers a way of living with it, knowing that assurance is but a reward that may or may not be given to the faithful, who in any event can rest assured that good works are not necessary for salvation.

> When I consider how my light is spent,
>   E're half my days, in this dark world and wide,
>   And that one Talent which is death to hide,
>   Lodg'd with me useless, though my Soul more bent
> To serve therewith my Maker, and present
>   My true account, least he returning chide,

> Doth God exact day-labour, light deny'd,
> I fondly ask; But patience to prevent
> That murmur, soon replies, God doth not need
> Either man's work or his own gifts, who best
> Bear his milde yoak, they serve him best, his State
> Is Kingly. Thousands at his bidding speed
> And post o're Land and Ocean without rest:
> They also serve who only stand and waite.

That final declarative pronouncement, "They also serve . . . ," suggests neither a grudging submission by a "domb . . . beast" whose master has no use for him (cf. *CPW,* I, 804–5), nor a triumphant proclamation by a writer who is certain that God will employ him as an instrument. The final line shows forth a Milton of negative capability whom we may, with the proper qualifications, identify once again with the speaker who began his consideration in line one. He is not yet certain of the future, but is poised at a moment in a dynamic process that he cannot hurry towards closure, even as he knows that he is responsible for the way in which it will develop.

Milton's sonnet does not validate the popular notion that a single biblical place may define one's eternal destiny. Nor does it conceive the nature of the problem so narrowly as to dismiss biblical categories as themselves the problem. By introducing a whole array of biblical language, the poet offers a model for those who have been steeped in the tradition of reading for experimental knowledge, showing how they may work creatively against its most damaging features. We have seen some of this, for instance, in the labeling of the "murmur." There is more of it when the considerer insists that his "bent" is for service, for this too distances him from the figure with whom he has been feeling an affinity. (In fact, this assertion implies that he is already among the converted.[32]) But the real turn comes not by way of substituting another, more consoling place. The fundamental change (conversion is after all literally a "turning") involves an invitation to learn how to read in a new way, one that does not fix meaning but allows for places to play off one another. When the voice of patience declares that "God doth not need / Either man's work or *his* own gifts" (italics added), it offers the considerer the possibility of delighting in an ambiguity, rather than being oppressed by his lack of evident productivity. The induced state of active waiting in the face of indeterminacy also introduces, like that final meditation in the volume by Quarles, a rather more searching test of faith.

Milton and the Tradition of the Auditing Sonnet

The ambiguity about the owner of the "gifts" that "God doth not need" constitutes what Stephen Booth has called, writing of one of Shakespeare's sonnets, "two paradoxically compatible alternatives." Booth's phrase is equally, and even more usefully, applicable to the two senses in which the considerer may be said to be foolish in the "fondly" asked question. The chiasmic relation between the beginning of the question ("Doth God . . .?") and the beginning of the answer that undermines its presupposition ("God doth . . .") calls attention to a close relation between these two points in the poem. These are the points where Milton, precisely as a writer of sonnets, enters most squarely into the tradition of sonnets descending from Sidney that Anne Ferry has studied in *The "Inward" Language*.[33]

Like many of Sidney's poems that involve the metaphors of examining account books and making an audit, Sonnet 19 posits a gap between an inward reality on which a "true account" might be based and an external representation in language. In Milton's poem this gap is a function of the initial speaker's reliance upon the language of a particular biblical text to interpret his situation. Like other accounting sonnets previously written by Sidney and Shakespeare, "When I consider . . ." proceeds in ways that call into question the applicability of accounting terms for getting at what is in the heart. The similarities between Milton's poem and earlier auditing sonnets have not been much studied, although some vague perception of them may help to explain why critics have sought to project the parable of the talents into Shakespeare's procreation sonnets. In any event, it is worthwhile to explore the ways in which Milton engaged and handled the conventions of the auditing motif when he brought the sonnet form together with the great biblical parable of auditing. We can begin at the point where we can see Milton himself first glimpsing the possibility of fusing the two models, in that letter of 1633 found in the Trinity Manuscript. There Milton confessed that he recognized "a certain belatedness" in himself and that he felt "bound though unask't, to give . . . an account . . . of [his] tardie moving."

Although the sonnet "How soon hath time . . ." is associated with the parable of the talents by virtue of Milton's including the poem in the letter of 1633, that early poem does not so obviously allude to the parable as Sonnet 19 does. It provides, however, an early instance of Milton's taking up the tradition of the auditing sonnet, and in just the manner that Shakespeare found so fascinating in Sidney, that is, using it to expose the gap between outward appearances, which show up in verse, and an "inward" condition that "doth much less appear":

> How soon hath time the suttle theef of youth,
>   Stoln on his wing my three and twentieth yeer!
>   My hasting dayes flie on with full career,
>   But my late spring no bud or blossom shew'th.
> Perhaps my semblance might deceive the truth,
>   That I to manhood am arriv'd so near,
>   And inward ripenes doth much less appear,
>   That som more timely-happy spirits indu'th.
> Yet be it less or more, or soon or slow,
>   It shall be still in strictest measure eev'n,
>   To that same lot, however mean or high,
> Toward which Time leads me, and the will of Heav'n;
>   All is, if I have grace to use it so,
>   As ever in my great task Masters eye.

If this sonnet is like previous sonnets in calling attention to a gap between inward and outward states, it is decidedly different from them in another respect. Both Sidney and Shakespeare wrote sonnets in which the speaker feels wrongly interpreted, even misunderstood, by his judges. In both instances the poets avoid, rather than rely on, the conventional sixteenth-century notion that "unseen and unuttered inward experience is nevertheless open and visible to God, and therefore ultimately knowable."[34] Milton's speaker is much more sanguine about the possibilities for self-knowledge. Although he laments the discrepancy between his "inward ripenes" and his lack of "bud or blossom," he reconciles himself to a Judge who will finally take a true account.

It may be that Milton's attempt to revivify the convention whereby inward experience was thought to be open to God's inspection, and thus potentially knowable, owes something to his bold revivifying of another feature of religious poetry from the 1590s, the substitution of God for the mistress. There is a sense in which Milton's religious sonnets took up the challenge posed anew by Herbert early in the seventeenth century, in the question to God, "Why are not sonnets made of thee?" Sonnet 7, coming after the Italian sonnets in the edition of 1645, conspicuously alters the object of the poet's service from the beautiful mistress to a God who compels his obedience.[35] Given the connotations of "task Master" that derive from the Book of Exodus, where the "taskmasters" impose "burdens" on the Israelites, it would seem logical that Milton would follow in the line of Sidney and Shakespeare, taking occasion to question, in a tone of bitterness and resentment, what Astrophil calls the "yoke of tyranny" imposed on the slave. This seems all the more likely, moreover, when we consider the possibility that the poem carries a buried allusion to the parable of the talents when the speaker acknowledges that he has "no bud or blossom" to show. For if he were in the frame of mind characteristic of the third figure in the parable, he could find a scriptural language for his poetic complaint in the terms used by the man who buried his talent: "Lord I knew thee that thou art an hard man, reaping where thou hast not sown, and gathering where thou hast not strawed." At this important point in the parable an agricultural metaphor temporarily displaces the dominant pattern of banking metaphors. In Sonnet 7 Milton works against this predictable course of action, however, when in the sestet he embeds the designation of God as "task Master" within a tone that otherwise suggests trusting submission. In this way the speaker swerves away from the premature application of the parable to his situation:

> Yet be it less or more, or soon or slow,
>   It shall be still in strictest measure eev'n,
>   To that same lot, however mean or high,
> Toward which Time leads me, and the will of Heav'n;
>   All is, if I have grace to use it so,
>   As ever in my great task Masters eye.

In the sestet Milton projects the image of a young man taking up his life's journey with none of the bitterness of the pilgrim whom Bunyan would launch on a progress. Far from desiring to be rid of his burden, this figure seeks to embrace it with equanimity. Yet by designating the object of his service a "task Master," Milton opens up a new possibility almost as soon as he has closed the issue which the octave introduced. The final three words of the poem serve to effect a second turn, one more reminiscent of the use of the couplet in the English tradition than of the sestet in the Italian. The designation "task Master," coming after the abstract language of lines 9–13, reintroduces into the poem a narrative element.

It is odd that Milton seems so casually to accept the image of a God who assigns particular tasks, perhaps ones such as the writing of a sonnet. This God would seem to be the opposite of the God of the later sonnet, who "doth not need / Either man's work or his own gifts." That God seems so remote that not only is the pressure to perform removed but the belief in the possibility of being accurately known, and therefore duly appreciated, is tested. Such testing is appropriate, I think, to the situation of the kind of person whose experience Sonnet 19, like the final Meditation in Quarles's *Judgement and Mercie,* explores. It may be contrasted with the sort of testing to which the more youthful figure of "How soon hath time . . ." is subjected by a "task Masters eye" that sees and judges everything. The maturity that the speaker of the earlier sonnet displays is that of recognizing his need, because he is immature, for an external guide, someone who will give him something manageable to do. But the maturity asked of the figure who is not provided with a definitive "place" and may never be required outwardly to perform is of a much higher order.

In any event, the maturity or immaturity of the speaker is decidedly at issue in both sonnets, as the temporal references ("my three and twentieth yeer," "E're half my days") in the second lines make clear. Both poems suggest that it is too soon for a final reckoning before God's throne. It is the earlier poem that makes, by way of biblical associations that it sets off in the final lines, claims for the speaker's prospects. The phrase "if I have grace to use it so," in a context where a gap between the speaker's outward stature and "inward ripeness" has been established, sets the poem in relation to a number of narratives about the early lives of biblical heroes: Isaac (Gen. 21: 8), Samson (Judg. 13: 24), Samuel (1 Sam. 2: 21), John the Baptist (Luke 1: 80), but above all Moses and Jesus. It was a convention of biblical narratives about the youth of heroes to mention both their physical growth and their favor with God, or "grace," as a prelude to recounting their mature exploits. Samuel "grew before the LORD" and "was in favour both with the LORD, and also with men" (1 Sam. 2: 20–26). Jesus in his childhood "grew, and waxed strong in spirit, filled with wisdom; and the grace of God was upon him" (Luke 2: 40). The evangelist subsequently adds, after narrating the unique episode in all the gospels that depicts Jesus in adolescence, that "Jesus increased in wisdom and stature, and in favour [*charis:* 'grace'] with God and man" (2: 52). By contrast, Moses was slow to reach maturity. The Greek word for "stature" (*helikia*) used by Luke is the same one that Josephus used when describing Moses's outward semblance: Moses's "growth in understanding was not in line with his growth in stature (*helikia*) but far outran the measure of his years."[36] Exodus (2: 11) connects Moses's maturing with his becoming attentive to his people's burdens. Conventional as the disclaimer of Milton's speaker may sound, then, the associations set off by the phrase "if I have grace to use it so" show then that he is actually making a large claim about his chosen status and his likely heroic future.

In Sonnet 7 Milton seems to have been challenging God, even courting the adversity that would test and prove him. In a passage that would contribute significantly to Milton's depiction of how paradise was to be regained, the Book of Proverbs (3: 11–12) advised a young man not to "despise . . . the chastening of the Lord," who "loveth [the one] he correcteth; even as a father the son *in whom* he delighteth." Moreover, calling God a "task Master" served to associate him with the torturers of His chosen people in Egypt, who forced the Hebrew slaves to make bricks without straw. Renaissance commentators on the passage from Exodus glossed "taskmasters" as *praefectos angarius,* the imposers of compulsory services, and called them *malefactores*. Cornelius à Lapide and others spoke of them in terms similar to those used by the third figure in the parable of the talents: they were "*exactores tributorum, non pecuniæ, sed laterum.*"[37] Behind this comment stood the old Greek proverb, which had been taken over into Latin, whereby "to make bricks" meant to waste one's labor. The Hebrews may have helped Pharaoh to build the pyramids, but the "task Master" God perhaps "doth not need . . . man's work." Beyond this, a God who allowed the Egyptians so sorely to try His chosen people could be identified with the One who struck a bargain with Satan to test Job; for in the commentaries the Books of Job and Exodus were sometimes closely associated. Attempting to date the incidents depicted in the Book of Job, the learned Hebraist John Lightfoot set out several reasons for thinking that Job's "great triall and affliction" took place during the very period of Israel's "bitter times of . . . misery" under the Egyptian taskmasters.[38]

If the speaker in Sonnet 7 could be confidently and in simply autobiographical ways identified with Milton himself, this might square with William Kerrigan's controversial thesis about Milton's later life, based partly on a reading of Sonnet 19: that Milton came to regard his blindness as a punishment administered in advance by God for his presumptuous transgression of the sacred in writing *Paradise Lost*.[39] But the Book of Job taught just the opposite lesson, that human misery though potentially educative is not necessarily a punishment. For his part, as Kerrigan recognizes, Milton had such a robust conscience and was so little likely to accuse himself of actual sins that it seems preferable to propose a less pretentious interpretation of the effects of the "task Master" image. This is best done by pointing out that the narrative which the final part of the poem begins to generate corresponds structurally to the archetypal conversion narrative that descends from Luther; that is, it envisages a period of afflication as a prelude to assurance. Even divines who were not enthusiastic puritans characteristically taught young persons to expect that such a structure would be operative in their lives. Lancelot Andrewes's lectures on the ten commandments, given in Cambridge in the 1630s, emphasized that obedience was at once an "honor" and a "burden" (he related the two words etymologically) and that a future minister needed to bear it. Eventually, he insisted, others would owe duties to "men of gifts," who therefore needed to be ready to have their "talents" and "gifts" used and "to make accompt," especially for *"the goods of the minde."*[40] Milton's sonnet, by suggesting that the speaker's youth was but a prelude to something that would be more decisive, already displayed the sort of ending that would become characteristic of his greatest poems: an ending that opens out to new possibilities.

One other feature of Milton's sonnet writing that is both continuous and discontinuous with the practice of Sidney and Shakespeare emerges when we consider his use of organic imagery. By contrast with Sonnet 7, in "When I consider . . . ," Milton refrained from using it, despite its presence in the biblical parable with which he was working. While there is no reason to think that Milton had Shakespeare's great "When I consider . . ." sonnet prominently in mind, his sonnet thus differs markedly from it. Milton would probably have known the poem as it was printed in 1640, where it constitutes the third part (after Sonnets 13 and 14) of a long poem under the heading *"Youthful glory."* That grouping brings Sonnet 15 into especially close contact with the theme of husbandry and the charge of unthriftiness.

> When I consider every thing that growes
> Holds in perfection but a little moment.
> That this huge stage presenteth nought but showes
> Whereon the Stars in secret influence comment.
> When I perceive that men as plants increase,
> Cheared and checkt even by the selfe-same skie:
> Vaunt in their youthfull sap, at height decrease,
> And were their brave state out of memory.
> Then the conceit of this inconstant stay,
> Sets you most rich in youth before my sight,
> Where wastfull time debateth with decay
> To change your day of youth to sullied night,

> And all in war with Time for love of you
> As he takes from you, I ingraft you new.[41]

One large difference between the two "When I consider . . ." sonnets lies in the status that they accord to human productions. Shakespeare's poem follows a whole series of sonnets in which the fair youth is enjoined to beget an heir, in order to pass on his beauty and insure his fame. Whereas the biblical parable explicitly distinguishes between talents and natural aptitude, these procreation sonnets conflate "Nature's bequest" to the youth with his own beautiful body, so that what he is expected to "use" is precisely his natural abilities. Milton's sonnet, by contrast, preserves a distinction between the "talent" and the speaker's "bent"; the advising voice insists that "God doth not need / Either man's work or his own gifts." The challenge in "They also serve who only stand and waite" is for the "I" to give up his longstanding belief in the importance of his own productions. In this respect Milton's poem has deeper thematic affinities with a poem like Herbert's sonnet "The Holdfast" ("I heard a friend expresse, / That all things were more ours by being his") than it does with Shakespeare's sonnets.[42] This is perhaps less surprising, however, when we consider that it employs the convention, which Milton does not use elsewhere except in "Lycidas," of a second voice intervening. This was a favorite device of Herbert that he borrowed from Sidney.

When we come to Shakespeare's Sonnet 15 after reading such procreation sonnets as 13 and 14, we find the poet himself taking up the obligation of preserving beauty and establishing lasting fame. While a preoccupation with the destructive effects of Time continues, and unites the poem with the ones that precede it, the concern with the social duties attendant upon exceptional natural gifts gives way at this point to a new concern: the poet's own quest for immortality by the exercise of his poetic power.

Milton's sonnet, by introducing the word "talent," engages the parable more deeply than other writings of the period and differently from the ways in which twentieth-century readers generally suppose. Framed in terms of a burden shared by everyone who accepted the twin task of searching the Scriptures and the conscience, the sonnet is not a merely personal meditation on a problem unique to an aspiring poet who, having gone blind, feared he would not be able to write his epic. If Milton thought it death to hide his poetic talent, this was not simply or even chiefly because not writing he would fail to gain that immortality which comes to those of consummate poetic achievement. Unlike Shakespeare's "When I consider . . ." sonnet, which culminates in a daring boast about the immortality of verse in the war against Time, Milton's poem suggests that the poet is struggling to make what is elsewhere designated "That last infirmity of Noble mind" a matter of indifference. Even as he exercises his poetic power to write the sonnet, Milton is still haunted, it seems, by the traditional way of interpreting the parable as an injunction to service that requires self-sacrifice. As he offers a model for dealing with the dreadful suspicion that it is too late, he accepts an intermediate position in a world of process. He is precariously, exhilaratingly, balanced between a deadening resignation to his cruel fate and a triumphant defiance of the ill effects which Time has wrought "E're half [his] days" have been lived out. For the Milton of "When I consider how my light is spent," the readiness would be all, but he does not quite have it — yet.

While both these great sonnets record an exemplary struggle, then, only Shakespeare's presents itself also as a monument to a victory already achieved. Milton, writing in a context where readers were inclined to look to what had already been written to find a "place" that defined their destiny in advance, made no boast comparable to Shakespeare's. For him, the truly exemplary person is not the one who achieves an assured position but rather one who refuses to impose a totalizing pattern. While Shakespeare's poem projects a future that will be in large part determined by the poet's accomplishment, Milton's invites patient waiting for a really decisive revelation that, in accord with his nearly ubiquitous emphasis on human freedom and responsibility, lies in a future yet to be determined.

5. Conferring Places with Mary, Seeking Closure with Manoa

> Ye shall lay vp these my words in your hearts, and in your soule. . . .
> And ye shall teach them your children, speaking of them, when thou sittest in thine house, and when thou walkest by the way, and when thou liest downe, and when thou risest vp.
> And thou shal write them vpon the posts of thine house, and vpon thy gates.
> That your dayes may be multiplied, and the daies of your children.
> —Deut. 11: 18–21; quoted from the title page of Eusebius Pagit's *Historie of the Bible* (1613 ed.)

In each of the poems that Milton published together in 1671, the narrative concludes with the return of the hero to his parental home. In *Paradise Regained*, having resisted Satan's temptations in the wilderness, the Son of God repairs to his "Mothers house" in "private" and "unobserv'd"; and "Angelic Quires" pronounce him ready now to "enter, and begin to save mankind." The situation in *Samson Agonistes* is just similar enough for differences to be striking. Having pulled down the Philistine temple, Samson is no longer an actor. His corpse is to be taken "Home to his Fathers house," where a monument will be erected, and the chorus declares "all passion spent." This contrast in the paired poems of 1671 may be seen to recapitulate the sort of struggle between two interpretive dispositions that the preceding chapter has shown to be operative in "When I consider how my light is spent." What the sonnet dramatizes in miniature is writ large in *Paradise Regained* and *Samson Agonistes*, where the figures of Mary and of Manoa serve to illustrate two opposing styles of interpretive practice: on the one hand a disposition to wait patiently, entertaining in memory a range of places that play freely and suggestively "without rest," and on the other an urge to invoke a definitive paradigm that serves to close one's case. A theoretical basis for this contrast is enunciated in passages in *De Doctrina Christiana* where Milton makes explicit some foundational assumptions of his own interpretive practice. It will be the work of the present chapter briefly to isolate these key interpretive principles and then more elaborately to work out the contrast of interpretive styles that is set in motion in the companion poems of 1671. In Chapter Six I will attempt to explore other, related features of these poems that are suggestive of Milton's mature practice as an interpreter, in particular his handling of the temptation of learning in *Paradise Regained* and his allusions to later biblical literature in *Samson Agonistes*. My assumption, in both chapters, is that the poems need to be considered together in order to carry out the sort of "conference of places" that served as Milton's principal interpretive method in composing them.

Before attending to *De Doctrina*, it is worth adverting to a significant difference between seventeenth-century interpreters and the characters shown in Milton's biblical poems to be performing interpretive tasks. The basis of this difference has been identified by Hugh MacCallum, who has demonstrated how in *Samson Agonistes* Milton represented "the religious culture of the age of Samson." In that period the few sacred texts that had thus far been written were "locked up in the ark of the covenant." Thus it is unsurprising, although important, that Milton's Samson "never refers to Scripture as a written document." What makes MacCallum's observation especially valuable is that he has foregrounded what readers of the Bible in the seventeenth century and of Milton's poetry in the twentieth often fail to reflect upon: that the "history" encoded in narrative had to be "made into literature."[1] In *Samson Agonistes* and *Paradise Regained* Milton prodded readers to reflect upon the process by which the canonical Scriptures had been produced. This he did by setting in motion contests of interpretation in which an urge for closure is pitted against a disciplined, responsible patience that delights in continuing interpretive activity.

Disciplining Interpretation

If we reflect on the fact that Protestantism made absolutely central the idea that Scriptures were necessary and sufficient for salvation, a significant contradiction emerges: it is striking that none of the characters in Milton's biblical poems had access to the full range of places that were available to belated Protestants through which they were able to search to make their callings and election sure. Certainly, none was able to apply the "analogy of faith," the ultimate interpretive principle by means of which difficult or obscure passages were to be clarified. These facts did not create trouble for

Milton, however, once he had come to identify the Word of God as something beyond the words in which the Scriptures were written. In fact, his imagination was emboldened by the fact that no biblical figure, or biblical writer, could have had complete knowledge of "the uniform tenor of Scripture" or the "internal consistency of the whole scripture." These are the phrases by which Sumner and Carey respectively have rendered Milton's own account, in *De Doctrina Christiana,* of the circular process by which an authoritative interpretive community first points out which writings constitute sacred Scripture and then the individual reader confirms the authority of the church and of the books themselves: ". . . *postea vero ecclesiæ ipsisque codicibus eorumque singulis partibus propter auctoritatem totius scripturæ secum collatæ*" (*Works,* XVI, 278–79). Both Sumner's translation of *totius scripturae secum collatæ,* "the uniform tenor of Scripture," and Carey's, the "internal consistency of the whole scripture" (*CPW,* VI, 590) cover over something that, in the divorce tracts and especially in *Areopagitica,* Milton had insisted upon as of primary importance in interpretation: the process of gathering or collating. By the time he wrote the three biblical poems published after the Restoration Milton was able to enlist to advantage what had become, in the 1640s, a cardinal rule of his interpretive procedures: that one ought not presume to know in advance, merely on the basis of custom and traditional interpretation, "the uniform tenor of Scripture."

In *De Doctrina Christiana,* the most conspicuous effect of Milton's refusal to enlist the analogy of faith to prop up currently accepted *doxa* is his rejection of the doctrine of the Trinity. One might have supposed that his thoroughgoing attention to biblical places—more than eight thousand are said to be quoted in the treatise (*CPW,* VI, 106–7)—would have yielded new and clearer insights into what the New Testament means when it calls Jesus the "Son of God." Yet in the long and idiosyncratic fifth chapter of Book I, Milton proves curiously reticent about this subject. He vigorously insists that the Father alone qualifies as the supreme and self-existent God of which Scripture speaks, and he goes on explicitly to rule out the traditional category of the "trinity" as a means of explaining the paradox whereby Jesus is sometimes said in Scripture also to be God. Without reviewing here the whole argument, which has given rise to considerable controversy,[2] two things should be noted for present purposes: first, that in *Paradise Regained* Milton calls attention, especially through the indecisive probing assigned to Satan, to the fact that the designation "Son of God" is highly ambiguous and "bears no single sence" (IV, 517); second, that the principles by which Milton felt obliged to reproduce the ambiguities of New Testament language about "the Son" are explicitly articulated in the theological treatise. Claiming conventionally enough that in every point of necessary doctrine "the scriptures are both in themselves and through God's illumination absolutely clear" (VI, 578), Milton also insists that great caution is necessary lest readers import metaphysical categories foreign to the assumptions of the biblical writers. "We should be afraid," he cautions in the chapter on the Incarnation (I, xiv) "to pry into things further than we are meant" (421). Elsewhere, in the chapter on the Son (I, v), he insists that it "is never permissible for us to say of Christ what scripture does not say" (248). Similarly, in the chapter on the Holy Spirit (I, vi), he explicitly acknowledges two cardinal interpretive principles:

> Let us assume that, appropriately enough, when God wants us to understand and thus believe in a particular doctrine as a primary point of faith, he teaches it to us not obscurely or confusedly, but simply and clearly, in plain words. Let us also take it for granted that, in religion, we should beware above all of exposing ourselves to the charge which Christ brought against the Samaritans in John iv. 22: *you worship something you do not know*. (287–88)

In short, Milton came to construe the Protestant insistence on *scriptura sola* not only as a means for jettisoning "mere human traditions" but as a negative hermeneutical criterion forbidding readers to force openings by "pry[ing] . . . further than we are meant." It was therefore imperative for him also to develop positive criteria for ascertaining what "God wants us to understand and thus believe . . . as a primary point of faith." For the principal index to how Scripture reveals this he looked to the practice of those biblical authors who were reinterpreting the work of earlier writers.

Milton recognized that the art of comparing biblical places had already been practiced by the later and more learned biblical writers, whose writings constituted interpretations of the Scriptures as they knew them, even before the Hebrew Bible had been transformed into the Christian Old Testament.[3] This was an art of reading before it was an art of writing, and *Paradise Regained* ascribes its practice not only to its hero, who had left behind no writings himself, but also to the hero's mother, from whom apparently he had learned to read. Before exploring some resemblances between Milton's portraits of Jesus and of Mary, it is worth noting that the poems of 1671 also posit certain resemblances between Jesus and Samson and between the heroes of both poems and the sort of Bible-readers whose experiences have been considered in Chapter One. The first book of *Para-*

dise Regained, in particular, presupposes familiarity with the introspective practices that were endorsed by experimentalist divines. At the outset Jesus has heard God's voice directly. It has informed him that he is God's "son" and that God is "well pleased" with him. This pronouncement, which may be said to constitute Jesus' "calling," creates an internal disequilibrium and provokes introspective "Meditations." It does not awaken in him memories of his sins nor does it set him on a quest for assurance. It does make him sharply aware of a discrepancy:

> O what a multitude of thoughts at once
> Awakn'd in me swarm, while I consider
> What from within I feel my self, and hear
> What from without comes often to my ears,
> Ill sorting with my present state compar'd.   (I, 196–200)

In *Samson Agonistes,* the psychological setting for the hero's opening soliloquy bears a striking similarity to Jesus' meditation upon entering the desert. For his part, Samson also hears reminders of his calling, which (according to Judges) was mediated by an angel to his mother and thence to him. It sorts ill with *his* "present state," because he thinks that he has fallen out of his calling and has abrogated his predestined role:

> restless thoughts, that like a deadly swarm
> Of Hornets arm'd, no sooner found alone,
> But rush upon me thronging, and present
> Times past, what once I was, and what am now.
> O wherefore was my birth from Heaven foretold
> Twice by an Angel . . . ?
> . . . .
> Why was my breeding order'd and prescrib'd
> As of a person separate to God,
> Design'd for great exploits; if I must dye
> Betray'd, Captiv'd, and both my Eyes put out,
> Made of my Enemies the scorn and gaze . . . ?   (19–24, 30–34)

Moreover, Samson's great lapse has become for him the occasion for an intense awareness that the story of his failure is being spread abroad. "[T]ell me Friends," he says when the chorus comes on, "Am I not sung and proverbd for a Fool / In every street . . . ?" (202–4). His awareness that his story is redounding to his humiliation confirms Samson's surmise that he has sinned irrevocably, and like the figure at the start of "When I consider . . ." he interprets his experience of darkness as a punishment.

In *Paradise Regained* the Son's experience differs from Samson's and differs decisively from the paradigmatic case of Luther and from many experiences reported in seventeenth-century conversion narratives. Introspection does not torture or imprison him. Jesus' "holy Meditations" are an occasion for remembering and reinterpreting his previous life, especially what he had learned from his mother. They are not themselves the locus of temptation, for Jesus' calling does not necessitate or entail a conversion. His temptations are *foris, non intus:* they come from an external tempter.[4] They are not represented as the sort of auto-suggested texts that had, for instance, plagued the writer of *Grace Abounding*, and which Bunyan retrospectively ascribed to the work of Satan. Instead of depicting a consciousness in which rival texts seem to present themselves, Milton allocates the work of suggestion to Satan, who turns out to be unable to make plausible applications of the texts that he quotes. Nor does the Son of God deny his own responsibility for interpreting texts and retreat into anything like a "disclaiming locution." Rather he draws on his learning to bring forward texts that he deems apt, thus countering every proposed short-cut to achieving his goal. In this respect Milton's hero provides a critique of many popular religious practices of the day, and the critique comes precisely from a religious conviction about the necessity of learning in the quest to regain paradise. From this perspective those who, like Bunyan, report having had difficulty in distinguishing the source of the scriptural texts that race round in their consciousness display a degree of ignorance and incompetence with which Milton had little patience. In *Paradise Regained* the hero has been well taught by his mother when and how to deal with scriptural texts, and in the wilderness Jesus puts into practice lessons that he first learned from Mary. If he receives "Light from above" and needs "no other doctrine," it is because he has assimilated the Hebrew Scriptures and reads them according to canons of interpretation that are not divinely infused but learned in accord with the idea, as Richard Baxter framed it for seventeenth-century readers, that "*Education* is God's ordinary way for the conveyence of his grace."[5]

A Portrait of the Hero's Mother in *Paradise Regained*

Milton's inclusion of an admiring portrait of Mary is surprising in that it had been one of the most dramatic successes of the Reformers that they managed, within the ninety years or so between Luther's first protests and

Milton's birth, nearly to eradicate the cult of the Virgin from mainstream Protestantism. For this reason the longstanding neglect of Mary in writing about Milton's poetry is explainable: it is in keeping with the persistent polemic against vestiges of popery that runs through Protestant literature of the sixteenth and seventeenth centuries. Moreover, it befits the fact that in his theological writings there is no indication that Milton took an interest in Mary in her own right. In seventeenth-century England, although the Magnificat remained in the Prayer Book, aversion to "unwritten traditions" had taken sufficient hold for many non-biblical features of Christian piety to have been largely jettisoned. In the case of Marian devotion in particular, the "Ave Maria" was suppressed as a prayer, and the apocryphal legends met with derisive scorn. Aversion to popular superstition issued into vociferous objection when it came to the doctrines of Mary's immaculate conception and bodily assumption. And while the biblically warranted doctrine of the virgin birth remained undisturbed, stories about the Virgin's apparitions and miracles met with downright hostility. Milton, for his part, never deigned to write about superstitious abuses of the Marian variety.[6]

Although the New Testament has little to say about Mary, and much of what it says seems demeaning, Milton bestowed upon Mary, without obvious biblical precedent, a significant role in a poem about the temptations of Jesus.[7] In light of Protestant antipathy to Mariolatry, we might predict that he would more likely have made Mary a different sort of "second Eve," a woman who tempts her son, for instance, to rest content with the comforts of domestic life, as in the companion poem both Dalila and Manoa invite the hero to retire from a public role in the service of God to enjoy private pleasures. The gospels provide ample warrant for supposing that Jesus had to resist such temptations: "The foxes have holes," says Jesus to a would-be follower, "and the birds of the air *have* nests; but the Son of man hath not where to lay *his* head" (Matt. 8: 20). Similarly, in the striking passage that lies behind Christian's departure from his family at the start of *The Pilgrim's Progress,* Jesus declares that he is "come to set a man at variance against his father, and the daughter against her mother. . . . He that loveth father or mother more than me," he concludes, "is not worthy of me" (Matt. 10: 35, 37). All this is in keeping with the synoptic picture of Mary and the brothers of Jesus as outsiders during the course of his public life. In Milton's poem, however, despite the emphasis on the single hero relying upon God alone, there is no rejection of family, nor any of the apparent coldness to his mother that several gospel passages depict in Jesus.

In fact, Milton risked importing some anachronistic assumptions when he came to depict Mary as a reader and interpreter. In biblical times women were frequently excluded from literate activity, and it was not until the late medieval and Renaissance periods that painters of the Virgin typically furnished her with a book. Some artists, perhaps inspired by Josephus's account of the obligation of Jewish parents to instruct their children in the Law, suggested that Mary had read to her son, or even that it was she who taught him to read. There were, however, Christians who considered heretical the idea that Mary or Joseph taught the boy anything, and in many other paintings the child is depicted turning the leaves of a book or pointing to letters on a page, possibly in the act of instructing his parents.[8]

It is in paintings of the Annunciation that Mary's reading took on a specifically religious coloring. From the late middle ages the Annunciation was almost always represented somewhere on the altarpiece in Western churches, no matter what the principal subject of the composition was. Whereas in Byzantine paintings of the scene Mary was typically engaged in manual tasks when the angel Gabriel appeared, in the West she was regularly shown with a book open beside her, and sometimes with other books in a niche beside or behind her. According to some Church Fathers, she had been studying the Book of Isaiah and had just come to the place where it was predicted that a virgin would conceive when, behold! the prophecy began to come true.[9]

In seventeenth-century England mothers reading to their children was an everyday occurrence, even in the homes of many working people. The popular handbook, *A Godly Form of Hovseholde Gouernment,* prescribed that parents read to their children from the Scriptures daily and teach them how to interpret them. Preachers commonly cited as a text to recommend the practice a verse from the Second Letter to Timothy (3: 15), where the recipients of the epistle are urged to stand fast in the knowledge of the Scriptures which they have had since childhood.[10] Oliver Heywood (c. 1629–1702) tells of his mother's taking her Bible round with her and spending the day reading and praying, and of her having seen not only to his education but to that of many poor children, for whom she promoted a knowledge of the Scriptures. When Heywood went up to Cambridge he sent his mother notes from sermons he heard there for her to meditate on: "it was her constant course in the night when she lay waking to roll them in her mind, and rivet them there." There is considerable evidence that in sixteenth- and seventeenth-century England many women learned to "think biblically" and, if they wrote, to write in a style that "modulates . . . between Biblical quotations or references and their own words." Anna Maria à Schurman developed an explicit argument that women do not need a "speciall Calling" to participate in a life of studies. She insisted that a woman who shows an aptitude for study needs "spare houres . . . from the Exercises of Piety and houshold Affairs."[11]

In *Paradise Regained* Jesus is made gratefully to recall his mother's timely teaching. In his "deep thoughts" (I, 190), he re-creates imaginatively what she had taught him about his origins. His memory dwells not on the information about the identity of his true Father, which he could never forget, but on his mother's attempt to help him interpret the implications of his divine paternity:

> high are thy thoughts
> O Son, but nourish them and let them soar
> To what highth sacred vertue and true worth
> Can raise them, though above example high;
> By matchless Deeds express thy matchless Sire.
> For know, thou art no Son of mortal man,
> Though men esteem thee low of Parentage,
> Thy Father is the Eternal King, who rules
> All Heaven and Earth, Angels and Sons of men,
> A messenger from God fore-told thy birth
> Conceiv'd in me a Virgin, he fore-told
> Thou shouldst be great and sit on *David*'s Throne,
> And of thy Kingdom there should be no end. (I, 229–41)

Although it might be thought that remembering all this would be quite enough to sustain him through the temptations, the Son does not break off his reminiscence of his mother's words here. He goes on, recalling the details surrounding his birth and earliest days, thus drawing strength from a deep identification with a human forebear who had herself known the loneliness of being divinely favored. Within the dramatic context of the poem, the hero's remembering these details in this way suggests that the strength he derives from his mother's words comes from his ability now, in his adulthood, to appreciate her experience, including the artful manner in which she had reviewed and supplemented at just the right time a story she had evidently told him previously and in part:

> At thy Nativity a glorious Quire
> Of Angels in the fields of *Bethlehem* sung

> To Shepherds watching at their folds by night,
> And told them the Messiah now was born,
> Where they might see him, and to thee they came;
> Directed to the Manger where thou lais't,
> For in the Inn was left no better room:
> A Star, not seen before in Heaven appearing
> Guided the Wise Men thither from the East,
> To honour thee with Incense, Myrrh, and Gold,
> By whose bright course led on they found the place,
> Affirming it thy Star new grav'n in Heaven,
> By which they knew thee King of *Israel* born.
> Just *Simeon* and Prophetic *Anna*, warn'd
> By Vision, found thee in the Temple, and spake
> Before the Altar and the vested Priest,
> Like things of thee to all that present stood.   (I, 242–58)

From one point of view the use of the definite article here in the phrases "the Manger" and "the Wise Men" suggests that the narrator (as he reports Mary's speech) is simply reminding seventeenth-century readers of details that they already know. If we consider, however, that the poet is representing the thirty-year-old Jesus remembering an incident from his adolescence, then the implication is that these definite articles mark old information, that is, when Mary told him who his "matchless Sire" actually was, he had already heard from her other details about the circumstances surrounding his infancy. It was only when he was old enough to probe the religious implications of the story that Mary revealed to him further information, including both the Virgin-birth and the predictions of his messiahship that sent him back to "revolv[e] . . . / The Law and Prophets," where he discerned (being now sufficiently mature) that his "way must lie / Through many a hard assay even to the death, / E're [he] the promis'd Kingdom can attain" (I, 259–65). In light of the lesson that the attainment of the Kingdom lies on the other side of death, he should be able to recognize that all of Satan's offers, which will be for kingdoms he may rule in this life, are out of sorts with the teaching of God's Word. This lesson the Son of God associates pre-eminently with his mother's teaching. Elsewhere in the poem we see her similarly reflecting that her "favour'd lot" is likewise "to Afflictions high" (II, 91–92). By thus according the hero's mother a timely and enduring role in her son's combat, Milton shows what it might mean in biblical terms to call her the "mother" of the Savior. As his poem unfolds we can infer that it was she who initiated Jesus into the process by which paradise is to be regained, insofar as this entails an interpretive quest to find one's place in, and in relation to, the saving Word of the Scriptures.

Eschewing both the riches and the potential crudities of medieval symbolism (whereby Mary was sometimes represented as the new ark containing the Word or as a tabernacle for the eucharistic Presence),[12] Milton suggested that the process by which paradise is regained was proleptically operative in the experience of Mary, herself a great repository of the biblical Word even before she conceived her son and long before the New Testament scriptures were written down. In other words, Milton inferred a good deal from reading the opening chapters of Luke's gospel, which, instead of giving the story of the virginal conception and birth from Joseph's point of view (as Matthew did), emphasized Mary's response to an extraordinary invitation. Mary was "troubled," Luke says, at the angel's greeting, "and cast in her mind what manner of salutation this should be" (1: 29). This response seems a natural prelude to her acceptance of the role of "handmaid of the Lord" when she declares, "be it unto me according to thy word" (1: 38). Mary is the common thread that runs through the whole collection of stories that Luke told in the first two chapters. While unsentimental biblical scholars in our day have been eager to deny Mary any role in the formation of the gospel tradition, thoughtful readers of the gospel have often supposed that the evangelist was referring especially to her when he announced that he had consulted "eyewitnesses, and ministers of the word" who knew the story "from the beginning" (1: 2).[13] It was in virtue of the Magnificat that in early modern England Mary was said to have been a prophet, that is, both a composer and, in accordance with the then current sense of "prophesying," an expounder of the Scriptures.[14] In a list of ancient women "Eminent for Poetry" compiled by Edward Phillips, Mary is called "the most Divine and Seraphic of all Poets," even "though her Heavenly Muse hath produc't but one single Hymn." *Paradise Regained* shows that Phillips's uncle and teacher likewise thought of Mary primarily in her creative capacity, as a singer in the line of Hannah and Deborah and Miriam, rather than as an uncomprehending obstacle to her son's mission. For Milton, Mary was a kind of interpreter and relater of the best and sagest things. More than any other writer of his era, he explored the implications of the ascription of the Magnificat to her and of Luke's hint that he had depended on Mary for his infancy narratives. This he did by comparing and relating a number of gathered of biblical places.[15]

Mary and Authentic Tradition

Besides being a figure around whom debates about proper womanly conduct were sometimes conducted, in early modern England Mary was also important in the context of debates about "tradition." Already in the sixteenth century learned Protestants recognized that the Scriptures had a prehistory in oral storytelling. Since this might seem to give some point to the Catholics' attempt to ascribe authority to Tradition, they had worked out ways of explaining how authentic tradition worked. John Boys acknowledged that both sides agreed "that *Traditions are doctrines deliuered from hand to hand, either by word of mouth, or by writing, beside the Canonicall Scriptures.*" The problem, according to Boys, is that papists "teach, *that beside the word written, there be certaine traditions vnwritten, which must be beleeued as necessarie to saluation.*" Commenting on Matthew's narrative about the temptations in the wilderness, Boys cites the advocacy of the "worship" of saints as precisely such an instance. The papists were to be answered as Jesus answered Satan, with "*worship the Lord thy God, . . . him only shalt thou serue.*"[16]

The two differing views on the status of unwritten traditions were presented in a similar way by Perkins, in a systematic account of the differences between the "Reformed and Romish" religions. The difference between, say, a legend about Mary's birth to Joachim and Anna and the traditions about Jesus' birth in the stable is that the latter came to be written down by the "sacred penmen," just as Moses eventually recorded things that God had revealed long before to Adam and to the Patriarchs. To rule out the accretions of unwarranted post-biblical traditions, Perkins cited a host of texts to support the contention that the Scriptures are utterly sufficient. He began with the *locus classicus,* Deut. 4.2, "*Thou shalt not adde to the words that I commaund thee, nor take any thing there-from.*" He concluded by dismissing the objection that disagreements about interpretation make appeals to Scripture indecisive. Here he set down the guidelines within which Protestant writers characteristically worked. Difficult matters are clarified, he explained, by means of "the analogie of faith, which is the summe of religion gathered out of the clearest places of Scripture," and by making "conference of place with place."[17]

Often this method was recommended also to preachers and their auditors, and the activity was explicitly connected with the multiplying of "talents." Commenting on the readings for the Second Sunday after Epiphany (which included the account of Mary's behavior at the wedding feast at Cana), Boys observed that the conference of places was to be used by the modern prophet, that is, by one who "vnder the Gospell . . . interprets the Prophets." After asserting the necessity of proceeding in accord with "faiths analogie," Boys urged that the interpreter "exercise his talent with faith and diligence, to the best edification of Gods people" and that none "suffer his talents to rust" by lack of activity. He went on to confer places himself, adducing "the text . . . in the second of Luke, *that Mary kept all those sayings and pondered them in her heart*" to explain how it was that she had sufficient faith to ask her son for a miracle: she had had the good sense "safely to lay . . . vp" her son's own sayings "as in a treasure house," so that at the opportune moment they would be "readie for . . . vse." John Preston also expressly connected the place about "laying up" one's treasure with Matthew's parable. He urged that "the time of youth, the time of education, is the seede-time of our life after," whereas maturity is "the time of making sure his Election, a time of *growing in grace and knowledge,* and of *growing rich in good workes.* He whose eyes *God* opens to see this time, he makes vse of it, he layes out those talents he hath." Milton, in the introduction to the *De Doctrina,* described a process that moved from a collation of the pertinent passages, to the storing up of a "treasure [*thesaurum*] which would be a provision for my future life."[18] He operated in a similar way in composing his brief epic.

The high estimate which, according to his nephew, Milton had for *Paradise Regained* was likely a function of the painstaking way in which he had gathered, compared, and synthesized diverse biblical passages to make a coherent narrative. As its origin in the Latin *conferre* indicates, "conference of place with place" involved a series of interpretive activities. These are suggested in the range of meaning given for the word in the *OED:* the "action of bringing [various texts, *locos*] together" into a "collection," making a "comparison" of them, with a view to their then "supplying" for future uses. All this was the prelude to finding an essentially biblical narrative about "deeds, / Above Heroic, though in secret done, / And unrecorded left through many an Age" (I, 15–16). The story was "Worthy t' have not remain'd so long unsung" (I, 17) because, without crediting unwritten traditions, a more comprehensive version than any of the evangelists told could be pieced together on the basis of "conference of place with place." In this respect, the poem adds nothing non-biblical to the object of Christian faith; and the interpretive work that stands behind it is of a piece with that which went into compiling a systematic Christian doctrine on the basis of the Bible alone. It is as a gatherer of places and as the mother of an interpretive quest, the process of "conferring place with place," that Mary figures most importantly in the poem.

Milton's Portrait of Mary as a Bearer of the Word

In *Paradise Regained*, while respecting Mary's characteristically maternal role and suggesting psychological and spiritual ways in which she had nourished her son, Milton depicted Mary as a model for all disciples, male and female. He saw in her a "minister of the Word," inferring, naturally enough in view of what Luke had said about his sources, that she was the primary source for the biblical stories about the savior's infancy. From the Son's first interior monologue in the poem, we learn that his mother had brought forth the Word *to* her child as well as *in* him.

In Book I, after Jesus has received what Milton's contemporaries thought of as his calling, he retreats into the desert, and he proceeds to "cast in his mind," we might say, "what manner of" saying had been pronounced at his baptism. He is doing what his mother had done when she received her calling from the angel Gabriel; as noted above, he brings to mind that his mother had told him the story of his divine conception when she recognized that his noble aspirations required to be "nourish[ed]" and also to be properly challenged (I, 227 ff.). Then, in relation to the Father's sudden declaration of his favor, the Son reviews the rest of what his mother had taught him after the incident in which she and Joseph found him teaching in the Temple. In this way, as Milton gives us access to Jesus' memory of his mother's actual words, he shows that Mary has woven together various details that came down to him and his readers piecemeal, from Matthew and Luke.[19] In the belated experience of Bible-readers these materials have been "scatter[ed] . . . like pearle heer and there" in the various gospels, according to the principle whereby the evangelists, like their Lord who did not give "continu'd discourses," sowed "the heavnly grain of his doctrin" the better to "require . . . a skilfull and laborious gatherer; who must compare the words he finds" (*CPW*, II, 338). Milton followed this process through various New Testament books in order to reconstruct the integrated account which Mary had once provided to her son. Mary had been a bearer of the Word, mediating to her son matter that required of him more than ordinary faith in his mother's reliability as a witness. This information proved timely for his mission long before the penmen wrote it down for aftertimes, not least because it required of him a growth in faith.

Beyond this, Milton suggests that Mary had first taught Jesus the work of conferring place with place. The information that she supplied him sent him back to the sacred scroll with new interpretive perspectives and new questions:

> This having heard, strait I again revolv'd
> The Law and Prophets, searching what was writ
> Concerning the Messiah, to our Scribes
> Known partly, and soon found of whom they spake
> I am; this chiefly, that my way must lie
> Through many a hard assay even to the death,
> E're I the promis'd Kingdom can attain,
> Or work Redemption for mankind, whose sins
> Full weight must be transferr'd upon my head. (I, 259–67)

In this way Jesus puts together the "texts" that his mother had given him orally with the ones "Concerning the Messiah" that he found when he "revolv'd / The Law and Prophets, searching what was writ." This work of conferring places then continues through the course of the temptations, and it is to be performed by the reader, just as it was performed by Mary, by Jesus, and by Milton.

Milton's inference that Mary was not only the source of the details about Jesus' infancy that the evangelists only wrote down but that she also taught her son to confer places rests upon his own conference of place with place. When, for instance, Luke tells of the angel's announcement that Mary would conceive virginally, he shows her responding with a disposition simultaneously to search for its meaning and to accept it as a mysterious expression of God's will. Moreover, he extends his treatment of Mary into subsequent narratives to record other similar responses to events in her son's life. He tells of her reaction to the choir of angels and the visit by the shepherds: "Mary kept all these things, and pondered *them* in her heart" (2: 19). Again, after remarking on her puzzlement when she and Joseph listened to the twelve-year-old in the temple going about his Father's business, Luke says that "his mother kept all these sayings in her heart" (2: 51). Taken together the two statements mean that Mary remembered both events ("these things") and speech ("these sayings"), and the context suggests that, because she did not understand everything that was going on, more than mere retention is meant. Just what Mary did "in her heart" is not immediately clear from Luke's word *symballousa* (2.19), rendered *conferens* in the Vulgate and "pondered" in the English versions. It is not surprising that some commentators, having compared places, associated her activity with that of the Bereans of Acts 17: 11, who "received the word with all readiness, and searched the Scriptures daily."[20] What needs to be emphasized, however, is that in seventeenth-century English, especially in religious usage, the "heart" was not contrasted with the head. The heart was often said to be the locus of one's most private and imitate thoughts. The opening collect of the Communion Service is richly illustrative:

> ALMIGHTY God, unto whom all hearts be open, all desires known, and from whom no secrets are hid: Cleanse the thoughts of our hearts by the inspiration of thy Holy Spirit, that we may perfectly love thee. . . .[21]

Also pertinent to understanding the dynamics of the process that Mary taught Jesus is the quotation from Deuteronomy that appears as an epigraph for this chapter. The passage appeared on the title page of a *Historie of the Bible* (1602) written by Eusebius Pagit out of twenty-six years' experience of talking daily with his children and servants about their understanding of the Scriptures: "lay vp these my words in your hearts . . . teach them [to] your children . . . write them vpon the posts of thine house . . . That your dayes may be multiplied. . . ."[22]

The ambiguity of Luke's word *symballousa* seems to have suggested to Milton a series of roles for Mary. Literally, *sym* "with" and *ballein* "throw" (the root of our English word *symbol*), suggest a particularly active and creative role. The word hints that she "combined" what she saw and heard and remembered in her heart into the coherent collection of narratives that Luke later recorded.[23] Still, it is also possible that *symballousa* carries a less literal sense and one that implies less mastery and control on the part of Mary. In Hellenistic literature, the word typically "refer[s] to an interpretation of dark or difficult matters, the right meaning of which is often ascertained only by means of divine help."[24] A more relevant context for understanding Milton's usage seems to be the Authorized Version.[25] Besides Luke 2: 19, the word *ponder* appears only in the Book of Proverbs. The five instances there suggest that the experience of Solomon stands in the background of Satan's scorning of sexual temptation in *Paradise Regained* (II, 172 ff.) and of his proposing the temptation of learning (IV, 195 ff.). Early in Proverbs, the writer recommends the activity of pondering (4: 26) as a means of avoiding sexual temptation (5: 6 and 5: 21). Later, he speaks of it as a particularly divine activity: the Lord is said to "ponder . . . the hearts" of his creatures (21: 2; 24: 12).

In any event, Milton concluded that Mary's encounter with God's mysterious word, which intensified with the announcement of the virginal conception, continued through the course of her life. The puzzling over texts anticipated her son's experience and that of later readers. Just as Mary did not fully understand all at once the meaning and implications of the text of her calling, so Jesus, having heard that he was the Father's "beloved Son," gradually works through the implications of his calling during the trials in the wilderness. He learns "the rudiments" (I, 157) of his mission by trying experiences analogous to those that Mary went through during his childhood—the slaughter of the innocents, the flight into Egypt, the predictions of trouble by aged Simeon, the loss of the child in the temple.

Mary's Magnificat also provides relevant background to *Paradise Regained*. From the temptations through which Satan puts her son, we can infer that Mary had been an active teacher of the values that she had voiced in her poetic composition. Most of the revolutionary sentiments that she expresses—

> He hath showed strength with his arm; he hath scattered the proud in the imagination of their hearts. He hath put down the mighty from *their* seats, and exalted them of low degree; . . . and the rich he hath sent empty away. (Luke 1: 51–53)

—prove to be prominent among the ideas that Satan calls into question. From start to finish, Satan tempts Jesus to make a superficial application not only of texts from the Hebrew Bible but also of "texts" that an alert reader can infer that the Son must have heard from his mother, texts such as "he that is mighty" does "great things" for his people and "fills the hungry with good things."

More important for Milton's purpose, the fact that Mary's hymn is a tissue of allusions and echoes from the Hebrew Bible illustrated that she was an interpreter who could reassemble scriptural texts into a personal synthesis. This is what Milton shows her doing in the two passages where she "Meekly compos[es]" her thoughts (II, 108) and we have access to her actual words (I, 229–58 and II, 66–104). Despite its conjunction with "Meekly," the word "compose" here does not so much refer to an act of settling down, or making calm and tranquil (*OED,* senses II and III), as it does to the putting together of various elements, to framing or fashioning thoughts to make up a whole (sense I.1), even to arranging them artistically (sense 8). Still, there is a suggestion that these various senses are deeply related; for Milton's inferences about Mary's methods and messages in the teaching of her son inform his portrait of her at the beginning of Book II, where he shows her to be more adept at dealing with delays and disappointments than Andrew and Simon, who have only recently had their hopes raised. Mary's soliloquy there is exemplary not in that it shows a person exempt from "cares and fears" (these are essential to her testing) but in that it dramatizes the inner struggle of one trying to make sense of her experience in relation to what she had previously heard from God. She recalls the things she has lately heard about her son — all of it matter drawn, as if by anticipation, from what will be recorded in the New Testament. She weaves it together into a new synthesis, making as much sense of it as she presently can, putting into question her previous interpretations in light of new data: "O what avails me now that honour high / To have conceiv'd of God, or that salute, / Hale highly favour'd, among women blest" (II, 66–68).

The characteristic method of Mary's interior monologue, that is, of what Milton shows going on with the things that she has kept in her heart, is a comparison of texts. The narrator points out that she has been "pondering oft, and oft to mind / Recalling what remarkably had pass'd / Since first her Salutation heard" (II, 105–7). In this way Milton projects into Mary's experience during Jesus' adult life both the method that she had practiced and something of the content that she had learned when Jesus was a boy. "But where delays he now?" she asks herself,

> some great intent
> Concealies him: when twelve years he scarce had seen,
> I lost him, but so found, as well I saw
> He could not lose himself; but went about
> His Father's business; what he meant I mus'd,
> Since understand; much more his absence now
> Thus long to some great purpose he obscures.
> But I to wait with patience am inur'd.... (II, 95–102)

The word *mus'd* here is particularly rich, suggesting as it does an alternative to "ponder" as a translation for the Greek *symballousa*. By Milton's time its older senses (*OED*, 5; 6) of "To wait or look expectantly" and "To murmur; to grumble, complain" were obsolete. Still, as a reminder of the two divergent responses to God's promises made by the Israelites during their wanderings through the wilderness, these meanings are part of the background to the activities of both mother and son. Another sense of the word (*OED*, 2) implies "be[ing] at a loss," and this perfectly befits the context in which Mary now finds herself. For her, unlike the new disciples, the experience of missing something turns out to be an inspiration, and Milton gives a longer speech to Mary here than she has in any of the canonical gospels.

Pondering over the meaning of God's words in the way the writer of *De Doctrina Christiana* says he "pondered" over the words of Scripture, Milton's Mary emerges as a portrait of the responsible reader. She is, in the phrase that Luke uses later in his gospel to provide a way to reinterpret Jesus' definition of his true family, one who, "in an honest and good heart, having heard the word, keep[s] *it,* and bring[s] forth fruit with patience" (8: 15). Perhaps even more to the point, she has understood by anticipation the saying that her son will pronounce before the crowds: "where your treasure is, there will your heart be also" (Luke 12: 34).

Beyond this Milton suggests that Mary had greater interpretive powers and privileges, in keeping with the notion that she exercised the power of symbol-making. There is already something of this activity in Book I, when Jesus recalls what his mother had told him and how it sent him back to reread the Scriptures (I, 259 ff.). This role is hinted at again and given a striking name at the close of Mary's speech in Book II. There she says that her "heart hath been a store-house long of things / And sayings laid up, portending strange events" (II, 103–04). This paraphrase of Luke 2: 19 and 2: 51, inserted at the end of the soliloquy in which she had demonstrated what she does with the things she keeps in her heart, makes it clear that Mary does what Milton does. More than a disciple who waits expectantly for further clarification of the texts that she does not understand,[26] Mary actively seeks out meaning.

Some typical uses of the word *storehouse* in Renaissance books on rhetoric and logic reinforce the notion that Milton looks upon Mary as a "chosen vessel" and her heart as a writer's commonplace book. The *storehouse* (sometimes described as a "chest" or "vessell") served as the standard image in rhetorical treatises for the container in which the topics, or places, were kept.[27] In his *Arte of Logique,* Thomas Wilson speaks of "the storehouse of places, wherin Arguments reste." He recommends that one "conferre" there matters that are to be "put to the profe," insisting meanwhile that this will require "a very diligent labourer." Raphe Lever, in *The Arte of Reason,* enumerates ten storehouses and spells out their uses. Moreover, translators of commonplace books often enlisted the word *storehouse* to render the Latin *thesaurus,* emphasizing more than they might by the word *treasury* the functional aspect of the collection. Other writers related the storehouse to the religious use of books. Robert Cawdray, in *A Treasvrie or Store-hovse of Similes,* spoke of the Word as a mine to be searched into from which readers could draw out "whatsoever is requisite & necessarie for the saluation of our soules." Closer to Milton's time, Henry Jessey presented his cases-of-conscience book, *A Storehouse of Provision,* as "*Collections* of various kinds of spirituall FOOD."[28] In any event, the storehouse and treasury which is Mary's heart makes her akin to the writer whose method Milton describes in the opening chapter of *De Doctrina Christiana,* where he cites Matthew 13: 52: "every scribe who has been instructed in the kingdom of heaven, is like a householder who brings out of his treasure new and old possessions" (*CPW,* VI, 127–28; italics omitted). This assimilation of Mary's heart to a thesaurus, upon which the scribe then draws to produce a work at once old and new,[29] makes a sort of signature in Milton's poem, even as it validates the storyteller's method. The words *symballousa, conferens,* and *pondered* apply to the activities of Milton and Mary alike, as they collect, compare, and recombine texts in a continuing search for meanings that cannot be permanently fixed. All this suggests why, at the end of Milton's poem, the victor returns to his mother's house, and it gives some indication of what he will do there.

In connection with the ending of *Paradise Regained,* it seems appropriate to notice that, if we were to make a harmony of the four gospels, it is not long after the temptations that Jesus is interpreting the Scriptures publicly in the synagogue and applying a biblical place to his own situation (Luke 4). Yet the event which follows even more closely upon Jesus' return from the desert is the wedding feast at Cana (John 2). There Mary will break through, we might say, the newly acquired lessons in detachment that her son has learned as he spurned Satan's various offers. She will use the fruits of her recent pondering to teach Jesus a new lesson about timing when she prods him to act in response to human needs: "They have no wine" (2: 3). For John, this is a way of introducing his guiding notion of the *kairos,* the right time, a notion that informs Milton's poem at virtually every turn.[30] For Milton, who sends his hero home to his mother's house in private after the temptations, this is a way of suggesting how waiting itself needs to be done *at the right time,* rather than simply *for* the right time: they also *serve* who only stand and wait.

Paradise Regained shows Mary nurturing and teaching Jesus at some times and learning from him at others. Without in any way implying that the papists had reason to see in her a mediatrix of divine grace, Milton presents Mary as one who mediates the Word—first to Jesus himself, then to the New Testament writers, and ultimately to Christians in every age. Beyond this, he has painted in her a portrait of the artist. She exercises the authorly roles of preserving, interpreting, and combining diverse texts into a unique personal synthesis. In this way Milton's Mary anticipates the activity of other bearers of the Word, that is, of both the evangelists like Luke and latter-day poets like Milton himself.

It is important to recognize that Milton has not painted a portrait of the Madonna by herself. Mary is a figure in a larger portrait; and her significance remains, as Protestant writers insisted that it should, a function of her relation to her son. This should not obscure, however, the degree to which Milton has painted the son to resemble his mother. The hero of *Paradise Regained* learns from his mother a whole range of virtues, including the ability to ponder texts patiently and persistently, searching out their implications for life. This family resemblance between mother and son places an unmistakable emphasis on the right uses of reading and of learning, and it tends to blur one of the distinctions between male and female roles that we have been accustomed to associating with the English seventeenth century.

The Father's House (and the Suppression of Samson's Mother)

In view of the prominence that Milton accorded to Mary, it is worth noticing that when we compare the companion poem to its biblical original in the Book of Judges, the hero's mother is conspicuously missing from *Samson Agonistes*. Whereas Milton suggests in *Paradise Regained* how much the Son of God owes to the woman who taught him to read and provided timely information in the light of which to interpret the Scriptures, in *Samson Agonistes* books and reading have almost no place in the characters' experience, and there is no mention of, and at best only an oblique reference (25) to, the hero's mother. This absence of the hero's mother constitutes an erasure, not an inadvertent omission. In the Bible the mother of Samson belongs to a group of women, including Sarah and Hannah and Elizabeth, who in their barrenness become recipients of the Lord's special favor. The narrative in Judges depicts her as a resourceful woman, who by contrast with her comically dull husband (Manoah, in the common spelling of the English versions) proves a shrewd interpreter of the actions and statements of an angelic messenger. In *Samson Agonistes* Milton assigns to his Manoa the unedifying work of effacing her.

In the thirteenth chapter of Judges, although the narrator tells the story chiefly from the man's point of view and does not give the woman's name, it is clear that Manoah's wife has the more prominent role. It is she who is said to be "barren" and she who is made to "bear" (this word play is unique to the English version) the burden of the angel's message, not just once but also when he appears "there the second time" (the meaning of Samson's name). Her husband evidently feels excluded when he learns that she has had a mysterious visitor. What makes sense of his prayer that the messenger come again to "teach us what we shall do unto the child" is the fact that his wife omits telling him the detail that will become, in Milton's version, Samson's "capital secret," the stipulation that "no razor shall come on his head." When the angel returns, he tells Manoah nothing about "how to order the child," nor anything about this prohibition. Nor does the narrator in Judges ever inform readers how or even whether Manoah learned the source of his son's strength.

In any event, the narrative in Judges develops several differences between Manoah and his much more canny wife. Whereas the woman had been content merely to accept the angel's message without interrogating him, Manoah seeks to detain the angel and boldly poses a question. This moment is reminiscent of a famous passage in Genesis (chap. 32) which recounts Jacob's attempt to detain another elusive figure, the angel with whom he wrestled and who, refusing to give his own name, blessed Jacob and changed his name to Israel. (Israel means "he who strives with God," or perhaps "God strives.") By contrast with Jacob, Manoah is rebuked for having pried further than is meant: "Why askest thou thus after my name, seeing it *is* secret?" The angel's answer calls further attention to Manoah's exclusion from the center of power and activity. The precedent involving Jacob, moreover, seems not to occur to him. Instead he draws confidently on his familiarity with another Israelite tradition to interpret the events: "We shall surely die," he tells his wife, "because we have seen God." She simply observes, however, that her husband's interpretation is unlikely: God would not have received their offering and shown them "all these *things*" if God were about to kill them. The episode concludes without Manoah:

And the woman bare a son, and called his name Samson: and the child grew, and the LORD blessed him. And the Spirit of the LORD began to move him at times in the camp of Dan between Zorah and Eshtaol.

Omitting Samson's mother from his version of the story, Milton made more prominent a contrast between the mother of Jesus and the father of Samson. When he took up the story of Samson's last day, he assigned to Manoa a fear of being left behind, evident from his opening speech when he contrasts the "younger feet" of the chorus to his belated self, "cast back" as he is "with age" and "lagging after" (335–37). It is operative to the end, when by contrast with the mother of Jesus, who according to the gospels was present at the cross, he is absent from his son's death. The suppression of Samson's mother is wholly of a piece with Milton's characterization of Samson's father; it emerges as a kind of revenge taken by Manoa for his belatedness and his exclusion from the center of the story in Judges. Constantly berating his son for his unfortunate nuptial choices, nowhere in *Samson Agonistes* does Manoa mention his wife. Even when he reviews with Samson the earliest part of the story, in which Samson's mother had so prominent a part, Manoa revises the narrative to get himself into its center:

> I pray'd for Children, and thought barrenness
> In wedlock a reproach; I gain'd a Son,
> And such a Son as all Men hail'd me happy;
> Who would be now a Father in my stead?
> O wherefore did God grant me my request,
> And as a blessing with such pomp adorn'd?
> Why are his gifts desirable, to tempt
> Our earnest Prayers, then giv'n with solemn hand
> As Graces, draw a Scorpions tail behind?
> For this did the Angel twice descend? for this
> Ordain'd thy nurture holy, as of a Plant
> Select, and Sacred, Glorious for a while,
> The miracle of men: then in an hour
> Ensnar'd, assaulted, overcome. . . .   (352–65)

Instead of calling attention to similarities between the mothers of the heroes in his companion poems, Milton avoided the sort of typological symbolism exploited by Luke in his narratives about Elizabeth and Mary.

Strictly speaking, he had no need to include Samson's father in the poem either. In the biblical account it seems that Manoah was already in his grave when Samson pulls down the pillars. The anonymous narrator of Judges reports that after the devastation, Samson's "brethren and all the house of his father came down, and took him, and brought *him* up, and buried him between Zorah and Eshtaol in the buryingplace of Manoah his father" (16: 31). This verse leaves just enough space to suppose that Manoah may have been living still, and Milton exploits this possibility to point certain contrasts with the mother of the hero in *Paradise Regained*. Through the figure of Manoa Milton dramatizes some parental pressures to which his Samson was subject until his dying day and some interpretive dispositions to which Samson's story has been subject ever since. Milton presents Manoa as a man of business and as a forerunner of seventeenth-century spiritual accountants: his Manoa weighs everything in terms of credits and debits and seeks to know whether his son's story ends with "crown or shame." "Tell us the sum," he says to the messenger who reports the catastrophe, "the circumstance defer" (1557). He is puzzled about how someone might turn out to have had what, in the terms of experimental predestinarianism, was called a merely temporary vocation. Seeing Samson in the prison, he asks:

> Why are [God's] gifts desirable, to tempt
> Our earnest Prayers, then giv'n with solemn hand
> As Graces, draw a Scorpions tail behind?
> For this did the Angel twice descend? for this
> Ordain'd thy nurture holy, as of a Plant;
> Select, and Sacred, Glorious for a while,
> The miracle of men: then in an hour
> Ensnar'd, assaulted, overcome, led bound,
> Thy Foes derision, Captive, Poor, and Blind
> Into a Dungeon thrust, to work with Slaves?   (358–67)

After thus piling this mass of nouns and verbs and adjectives upon his son (each part of speech blurring into the other, all fixing Samson in the present perfect tense), and then recurring repeatedly to the unfortunate "Marriage choices," at the end of the poem Manoa seizes the occasion to define an alternative version of the story. It is his eagerness for closure that surfaces, as he seeks to pronounce a final interpretation of his son's story that not only redounds to the father's credit but reveals his personal stake in believing that Samson acted in concert with God:

> *Samson* hath quit himself
> Like *Samson,* and heroicly hath finish'd
> A life Heroic, on his Enemies
> Fully reveng'd, hath left them years of mourning,
> And lamentation to the Sons of *Caphtor*
> Through all *Philistian* bounds. To *Israel*
> Honour hath left, and freedom, let but them
> Find courage to lay hold on this occasion,
> To himself and Fathers House eternal fame;
> And which is best and happiest yet, all this
> With God not parted from him, as was feard,
> But favouring and assisting to the end.   (1709–20)

Concerned with the reputation of his "house" in posterity, Manoa knows nothing about the sort of eternal salvation or damnation that preoccupied many seventeenth-century Protestants. (It is an aspect of the "verisimilitude and decorum" to which Milton's preface refers that the poet thus preserves the ancient Israelites' historic skepticism about an afterlife in another world.) For Manoa the issue is worldly honor. He responds enthusiastically to the semi-chorus's comparison of his son to the phoenix, who, "though her body die, her fame survives / A secular bird ages of lives" (1706–07). Yet the desire for fame turns out to be only the penultimate infirmity of his mind, as his plan to build his son a "Monument" gives way to his final words. They are words of regret, harping on Samson's "lot unfortunate in nuptial choice," and Manoa persists in ascribing his son's "captivity and loss of eyes" (1743–44) to disobedience of his parents and of tribal law. In this way Samson's father, even as he evades the possibility that the death may be deemed a suicide, is made ironically to give the last word to the problematic period in Samson's life when he, perhaps only for a time, "fell away."

Readers who make a conference of places while reading *Paradise Regained* and *Samson Agonistes* can notice that by including portraits of their parents and of their "houses" Milton has set up a number of telling contrasts between the two heroes. Mary's real home is the "store-house" which is her heart, the place where she treasures up deeds and sayings on which to muse. This is the place to which the Son of God finally repairs. Manoa's treasure is the reputation of his "house," and this he defines above all in terms of his son's achievements. To save his son from public ignominy, as he tells the chorus, he is willing to sacrifice all his wealth and to incur poverty:

> His ransom, if my whole inheritance
> May compass it, shall willingly be paid
> And numbered down: much rather I shall chuse
> To live the poorest in my Tribe, then richest.
> . . . .
> For his redemption all my Patrimony,
> If need be, I am ready to forgo
> And quit: not wanting him, I shall want nothing.
>
> (1476–79, 1482–84)

When the chorus goes on to observe that "Fathers are wont to lay up for thir Sons, / Thou for thy Son art bent to lay out all" (1485–86), readers may remember Mary's having laid up "sayings . . . portending strange events" (II, 104). Samson's father seeks to minimize the possibility of strange events by managing his son's story with "a Fathers timely care" (602). His very willingness to lay out his treasure to buy his son's release from prison suggests that he would be unlikely to appreciate the more inward conception of the locus of value that Mary has. That is how one attempt to put Milton's poem on the stage interpreted him, as Manoa was made prominently to carry round a treasure box.[31]

References to the "Fathers house" recur twice in the closing section of *Samson Agonistes* (1717, 1733), recalling Manoa's earlier charge that his son had dishonored "thy Fathers house" (447) and making a kind of refrain. For readers who hear an echo of Jesus' references to his "Father's house" in the gospels, and of Satan's reference to the Temple as "thy Fathers house" in *Paradise Regained* (IV, 552), this phrase serves to direct irony at Manoa and all those whose conception of religion is decidedly materialistic. In particular, Manoa's phrase the "Fathers house" involves submerged references to two particular episodes. The first is the scene of conflict between Jesus and his parents, uniquely reported by Luke (2: 41–52), in which Joseph and Mary, having lost their twelve-year-old boy, find him "in the temple, sitting in the midst of the doctors, both hearing them, and asking them questions." For their pains they are greeted by Jesus with a sort of rebuke that Protestant denigrators of Mary liked to quote, "How is it that ye sought me? wist ye not that I must be about my Father's business?" It is immediately after this saying that Luke reports that "his mother kept all these sayings in her heart"; in *Paradise Regained* (II, 95–100) Mary is shown to have pondered the meaning of this phrase in particular. The Greek phrase (ἐν τοῖς τοῦ πατρός μου) rendered "Father's business" in the Authorized Version and

Geneva Bible was imprecise enough that, in other English versions, the verse was sometimes translated to make Jesus' second question seem more closely related to his first by using terms that establish the verbal parallel, "my Father's house."[32] It is this fusion the "Father's business" and the "Father's house" that, for readers whose memories were storehouses of biblical phrases, makes a second allusion particularly telling in interpreting the workings of irony in Milton's *Samson*.

Early in John's Gospel, occupying a position functionally equivalent to the temptations in the desert in the Synoptic gospels, the evangelist reports the incident in which Jesus overthrows the tables of the money-changers and upbraids those who have set up shop in the Temple: "make not my Father's house an house of merchandise" (2: 16). Jesus then propounds a riddle worthy of Samson and fraught with imagery reminiscent of Samson's final day. He is reported to have gone on cryptically to say, "Destroy this temple, and in three days I will raise it up." This provokes puzzlement and hostility among his auditors: "Then said the Jews, Forty and six years was this temple in building, and wilt thou rear it up in three days?" Yet John's principal interest lies in a figurative interpretation of the word "temple," to which he provides access for his readers: "But he spake of the temple of his body. When therefore he was risen from the dead, his disciples remembered that he had said this unto them; and they believed the Scripture, and the word which Jesus had said" (John 2: 19–22). Here the evangelist provides a model for understanding how Milton's redaction of the Samson story works for readers familiar, as the characters in the narrative are not, with biblical texts written after the close of the story. And yet there is an operative contrast as well. For in *Samson Agonistes* Milton eschewed the use of a narrator's voice, which in *Paradise Lost* and *Paradise Regained* frequently serve to direct his readers' understanding.

By depicting Manoa as an interpreter overly intent on establishing meanings that would nevertheless, in biblical literature composed long after the period of the Judges, take on new and ironic senses, Milton, rather than seeking himself utterly to fix the meaning of Samson's story, counted on cooperation from readers able to see that the Word of God lies behind or beyond any words written in the Bible. By dexterous allusion to New Testament passages, he was able to suggest that the words of the narrative in Judges cannot be utterly isolated from the rest of Scripture but "require" reconfiguration at the hands of "skilfull and laborious" gatherers. This is to say more, then, than Stanley Fish has in his indictment of Manoa as a co-conspirator with the chorus (and with many readers of *Samson Agonistes*) in a plot to "domesticate Samson by placing him in a tradition that makes his life intelligible." Even without reference to the extensive and subtle workings of allusions to biblical paradigms and places, Fish has shown Manoa to be an epitome of the sort of interpreter who seeks to evade discontinuity, incoherence, and indeterminacy, who cannot bear the idea that Samson's story might remain "fragmentary" and unintelligible.³³ The chapter to follow will examine biblical evidence that confirms Fish's demonstration that Milton wrote his version of the Samson story to multiply rather than settle the troubles found in previous versions, but it will attempt to point a way beyond Fish's summary conclusion. Taking into account the contrast Milton created between Manoa, who seeks reassuring closure, and Mary, who waits patiently comparing text with text, it will show that while Milton displayed remarkable respect for genuine ambiguities in the biblical materials, he also enlisted a conference of places to tease out secrets that had long been buried in the scriptural texts. In due course this work will also entail renewed attention to the parable of the talents, a biblical place that John Guillory, in his materialist treatment of Milton's poem in relation to the celebrated thesis of Max Weber, has aptly denominated "the most active subtext in the drama."³⁴

Before concluding this chapter, it is worth noting one specific passage in *Samson Agonistes* in which the parable of the talents works to tie the poem to the biblical places about Mary's storehouse. When Milton's Samson rehearses the events that led up to his blinding, imprisonment, and degradation, he sustains a pattern of financial metaphors that have been introduced in his businessman father's language. In referring to what Dalila got from him he also uses terms in ways curiously continuous with language that appears in *Paradise Regained*:

Thrice she assay'd with flattering prayers and sighs,
And amorous reproaches to win from me
My capital secret, in what part my strength
Lay stor'd, in what part summ'd. . . .   (*Samson Agonistes*, 392–95)

Like Mary's heart, Samson's, it seems, had been a "store-house." Eventually he gave Dalila access to it, when he "unlock'd her all [his] heart" (407). This points up something striking about Samson's case: it is in Milton's poem, and not in the story in Judges, that Samson's treasure is said (by Manoa) to have been a "sacred trust of silence / Deposited within" and not to be "divulg'd" or "publish'd" under pain of breaking a vow. Milton's

Mary, although she transmitted oral culture to her son from her breast,[35] also "kept . . . things in her heart" until the opportune time, and eventually revealed to her son, and then to the evangelists, details that came to be recorded in the Scriptures. But Milton's Manoa seems to have kept to himself the prerogative of making definitive interpretations and to have encouraged his son to think *his* publishing of a family secret a sinful profanation. Samson, unlike "every scribe . . . instructed unto the kingdom of heaven," does not understand himself as "a householder, which bringeth forth out of his treasure things new and old" for the entertainment and instruction of his guests. In this respect, he bears a family resemblance not to his mother (about whom Milton's poem is so silent) but to his father, who works hard to close down the process of interpretation.

* * *

Try as many people in seventeenth-century England did to fashion their "selves" according to biblical paradigms and to base their moral lives on biblical teachings, the Bible did not and could not serve as an utterly stable frame of reference. So much might have been predicted by any literary theory that posits the illusory nature of all attempts to fix meaning in language or to produce a totalizing world picture. What is of interest, and of importance for understanding his mature biblical poetry, is that Milton developed a view of the Scriptures as a copious storehouse of places the very nature of which required that they be drawn out and put to new uses. Far from understanding a commitment to "the Bible only" as implicating readers in a fixed system, Milton understood it in terms epitomized in the parable of the talents, as requiring a diligent investment of interpretive energies and enabling a productive reconfiguration of authorized places. Having come to suppose that the Scriptures are "meant" to be appropriated and assimilated by individual readers, Milton did not conceive the work of interpretation as simply conforming one's views to an already given meaning, nor as constituting an addition to the Scriptures. He did not understand interpretive work on a model of supplementation. The canonical texts *became* for him the Scriptures when they were interpreted with disciplined reserve as well as "experimentally."

6. Keeping Secrets, Telling Secrets in *Paradise Regained* and *Samson Agonistes*

> . . . full summ'd to tell of deeds
> Above Heroic, though in secret done,
> And unrecorded left through many an Age,
> Worthy t' have not remain'd so long unsung.
> —*Paradise Regained*, I, 14–17

By contrast with critical work on *Paradise Regained,* the most telling criticism of *Samson Agonistes* in recent years has claimed little for the importance of biblical texts, and it has advocated strong skepticism in the face of the pretensions of interpreters. That various characters in Milton's poem, as well as readers of it, seek by questionable interpretive methods to fill in a number of gaps in the story of Samson has been demonstrated in impressive detail by Stanley Fish. Without explicitly committing himself to the hypothesis that *Samson* was Milton's last poem, Fish has asserted that it represents the culmination of an interpretive "progress" on which Milton had set out in 1644 when he wrote *Areopagitica.* The "perpetuall progress" that Milton advocated in the pamphlet came to entail for him, Fish proposes, giving up all certainty, so that Milton came finally to live with "radical incompleteness," glorying in a "strenuous" Christian liberty as "terrifying" as it is "liberating."[1]

One conclusion to be drawn in the course of this chapter will prove largely congruent with what Fish has demonstrated about *Samson Agonistes,* that it "renders us incapable of performing the task we are assigned" by it, above all "the task of interpreting" Samson's final action. In Milton's representation of the hero's last hours, he drew on the criterion for interpretation whereby readers ought not to "pry . . . further" than is "meant," and recapitulated many ambiguities in Scripture concerning Samson's status and mission rather than resolving them. Milton's Samson, "immixed, inevitably" in conflicting estimates of his person and conduct, lies finally "tangled in the fold, / Of dire necessity."

Other conclusions to be drawn in this chapter should help to unsettle Fish's theory that the foregrounding of indeterminacy in *Samson Agonistes* represents the culmination of Milton's "progress." The preceding chapter has documented, in its discussion of Milton's representation of Mary as a model interpreter, some results of the positive criteria for reading Scripture that Milton developed in his maturity. Next I want to examine how he drew on various Pauline materials to project into the experience of Jesus a proleptic encounter between the classical and biblical traditions. This examination will present further evidence that while Milton faced with equanimity the fact that Scripture does not provide metaphysical clarity about what it means to call Jesus the "son of God," he nonetheless discovered a good deal about Jesus that the individual "penman" had left "unrecorded." In other words, he was not making a steady "progress" towards finding radical indeterminacy everywhere he looked. Milton's major poems demonstrate that as an interpreter he was not immobilized by his having achieved the courage squarely to face indeterminacies in biblical literature. In particular, Milton's own painstaking conference of places helped him to unlock long hidden secrets in the biblical stories he sought to retell. This does not mean that he recoiled from a courageous embrace of "strenuous liberty." It shows rather that as an interpreter he was liberated both negatively, from an obsession with certainty and closure, and positively, to glimpse in imagination new interpretive possibilities.

The Temptation of Learning

In recent years a good deal of writing about *Paradise Regained* has called attention to ways in which that poem in particular dramatizes a veritable "hermeneutic combat." No doubt some have claimed too much for the efficacy of the activity that all readers of the poem inevitably share with the hero, as if "the right interpretation of the Scriptures . . . [is] the key to overcoming the forces of evil" and the preeminent means by which paradise is to be regained.[2] In this body of criticism much is often claimed as well for the importance to Milton of one or other book of the Bible. Luke's Gospel has been said to provide the narrative outline for *Paradise Regained;* the Book of Job its generic model; John's Gospel its theological framework and "primary inspiration"; the Pauline letters, the Epistle to the Hebrews, and the Book of Revelation important thematic materials; and certain Psalms the principal texts which the antagonists try to interpret.[3] Individually, such studies provide valuable insights into aspects of Milton's literary and theological debts. It is their collective significance, however, that needs probing. The discovery of so many different keys to the poem points directly to unresolved—sometimes even unasked—questions about what principles of selection and omission operate in Milton's choice of biblical materials and about what effects are created by the combinations of these materials from various biblical sources. These are questions about the poet's use of his learning, especially his knowledge of the Scriptures. One way to begin exploring them is to attend to the episode in Book IV in which, without obvious scriptural precedent, he records the temptation of learning.

In *Paradise Regained,* in addition to the scriptural learning bequeathed to him by his mother's teaching and example, it is striking that the Son of God has also acquired classical *scientia*. This detail of Milton's portrait was not inspired by places from the gospels, nor does it derive from "human tradition." Rather it may be seen as an aspect of Milton's anticipation of historic developments in Christianity to which other parts of the New Testament bear witness. The license Milton thus accorded himself requires interpretation in relation to his theme. Jesus' familiarity with classical culture in not merely an "imaginative detail," to be accepted in the same way that we accept the fact that the poem reports his speeches in English and casts them into blank verse. For classical *paideia* contributed substantially to Milton's conception of his hero, to his "words and images," and beyond them to the form taken both by the questions that he faces and the answers that he devises. Yet *Paradise Regained* is remarkable among biblical epics of the Renaissance in its spare style and in its close adherence to its scriptural source, on which it is a kind of meditation. Far more than seventeenth-century biblical epics in French, and more than other biblical epics in English, including *Paradise Lost,* the poem follows a single scriptural narrative.[4] This makes its expansions and additions, such as the banquet, the storm, and the temptation of learning, the more striking. Modifications of the biblical original are particularly significant here because the whole poem seems to represent an heroic attempt at restoring what Milton considered an authentically biblical perspective on the relations between the biblical and classical traditions. The act of writing the poem contributes to a conception of how paradise may be regained imaginatively by someone who is de facto learned.

Despite the remark in the Epistle to the Hebrews that Jesus had been "in all points tempted like as *we are, yet* without sin" (4: 15), there is no temptation of learning in the Synoptic accounts of the trials in the wilderness, and apparently no precedent for it in the exegetical tradition. Yet Milton allowed this temptation more scope than any other and placed it in a climactic position, at the end of the temptations concerning the kingdoms of the world. He likely inferred its historic existence both from the Pauline literature (to be considered below) and from relevant passages in other parts of the gospels. The evangelists characteristically assign the role of adversary to the scribes and Pharisees, who test the teacher by asking him to apply his learning to specific situations, such as the case of divorce or the question of paying taxes to Caesar. When Milton includes in his poem a temptation by learning, he provides a prolepsis of and variation on these public temptations.[5] What is most striking, however, is Satan's extension of the temptation to include classical learning:

> All knowledge is not couch't in *Moses* law,
> The *Pentateuch* or what the Prophets wrote,
> The *Gentiles* also know, and write, and teach
> To admiration, led by Natures light;
> And with the *Gentiles* much thou must converse. . . .   (IV, 225–29)

There is little indication in the gospels that Jesus had a mission to the Gentiles. Nor is there evidence that he ever went far beyond the borders of Palestine (the narrative about a descent into Egypt as a baby has a chiefly typological significance), or that he was acquainted with classical cultures and civilizations. This was, at least potentially, something of a scandal to Milton and his fit readers. To counteract it some other writer might have drawn upon Erasmus's *philosophia Christi*, with its celebration of the foolishness of God and its denigration of the wisdom of the world. Milton, when he introduced the temptations of Athens and Rome as part of the kingdoms of the world, took a still bolder course. Making the human Jesus aware of the broader world, including the cultivated world, Milton gives him the opportunity to respond to the greatest pagan accomplishments of the ancient world and to erect a heroism of renunciation above the active heroism of noble Romans and the contemplative heroism of learned Greeks.[6]

Mid-twentieth-century commentators on this aspect of *Paradise Regained* often expressed worry about what they took to be Milton's uncharacteristic outburst against classical learning. Tillyard went so far as to accuse the poet of "masochism," claiming that Milton went "out of his way to hurt the dearest and oldest inhabitants of his mind: the Greek philosophers — his early love Plato included, the disinterested thirst for knowledge, the poets and orators of Greece and Rome." Even the poet's defenders have often seemed embarrassed by the rejection of classical learning, Douglas Bush confessing that he found it painful "to watch Milton turn and rend some main roots of his being."[7] What warrants attention, however, is the more curious and fundamental fact that Milton ascribed a rather considerable degree of learning to his hero. In his debate with Satan the Son seems to equivocate about the degree of his classical learning: "Think not but that I know these things, or think / I know them not" (IV, 286–87). Yet elsewhere he demonstrates a familiarity with classical culture in the course of his denunciation of various philosophic schools and of Greek poets. He even enlists classical *paideia* at various points, as when he praises Socrates for being second only to Job in patient endurance for the cause of truth (III, 96–99). Moreover, the hero shares a great deal with the stoical heroes of Seneca, intelligent and sensitive men living under oppression in the Roman Empire, who often exercised their wisdom by withdrawing from confrontation with military might.[8] In short, Milton's hero possesses both *scientia* and a cosmopolitan sensibility that the four canonical evangelists seem to have been unconcerned to include in their portraits.

When Milton made his hero familiar with classical culture, he employed a characteristic imaginative technique that he learned early from his own Bible-reading. Milton seems to have thought of it as a mode of "prevention." It involves placing a familiar bit of material into an earlier context in order to bring to light its wider significance. Already in the Paraphrase on Psalm 114, "done by the Author at fifteen years old," the "Israel" of the Geneva Bible and the Authorized Version is rendered "the blest seed of *Terah*'s faithful Son." The mention of Abraham's father takes readers back to earlier generations and may remind us, obliquely, of the promise made to the grandfather of Israel's eponymous ancestor. In the Bible this technique of anticipation was used most dramatically by the author of the Fourth Gospel, who takes readers back before the "beginning" of the Book of Genesis and identifies Jesus as the Logos by whom "All things were made." It is a technique that informs *Paradise Lost* at nearly every point,[9] and one that, since it inevitably risks anachronism, requires imaginative discipline on the part of a reader who is comparing biblical places.

The New Testament locates the encounter between the classical and biblical traditions in the generation after the Savior's earthly career. As he is depicted in the Synoptic gospels, Jesus, though a teacher, comes from a social group in which he is unlikely to have mixed with Hellenistic savants and rhetors. According to the author of the Acts of the Apostles, the decisive moment when an inchoate Christianity met with Greek culture is to be found in the experience of Paul, the apostle to the Gentiles.[10] As he appears in the pages written by Luke, Paul visits the Areopagus (Acts 17) and speaks to an audience of Stoic and Epicurean philosophers of "the unknown God." He even quotes, as Milton pointed out in his introduction to *Samson Agonistes,* a verse from Greek poetry. In the context of *Paradise Regained* the verse would have been of interest to Satan: "we are also his offspring" (17: 28).

If Luke, who understood that addressing the Gospel to Greeks had profoundly influenced the development of Christianity, assigned the crucial initiative to Paul, some evidence from Paul's own letters points in a different direction. In the biblical passage that stands most squarely behind the Son's refusal in *Paradise Regained* to rule on the basis of consummate classical learning, Paul warns the Colossians against "philosophy and vain deceit, after the tradition of men, after the rudiments of the world" (2: 8). Only a few generations after Paul's death the situation would be reversed. As Luke partly foresaw, Christians began to present the gospel as *paideia,* to formulate its teachings in the language of Heraclitus and Plato, even to proclaim that "Nobody can deny that our Saviour and Lord was a philosopher."[11]

Milton was in several respects remarkably unsympathetic to the wedding of the gospel to philosophy, and the *De Doctrina* stands as a sort of divorce pamphlet attempting by its returning to "the Scriptures alone" to annul a disastrous marriage. In discussing the interpretation of Scripture there, Milton insists that "we should not rely upon our predecessors or upon antiquity" but stick to "the Bible only." "Human traditions, written or unwritten," he echoes Paul (and the magisterial Reformers), "are expressly forbidden," citing the standard text, Deuteronomy 4: 2 (*CPW,* VI, 591). In fact, Milton even locates the Fall of the church from its "pure original state" in the late second or early third century (117), probably in reference to the patristic introduction of speculation about the two-stage Logos into discussions of Christ and the Trinity. Whatever *Paradise Regained* owes to the Fourth Gospel, Milton's hero is not the Logos of St. John, a nearly Docetic Christ who possesses all sorts of knowledge unavailable to his auditors. That the Son of God should know about Socrates and Plato and the Epicureans is nowhere said or implied to be a matter of divine knowledge, nor even of infused human knowledge.[12] It is not that "Light from above" which is ethically and religiously necessary to the regaining of paradise. For all his learning, the Son of God in *Paradise Regained* is thoroughly human and does not possess any advantage of superhuman knowledge. He is the figure of the Synoptic tradition who "increased in wisdom and stature, and in favour with God and man" (Luke 2: 52).

Perhaps the principal reason that the temptation of learning has provoked widespread commentary in our century, both disapproving and defensive, is that it resists the sort of allegorizing with which critics are now accustomed to dealing with the poet's religious commitments. That is, the episode anticipates not only the confrontation between biblical and classical cultures that began in the generation after Jesus' earthly career and came memorably to be formulated in Tertullian's question, *Quid Athenis et Hierosolymis?* It also anticipates the development of views that have become commonplace only since the nineteenth century: the habit of seeing religious issues as displaced instances of aesthetic ones, and the erection of an ideal of "disinterested" knowledge that separates that knowledge from religious faith.

Satan's offer of a kingdom of the mind has a decided "spiritual" appeal: "let pass," he says, "as they are transitory, / The Kingdoms of this world" (IV, 209–10). He goes on to speak to what he has surmised to be a deep love of learning and of learned exchange. Displacing a biblical understanding of the nature of spiritual reality, Satan offers the possibility of defining the non-worldly kingdom in philosophic and aesthetic terms. "Be famous then / By wisdom," he proposes; "as thy Empire must extend, / So let extend thy mind o're all the world, / In knowledge, all things in it comprehend" (IV, 221–24). This is not simply a matter of offering Fame, although it is of interest that Satan places this offer after all the kingdoms of the world, as if he has discovered the "last infirmity of noble mind." Satan holds out the possibility of understanding the realm of "grace" as a realm of art and culture.

St. Paul as a Model for Jesus

According to the Acts of the Apostles, the rapprochement of early Christian religion, with its distinctive sense of history, and classical culture, with its propensity for abstracting the timeless from the particular, took place in the experience of St. Paul. In other words, it occurred in the generation after Jesus' earthly career, when the expectation of an imminent close to human history was receding. The very existence of a Book of Acts, and of written gospels, attests to a growing recognition that the church was settling down in history and that the gospel would be addressed to future generations. I have been proposing that Milton, on the basis of this awareness about the extension of the gospel in time and space, which was written into the New Testament itself, reprojected the encounter between the classical and biblical traditions back into the experience of Jesus. This enabled him to explore what might be the legitimate and fruitful accommodations of the scriptural data to classical culture and also, as the temptation of learning indicates, to insist upon the limits within which the marriage was to be made.

The first major accommodation of the scriptural data about Jesus that Milton was willing to allow owed something to the tradition of presenting Jesus as a model believer. Seeing Jesus as an example had roots of course in the New Testament itself, and the church Fathers had developed this perspective when they sought to work out a basis for presenting Christ to the already converted as well as to pagans.[13] Milton took the process still further, however, when he refashioned the figure of Synoptic tradition to look something like St. Paul. He emphasized, as the New Testament (Acts 22: 3; 26: 4–5; Gal. 1: 14; Phil. 3: 4–6) emphasizes about Paul, his hero's thorough grounding in Jewish learning. He assigned to him familiarity with classical learning as well.

What Milton did not do was to devise a "conversion" for Jesus, as Luther had done for Saul of Tarsus when he had interpreted the story of Paul's calling (Acts 9) as a moment of moral transformation. Chapter Two has indicated that Milton was not much interested in the phenomenon of conversion, at least by comparison with many of his contemporaries. Yet he took as the subject for a poem on the regaining of paradise the episode in the life of Christ that, as Perkins's treatise on it had shown, seemed especially promising to those who wished to find a model for how to make one's calling and election sure. The fact that Milton chose to tell about Jesus' private, personal temptations indicates that he may have been thinking about Jesus' likely internal experiences in reference to the standard Protestant map of the saint's spiritual life.[14] When the poem opens Jesus has recently heard, from the greatest preacher of his day, what Protestant tradition would call an awakening sermon. Through it he had received his calling. He dutifully searches the Scriptures in accord with the directions given in passages (2 Pet. 1: 10; Acts 17: 11; John 5: 39) that proved of great importance in the practical divinity of seventeenth-century England. His rereading of the Hebrew Bible reminds him that he has experienced just those early providential mercies that later autobiographers would regularly include in their personal narratives. Once he lives his public life, the gospels will in due course provide the standard account of the ministry which would conclude works like *Grace Abounding*. What is most prominently missing, however, is any account of a conversion.

If in his learning and in the readiness with which some aspects of his life can be considered as an exemplary pattern, Milton's hero is rather more like Paul than the Synoptic Jesus, he is also like Paul in the scope of his experience. It is true that Satan charges that Jesus has been "Bred up in . . . streights at home" (II, 415) and that he has not seen the wide world (III, 232–38). Yet the very fact that Milton includes extensive details about the larger world, including the world of learning, implies that Jesus is sufficiently informed about the larger world to make him susceptible to a wide range of temptations. Commentators on the Synoptic narratives admitted that some temptations "were not set downe by any Euangelist."[15] In accord with the relevant verse in Hebrews (4: 15) and with Luke's closing remark that "the devil had ended *all* the temptation" (4: 13; emphasis added), Milton thus presents his hero as one "fully tri'd / Through all temptation" (I, 4–5), expanding the Synoptic accounts chiefly by drawing upon data gleaned from a scrupulous comparison with other biblical places. The prominence that the poem gives to the period which Jesus spent in the wilderness calls attention to another, more personal aspect of the hero's learning: the personal lessons that he learned by suffering the temptations.

The parallel between Jesus' retreat into the wilderness and Paul's removal to Arabia after his conversion (Gal. 1: 17) was not lost on commentators. Perkins claimed that God characteristically prepares his ministers to be teachers by trying them privately. Paul's journey to Arabia was "a sharpe and weighty triall" analogous to one that God imposed on Moses, David, Jonas, and Christ himself, pre-eminently "the Doctour of the Church." The experience of all these biblical figures was said to confirm the maxim, "Reading, prayer, & temptation, make a Divine." In *Paradise Regained,* it is as if the Most High shows himself conversant with this theory when he explains to Gabriel, in accord with Hebrews 12: 6–7, that the temptations are a means of education and discipline which God gives his sons. They are an "exercise" in the "rudiments" of the lesson that human "weakness shall o'recome Satanic strength / And all the world" (I, 156–62).

Before considering the curious manner in which *Paradise Regained* defines the Son's "weakness," it will be useful to advert to something about this exemplary hero's strength, or virtue. The son uses the power of God to resist temptation and thus to reverse the course of human history. The ascription of such power to him comes chiefly from St. Paul, who set up the typological relationship between Adam and Christ to which the opening lines of Milton's poem alludes and on which the conception of the whole poem is built.[16] That Milton did not tell of a paradise regained through Christ's death on the Cross did not, as Tillyard claimed, ruin the "Pauline fabric of fall, grace, redemption, and regeneration." It redefined it. Milton used Pauline materials to play down what Paul had called the "folly" of the Cross. Although Paul admitted that a suffering Messiah was a scandal to the Greeks (1 Cor. 1: 23), he elsewhere (2 Cor. 4: 7–10) suggested that the experience of temptation was analogous to the crucifixion. Perkins made the connection explicit: in the wilderness "Christ stood in our roome and sted (as he did upon the Cross) encountering with Satan for us, as if we in our owne persons had been tempted." Milton knew all about using prolepsis, and the fact that there was no biblical basis for the legend of the harrowing of hell gave him an added reason to depict the temptations as the crucial battle with the Prince of Darkness.[17]

If seeing an anticipation of the passion narrative in the wilderness temptations rests upon Paul's typological reading of Genesis, it owes a good deal to his reading of Exodus and Deuteronomy as well. The most relevant passage appears in 1 Corinthians (10: 1–13) and serves as a Pauline commentary on the Synoptic accounts of the temptations. Paul proposes that Christ's triumph over Satan reversed the sins of the wandering Israelites as well as the sin of Adam. Enlisting the metaphors of standing and falling, Paul encourages his readers not to recapitulate their wandering forefathers' sins. If Christ reversed the course of history with his triumph over the "destroyer," he did not do so in a manner that precludes others' falling.

Beyond creating an exemplary hero who would not be so much a scandal to the Greek in himself and his readers, Milton made another major modification of the biblical tradition in his handling of the Pauline theme of weakness. For Milton, the Son's "weakness" is not intellectual, nor physical, nor moral; it seems to consist only in the fact that he can be afflicted with temptations. This conception of epic heroism was revolutionary, John Steadman has argued, in its distinctive emphasis on the paradox of divine strength working through human frailty. Milton subverted the classical conception of heroic strength, and "the Christ of *Paradise Regain'd* rejects the strength and wisdom of the world," in this view, because he has no need for them. "Through his complete dependence on providence and the divine will," says Steadman, "his frailty is stronger than the Parthian armies and wiser than the philosophy of the Greeks."[18] True as far as it goes, this does not explain why Milton should have troubled to give his hero a knowledge of the classics of which he has no need.

There were three rather different understandings of the Pauline term "weakness" available in the seventeenth century, none of which is precisely relevant to Milton's conception of heroism in *Paradise Regained*. One appears in 1 Corinthians, where it is associated with intellectual weakness, the folly of the Cross: "we preach Christ crucified, unto the Jews a stumblingblock, and unto the Greeks foolishness" (1: 23). Paul reminds his readers that God destroys worldly wisdom (he cites Isa. 29: 14) and chooses the unlettered for his purposes:

> For ye see your calling, brethren, how that not many wise men after the flesh, not many mighty, not many noble, *are called*: But God hath chosen the foolish things of the world to confound the wise; and God hath chosen the weak things of the world to confound the things which are mighty. (1: 26–27)

Elsewhere in the letter (2: 1–5), Paul associates his own "weakness" with a lack of rhetorical eloquence and human wisdom. This understanding of weakness as a lack of learning and eloquence does not usefully apply to the relatively learned hero and the decidedly learned poet of *Paradise Regained*.

Nor does a second understanding of weakness as a physical affliction, though Milton elsewhere associated his own blindness with the "weakness" of which Paul speaks in a particularly rich passage from 2 Corinthians (12: 2–21). After Paul tells of an extraordinary ecstatic experience of being "caught up into paradise," he goes on to report about his "thorn in the flesh, the messenger of Satan to buffet" him. It may well be that this was a physical affliction, perhaps even severe ophthalmia (cf. Gal. 4: 13–15).[19] In any event, Paul explains that this "thorn" kept him from feeling that the exalted experience of mounting up to the third heaven could be a permanent regaining of paradise in life, and that it brought him to a more thorough reliance upon divine grace and a more personal appreciation of the message of the Cross, whereby Christians receive no exemption from the need to suffer.

There is no indication in *Paradise Regained* that the hero has any physical weakness, and there are no poignant passages about the narrator's "ever-during dark" or about his inability to see the "human face divine." Nor is weakness defined as Luther generally understood it, that is, in moral terms. For the Reformers, Paul was the paradigmatic example of the Christian who found himself in a continuing struggle with the flesh, with human depravity, the effects of original sin. Luther's epigraph for his *Commentarie vpon Galathians* was "My power is made perfect through weakness." Throughout the commentary, which enjoyed wide popularity in England well into the seventeenth century, Luther treated weakness primarily as that inherent human sinfulness from which each person must be delivered by the power of God in Christ. In this view, it is utterly necessary that a person become conscious of personal sinfulness by passing through the trials and afflictions characteristic of the "time of the Law," before it is possible to know that God's "grace is sufficient."[20] It was in just this way that Paul was made the great model for Christians: he was said to have gone through a sinful period of "works-righteousness" before achieving the abundant grace of his Christian conversion. The Lutheran *Commentarie* proved an immense comfort to the author of *Grace Abounding to the Chief of Sinners*, who recounted his life in terms of this Pauline paradigm. No doubt it was a help to many others who had, as the title to the preface put it, "AFFLICTED CONSCIENCES WHICH GRONE for Salvation, and wrastle under the crosse for the Kingdome of Christ." This understanding of weakness as a metaphor for sinfulness, widespread as it was, is also irrelevant to Milton's hero, who was "in all points tempted like as we are, *but without sin*" (emphasis added).

There is, however, another way in which Milton likened Jesus to Paul that is worth pondering. We have previously adverted to the fact that early in *Paradise Regained* the narrator gives us access to the Son's consciousness by way of the interior monologue in which he recalls what he had learned from his mother. In *Paradise Lost* the soliloquy and interior monologue are associated with the experience of fallen creatures, particularly with Satan but also, in Book IX, conspicuously with Adam and Eve. Satan's great soliloquy in Book IV is at once an index of a powerful introspection and a divided self.[21] What is different about the Son's interior monologue in *Paradise Regained* is that he does not experience himself as divided; rather, Milton uses the form to illustrate the workings of "pondering in the heart." Although Milton's hero has something of an introspective conscience, he displays no anxiety about the search to make his calling and election sure, and he has no claim to having been "chief of sinners."

It is important for understanding Milton's idea of recovered paradise to reflect on the fact that the temptations in *Paradise Regained* are *foris, non intus*, the work of an external tempter. "[T]houghts of sinne arising out of our lusts," wrote Richard Capel in a thorough treatment of *Tentations: Their Nature/Danger/Cure* (1633), "are sinful thoughts." But a "meere and single apprehension or cogitation of a sin suggested by another, is not straight sin: for this was, or I know might have beene in Christ" and in "*Adam* before his fal." Or, as Milton's Adam says of the prelapsarian condition: "Evil into the mind of God or Man / May come and go, so unapprov'd, and leave / No spot or blame behind" (*PL*, V, 117–19). Capel observed that this meant that Jesus' interior experience was different from that of Paul (as understood in the tradition descending from Luther), for Paul "did sin against his judgement."[22]

Instead of depicting the youthful Jesus as a sinner, *Paradise Regained* emphasizes his vulnerability to the assaults of a tempter. It assigns the temptations not to the "lusts" of a fallen nature but to an external Adversary. While the whole poem is devoted to a struggle with temptation, it does not show us in Jesus the sort of imprisoned introspective conscience that Luther had made the privileged locus for the workings of grace. It is, rather, Satan who has an introspective conscience. Jesus has a robust conscience. When he does turn momentarily introspective, there is nothing morbid or neurotic about his reflections. In his interior monologue, without accusing himself of sin or of "works-righteousness," he simply acknowledges those Pelagian proclivities that Luther had associated with the "time of the Law," with Paul's intensely active persecution of the church, and with his own life as a monk.[23] Jesus admits that as a boy he scorned "childish play" and had with exceeding earnestness devoted himself to studies that were to prepare him to perform "victorious deeds" and "heroic acts," rescuing "*Israel* from *Roman* yoke" (I, 201–20). On the basis of the brief anecdote about the twelve-year-old's precocious activity in the Temple, Milton gives us an adult Jesus who looks back on his youth as an unripe time of strenuous and slightly misguided efforts to go about his "Father's business." Jesus is not a repenting sinner. Rather, by being tempted, he learns the humility that it often takes an actual fall to reveal to others: that human weakness, understood as vulnerability to assaults on one's spirit, opens one up to the power of God.

Paradise Regained then extends the doctrine of justification by faith alone, rendering it specially applicable to the situation of learned Christians. This represents another major accommodation of the biblical data to the classical tradition which, on the basis of careful conference of places, Milton authorizes. It also provides a helpful context within which to understand the hero's resisting the temptation of classical learning. He repudiates the wisdom of the Greeks insofar as it is a "work" analogous to the Jews' Law and the papists' sacramental system as these were defined in classic Protestantism.

There was precedent of course in Luther's writings for such a view, although Luther had taken as the principal threat to the Pauline gospel in his day the "merit-mongering" of the papal church. "Without faith in" Christ, wrote Luther in the *Commentarie vpon Galathians,* "neither shall the Jew be saved by the law, nor the Monke by his order, nor the Grecian by his wisdome, nor the Magistrate or Master by his upright government, nor the servant by his obedience." The authors of the anonymous preface for the English translation developed the point. No one will understand this "comfortable doctrine of faith and justification," they asserted, by means of learning or "human traditions": "except the Spirit of God from above do reveale it, learning cannot reach it, wisdome is offended." Yet this doctrine is said to be the key to Truth in all times and circumstances: "The ignorance whereof is the roote of all errours, sects and divisions, not onely in all Christendome, but also in the whole world." This seems sadly simplistic when we consider it along with the optimism about the rise of the sects that informs Milton's *Areopagitica,* itself a young man's idealistic utterance. The sentence that follows in the preface to Luther's *Commentarie* announces, however, the principle that Milton would seek to apply anew in *Paradise Regained*: "The Iew thinketh to be saved by his *Moses* Lavv, the Turke by his Alcoran, the Philosopher by his morrall vertues."[24]

It was just the discovery of a general principle in the Pauline teaching about Jewish Law that represents the most powerful adaptation of the biblical tradition in the period of the Renaissance and Reformation. Luther's reform rested on his reading of Paul's letters as containing a general principle about legalism. In Galatians and Romans, Paul had devised a theory for making sense of the fact that the Gentiles, not the Jewish people chosen of old, were accepting Jesus as Messiah: the works of the Law count for nothing, and "he is a Jew, which is one inwardly" (Rom. 2: 29). For Luther and those in the reformed tradition, this became a timeless truth about the perniciousness of "works-righteousness," to be applied analogously in every culture. This generalization, more Greek than strictly biblical (although it was said to be found "in the Bible only"), did not entail a thorough condemnation of classical learning. It made it possible to see learning, however, as a potential temptation. Luther did not hesitate to pay tribute to the accomplishments of "many notable" Gentiles of the ancient world, including Xenophon and Cicero, whose learning, virtue, and good government were deemed utterly necessary to the preservation of order in their "common-weales."[25] Insofar as intellectual efforts might be supposed a means to the recovery of prelapsarian innocence, however, both the efforts and their fruits were to be resisted.

Timely as the Epistles to the Galatians and Romans had been in the sixteenth century for effecting a disengagement from "merit-mongering," the First Epistle to the Corinthians, read in light of Galatians and Romans, seemed a biblical message newly addressed to the learned in the Renaissance. To the recorder of temptations resisted "in secret" and "unrecorded left through many an Age," the temptation of learning seemed "Worthy t' have not remain'd so long unsung." The Pauline condemnation of the wisdom of the world, understood now as a function of the doctrine of justification by faith alone, was the principal biblical source for the temptation of classical learning in *Paradise Regained*. It also provided a powerful principle governing Milton's selection and arrangement of biblical places in his reconfiguration of the biblical story.

When Satan offers Athens to the Son of God, then, he offers the possibility of accepting a worldly wisdom that defines spiritual experience wholly in philosophic and aesthetic terms. Milton's hero resists this temptation on two related grounds: first, that the empire of the mind is not the spiritual kingdom which he is to initiate, and secondly, that it is not a means to bring that kingdom about. In the context of the debate with Satan about the means of achieving God's Kingdom, the lines in which the Son asserts that one "who receives / Light from above . . . / No other doctrine needs" (IV, 288–90) are not likely to have been the least masochistic or to have caused Milton to "rend some main roots of his being." The "living Oracle" (I, 460) is made simply to proclaim an utter discontinuity between a religious and an aesthetic understanding of spiritual experience in accord with the canons of biblical monotheism. These canons do not include, however, a notion of infused knowledge. When the Son makes his comments about one

> who reads
> Incessantly, and to his reading brings not
> A spirit and judgment equal or superior,
> (And what he brings, what needs he elsewhere seek)
> Uncertain and unsettl'd still remains,
> Deep verst in books and shallow in himself,   (IV, 322–27)

he is concluding his reflections on pagan literature and making a transition to talking about the "delight" to be found in literature written in his "native Language," his mother tongue.

The writing of the poem represents a fourth major accommodation of the biblical to the classical tradition. Employing the language and art of his own culture, which had drawn a good deal from both traditions, Milton reimagines Jesus as he appears in the Synoptic gospels in the light of data available from other parts of the Bible, especially from Paul. He fashions a hero whom he does not call by the Greek title, "Christ," but by the Hebrew title, "Messiah," and by the biblical English title, "Son of God." This hero is emphatically not the Logos of philosophical speculation. He is, however, a composite being, at once the product of a common Renaissance desire to effect a synthesis of all knowledge and Miltonic challenge to that desire. In him are combined Jesus as he appears in the Synoptic narratives, with their distinctive sense of history and their claim to an unique revelation, and the universal "Son of God," rendered present and timely by the imagination of the poet.

Accommodating potentially contradictory facets of the biblical and classical traditions to one another, *Paradise Regained* illustrates, then, Milton's mature sense of the "experimentally" read Bible as a storehouse of places for gathering and framing. The workings of the poem embody the multiplying of "talents," understood both as the rudiments out of which a reader newly constructs the authentic Scriptures and as the natural, God-given abilities that the reader uses to do so. Ultimately, therefore, the accomplishment of *Paradise Regained* lies in the model that it offers when it constructs a symbiotic relationship between the process of conferring places and the product that results from and embodies that process. In this way the poem demonstrates that a commitment to "the Bible only" not only does not preclude producing one's own work but requires and inspires it.

Tragedy in the Story of Samson

In view of the numerous constraints that *Paradise Regained* places upon the accommodation of biblical literature to the classical tradition, perhaps it is unremarkable that so much energy should have been expended to keep the story of Samson from being understood as a tragedy. Until recently the dominant ways of reading *Samson Agonistes* have denied fully tragic force to the drama by urging typological parallels between Samson and Christ or by insisting that the hero achieves spiritual regeneration. But as Stanley Fish pointed out some years ago, even if it could be established that Samson recovers from the sinful state into which he has fallen, the poem does not demonstrate a necessary connection between the hero's spiritual recovery and the return of his physical strength.[26] Moreover, as Fish has argued more recently, Milton wrote *Samson Agonistes* in ways that highlight the ambiguity of Samson's story, which remains radically indeterminate, try as characters in the poem and readers of the poem may to fix its meaning. To Fish's demonstration that Milton left important gaps in the story and showed how unwilling various characters were to acknowledge this, it should be added that the Bible itself, as Milton had come to read it, had already rendered the interpretation of Samson acutely difficult. In fact, it was the intractable ambiguity in the biblical records that made the story of Samson especially apt for treatment as a tragedy in terms developed and perfected in the classical tradition.

Set in an early period of Israelite history, long before the emergence of the perspectives on Law developed by the high prophets, *Samson Agonistes* deserves to be recognized as unusually ambiguous among Milton's poems. The story of Samson had, in fact, become increasingly controversial in seventeenth-century England, and it was being interpreted in strikingly diverse ways.[27] Milton's poem does not constitute an intervention aimed at bolstering one or other side in debates about whether Samson was saved or damned. Rather it highlights a theme of secrecy that was already present in the Book of Judges and reinvigorates that theme by replicating the indeterminacies in the biblical record. Moreover, in ways reminiscent of *Hamlet* Milton's tragedy posits a large and possibly unbridgeable gap between the inward experience of the hero and the language available for expressing what that experience consists in. This stylistic feature is especially apparent in the persistent imagery of enclosure, confinement, and separation (exaggerating the fact that Samson is after all a Nazarite, "separate" to God) and above all in the large scope that the poet gives to the motif of secrecy.[28] The fact that the isolated hero struggles to understand his own story serves to define one important sense in which Samson is "agonistes," a wrestler with God and God's Word in the tradition of his eponymous ancestor "Israel."

While there has been wide appreciation that in matters of style and especially of versification *Samson* is unusual, its discontinuities from the rest of Milton's corpus have been obscured by attempts to find in it Milton's final testament or the culmination of his poetic development. Moreover, for more than a generation now critics have often sought to disambiguate the poem by proposing that the system of biblical symbolism known as typology provides a key to interpreting it. Biblical typology theoretically makes room for contrasts and even for the possibility of significant discontinuities. The famous Pauline passage to which the opening lines of *Paradise Regained* allude, where Adam is presented as a "type" of Christ, culminates in a startling denial of likeness even as its grammar seems to be working in an opposite direction. The language of the Authorized Version aptly reflects Paul's Greek (and the Vulgate, as well) when it points simultaneously to continuity and almost utter discontinuity between the two dispensations: "But not as the offence, so also *is* the free gift" (Rom. 5: 15). Nonetheless, in practice, those who read typologically tend to call attention to continuity and to see in Milton's Samson a *homo victor* who complements the *Christus victor* of the companion poem.[29]

Far from settling the matter, the invocation of typology raises large questions. Milton's volume of 1671 calls attention to problems inherent in thinking typologically even as it invites typological interpretations. On the one hand, the arrangement of the poems places first a story that is set more than a thousand years *after* the story that is made to follow it. On the other hand, while the title page says that *Samson Agonistes* has been "added," perhaps suggesting that it thus fills out an otherwise fairly slim volume, the poem with the earlier setting may be seen to occupy a climactic position. Its story of the death of Samson stands in the place where, had Milton given a whole volume of the same size to the life of Christ, the story of the Crucifixion would have occurred.[30] The placement of *Samson Agonistes* out of chronological order should make it more difficult for readers to suppose that the emergence of an antitype closes a narrative and fixes the meaning of the antecedent type.

It was fateful for the history of interpreting the narrative of Samson's life, however, that when the doctrine of double predestination was made prominent in early Protestantism, readers were able, by making even a casual comparison of biblical places, to notice that the figure from the Book of Judges is enrolled among the heroes of faith named in the Epistle to the Hebrews (11: 32). In the seventeenth century, the eleventh chapter of Hebrews proved a rich source of narrative possibilities. It offered Milton a roll of faithful heroes for inclusion in Michael's revelation of the future at the end of *Paradise Lost*, and it provided Bunyan with the leading metaphors for his account of the progress of pilgrims towards the "world to come."[31] Although Milton dissented in several important respects from the experimental predestinarian model that informed the writings of many of his contemporaries, including Bunyan, he had enough in common with predestinarians that in his major poems he engaged their presuppositions and often pointed up what was most problematic about their thinking. Attempts to see in Milton's Samson an "honorary puritan saint" whose experience conforms to "the Protestant paradigm of salvation" obscure the degree to which *Samson Agonistes* works against, as well as with, the ideas that all of humanity is divided into two eternally distinguishable groups and that the truly elect need to find in the Bible a basis for assurance of their calling and election.[32] In this respect it is of interest that at the time in which Samson lived, little of the Bible had been written, and many of the events which the Bible records had not yet occurred. Or, as the author of Hebrews goes on to say in the passage about the heroes of faith, from Abel to Moses and on down through Samson and David, "And these all, having obtained a good report through faith, received not the promise: God having provided some better thing for us, that they without us should not be made perfect" (11: 39–40). From this perspective, the "good reports" that accumulate at the close of *Samson Agonistes* are all partial and unfinished, at once open to and in need of completion.

Samson and the Parable of the Talents

If Hebrews 11: 32 cannot provide a stabilizing perspective from which to interpret the story of Samson, neither can the parable of the talents, which is often invoked as if it has explanatory power with respect to *Samson Agonistes*.[33] The word "talent" does not appear anywhere in the tragedy, and Milton was sufficiently scrupulous about what his preface calls "verisimilitude and decorum" so as not overtly to intrude into the knowledge of his characters an awareness of biblical events and concepts that emerged after the period of the Judges. When Manoa seeks, for instance, to "ransom" his son, neither he nor any other character has knowledge that this concept will come, more than a millennium later, to serve St. Paul as a principal metaphor for presenting his understanding of what God has done in Christ. In many instances besides Manoa's use of the phrase "thy Fathers house" the language of the poem anticipates that of English Bible passages created long after the period in which the story is ostensibly set. Mary Ann Radzinowicz has shown that *Samson* is filled with references to certain features of the Psalms, such as an intense desire for justice. Given the idea that the Psalms were the work of David, who lived near the end of the period of Philistine domination, it may be appreciated that the "psalmic texture" of the poem is an especially subtle aspect of Milton's concern with verisimilitude. "Milton's keen sense of historical and cultural evolution is evident here," Hugh MacCallum points out, "for he implies that the experience of the servants of God in the early books of scripture lies behind the psalmist's treatment of the human condition," so that "the play suggests the historical growth of religious consciousness."[34] Some especially difficult questions arise, however, when readers in a position to know that history seek to use later scriptural materials to understand the earlier stories.

The messy interpretive questions began to emerge, therefore, already in the era when the later books of the Bible were being written. They became messier through the course of centuries of exegetical activity. In the time of Samson, as MacCallum has helpfully observed, the Law was kept in the ark, written texts were largely unknown, and people relied chiefly on memory and tradition to mediate their religious and historical consciousness. Often their memory and sense of tradition were highly selective and narrowly trained on features of Israel's previous experience, especially their election, that from an ampler biblical and human perspective seem crudely ethnocentric. The fact that, in addition to memory and tradition, some extraordinary individuals called "judges" were said to have more direct access to "the Spirit of the LORD" in no way seems to have threatened this tendency to think that the Israelites were uniquely favored by God, and that the Gentiles were, quite simply, God's enemies. The parable of the talents proved newly attractive to Milton and others in the seventeenth century, when criteria for understanding the nature and implications of "election" had become the object of considerable debate. The author of the parable, whether Jesus or Matthew, or some anonymous early Christian(s), had used it to reinterpret the story of Israel's election and vocation. By the sixteenth and seventeenth centuries, when biblical places had been quite thoroughly dislodged from the context of a world in which literal master-slave relationships were common and from debates about the relative places of Jews and Gentiles in God's plan, the parable was characteristically redeployed as an authoritative text about "callings." Luke's version of the parable, in which all participants received an equal number of pounds, was commonly taken as a parable concerning the general calling, Matthew's version as a parable about the responsibilities attendant upon particular callings.

Already in the sixteenth century the potential for aligning the story of Samson and the parable of the talents had been clear in the Geneva Bible, where marginal comments explicitly ascribed Samson's enslavement to his having neglected his "vocacion." In *A Treatise of Callings,* Perkins interpreted "Sampson's strength" as a mark of his "extraordinary calling" and proposed that he lost his strength "because hee went out of his calling." From this perspective it was only a short step to see Samson's final act as evidence that he had returned to his calling, which then helped to explain how he had come to be numbered in the Epistle to the Hebrews among the heroes of faith. It is scarcely possible to suppose that Milton drew upon this line of interpretation in uncontroversial ways. His concern with "verisimilitude" required him to consider that, in the period of the Judges, the coming of Christ was more than a millennium away and that Israel had not yet been instructed by prophets predicting a New Dispensation. Nor had the Israelites heard of the Isaian "suffering servant."[35] Still, they were manifestly in need of a deliverer. It was knowledge of the whole of biblical literature that enabled Milton to prompt readers to consider the history of the concept of "deliverance." In the New Testament "deliverance" was redefined in ways that were largely discontinuous with what the early Israelites seem to have understood by the concept.

Samson could not know the parable of the talents or be able, like the figure at the start of "When I consider . . . ," to think of himself explicitly in its terms. Yet, as Guillory has shown in detail, Milton's Samson is unmistakably like the unprofitable servant who thinks of his master's demands on him as a strict rational calculus, in the light of which he stands condemned. Samson thinks of his body, the locus of his strength, as prematurely "buried" (101). He even recognizes that his punishment has been tailored to the consciousness he has created for himself:

> O indignity, O blot
> To Honour and Religion! servil mind
> Rewarded well with servil punishment!
> The base degree to which I now am fall'n,
> These rags, this grinding, is not yet so base
> As was my former servitude, ignoble,
> Unmanly, ignominious, infamous,
> True slavery, and that blindness worse then this,
> That saw not how degenerately I serv'd.   (411–19)

In the course of the poem, particularly during the exchange with Harapha, Samson does seem to recover the sense that he remains potentially "useful." He continues, however, to think of his utility in political and military terms, in accord with his habitual interpretation of the oral calling by which it was predicted that he would "begin Israel's deliverance." When he finally acts to pull down the temple, so far as one can tell from the text of Milton's poem, he persists in thinking in these political terms. In this respect Samson is quite different from the figure who at the end of the companion poem is urged to "begin to save mankind." The Son of God in *Paradise Regained* resists political power and repeatedly seeks to avoid being understood as a political messiah. For just this reason readers of Milton's poems have sometimes felt that Samson is "unchristian," even when they have found ways to evade puzzling over the evident fact that his final act, although perhaps meant to liberate his people from unjust oppressors, involves wholesale slaughter and destruction.

For readers eager to see in Samson a type of the Deliverer, the parable would seem to support a regenerationist reading. Samson is convinced that he was "Heav'n-gifted" with "glorious strength" (36) and that it was by God's "special favour" that he has been designated Israel's "Deliverer" (273–74). The Chorus and Samson's father concur in this interpretation, the Chorus unwittingly speaking in biblical language that had been newly inflected in classic Protestant soteriology: God has "solemnly elected" Samson "With gifts and graces" for the sake of "some great work" (678–80). Samson, having lost the gift of strength, tends to assume that he will never fulfill the role "prescrib'd" (30) for him from his mother's womb. In seventeenth-century terms, his plight seems to show that he has had a merely temporary faith. Samson's consciousness that he nonetheless remains accountable for his extraordinary "gift of strength" suggests that he is inclined to think of himself as a person whose life-narrative has effectively ended before the death of his body. Having been blinded, "exil'd from light" (98) and cast into "real darkness" (159), figuratively "Buried" (103), he himself poses what those familiar with the parable of the talents might suppose to be the key question:

> To what can I be useful, wherein serve
> My Nation, and the work from Heav'n impos'd . . . ?   (564–65)

While Samson fears that at best he is condemned now to "sit idle" and prove a "burdenous drone" (566–67), his father, thinking more literally about Samson's work, urges him not to serve the Philistines but to sit home "idle" and "unimploy'd" (579–80). Later, however, even before hearing of his son's end, Manoa speaks in terms that would encourage us to think that his son will fulfill the injunctions about working in one's vocation that in the seventeenth century were commonly associated with the doctrine of the calling: God's "purpose" is surely "To use him further yet in some great service, / Not to sit idle with so great a gift / Useless" (1498–1501). At the close of the drama then Manoa produces a flattering interpretation of Samson's story, at once ruling out the dread hypothesis of temporary faith and transforming his son's life-narrative into a success story.

Samson Agonistes can be related then to two contexts that have been shown in Chapter One to have been closely tied to one another in the English seventeenth century: life-narratives, in which the parable of the talents was sometimes invoked as a master-text in relation to which a person such as M. K. might plot the course of her life, and the doctrine of callings, of which Weber made so much in his classic study of "the Protestant ethic." Guillory has shown some ways in which *Samson Agonistes* brings these two contexts together. Yet for all his patient tracing of the history of the concept of "vocation," it is notable that in his eagerness to make *Samson Agonistes* into a parable of a decisive historical "moment" in the early modern transition to capitalism, he omits to consider several ways in which the subterranean workings of the parable of the talents are complicated by its interaction with other biblical subtexts in Milton's poem.

Guillory puts his discussion of the parable at the service of a claim that Milton's narrative is "determined by a contradiction between the demands emanating from the poem's two fathers," Manoa and God. In his view, the "psychic economy" of Milton's poem ultimately negotiates a way between two sets of contradictory paternal demands. Samson is said to have satisfied God by fulfilling the parable of the talents, which the poem has set into a "contest" with the parable of the laborers in the vineyard (Matt. 20: 1–16). Both parables, Guillory maintains, depict "the relation between God and man as that of a master-employer to a servant-employee" (p. 158).

If these parables posit a model of the relations between God and humankind that draws on the experiences of servants with their master, it is worth noting that both parables tend, nonetheless, to subvert the ways of thinking about God that have to do with satisfying His demands. (In the parable of the talents the only figure who fails is the one who thinks of his benefactor as a demanding master.) In fact, readers of Milton's *Samson* cannot invoke the parable of the talents in isolation from the fact that New Testament writers repeatedly contrast the servants-master model with another that derives from experiences of children with a loving parent. We are, St. Paul urges in several places and at length in the eighth chapter of Romans, not servants or slaves living under bondage but "joint-heirs with Christ." To think of God as one who makes demands is to reveal one's lack of understanding of a radically new "dispensation," in which God's unconditional love precedes all human efforts and renders them superfluous. This is powerfully illustrated in the parable of the prodigal son, a story that points up the limited generosity of the older brother and yet leaves open the possibility that he too will enter the father's banquet. By a similar token the parable of the laborers in the vineyard exposes the niggardliness of those who resent equal pay for the belated.

In *Samson Agonistes,* it remains unclear whether Samson ever "satisfies" God, and in any event God is never thought by any of the characters to be Samson's "father." The play of the phrase "Father's house" points a sharp contrast between the mode of thinking available to Manoa and the Chorus and even Samson himself and another "dispensation" altogether. There are suggestions, as Guillory elsewhere notes without allowing for the critique of his argument thus set in motion, that Samson experiences "release" from a "calculus of economic rationality" (p. 171) and readers glimpse, though quite imperfectly, "an image of the abolition of all structural domination" (p. 167). Valuable as Guillory's study is for reminding us of later sedimentations in the history of the concepts of "talent" and of "vocation," it blurs the ways in which this New Testament perspective poses a radical challenge to a work-centered consciousness. As a story promising lasting joys to those who trust that their relations with God cannot be understood according to a rational calculus, Jesus' parable stands as a powerful reinterpretation of the terms that had previously been available for telling the story of Samson's "election." The parable also stands as a potential challenge to the values that materialist and psychoanalytic approaches ascribe to "work."

There remains a curious incompatibility between *Samson Agonistes* and the parable of the talents. It arises out of the unprecedented insistence that runs through Milton's poem that, in addition to his Nazarite vow, Samson was obliged to keep a vow of silence. In Chapter Three it has been shown that in the exegetical tradition the principal violation against the lessons of the parable of the talents was said precisely to be keeping silent about God's gifts. Near the end of the parable of the talents, it will be recalled, there emerges from the mind of the servant who has buried his talent a particularly harsh image of the master, who then pronounces, as if to confirm the condemned man's worst surmise, a shocking punishment: "Take therefore the talent from him, and give *it* unto him which hath ten talents." The narrator then raises this conclusion to a general principle, and it bears an uncanny resemblance to one of the most unjust tendencies of ancient economies as well as modern: "For unto every one that hath shall be given, and he shall have abundance: but from him that hath not shall be taken away even that which he hath" (Matt. 25: 28–29).

By an exegetical conference of places this general principle proves potentially relevant to interpreting *Samson Agonistes*. When it appears in the parable of the talents, this verse repeats a verse that had appeared earlier in Matthew's gospel, in the chapter where Jesus speaks of entrusting his disciples with "the mysteries of the kingdom of heaven" (13: 11) and where he delivers the saying about the "householder, which bringeth forth out of his treasure *things* old and new" (13: 52). It is also the chapter in which Jesus compares the kingdom to "hidden treasure," in which he tells the parable of the sower, and in which he is made to explain why he teaches in parables. In the course of explaining why some hearers understand his teaching and others do not, Jesus pronounces the principle whereby "whosoever hath, to him shall be given," whereas "whosoever hath not, from him shall be taken away even that he hath" (13: 12). The reappearance of this verse in the parable of the talents links that parable, where the offending figure hides his talent, with Jesus' earlier explanation that he teaches in parables in order to "utter things which have been kept secret from the foundation of the world" (13: 35). In seventeenth-century England these places had been conferred in order to interpret what it means to bury a talent. The unprofitable servant was said to have been hoarding the secrets of the kingdom, and his behavior was sometimes interpreted as failing to develop an "experimental knowledge" of the revelation God had entrusted to him.[36] Milton, for his part, seeking in *De Doctrina Christiana* to rule out a view of Predestination that abrogates human responsibility, twice considers "The famous quotation, *to him that has shall be given*" (*CPW*, VI, 187) and maintains that the punishment spelled out in this repeated biblical place applies to those who reject or neglect divine grace (200). In view of this concurrence with the common interpretation of hiding one's talent as failing to disseminate God's Word, it should seem particularly odd then that the parable of talents should be so frequently invoked to interpret *Samson Agonistes*, in which the hero is accused of having violated a "sacred trust of silence / Deposited within" him (428–29) when he "divulg'd the secret gift of God" (201).

Milton's own most extensive treatment of the parable, it will be recalled from Chapter Two, had appeared in *The Reason of Church Government*. In order to justify his intervention in the controversy over prelacy, Milton presents himself there, by virtue of his natural disposition and education, as a repository containing the knowledge of God and of God's true worship. He insists, by way of alluding to the parable, that he is obliged to speak up. To this end he exploits the financial metaphor lodged in the history of the word, to insist that "talents" must be put into trade. He associates himself with God's "dispensers of treasure inestimable without price" when he urges that in the current circumstances one "entrusted" with a knowledge of the Scriptures,

> remembring also that God even to a strictnesse requires the improvment of these his entrusted gifts, cannot but sustain a sorer burden of mind, and more pressing then any supportable toil, or waight, which the body can labour under; how and in what manner he shall dispose and employ those summes of knowledge and illumination, which God hath sent him into this world to trade with. (*CPW*, I, 801)

Milton goes on to insist that the "burden" of "divine inspiration" requires him to speak up, since "when God commands . . . , it lies not in mans will what he shall say, or what he shall conceal"; he instances Jeremiah as one who had to overcome a tendency to "silence" born of fear of daily "reproach and derision" (803). By contrast with the prelates, who are hoarders, "striv[ing] to keep to themselves to their great pleasure and commodity those things which they ought to render up," he wishes to make a "contribution of those few talents which God" has "lent" him (804). For it is by sharing his "knowledge and illumination" that he expects "to store up to [him] self the good provision of peacefull hours" (806) and "to lay up . . . the best treasure, and solace of a good old age," defined here as the memory of having used "the honest liberty of free speech from [his] youth" (804). The thrust of the argument runs clean contrary to the idea that anyone who has been given a talent might fail to bring it into a public forum.

In *Samson Agonistes*, the hero bears no such burden of publicly interpreting the best and sagest things. On the contrary, Samson thinks that to have "divulg'd" his "capital secret" was a heinous sin and regrets the "publishing" of that secret, by Dalila, as the source of his lasting humiliation. He loathes himself as a foolish "blab." When Dalila seeks reconciliation, offering to nurse him with "redoubl'd love and care" (923), he pronounces a sort of decree of divorce, based on the fact that she has been and would continue to be a bearer of his words to those unwilling to interpret him sympathetically:

> again [thou wouldst] betray me,
> Bearing my words and doing to the Lords
> To gloss upon, and censuring, frown or smile.   (946–48)

Nonetheless, once his "capital secret" has been "published," Samson makes no attempt to suppress its further dissemination. He even declares quite openly to Harapha that

> My trust is in the living God who gave me
> At my Nativity this strength, diffus'd
> No less through all my sinews, joints and bones,
> Then thine, while I preserv'd these locks unshorn,
> The pledge of my unviolated vow. (1140–44)

In view of the ending of Samson's story, however, this declaration may be much more evasive than it first seems. Samson had been thinking that, having sinned, he has written himself out of the destiny which God had planned for him. At the time he meets Harapha, whether or not he has fully recovered a sense of his potential usefulness, he is certainly content to let his adversary see that he thinks his story is effectively over. When he goes off to the Dagonalia with the Public Officer, however, he has a new secret which he is keeping to himself, only to reveal it at what he now considers the proper time.

Jesus, Samson, and Secrecy

Milton's subtle infusion of a sense of the proper time into his redaction provides a significant point of contact between *Samson Agonistes* and its companion poem, in which *kairos* is so important a theme.[37] Samson's overwhelming sense of his vulnerability, his fear of being misinterpreted and of proving a "scandal" to "feeble hearts" (453–55) all connect him to Jesus in the gospels in a way that, so far as I know, has not been much contemplated by those writing about Milton's poetry. From the first chapter of Mark's gospel, when Jesus cures a leper and commands him to "say nothing to any man" and yet the man proceeds to "publish it much, and blaze abroad the matter," there is an increasing sense that a secret is erupting and escaping control and Jesus keeps telling everyone from the devils and the lepers to his own disciples not to reveal his miracles or identity. Mark later reports that when Jesus healed a man who is deaf and dumb, "he charged" those who witnessed the healing "that they should tell no man: but the more he charged them, so much the more a great deal they published *it*" (7: 36). This motif of secrecy provided the Synoptic evangelists with a powerful means of organizing the materials about Jesus' life and teaching. In the gospels of Matthew and Mark, it receives considerable play in the places that explain why Jesus teaches in parables, and it serves as a structuring device to help account for how the messiah could have been unrecognized and even put to death.

The Greek word *parabola*, rendered "parable" in the Authorized Version, could be translated as "comparison" or "analogy." It was the term regularly used to render the Hebrew *mashal* ("dark saying" or "riddle"). Occasionally it was used as a translation for *hidah* ("riddle"), which is the word that appears in the episodes about Samson in Judges. The famous biblical places in which Jesus is made to explain his reason for speaking in parables are themselves notoriously cryptic. As Mark uses the motif of secrecy most extensively and it is now thought that Mark's is the earliest of the canonical gospels, it makes sense to quote his version of the saying. In his gospel (4: 11–12), the explanation is occasioned by the disciples' request that Jesus explain the parable of the sower, and it includes a quotation from the prophet Isaiah:

> And he said unto them, Unto you it is given to know the mystery of the kingdom of God: but unto them that are without, all *these* things are done in parables: That [Greek: *hina*] seeing they may see, and not perceive; and hearing they may hear, and not understand; lest at any time they should be converted, and *their* sins be forgiven them.

So shocking is the possible implication here that the teacher may perversely desire that most of his students fail that it seems that Matthew, writing after Mark, altered the whole line of reasoning. Where Mark's Greek has Jesus teaching in parables in order to (*hina*) exclude outsiders, Matthew's has Jesus teaching in parables because (*hoti*) his auditors have only low capacities and he wishes to accommodate them (13: 13).

Some years ago this pair of passages served Frank Kermode as the starting point for a whole theory about the property of secrecy not only in the gospels but in narratives generally. Kermode proposed that interpreters are so in need of a hypothesis of secrecy, so committed to the priority of the latent sense over the literal, and so invested in being able to produce original interpretations, that "finally all stories are *hina* stories," inevitably interpreted as if they were meant to be obscure, "even the story that they are all *hoti*."[38] Kermode went on to remark that there was nothing new about his theory. Calvin, for instance, was quite ready to agree "with Mark that the divine author made his stories obscure in order to prevent the reprobate from understanding them." Consulting seventeenth-century commentaries tends to confirm Kermode's point.[39]

Seventeenth-century commentary on the saying about parables was of course not monolithic. Some commentators pointed out that, instead of closing questions, the saying did what the parables do: it provided a "spur or preparation" for readers who would respond to obscurity with a genuine curiosity to find out God's secrets.[40] Henry Hammond related the secrecy of the parables to "the secret manner of Gods dispensing of his grace" and pointed out that, while "parables are a way of obscuring doctrine to the careless," they also "have a special energy in them" that sets the "diligent" hearer to work. His comment on Jesus' saying that "there is nothing covered, that shall not be revealed; and hid, that shall not be known" emphasized that parables motivate "industrious" searching and a desire to share one's findings. He paraphrased Jesus precisely as requiring his disciples to "publish" the results of their "industrious" quest:

> For the doctrine which is taught you by me in, or out of parables, must be both practiced and published by you, and therefore (for no other reason) it is revealed to you, and that by way of parables, which are the obscuring of it, that having acquired the understanding of them you may set the more value on them for your own practice, and be more industrious to communicate them to others.[41]

For those committed to the doctrine whereby saving faith consisted in an explicit knowledge of Christ and of the Word of God, the fact that the gospels frequently report that Jesus forbade "publication" of his identity was especially troubling. The most notorious instance was Jesus' response to Peter's declaration, "Thou art the Christ, the Son of the living God": as Matthew has it, "Then charged he his disciples that they should tell no man that he was Jesus the Christ" (16: 13–20).

It was not until the end of the nineteenth century that interpreters developed a full-blown hypothesis about the implications of the motif of secrecy for the entire gospel narrative. Wilhelm Wrede proposed that Jesus had never claimed to be the messiah but that after his death the disciples invented the idea and read it back into his life, using the idea of secrecy to cover their tracks.[42] Long before Wrede, however, Bible-readers were having to reckon with this puzzling secrecy motif. In seventeenth-century England there was a large body of commentary on the many passages in which Jesus commanded concealment. This commentary regularly referred to the problems created by Jesus' repeated commands not to "divulge" or "publish" his miracles and identity. For experimentalists, in particular, the problems were not merely exegetical. Remarking on the difference between the injunction recorded in Matthew 16: 20 ("Then charged he his disciples that they should tell no man that he was Jesus the Christ") and the injunctions given elsewhere in the gospels "to those whom he had miraculously Cured," one group of commentators admitted that they were simply "not able to give an account" of how Jesus could have forbidden "Preaching . . . a Doctrine necessary to be believed, in order to Peoples Salvation." Yet they went on to propose five possible reasons for Jesus having so often forbidden the publishing abroad of his miracles and messiahship. The list is worth citing for its relevance to understanding the use of the secrecy motif in Milton's retelling of the tale of Samson, where he assimilated the stories of two riddlers whose secret identities put them both in physical danger.

The commentators express certainty that the injunction against publication was "but of a Temporary Force and Obligation" and at the same time acknowledge that they "cannot certainly determine" why Jesus even temporarily forbade his disciples to "publish" his messiahship. These are the enumerated possibilities:

> 1. Because they were not yet fit to publish so great a Truth. Or, 2. Because the time was not yet come, for the Publication of it. Or, 3. He would not have it published, till he rose again from the dead, having Triumphed over Death, lest People hearing of it before, should have had their Faith shaken by his Death; which seemeth very probable, because in the next Words, he begins to speak of Death. Or, 4. That he might hereby (as much as might be) avoid the *Odium* and *Envy* of the Pharisees. Or, 5. That himself might publish first this great truth of the Gospel, and confirm it by his Miracles.[43]

Since this commentary was meant to gather up and distill various interpretations, there is nothing surprising about the fact that all these possibilities can be found in other commentaries (not all possibilities in all commentaries). All five explanations, *mutatis mutandi,* might have been invoked by someone attempting to make sense of a near obsession with secrecy on the part of Milton's Samson. In *De Doctrina Christiana,* Milton himself cited a verse in which Jesus "*forbade his disciples to tell anyone that he was Jesus, the Christ*" as an illustration of "profession of one's faith at the wrong time" (*CPW,* VI, 702), precisely in the context of enumerating actions that are opposed to true martyrdom. What is most striking with reference to the language of *Samson Agonistes,* however, is the recurrence

Keeping Secrets, Telling Secrets   177

through the whole body of seventeenth-century exegesis of the same terms "divulge" and "publish" which Jesus used to refer to the forbidden activities.[44] One feature of the commentary by Hammond is of particular interest for the way in which it establishes a network of biblical terms and references that also organizes Milton's companion poems of 1671. Commenting on the fact that, after the Transfiguration, Jesus forbade the disciples to "publish" the "clear testimony by *a voice from heaven, This is my beloved Son,*" Hammond remarks that the Apostles "had store" of various "evidences" of Jesus' messianic identity, which "should be reserved and not yet publish'd, till after his death and ressurection." Hammond goes on to propose that the parable of the talents (he cites Luke's version, chap. 19) provides a model of proper timing: there only after a long delay does the King "proceed . . . to execution against his enemies," as Christ first retreated to heaven before the gospels were disseminated. In Hammond's view, the publication of Christ's true identity had to be delayed until after his death, resurrection, and ascension, in order to strike the crowning blow against "his enemies."[45] For all the verbal parallels and suggestive analogies, however, neither the body of seventeenth-century exegesis nor Milton's own writing provides a control that fixes or stabilizes the workings of the allusions to New Testament literature in *Samson Agonistes*.

Glimpsing New Possibilities

More than the workings of subtle allusions and alleged typological parallels, what renders *Samson Agonistes* similar to *Paradise Regained* is the writer's method of invention, Milton's way of coming upon the details of Samson's last day. In the brief epic the poet claims to have been able to discover (by comparing places) things that had been done "in secret" and had long remained "unrecorded." Much as he inferred, on the basis of Jesus' later confrontations with the Scribes and Pharisees and of Paul's condemnation of the wisdom of the world, that in the desert "all temptation" must have included a temptation of learning, similarly, on the basis of Samson's earlier experience on the day when the Spirit of God had "departed from him," Milton constructed for the last day of Samson's life a recapitulation of several key features of his previous experience. In this respect it is worth remembering that the etymology of Samson's name is "there the second time." For in handling the final episode in Samson's life Milton reinscribes ambiguities that his poem shows were present in an earlier episode: Samson's appearance at the Dagonalia, which culminates in his death, stands in relation to his capture and blinding as ambiguous antitype to ambiguous type.

When we notice that in Milton's redaction on the last day of Samson's life each of his four visitors comes with certain designs on him, and that he resists them, then it is possible also to see, as William Kerrigan has astutely suggested,[46] that Milton's Samson has the opportunity to replay the events of the day in his previous life that has been most fateful. Without pressing the parallel too closely, it is possible to take Samson's resistance to Manoa's plan for ransom, Dalila's attempt at reconciliation, and Harapha's prodding to despair as a recapitulation of the threefold resistance to Dalila's earlier pleas which Samson explicitly recalls early on in the drama:

> Thrice she assay'd with flattering prayers and sighs,
> And amorous reproaches to win from me
> My capital secret, in what part my strength
> Lay stor'd, in what part summ'd, that she might know:
> Thrice I deluded her, and turn'd to sport
> Her importunity, each time perceiving
> How openly, and with what impudence
> She purpos'd to betray me, and (which was worse
> Then undissembl'd hate) with what contempt
> She sought to make me Traytor to my self.   (392–401)

When the fourth visitor arrives, Samson has the opportunity to revise the previous error, which he made "the fourth time" (402) he was beseeched. Intent not to make the same mistake twice, Samson refuses to accompany the Officer to the feast, confiding his reasoning (he will not abuse his "Consecrated gift," "prostituting holy things to Idols," 1354–62) to the chorus only after the man has left. Then, extraordinarily, having felt "rouzing motions" (1382), he reverses himself, so that his going along with the officer looks as if it may be a reaffirmation of the fateful decision he had made, under pressure, to yield to Dalila. It may or may not be repetition with a difference.[47] Yet this time Samson seems to have worked out, in discussion with the chorus, a rational explanation and justification for his action:

> The *Philistian* Lords command.
> Commands are no constraints. If I obey them,

> I do it freely; venturing to displease
> God for the fear of Man, and Man prefer,
> Set God behind: which in his jealousie
> Shall never, unrepented, find forgiveness.
> Yet that he may dispense with me or thee
> Present in Temples at Idolatrous Rites
> For some important cause, thou needst not doubt. (1371–79)

It may be that here, when he speaks of preferring Man to God and of the need for repentance after sinning, Samson is differentiating between the situation he now finds himself in and the previous one, when he yielded to Dalila.[48] Yet it may also be that here, having had time to reflect and to consult with a body of sympathetic tribesmen, he is sinning more gravely still, acknowledging the ways in which God may work, but applying this divinity in a way that masks a secret determination to act in any event of his "own accord." While Milton has eschewed the use of a narrator's perspective of the sort that operates in *Paradise Lost* and *Paradise Regained,* the report by the messenger serves to open up the possibility that Samson's final action was *not* preceded by prayer: "with head a while enclin'd, / And eyes fast fixt he stood, as one who pray'd, / Or some great matter in his mind revolv'd" (1636–38). Then it leaves open the further possibility that he who is "there the second time" is again the "sole Author" of a still more heinous sin:

> Hitherto, Lords, what your commands impos'd
> I have perform'd, as reason was, obeying,
> Not without wonder or delight beheld.
> Now of my own accord such other tryal
> I mean to shew you of my strength, yet greater;
> As with amaze shall strike all who behold. (1640–45)

Samson's emphasis on what he does of his "own accord" does not necessarily preclude the possibility of divine inspiration and approbation. In context it sets up a contrast between the springs of his action and the "commands impos'd" by the Philistine Lords. Still, by having Samson himself make the claim that he feels "rouzing motions" within him, Milton's poem reproduces and intensifies, rather than eliminates, an ambiguity about the relation of Samson's deliberate action to divine inspiration that is already present in Judges. Samson experiences his "rouzing motions" privately, although he proclaims publicly that he has felt them. The "motions" themselves are non-verbal.

None of this means that Milton's intensification of the ambiguities already found in the Bible cannot be probed further and understood more adequately. There is at least one other way of thinking about the four-part verbal interaction between Samson and Dalila on the fateful day when the "fort of silence" was given over. It is clear to readers of the narrative in Judges that, especially in his captive state, Samson is an epitome of his people. What is more oblique, a kind of secret in the biblical text which Milton's poem has begun to tease out, is that Samson is at times also a figure of the Lord Himself. Such an interpretation is readily plausible with respect to the actions Samson performs in Judges, often by the prompting of the Spirit, against the enemies of his people and of the Lord of hosts, who is said to lead Israel in battle. Yet Milton, by stressing that Samson loved Dalila and that he had married her, also associates Samson with the Lord in a subtler way, and one which, if one compares various passages from the Hebrew Bible, helps to explain the connection that Milton's Samson makes between his betrayal by Dalila and his having subsequently become the Philistines' enemy.

In his exchange with Dalila, just after she has told Samson she had acted in order "glorious[ly] to entrap / A common enemy, who had destroy'd / Such numbers of our Nation" (855–57), Samson replies in tones that anticipate the prophetic literature, where the Lord will complain about Israel's idolatry under the figure of marital infidelity. When for instance the breaking of the Covenant is expounded by a parable in the sixteenth chapter of Ezekiel, the Lord will be quoted as telling Israel at length how He had chosen her and cared for her only to be betrayed by her: "thou didst trust in thine own beauty, and playedst the harlot because of thy renown, and pouredst out thy fornications on every one that passed by" (16: 15).[49] As if he is unknowingly anticipating the Lord's choice of Israel from among the nations, Samson reminds Dalila

> I before all the daughters of my Tribe
> And of my Nation chose thee from among
> My enemies, lov'd thee, as too well thou knew'st,
> Too well, unbosom'd all my secrets to thee,
> Not out of levity, but over-powr'd
> By thy request, who could deny thee nothing;
> Yet now am judg'd an enemy. (876–82)

The parallel between cuckolds ought not to be pressed, for Samson's language suggests particular hurts in the context of a unique relationship. Yet the biblical convention whereby the Lord's love for Israel is figured in marriage provides a basis for Milton's unprecedented portrayal of Samson and Dalila as married and the background of his making the revelation of Samson's secret a function more of his love than his foolishness. Milton's Samson tells his father that each time Dalila besought his secret, he "perceiv[ed] / How openly, and with what impudence / She purpos'd to betray" him (397–99). It was not so much that Dalila was tempting Samson, then, but that (as in the case of the Lord and Israel) he was trying her, trusting her even to the point of "unlock[ing] all [his] heart" (407) in hopes that she would prove worthy of his "Faith" and "love" (388). When Dalila subsequently became a bearer of his secrets to the Philistines, she proved herself, in language now widely acknowledged to be reminiscent of Milton's divorce tracts, an "unfit" wife. "No, no, of my condition take no care," Samson insists. "It fits not; thou and I long since are twain" (928–29). Samson's conviction may be reminiscent, for readers who know the whole Bible, of the decrees of "divorce" subsequently voiced by God against an unfaithful Israel.[50] Nonetheless, typological interpretation invites contemplation of discontinuities as well as similarities, and Samson cannot be said to be an innocent party.

At any rate, in the categories of the experimentalists, which echo obliquely in the words of the chorus, Dalila has had a merely temporary faith, seeming worthy for a time but "Discover'd in the end, till now conceal'd" (998). Whether Samson finally has a "saving faith" or only a temporary one is not answered by Milton's poem. It was no part of Milton's concern to settle this question, although other interpreters, both *of* Milton's poem and *in* it, have been less willing to rest content with the ambiguities inherent in the biblical data.

* * *

The argument of this and the preceding chapter entails a recognition that Milton's biblical poetry sometimes works by reapplying techniques used by the relatively belated biblical authors, and implies that Milton frequently enlisted these techniques to undermine a dogmatic cast of mind by prompting readers to reflect upon the historical limitations within which the biblical texts had come to be written. Milton himself had come to read the Bible as a divinely authorized collection of fragments. While he regularly attended to the context of any given biblical place within the book into which it had been inscribed, he understood that biblical places had been written down in various times and places by human "penmen" who had only a limited knowledge of the divine Author's larger design. He did not place above the Bible some faculty of reason which could operate independently of Scripture. Nor did he subscribe to notions, which were becoming increasingly available, whereby the Scriptures were to be left behind to follow an inward light. Rather, he continued to interpret the biblical texts, allowing that they have at least the priority of existing before though not apart from interpretive activity. The choice of biblical fables for *Paradise Lost, Paradise Regained,* and *Samson Agonistes* reveals an abiding disposition to keep working with a particular storehouse of provision.

The poems of 1671, in ways different from the prose works but complementary to their consistent pleas for freedom in interpretation, provide lessons in discovering and bearing the burdens of biblical interpretation. The placement of the two poems in an order that complicates the workings of typological symbolism not only invites a rethinking of the relations between the two testaments, but also requires discrimination about the ways in which materials from one part of the Bible may be brought to bear to discover things which have remained diffusely scattered and in that sense "unrecorded." In *Samson Agonistes,* as in *Paradise Regained,* Milton took the dispersal of materials through the various parts of the Bible as an invitation to enjoy the sorts of interpretive pleasures that accrue to a "gatherer," who by carefully combining place with place discovers things that had long seemed to have been "in secret done." In his retelling of Samson's story he drew upon the New Testament not so much to establish typological symbolism as to clarify the nature of the tragedy. With great discretion, and with care not to disturb "verisimilitude and decorum," he used that literature to clarify what he called in his preface the "œconomy, or disposition of the fable." In particular, the complex effects that the motif of secrecy had set in motion in the gospels provided a model with which to explore and evaluate Samson's habitual silence and secrecy. Seen in light of later biblical writers' treatment of the dynamics of secrecy and revelation, Samson's obsessive worry about having allowed the secret of his strength to be published abroad seems both warranted and unnecessary. His final action, including his death, seems at once a fulfillment of his predestined role and a precipitous and presumptuous fulfilling of it, his attempt to take decisive action proving to be both understandable and also tragically premature.

7. The Bookish Burden Before the Fall

> To ask or search I blame thee not, for Heav'n
> Is as the Book of God before thee set,
> Wherein to read his wondrous Works, and learne
> His Seasons, Hours, or Dayes, or Months, or Yeares:
> This to attain, whether Heav'n move or Earth,
> Imports not, if thou reck'n right, the rest
> From Man or Angel the great Architect
> Did wisely to conceal, and not divulge
> His secrets to be scann'd by them who ought
> Rather admire. . . .   —*Paradise Lost* VIII, 66–75

The attention to ambiguities that in conceiving *Paradise Regained* and *Samson Agonistes* Milton accorded to the Scriptures was not unprecedented in his reading and writing. Earlier chapters have shown that a fascination with "tangles" in biblical texts dates back to the mid-1640s. Having been accustomed in his early education to thinking that the plain words of the Bible provide the ultimate criterion for judgment in spiritual matters, in *Of Reformation* (1641) Milton proclaimed that the Scriptures "protest . . . their own plainnes, and perspicuity, calling to them to be instructed, not only the *wise*, and *learned*, but the *simple*, the *poor*, the *babes*, foretelling an extraordinary effusion of *Gods* Spirit upon every age, and sexe" (*CPW*, I, 566). Yet within a matter of months in *The Doctrine and Discipline of Divorce* (1643) he was proposing that most biblical places "must be read with limitations and distinctions to be rightly understood" (*CPW*, II, 338). Now he was urging that "the strictnes of a literall interpreting" leads to the "overburdning" and "sad oppression" of those specially in need of "considerate care" (242). He insisted, moreover, that interpretation is "no every daies work" (340). An interpreter requires not only "help" from God's "illuminating Spirit," but personal "diligence" and a charitable disposition in order to restore Scripture passages "to their native lustre and consent between each other." For ungenerous habits of interpretation have infected the word of God with "burdensom & remorsles obscurity, tangl'd with manifold repugnances" (340). *Tetrachordon* (1645) pointed out that even the first disciples were often so dull that Christ had the good sense to let his hard sayings continue to trouble them, as a way of gradually breaking through "the thick prejudice and tradition wherein they were" (679). In short, during the period from 1643 to 1645 Milton came to realize that the traditional Protestant insistence on the perspicuity of Scripture encouraged readers to think that unexamined interpretations were "clear" just because they were commonplace. He came to understand, moreover, that the doctrine of Scriptural "plainness" bestowed on merely habitual readings a presumption of accuracy and of timeless stability.

By some time in the 1650s, the new dispositions toward interpretation articulated in the divorce pamphlets and in *Areopagitica* had made thinkable and even necessary the compiling of a theological treatise that would display the fruits of a detailed conference of places. In the event, Milton wrote an introduction for the treatise that presents it as a Herculean labor of many years. Yet *De Doctrina Christiana* also testifies to its author's having passed into the phase of his career as an interpreter in which he acknowledged radical limits to what the conference of places can be made to turn up. The treatise does not always and everywhere demonstrate "the consent between each other" of the numerous scriptural places that it gathers. At many points the discussion is bounded by a principle whereby readers ought not to "pry . . . further" for meaning than the sacred texts warrant (*CPW*, VI, 421).[1] Milton took this to be the case especially in some matters for which the "analogy of faith" might have been invoked by others to fill in lacunae, to clear up ambiguities, to provide closure, or to establish certainty. His conviction that the biblical record does "not divulge" all God's "secrets" but needs to be read with a respect for its tangled obscurities and with a willingness to forbear drawing premature conclusions also had important implications for the writing of *Paradise Lost*.

Interpretation and the Tangles of Language

When Milton expanded the biblical narrative of the first parents into an epic poem, he placed great emphasis on the extent and degree to which Adam and Eve were involved in interpretive activities both before and after their Fall. Conspicuously, interpretation in *Paradise Lost* is a matter of their following the revelations mediated by Raphael and Michael. Yet virtually every episode in which Adam and Eve appear shows them performing some

The Bookish Burden Before the Fall   185

work of interpretation. Sometimes they interpret before our very eyes: Eve recounting her ominous dream and Adam attempting to reassure her; or later, the two of them debating Eve's proposal that they work separately, the better to accomplish the gardening tasks whereby they seek to interpret and fulfill the injunction to be fruitful and multiply.[2] At other times they are more reflexively conscious about, and they are more evidently able to take pleasure in, the twin facts that meanings unfold gradually and that new contexts make *re*interpretations possible: Eve rehearsing her experience at the "wat'ry" mirror in the context of recalling her first meeting with Adam, and Adam recounting for Raphael his conversation with God about the experience of loneliness. Beyond all this, the angelic narrators Raphael and Michael serve as interpreters as well. So does Milton's Satan.

After the Fall, interpretive activities become less playful and interpretive disagreements are for a time quite vituperative. This feature of the poem would seem wholly in keeping with an idea articulated in *Areopagitica*, that a principal effect of the Fall was the introduction into human experience of a massive interpretive burden on the order of Psyche's "incessant labour" sorting through many kinds of small seeds.[3] The passage has been invoked especially by readers who wish to see the discontinuities between fallen and unfallen experience in *Paradise Lost*. I cite it because its supposed relevance to interpreting Milton's epic needs thoroughly to be rethought:

> Good and evil we know in the field of this World grow up together almost inseparably; and the knowledge of good is so involv'd and interwoven with the knowledge of evil, and in so many cunning resemblances hardly to be discern'd, that those confused seeds which were impos'd on *Psyche* as an incessant labour to cull out, and sort asunder, were not more intermixt. It was from out the rinde of one apple tasted, that the knowledge of good and evil as two twins cleaving together leapt forth into the World. (*CPW*, II, 514)

When at the end of *Paradise Lost* Adam and Eve, after tasting the "one apple," begin to make their way through the "wilderness of the world," it should be striking that that "wilderness" was not brought into being by their transgression. It has been there from the original creation. The landscape of the world before the Fall already included features that are described in language and imagery which suggest that Milton was thinking of the material world as a text. In fact the text has large patches of difficulty for interpreters. The epic bard depicts the prelapsarian terrain as including thickets and tangles and vegetation ever "Tending to wilde" (IX, 212).

Doing so, he borrows imagery that in Milton's prose works published between 1643 and 1645 had sometimes been used to describe problems of interpretation. In *Tetrachordon,* for instance, Milton had observed that Christ had often been required by the close-minded disposition of his auditors to lay "aside the facil vein of perspicuity" and "to utter clouds and riddles." Christ sought "to perplex and stumble them purposely with contriv'd obscurities," providing "not so much a teaching, as an intangling" (*CPW,* II, 642–43).

That Milton in *Paradise Lost* was working against the idea that verbal complexity had been ushered into the world with the Fall has not been well understood. It seems to have been missed by every reader who has followed Dryden and Johnson in thinking that the poem's having been written through the spectacles of books counts against Milton's project. In recent years Milton's having written against the grain has been made almost invisible. The widely popular doctrine according to which the whole Western tradition is pervaded by linguistic ambiguities and structured by binary oppositions has proved readily available for leveling the charge that Milton's Adam and Eve are "always already fallen." At first blush, it might seem that the emphasis that will be placed in this chapter on the degree to which Milton imagined paradise in bookish terms will merely reinforce this predictable line of reading. From a Derridean perspective, the passage that stands as epigraph for this chapter, in which Raphael describes the heavens by way of a simile involving a book, seems to be just another instance when "so-called living discourse" is "described by a 'metaphor' borrowed from the order of the very thing one is trying to exclude from it," namely writing. If writing is a fallen form of discourse, a negative, corrupt, and undesirable version of speech, then Milton's projection of writerly categories into his picture of the unfallen world compromised his attempt to present prelapsarian complexities as an aspect of the world's perfection. Moreover, any continuity that may be discerned in *Paradise Lost* between representations of the Book of the Scriptures and the Book of Nature would only confirm that the unfallen world-as-book is "always already" a dangerous "supplement." Like the *pharmakon* of Plato's *Phaedrus,* which means both "remedy" and "poison," Milton's picture of the Book of Nature would seem inevitably to involve that sort of "confused" intermixture of which he had spoken in *Areopagitica,* a "mixture" that is at once "helpful to the soul" and also "harmful," and in any event so contradictory as seriously to flaw the project of imagining unfallen experience.[4]

It is true of *Paradise Lost* that the imagery of tangles and thick obscurity that Milton infused into his picture of the Book of Nature generally shows up in contexts where harm seems to be lurking, for Satan is present. It is used to describe features of the material world that seem promising for Satan's purposes. Having journeyed to the new world, he finds that Eden is surrounded by a high wall "thick entwin'd" with an "undergrowth / Of shrubs and tangling bushes . . . [which] perplext / All path of Man or Beast" (IV, 174–77). The serpent, whose form will be available for him to assume, appears "Insinuating," and weaves "with Gordian twine / His breaded train" (IV, 348–49).[5] Later, Satan is able to lead Eve through "tangles" in the landscape and to make what is inherently "intricate seem strait" (IX, 632–33). Remembering Derrida and repeating the commonplace idea that all language requires interpretation, Regina Schwartz has argued that Satan first exploits this condition when he examines for Eve the sense and force of the prohibition: "Between utterance and reception, Satan infuses the problematics of interpretation."[6] The problematics, we have been noticing, are already present in creation. What proves interesting is that they are defined by Satan in a particular way. He asks Eve to assume that she can know all about what God is like. He encourages her, moreover, to think that what she really knows, or can infer, about God is at odds with what she has been thinking she knew. Satan's version of a hermeneutics of suspicion thus provides a framework within which to reinterpret the prohibition of the tree of knowledge. This framework, like the analogy of faith when it was invoked prematurely to pre-empt interpretive questions, allows virtually no room for God to have a currently unfathomable purpose or for Adam and Eve to grow towards a more mature understanding in a future yet to be conceived.

    Many features of the world that had been "fram'd . . . to mans delightful use" by the "sovran Planter" (IV, 691–92) are, in fact, ready for Satan to exploit to his own ends. As Schwartz goes on aptly to observe, "His barrage of questions releases the uncertainties of interpretation with a vengeance," and not so aptly, "ultimately rendering the command powerless." The uncertainties are already there in Eden, and Adam and Eve have been living with them. Satan gets Eve to think that by distrusting God she can divine the secret meaning of whatever God has tried to keep her from understanding. The terms by which uncertainties in the unfallen world are evoked belong to a network that includes the words "mazie error," "lapse," "wander," "luxurious," "wanton," and "disshevl'd." The presence of this semantic field in the prelapsarian section of the poem has attracted a good deal of attention and has been made to contribute to the hypothesis, which long antedates the application of deconstructive theory to the poem, that Milton represents Adam and Eve as "fallen before the Fall."[7] This charge rests on the twin notions that the language of entanglement signals "untamed" moral corruption and that Milton is a moralist, whose "intention" should be understood "to differ little," as Stanley Fish urged at the outset of *Surprised by Sin,* "from that of so many devotional writers, 'to discover to us our miserable and wretched estate through corruption of nature.'" Predictably, these widely held notions inform a popularizing "demonstration" that *Paradise Lost* is eminently ripe for deconstruction: the tangled network of exuberant terms with which aspects of the prelapsarian world are described in *Paradise Lost* have been said by Hillis Miller to exceed authorial control and to undermine Milton's project.[8]

The interpretive perspective called for by deconstruction bears a family resemblance, then, to one that is sometimes abstracted from *Areopagitica,* which for some years has been routinely cited by critics as if its moral perspective has explanatory power for interpreting *Paradise Lost.* As suggested above, there will be occasion later in this chapter to question the validity of glossing the epic with the well-known passage about Psyche's "incessant labour." Here by anticipation it may be said, however, that if the broad lines of my argument are valid, by the time Milton wrote *Paradise Lost* he had broken with some interpretive dispositions expressed in *Areopagitica,* in particular with the notion that difficulties of interpretation were a function of human depravity and were introduced into the world "from out the rinde of one apple tasted." In *Paradise Lost,* when Milton represented aspects of the unfallen world in language akin to what he had once used to describe interpretive difficulties, he asked readers radically to reconsider the boundaries conventionally constructed between so-called fallen and unfallen modes of existence and to imagine that before the Fall Adam and Eve were already faced with the burden of interpreting a partially tangled text. My argument here is meant to augment, therefore, the important study by Victoria Kahn of ways in which, especially in the episode in Book II where Sin and Death appear, Milton made "programmatic rhetorical ambivalence" central to his project of representing responsible prelapsarian agency. Kahn has provided a valuable corrective against the facile inference that prelapsarian interpretive difficulties show that "Adam and Eve are somehow fallen before their acts of disobedience." She has shown that in Milton's Eden "signs" (including the prohibition) are inherently ambiguous from the start and not "a consequence of the fall but the precondition of any genuine ethical choice."[9] Without the prohibition as a boundary line for their imaginations to encounter, Adam and Eve would not face indeterminacy, which is boldly included by Milton as a constituent of their prelapsarian experience of choice.

Whatever experiences seventeenth-century readers of *Paradise Lost* may or may not have had appreciating Milton's boldness, by the eighteenth century it had become difficult to perceive that Milton's picture of the unfallen world is at once linguistically complex and yet morally indifferent. The appropriation of Calvinist moral rhetoric for secular purposes is powerfully attested, for instance, in the language used by Samuel Johnson to characterize the metier of the lexicographer. Johnson described language itself in terms curiously reminiscent of those that Milton had used to depict the landscape bordering on Eden. The English language is said by Johnson to be an intricate and perplexing "maze" of tangles, which has been "suffered to spread . . . into wild exuberance." The lexicographer's work is precisely to untangle confused strands that admit of no inherent principles of organization:

> When I took the first survey of my undertaking, I found our speech copious without order, and energetick without rules: wherever I turned my view, there was perplexity to be disentangled, and confusion to be regulated; choice was to be made out of boundless variety, without any established principle of selection.[10]

Sometimes, Johnson observed, "kindred senses may be so interwoven, that the perplexity cannot be disentangled." These and other observations by Johnson reveal a habit of thinking about verbal complexity in terms that Milton had used in *Areopagitica* to characterize interpretive difficulties.

Yet the setting of *Paradise Lost* in a prehistoric period tends to obscure how much the poet's conception of the process by which paradise is lost and regained owes to early modern conceptions of the importance of interpretive activities. In a matter particularly relevant to the theme of this study Milton sought to depict the first parents in ways that suggested that their lives were similar, and pertinent, to the lives of his contemporaries.[11] He accommodated earnest Bible-readers by circumventing a feature of the story in Genesis 1–3 that has been foreign to the experience of every reader since it was first written down: Adam and Eve live in a world without books and writing. In this respect it is valuable to note that Milton retold the biblical story in the context of a decisive change in Western *episteme* described by Michel Foucault in *The Order of Things*. According to Foucault, the early modern period in European history was marked by the assumption that writing has an "absolute priority" in understanding how meaning is constructed. *Paradise Lost* is implicated in what Foucault has proposed to be characteristic of the new *episteme:* for the most part the poem rests on, and credits, the assumption that meaning is located in a specifically verbal realm. This assumption seems to be made explicit in the passage from Book VIII in which Raphael compares the heavens to a book.

The Unfallen World as a Book

Some implications of Foucault's thesis about the priority accorded to writing in the Renaissance period are hidden rather than illuminated if we suppose that in the passage quoted here from Book VIII Milton was simply incorporating a commonplace of his intellectual milieu. This is the impression that one might glean by turning to the well-known work of E. R. Curtius, who, in order to illustrate the continuity of the world-as-book topos through many centuries, cites the passage as if it were a bit of residue from earlier periods in cultural history. Curtius, it should be said, helpfully traces back to the ancient Near East the idea that books are sacred. He observes that this was the case especially in Egypt, where writing, in the possession of a literate priestly class, was often regarded as something mysterious. This attitude toward books differs from views common among the Romans and Greeks. (Derrida, of course, emphasizes that Socrates assigned primacy to oral instruction.[12]) The dissemination of more prestigious estimates of books and writing was owing, Curtius has shown, chiefly to Christianity. In the Christian Middle Ages metaphors drawn from books and writing proliferated, and "the concept of the world or nature as a 'book,'" which had "originated in pulpit oratory," then "passed into common usage" in the phrases *scientia creaturarum* and *liber naturae*.[13]

Although Curtius shows that from the fourteenth century the idea that the world is a book was sometimes alienated from its theological provenance, the evidence that he gathers from seventeenth-century England suggests that, when Milton took up the topos, a good deal of cultural work was going on to reclaim it in specifically religious contexts. From Foucault's thesis about the emergence of a new European *episteme* in the sixteenth century, we should expect that early modern writers did not so much preserve the ancient commonplace as they transformed it in accord with the new prominence bestowed upon the Book in reformed religion. Indeed this seems to be the case when the topos appears in passages to which Curtius refers from Donne and Herbert, Crashaw and Vaughan and Quarles. Most memorably, the idea that the whole world constitutes a book is cited from the *Religio Medici* of Thomas Browne, where it justifies the writer's whole endeavor:

> Thus there are two bookes from whence I collect my Divinity; besides that written one of God, another of his servant Nature, that universall and publik Manuscript, that lies expans'd unto the eyes of all; those that never saw him in the one, have discovered him in the other: This was the Scripture and Theology of the Heathens; the naturall motion of the Sun made them more admire him, than its supernaturall station did the Children of Israel; the ordinary effects of nature wrought more admiration in them, than in the other all his miracles; surely the Heathens knew better how to joyne and reade these mysticall letters, than wee Christians, who cast a more carelesse eye on these common Hieroglyphicks, and disdain to suck Divinity from the flowers of nature.[14]

These observations do more than imply that writing provides an especially apt metaphor for understanding the nature of the physical world. Browne compares the material universe to the best-known book in his culture and urges that the fundamental position of humans in the world is that of readers who seek pleasure and nourishment from their interpretive activity. Yet there is here the further implication that the world is written in a language that Christians do not know how to read. Throughout the passage, and elsewhere in *Religio Medici,* Browne offers a challenge to readers who try to make the Bible a short-cut to all knowledge. In this important respect his work provides an indicator of profound changes in epistemology underway in the mid-seventeenth century, especially with the growth of "experimental philosophy."[15]

Although in *De Doctrina Christiana* Milton claimed to have collected his divinity from the Bible only, in *Paradise Lost* the handling of the world-as-book topos offers an even more thoroughgoing challenge to Bible-readers than Browne had. Milton not only took seriously the idea that the Scriptures were often difficult to interpret; he drew on the Scriptures in *Paradise Lost* to suggest that even before the Fall much of the world-as-book was unreadable, if not absolutely, at least at that moment in time before the appearance of many more persons to participate in the human construction of knowledge. Reflection on Milton's treatment of the topos may begin but ought not to end with Foucault's thesis about the ways in which Europeans of the period conceived the relations between words and things. According to Foucault, the privilege of writing over speech characterized the entire

Renaissance period and transformed the common understanding of Genesis. By the sixteenth century it was widely taken for granted that

> it is the primal nature of language to be written. The sounds made by voices provide no more than a transitory and precarious translation of it. What God introduced into the world was written words; Adam, when he imposed their first names upon the animals, did no more than read those visible and silent marks; the Law was entrusted to the Tables, not to men's memories; and it is in a book that the true Word must be found again.[16]

At several points in Book VIII of *Paradise Lost* it would seem that writing is assumed to enjoy this sort of primacy. When, for example, Adam lists his first conscious activities, he says that he "perus'd" himself (267). Elsewhere, we learn that the first designation by which God introduced Himself to Adam was as an "Author" (317). Moreover, it seems clear that, although Adam is given the prerogative of naming, the names that he confers are not merely arbitrary but correspond to some pre-existing language. God pronounces that Adam has "rightly nam'd" the animals (439). Then "Adam's naming of 'Woman' crowns and completes the trial of his wisdom," as John Leonard has pointed out, and "Adam shares God's way of speaking."[17] This is certainly not to say that Adam knows all that God knows or that he knows as God knows.

The implication of *Paradise Lost* in a view of reality that accords primacy to *writing* is nonetheless both more belated, and more complex, than Foucault's thesis would lead us to think. At many points in the poem the treatment of *reading* is laced with earlier views of language and reality, views that are at odds with the tendency to think of writing as primary. When Adam first attempts to address God as "Author," he has a radically different experience from the one he had had when he named various material creatures (271 ff., 349–54). He finds the God-given designation inadequate:

> O by what Name, for thou above all these,
> Above mankinde, or aught then mankinde higher,
> Surpassest farr my naming, how may I
> Adore thee, Author of this Universe . . . ?   (357–60).

Adam's experience suggests that the term "author," which is elsewhere in the poem used of Satan and of Adam and Eve themselves, cannot be predicated of God in any simple fashion.[18] Adam's discovery of its inadequacy should prompt recognition that "author" has several senses that do not necessarily involve written language. All of them date to the late fourteenth century and (according to the *OED*) they include "The person who orginates or gives existence to anything," "The Creator," "One who begets," and "an authority." Since the sixteenth century these senses have been largely folded into a conception of the world that bestows a privileged status upon writing, and the sense whereby an "author" is thought to be "One who sets forth written statements" has largely driven them out of currency or made them seem merely metaphorical.

By a similar token, in the sixteenth century the word "peruse" sometimes referred to an activity involving written documents. It was used in the sense "to read thoroughly and carefully." Still, an older sense dating to the fifteenth century remained current, and "peruse" continued to be employed to refer to the activity of examining a number of things one by one. From the early sixteenth century it could also mean "to name or recount in order" and to "survey, inspect, examine, or consider in detail." (The *OED* cites *PL* VIII, 267 to illustrate this last sense.) In short, it is not clear whether in *Paradise Lost* the concepts of authoring and perusing necessarily entail correlative concepts of writing and reading, or whether Adam's naming of the animals involves reading "visible and silent marks" in any sense that implies the existence of a prior written text. Purporting to represent actions that antedate the human invention of writing, *Paradise Lost* offers a highly ambiguous representation of the activity of reading.

These ambiguities in Book VIII gain interest when we consider two fields of data that call into question the blanket proposition that Europeans of the sixteenth and seventeenth centuries ascribed an "absolute priority" to writing: a growing body of literature which deverbalized the Book of Nature (to be considered later in this chapter) and the practice of sixteenth-century English poets, including Spenser, whose thinking about language, as Anne Ferry has shown in *The Art of Naming*, is "predicated on assumptions often very unlike those ascribed generally to this period by Foucault."[19] In taking up the second of these contexts first, we should note that Foucault's references give no indication that he took into account evidence from England. Mrs. Ferry, whose study is confined to the practice of poets in sixteenth-century England, has not claimed that seventeenth-century English poetry, or thinking about language, does not fit the paradigm whereby writing is privileged over speech. Nor does she suggest grounds for supposing that Milton's theory and practice were out of keeping with the more modern conceptions of language which, in the seventeenth century, may have displaced the ones her study has unearthed. Yet when we consider that Milton was consciously attempting to represent antique experiences, as Spenser had, it is important to consider whether and to what extent older conceptions of "reading" that inform *The Faerie Queene* may have been borrowed and transformed in *Paradise Lost*.[20]

Books and "Reading"

As the first human beings, by definition Adam and Eve inhabit a world lacking other human stories with which they may compare their experience. Yet in *Paradise Lost* the first parents are not without stories: nearly half the poem consists of narrative materials provided ultimately by God for their entertainment and instruction. Exploring the implications of this fact, Marshall Grossman has proposed that Milton accommodated his representations of Adam and Eve to modern conceptions of a developing "self" and assimilated their experience to that of seventeenth-century readers of narratives. By providing his poem with the revelations given by Raphael and Michael, Milton showed that Adam and Eve had paradigms for thinking about the possible courses their lives might take. More than any previous writer, it seems, Milton exploited "the metaphor of authorship" to reflect and promote a new conception of the self as developing over time. To this end he enlisted a fundamental analogy between "writing a narrative and living a life."[21] Adam and Eve learn, in short, to construct meaning in the sort of language that is organized into narrative patterns.

There remains, however, a potentially important difference between the ways in which the Miltonic first parents experience narratives and the ways in which literate persons do. Given orally or in visions, the stories with which Adam and Eve become familiar do not entail "reading" in senses of that word which have been given priority since the seventeenth century, all of which have to do with discerning meaning in written materials. They involve "reading" experience in some older senses of the term which are closely related to the derivation of the word from Old English, where it meant chiefly to "advise" or "explain." These older senses are largely continuous with some ways in which the verb "to read" is used in *The Faerie Queene*, where the activity of reading is frequently associated with "speaking, answering, explaining, [and] describing rather than with the comprehension of writing." These associations, Mrs. Ferry has observed, reflect Spenser's "reverence for original and antique meanings which embody the ideals celebrated in fairyland." They do not presuppose that meaning is necessarily a function of verbal activity—or that tangledness and ambiguity are necessarily marks of fallenness.[22]

Forms of the verb "to read" occur fewer than half a dozen times in *Paradise Lost*. The incidence is slight when compared to *The Faerie Queene* and may be explained partly by the fact that the central actions of Milton's poem are set in prehistoric times and partly by the fact that by the seventeenth century senses unconnected to writing were fading from usage. Nonetheless, at least one instance in *Paradise Lost* shows that "reading" could still be conceived in terms that do not presuppose the existence of writing. In Book II, when Satan has asked for a volunteer to undertake the dangerous journey to the "new world," the Bard tells us that all the fallen angels

> sat mute,
> Pondering the danger with deep thoughts; and each
> In others count'nance read his own dismay
> Astonisht.   (II, 420–23)

Elsewhere, in Book IV, the word is similarly used in a context where it does not necessarily involve writing, as Gabriel counsels Satan to "look up, / And read thy Lot in yon celestial Sign / Where thou art weigh'd, and shown how light, how weak, / If thou resist" (IV, 1010–13). Here, anyone unacquainted with the older senses of the word is likely to project modern assumptions about language back onto the passage, and to take the usage as metaphorical, assimilating it to Raphael's figure in Book VIII. Yet it is entirely possible to take "read" here in senses that do not involve writing: to guess, or tell by conjecture; to discover the meaning (as of a riddle or dream); to discern, or discover; and (what is most apt) to foresee, foretell, or predict. Not long before this instance Gabriel had used the word "arreede" in his rebuff to Satan: "But mark what I arreede thee now, avant" (IV, 962). Here the sense recalls the use to which Milton had put the word in *The Doctrine and Discipline of Divorce* (*CPW*, II, 224), which is cited in the *OED* to illustrate the sense "to advise." (The word may also be equivocal here, however, suggesting the sense "to divine" or "conjecture."[23]) Of the instances of the word "read" in *Paradise Lost* the one most readily connected to writing is the Bard's reference to the commencement of the "great consult" in hell after a "summons [was] read," where the sense of uttering aloud seems to imply a written record of the participants' names. Still, when we consider how the word "book" is used in the poem, the existence of a document in which the names of the fallen spirits are recorded proves more problematic.

Unlike the word "read," the word "book" appears prominently on virtually every page of the seventeenth-century editions of *Paradise Lost*. It is to be found on the title page of both the ten-book and the twelve-book versions, and it is printed above the verse on both recto and verso pages, where it serves immediately to identify the numbered divisions of the poem. Within the actual blank verse lines, however, the word "book" appears only three times. The first occurrence is in Book I, where the Bard displays a certain fascination with the "multitude" (351) of "Innumerable" (338) and "numberless" (344) fallen angels, whose rebellious action has removed them from the realm of that providence which is conceived in specifically writerly terms: "thir Names in heav'nly Records now / [Have] no memorial, blotted out and ras'd / By thir Rebellion" (361–63). Curiously, their loss is depicted as in some respects only temporary, as they are later to receive "new Names" on earth, "among the Sons of *Eve*" (364–65). In any event, the projection of "Books of Life" (363) back into an original realm before history suggests an intense form of the modern bias towards writing, which according to Foucault has primacy when it comes to constructing meaning. The existence of these "Books" would seem also to reinforce the idea that selfhood is constituted in verbal and specifically in narrative terms.

The second instance of the word "book" in the actual lines of the poem similarly posits the priority of writing, although it does not necessarily imply narrative form. It occurs near the climax of the powerful opening of Book III, when the Bard describes his having gone blind. The loss made him feel as if the best and most beautiful of all books has been utterly erased:

> Thus with the Year
> Seasons return, but not to me returns
> Day, or the sweet approach of Ev'n or Morn,
> Or sight of vernal bloom, or Summers Rose,
> Or flocks, or heards, or human face divine;
> But cloud in stead, and ever-during dark
> Surrounds me, from the chearful wayes of men
> Cut off, and for the Book of knowledg fair
> Presented with a Universal blanc
> Of Natures works to mee expung'd and ras'd. . . .   (III, 40–49)

The poet avoids rather than indulges self-pity at this poignant moment, however, first by saying that thus "wisdome at one entrance [is] quite shut out," implying that there are other entrances, then by going on to invoke the "Celestial light" that can "Shine inward" and provide a compensating vision of "things invisible to mortal sight" (50–55). It is just such an experience of the whole Book of Nature having been erased that gives him the opportunity to fill it up again with his own re-creation of "Natures works" and just such a vision, he implies, that gives him the authority to write. In this way the blind Bard presents his poem as a kind of palimpsest, and suggests that his experience involves a recapitulation of the story he is telling: his depiction of paradise is written over the lines that were erased when the original "Book of knowledg fair" was lost.[24]

If the first mention of a "book" in *Paradise Lost* suggests that erasure may be a prelude to newer and still beautiful fictions, the second promotes the idea that reading and writing may contribute to the regaining of paradise, inasmuch as the unfallen world had been written. This makes the third mention of a "book" (to return now to the epigraph for this chapter) somewhat less odd than it might seem if it is read out of this context. Fully to appreciate the apparently anomalous idea that Adam and Eve might "read" the unfallen world, it is worth considering Raphael's comparison of the heavens to a book both in its immediate context and in relation to the persistent theme of knowledge that informs the poem more generally. Near the beginning of Book VIII, Adam, having just heard the account of the creation of the world, puts to Raphael the sort of question to which he seems previously to have supposed he knew the answer. When Eve had asked him why the beautiful stars shine at night, "when sleep hath shut all eyes," Adam had replied in confident tones that they serve a cosmic purpose:

> Those have thir course to finish, round the Earth,
> By morrow Eevning, and from Land to Land
> In order, though to Nations yet unborn,
> Ministring light prepar'd, they set and rise;
> Least total darkness should by Night regaine
> Her old possession, and extinguish life
> In Nature and all things. . . .   (IV, 661–67)

Beyond this, Adam continued, by their very existence the stars serve to praise the Creator, and he went on to evoke the sense of a world populated by "Millions of spiritual Creatures" (677) invisible even to humankind's immortal sight and beyond the present ability of the first humans to name.[25] As in the case of the "lovely . . . Lantskip" mentioned some lines earlier (IV, 152–53), which may refer to Eden proper or to some other part of the natural world, it is unclear where these creatures have their proper place. Yet they too seem, in Keith Stavely's terms, "not only very attractive" but "dense with benign significance," further evidence that out of His "generosity" God has fertilized "ordinary" nature with "providential design." In any event, the borders around Eden are not precisely drawn, and in their exceeding density they seem to anticipate the sort of excess signification on the edges of all printed texts to which Derrida has given the name *débordement*.[26] Adam locates these creatures in places that are at once difficult of access and teeming with creative energies:

> All these with ceasless praise his works behold
> Both day and night: how often from the steep
> Of echoing Hill or Thicket have we heard
> Celestial voices to the midnight air,
> Sole, or responsive each to others note
> Singing thir great Creator. . . .   (IV, 679–84)

For all this, in Book VIII, having heard Raphael's marvelous account of the creation, Adam is no longer confident of the adequacy of his previous explanation, and he poses a version of Eve's question:

> When I behold this goodly Frame, this World
> Of Heav'n and Earth consisting, and compute,
> Thir magnitudes, this Earth a spot, a graine,
> An Atom, with the Firmament compar'd
> And all her numberd Starrs, that seem to rowle
> Spaces incomprehensible . . .
> . . . .
> . . . . in all thir vast survey
> Useless besides, reasoning I oft admire,
> How Nature wise and frugal could commit
> Such disproportions, with superfluous hand
> So many nobler Bodies to create. . . .   (VIII, 15–20, 24–28)

It is in response to Adam's presentation of these observations as "something yet of doubt . . . / Which onely thy solution can resolve" (13–

14) that the third instance of the word "book" occurs in the poem. Raphael appeals to the book as a simile, as if to explain something of which we know that Adam has some first-hand experience by way of something that would seem, curiously, to be altogether outside his experience:

> To ask or search I blame thee not, for Heav'n
> Is as the Book of God before thee set,
> Wherein to read his wondrous Works, and learne
> His Seasons, Hours, or Dayes, or Months, or Yeares.   (66–69)

It is easy to glide over the anomaly here, supposing that Milton is enlisting a familiar topos and assuming that the idea was unproblematic and in any event not vital to the subject of the poem. Yet we should be suspicious when we notice that elsewhere Raphael is represented as being alert to the limits of Adam's experience and, typically, as using much simpler comparisons than does the narrator of the poem.[27] Moreover, in the work of Spenser the verb "to read" was still being used in senses that have nothing to do with books and do not depend upon a view of language that bestows priority upon writing. While "Scripture" would seem to require "reading" in senses that involve deciphering written materials, the *liber naturae* could apparently be "read" in older senses of the word.

The idea that the Book of the World was inherently difficult to read, which appears in the passage quoted from *Religio Medici*, had become increasingly available by the mid-seventeenth century. Moralists often proposed of course that the difficulties were a function of human sinfulness, that they had begun with Original Sin and had been compounded at Babel. For other thinkers, however, it did not matter so much what the origin of the difficulties was; what mattered were the effects. This is especially the case with the growing body of "experimental" philosophers, many of whom, however great their differences from one another, sought to appropriate the cultural authority that attached to the name of Bacon and, in various ways, radically to reconsider the relationship between creation and the Creator. As the work of Karen Edwards has begun to show in fascinating detail, it is naive to suppose that Milton's complex relation to the "new science" of the mid-seventeenth century is to be discerned merely or even chiefly in his handling of astronomy. The new "science" (that is, in seventeenth-century usage, "way of knowing") had such pervasive and thoroughgoing effects that virtually every line of *Paradise Lost* may be said to "register" some epistemological aspect of the "collision between the old science and the new." For our purposes here, the most important of these effects was a new and "different way of reading the book of the world."[28]

In critical writing on *Paradise Lost* the epistemological problems entailed in the emergence of the new science are not often brought squarely to the fore. In the 1920s and 1930s interest in the problems was largely delimited by questions about Milton's position in relation to sixteenth- and seventeenth-century debates about cosmology, or more narrowly about astronomy. Whereas that earlier work tended to see the mentions of Galileo in the poem (viz., I, 286–91, and V, 257–63) as an invitation to measure whether the cosmology of *Paradise Lost* was up-to-date (it was found by Svendsen to be old-fashioned), recent work has been more concerned to define Milton's estimate of Galileo as a sort of representative of the early modern world. (Milton is known to have read Galileo, although not enough is known about how he read Galileo, as is evident in recent debates about whether the "Tuscan artist" appears in the poem as a Satanic figure.[29]) The best of this work has encouraged a recognition that Galileo belongs in *Paradise Lost,* along with the narrator, as an instance of Milton's powerful transformation of belatedness into opportunity: his presence calls attention, we might say, to some substantial advantages that belated readers have over their predecessors. In particular, Judith Scherer Herz has observed that the many echoes and allusions to Galileo that may be found in the poem contribute to establishing the narrator's openness to learning, which is reprojected into the experience of the unfallen first parents. This is one way in which "scientific speculation is established as an aspect of Adam's humanness from the start," and "the problematizing of knowledge is [made] not an unfortunate result but the essential condition of the poem's undertaking."[30]

While it has long been clear that in *Paradise Lost* Milton took an interest in astronomy at least insofar as he could abstract moral implications for a poem about "forbidden knowledge," recent work has also shown that he recognized that the new knowledge raised new and more difficult questions. Amy Boesky has proposed that Galileo's *Letters on Sunspots* underlie the dialogue between Raphael and Adam, and her work suggests that the intertextuality of this incident encourages readers to probe the questions further than is appropriate for Adam to do "thus farr" (VIII, 177) in the course of constructing human knowledge. Donald Friedman has pointed out another particularly salutary effect of the sort of work done by Galileo, that it helped Milton to imagine "perfection" in more open terms than the Latin root of the word ("completed") might have allowed. Friedman has also cited a crucial passage from *The Assayer* that greatly complicated the understanding of the world as a book. Galileo had proposed there that while Nature is a Book, it does not use verbal language and cannot be understood on the model of a written composition:

> Philosophy is written in this grand book, the universe, which stands continually open to our gaze. But the book cannot be understood unless one first learns to comprehend the language and read the letters in which it is composed. It is written in the language of mathematics and its characters are triangles, circles, and other geometric figures without which it is humanly impossible to understand a single word of it; without these, one wanders about in a dark labyrinth.[31]

Increasingly, intellectuals from Bacon and Kepler to Descartes and the members of the Royal Society conceived the Book of the World in mathematical terms. The belief that mathematics offered the proper system for describing the Book of Nature meant for some a devaluing of human language, as when the historian of the Royal Society compared the "inveterate" corruption of human language to "the *want of paradise* in Religion" and called for "all things" to be brought "as near the Mathematical plainness, as they can." John Locke urged that "the study of mathematics has opened, and dis-entangled [its practitioners' minds] from the cheat of words" since "Mathematicians abstracting their Thoughts from Names . . . have avoided thereby a great part of that perplexity, puddering, and confusion, which has so much hindered Mens progress in other parts of Knowledge."[32] Such views contributed greatly to renewing old debates about the relative value and significance of the Book of the World and the Scriptures. Whereas Protestant divines typically maintained that the Scriptures are clear and capable of clarifying the other Book, Galileo and other "experimental philosophers" took the Book of Nature to be authoritative and the Scriptures to be but an imperfect supplement. In fact, increasing suspicion of the adequacy of human language posed a threat to the idea that the Bible could accurately communicate God's Word, especially with the emergence of the idea that all language, even that originally instituted by God, was arbitrarily imposed onto things.

The lines that Milton gives to Raphael about heaven as "the Book of God" evoke seventeenth-century discussions about the nature, significance, and relative authority of the different books that God was said to have written. It is well beyond the scope of the present study to review these debates, but I want to focus here on some indications of the collision of different epistemologies that was anticipated in Protestant Bible-commentary of the preceding century. Already in the sixteenth century, although divines were slow to acknowledge this fully, the new priority ascribed to writing raised new questions for those who wished to collect their divinity from a book that was apparently open to the eyes of all people. Milton's handling of this controversial subject in *Paradise Lost* represents a powerful intervention in the history of interpreting a particular biblical place.

In the early modern period the opening of Psalm 19 had become a favored ground for attempting to define the relations among God's books. It is this biblical place to which Browne's remarks about the Heathens' admiration for "the naturall motion of the Sun" allude, and it is on this place that Raphael's comparison of the heavens to a book is grounded. This psalm, as it could now be read in a Protestant culture that insisted on the priority of the written Bible over oral tradition, provided Milton with a lens for reinterpreting the first three chapters of Genesis in unusually bookish terms. (In attending to the passage here, as elsewhere, it is helpful to recall that the translators italicized words which they had added in rendering the Hebrew. I have divided the poem into sense-lines.)

> THE heavens declare the glory of God;
>   and the firmament sheweth his handywork.
> 2 Day unto day uttereth speech,
>   and night unto night sheweth knowledge.
> 3 *There is* no speech nor language,
>   *where* their voice is not heard.
> 4 Their line is gone out through all the earth,
>   and their words to the end of the world.
> In them hath he set a tabernacle for the sun,
>   5 Which *is* as a bridegroom coming out of his chamber,
>   *and* rejoiceth as a strong man to run a race.
> 6 His going forth *is* from the end of the heaven,
>   and his circuit unto the ends of it:
>   and there is nothing hid from the heat thereof.

For many centuries these verses were interpreted as if they give a priority to voice, and exegetes endeavored to explain in what sense the heavens might be understood to be speakers. In *Paradise Lost,* at least as Adam recounts his experience to Raphael, they seem at first to have been mute. The relevant passage, which suggests that the earliest human utterance was an interpretive question, is made to anticipate the opening of Psalm 19, where the heavens are said to "tell" of the glory of God:

> Thou Sun, said I, faire Light,
> And thou enlight'nd Earth, so fresh and gay,
> Ye Hills and Dales, ye Rivers, Woods, and Plaines,
> And ye that live and move, fair Creatures, tell,
> Tell, if ye saw, how came I thus, how here?
> Not of my self; by some great Maker then,
> In goodness and in power præeminent;
> Tell me, how may I know him, how adore,
> From whom I have that thus I move and live,
> And feel that I am happier then I know.

Yet the anticipatory allusion to a passage that will sing God's manifest glories in the creation serves here to underscore, it seems, Adam's disappointment at not receiving a reply from these natural creatures:

> While thus I call'd, and stray'd I knew not whither,
> From where I first drew Aire, and first beheld
> This happie Light, when answer none return'd,
> On a green and shadie Bank profuse of Flours
> Pensive I sate me down. (VIII, 273–87)

Karen Edwards has astutely pointed out that Adam had actually asked two separate questions, and it was to the second ("how may I know him, how adore"?) that "answer none return'd." This particular silence, she contends quite aptly, signals a stressmark in seventeenth-century epistemology, when intellectuals felt increasingly uncertain that the natural world could provide knowledge of God.[33] If we attend to the history of commentary on Psalm 19, we can see that the epistemological crisis wrought by the rise of "experimental" philosophy in the seventeenth century was to some significant extent anticipated in the sixteenth, when Calvin and other commentators developed the idea that the opening verses provide a scriptural instance of the world-as-book topos. These commentators were generally reluctant to countenance the possibility that the heavens were, as Milton's Adam found them, silent in response to questions about how to know God. When they did allow this reading of the Psalm, however, they were quick to situate it within a doctrinal context that emphasized human sinfulness.

Milton's reading of Psalm 19 will be seen to have been in some ways continuous with a more optimistic line of interpretation, whereby the opening verses were thought to concern, as in the Sidneys' rendering, a "faire booke" written "in letters greate / For ev'ry bodies reading."[34] Yet as he inscribed his reading in *Paradise Lost*, using the Psalm as a lens with which to read beneath or behind the lines of the account of creation in Genesis, it was anything but commonplace. Milton did not merely allude to this psalm as if it guaranteed the validity of a classical topos. Rather he discerned in it the grounds for imagining the material creation before the Fall as dense with potential for meaning. Psalm 19 helped to inspire his depiction of the unfallen world as a realm that included, as its Creator's "Master work" (VII, 505), creatures whose own work involved untangling and pruning, gathering and forbearing to gather, and whose unfallen pleasures entailed their living with interpretive difficulties and tangles. The boldness of the reading of Psalm 19 offered by the narrator of *Paradise Lost* is to be seen in his depiction of a physical world that does not "declare" clearly and simply in plain language all that the first parents desire to know about the divine "Author." The distinctiveness of this reading is best appreciated if we consider the broad lines of how the poem had been interpreted previously. We need also recall that the ascription of priority to writing was a relatively recent phenomenon and to recognize that proponents of the idea that the heavens are a book had a good deal of work to do to make that metaphor serviceable, since this idea inevitably raised a number of new questions.

Psalm 19 Before the Early Modern Era

Thanks above all to studies by Mary Ann Radzinowicz, a "history of the intertwined growth of Milton's poetical creativity and admiration for Psalms is well known." In his epics Milton drew on psalms for themes, for generic models, and for poetic styles. In particular Psalm 19 has been shown to have been one of eight psalms that occupied Milton's attention most frequently.[35] Yet this psalm stands out for two contributions to *Paradise Lost* which have gone largely unremarked: "conferred" with Genesis 1–3, it offered Milton a model for the transition to the more chastened style found in the last books, and it helped him to imagine the prelapsarian world as a site of complex interpretive activity. Of these two points the latter requires a more elaborate demonstration than the former, which will be taken up momentarily and then only briefly.

Before the early modern era, the opening verses of Psalm 19 were typically interpreted in ways congruent with the explanation that Milton's Adam would give to Eve about how the heavenly bodies "have thir course to finish" and "All these with ceaseless praise his works behold / Both day and night." These verses were read, that is, rather as Adam and Eve might seem to be interpreting them (long before they were written down) when they sing their morning hymn. The hymn, in which Adam and Eve echo biblical poetry *sotto voce,* as John Hollander has beautifully illustrated, is made to stand as the original behind a great song of creation such as Psalm 148.[36] From the glories of material creation, Adam and Eve spontaneously infer the goodness of their "Author," the term understood now in the non-writerly sense of "parent":

> These are thy glorious works, Parent of good,
> Almightie, thine this universal Frame,
> Thus wondrous fair; thy self how wondrous then!
> Unspeakable, who sitst above these Heavens
> To us invisible or dimly seen
> In these thy lowest works, yet these declare
> Thy goodness beyond thought, and Power Divine.   (V, 153–59)

The lines that precede this passage have given readers to understand that God's "lowest works" include the "wide Lantskip" containing "*Edens* happie Plains" and that the plains "come to open sight" through the agency of the sun.

If the privilege of writing over speech characterized at least the later Renaissance period and transformed the common understanding of Genesis, something similar may be said about what happened to the understanding of Psalm 19, a poem that, like the Pentateuch, concerns creation, language, and law. Whereas before the sixteenth century it was not common to think about this psalm in the sorts of terms provided by the topos of the world-as-book, Calvin's commentary shows that it became possible to understand the opening verses as a celebration of God's writing in nature. This possibility owed something to the changes in *episteme* that Foucault has sought to demonstrate. Yet the realization of this possibility, which overturned a long history of reading the poem allegorically, required a good deal of interpretive work. Exegetes had to attend to a series of linguistic and stylistic features of the psalm that had previously seemed unproblematic, and they constructed readings that made the poem into a commentary on the relations between the Book of Nature and the Book of the Scriptures.

Chief among the stylistic considerations was a recognition that the opening lines are somewhat discontinuous from what follows, beginning with verse 7, in praise of the virtues of Torah. (The phrase "the Law" was widely understood to apply not merely to the commandments but to the entire Pentateuch, and by some readers to the whole Christian Bible.[37])

> 7 The law of the LORD *is* perfect,
>   converting the soul:
>   The testimony of the LORD *is* sure,
>   making wise the simple.
> 8 The statutes of the LORD *are* right,
>   rejoicing the heart:
>   The commandment of the LORD *is* pure,
>   enlightening the eyes.
> 9 The fear of the LORD *is* clean,
>   enduring for ever:
>   The judgments of the LORD *are* true
>   *and* righteous altogether.
> 10 More to be desired *are they* than gold,
>   yea, than much fine gold:
>   sweeter also than honey and the honeycomb.
> 11 Moreover by them is thy servant warned:
>   *and* in keeping of them *there is* great reward.
> 12 Who can understand *his* errors?
>   cleanse thou me from secret *faults.*
> 13 Keep back thy servant also from presumptuous *sins;*
>   let them not have dominion over me:
>   then shall I be upright,
>   and I shall be innocent from the great transgression.
> 14 Let the words of my mouth,
>   and the meditation of my heart,
>   be acceptable in thy sight,
>   O LORD, my strength, and my redeemer.

Of course, earlier readers of the Psalm had already recognized a sharp discontinuity beginning at verse 7. In the medieval period it was characteristic to speak of the poem as falling into two, or sometimes three, distinctive parts. (The third part was thought to begin at verse 11.) But until the mid-sixteenth century, the first part of Psalm 19 was not contrasted with the rest on the grounds that the different parts concern alternative forms of writing. Medieval rabbis, discerning a contrast, often took occasion to urge that Torah is far superior to the heavens and to the sun. Torah, said Radak (c. 1160–c. 1235), provides a surer guide about how to come close to God. Verse 11b ("in keeping of them *there is* great reward") was taken to mean that Torah is more valuable than earthly possessions. The study of Torah, it was claimed, can make the student resemble Adam before the Fall.[38]

At least since the eighteenth century, however, many critics of *Paradise Lost* have thought that Milton accomplished just the opposite: the modulation of the last two books into a decidedly chastened style evinces Adam's new status after the Fall, when he has been reduced to a kind of schoolboy, required now to repair the ruins he and Eve have wrought. Adam's puzzlement is augmented by a dizzying array of materials that he must learn to interpret. To make matters more difficult, there are at least three different descriptions or designations of what is supposed to be going on. The first description comes within God's instructions to Michael, and it emphasizes the value of revelation as a kind of consolation:

> least they faint
> At the sad Sentence rigorously urg'd,
> For I behold them softn'd and with tears
> Bewailing thir excess, all terror hide.
> If patiently thy bidding they obey,
> Dismiss them not disconsolate; reveale
> To *Adam* what shall come in future dayes,
> As I shall thee enlighten, intermix
> My Cov'nant in the womans seed renewd;
> So send them forth, though sorrowing, yet in peace. . . .
>   (XI, 108–17)

A second description, emphasizing that revelation provides an opportunity for growth in faith, is provided by Michael himself, as he tells Adam what he is about to show him and why:

> . . . that thou mayst beleeve, and be confirmd,
> Ere thou from hence depart, know I am sent
> To shew thee what shall come in future dayes
> To thee and to thy Ofspring. . . .   (XI, 355–58)

Milton provided a third description in the argument for Book XII added in the 1668 reprinting and appearing in the subsequent editions:

> *The Angel* Michael *continues from the Flood to relate what shall succeed; then, in the mention of* Abraham, *comes by degrees to explain, who that Seed of the Woman shall be, which was promised* Adam *and* Eve *in the Fall; his Incarnation, Death, Resurrection, and Ascention; the state of the Church till his second Coming.* Adam *greatly satisfied and recomforted by these Relations and Promises descends the Hill.* . . . (*Works*, II, 378)

Writing about the final books of the poem, Louis Martz has observed that all three descriptions sort rather oddly with the bulk of what Adam actually sees and hears. Visions of murder, disease, pestilence, and treachery give way to narratives which amplify "the sombre history of the world from after the Flood through the Day of Doom." Although there are of course a few scenes which illustrate virtuous human conduct, there seems to be an enormous gap between what God and Michael and Milton say the books contain and "[w]hat happens in the poetry."[39] And the gap is hardly bridged by the fact that Michael warns Adam that he may expect to hear "good with bad" mixed together (XI, 358–59).

Martz's explanation for the anomaly created by the preponderance of evil actions in human history involves an expansion of the account of the final books given by Stanley Fish, and like Fish's argument it is a good one.[40] Adam, says Martz, is experiencing a trial of his faith. But to Martz's way of thinking, which extends Addison's charge that in the final books "the Author has been so attentive to his Divinity, that he has neglected his Poetry," this yielding of poetry to theology accounts for the falling off of Milton's style in the final books. This rather unfortunate mixture of theology and poetry can be described, Martz proposes, citing Dryden's preface to *Religio Laici*, as "the Legislative style":

> The Expressions of a Poem, design'd purely for Instruction, ought to be Plain and Natural, and yet Majestick: for here the Poet is presum'd to be a kind of Law-giver.[41]

Martz's disappointment with the legislative style of the final books has been shared by many readers, and his account of the reason for Milton's having checked his exuberance is suggestive. Still, the argument needs refining. Adam's task is to learn how to interpret the new style that he encounters when he meets Michael, a style which is markedly different from that which Raphael had used to tell of the war in heaven and the subsequent creation.

The kind of interpretation for which such a style calls elicits in its turn a new style, or at least a new tone, in Adam's speech, one that is more appropriate to life in the fallen world. These changes are epitomized in Psalm 19, the biblical text which dramatizes and accounts for the allocation of styles to prelapsarian and postlapsarian experience.

There is of course a certain mixing of styles in Books XI and XII, and there are occasions, even in the parts assigned to Michael, when the tone is exalted. Michael ends his series of revelations with a promise that with the coming of the "Womans seed," there will follow "Ages of endless date," which will "bring forth fruits Joy and eternal Bliss" (XII, 543–51). Then, when Adam announces that he has learned from the example of the Redeemer his ultimate lesson, Michael explains the reason that a relatively chastened style is appropriate after the Fall. He suggests that the Book of the Creatures does not reveal the sort of knowledge that Adam will need: "hope [for] no higher [knowledge]," he counsels Adam,

> though all the Starrs
> Thou knewst by name, and all th' ethereal Powers,
> All secrets of the deep, all Natures works,
> Or works of God in Heav'n, Aire, Earth, or Sea. . . .
>
> (XII, 576–79)

Instead, urging what seventeenth-century divines called reading for "experimental" knowledge, Michael proposes that for Adam fully to know the lesson he thinks he has learned from hearing what will be in the Scriptures, he must "add / Deeds to [his] knowledge answerable, add Faith" and other virtues. Only then will he know the fruits of that new internal garden, the "paradise within" (XII, 581–87). Such "experimental" knowledge must now replace the knowledge of God to which Adam once had spontaneous access. That knowledge, as Raphael had explained, might come in time through "the Book of God," the heavens themselves, "Wherein [Adam was] to read [God's] wondrous Works, and learne . . ." (VIII, 67–68). In the fallen world it would take much too long and it would require more than Herculean labors to gather a precise knowledge of God from the Book of the Creatures. The Book of the Law is therefore offered in its place, a translation into an accommodated language appropriate to a fallen world. In this sense the stylistic shift in Psalm 19 is made to provide not only a model but a rationale for the stylistic modulation into the quieter, more chastened tones that predominate at the end of *Paradise Lost*.

As for the more exalted metaphors in the opening lines of Psalm 19, medieval rabbis debated whether the heavens are capable of speech, and some attempted to make sense of them by maintaining that the heavens stimulate humans to express praises. Ibn Ezra said that although the heavens possess no means of verbal communication, human perception can discern their message clearly. Among Christians, Psalm 19 was of particular interest because the Fourth Gospel had identified the creative Logos with the Son. This identification stands in the background of a line of interpretation developed out of Paul and Augustine that became standard among the schoolmen: the poem was taken to concern the spread of the gospel through the whole world. In the tenth chapter of Romans, Paul incorporated verse 4 when he referred to the apostles' preaching: "But I say, Have they not heard? Yes verily, their sound went into all the earth, and their words unto the ends of the world" (10: 18). It was not until the sixteenth century, however, with the growth of a body of Christian Hebraists, that interpreters troubled themselves in detail over the fact that the verse in Romans gives preference to the Septuagint, which Jerome had rendered as *sonus eorum* ("their sound"), over the Hebrew. The Hebrew *kav* or *qwm* (as pointed by the Masoretes) gave rise in sixteenth-century Latin translations to various new renderings, including *linea* and *regula*.[42]

In the medieval period, Paul's reading was widely taken as giving access to the *literal* sense of the psalm. By an elaborate allegory, which was not acknowledged to be allegorical, "the heavens" were said to represent the apostles, "declaring" referred to their preaching, and "the glory of God" was Christ. (It was in this vein of interpretation that "the Law" was taken almost casually to refer to the New Testament as well as the old.) Even with Luther, who was known for his Christological and soteriological approach to the Psalms, there was still no disposition to read the first part of the poem as referring by way of metaphor to God's writing. Luther proposed that the psalm was a prophecy that the gospel will be preached in the whole world, God's "handiwork" being nothing so physical as the material world but rather all that is accomplished by the gospel. The "sun" of verses 4–5 was referred to Christ, while the "Law" was taken as the Word of God and contrasted with human statutes; "reviving the soul" was said to be what the Word offers to burdened consciences.[43] Here were the roots of a division of the poem into three parts on new grounds, in which the third part might be said to train the whole weight of the first two upon the individual. Seen in this light, the "feeling" words beginning in verse 11 thus illustrated the process of applying the preceding verses "experimentally." In the mid-seventeenth century, Obadiah Sedgwick (1600–1658), for instance, proposed that in the final part of the psalm David communicated a *"singular and experimental knowledge of himself,"* which the Law, "like the light of the Sunne," had opened within him.⁴⁴ If they wished, readers could find here God's third book, written upon the human soul or heart.

Psalm 19 and God's Books

The rudiments of an interpretation that would prove especially serviceable to the writer of *Paradise Lost* are to be found amidst the variety of sixteenth-century commentary. Whereas previously the opening verses of Psalm 19 had been read in ways that depict God as a speaker and the physical creation as preachers, a new line of interpretation suggested that God was a writer. This approach was distilled in a bold declaration printed in the Geneva Bible: "The heauens are as a line of great capital letters to shewe vnto vs Gods glorie."⁴⁵ The production of this reading required close attention to the metaphorical possibilities of "declaring" and "proclaiming" in verse 1. Some Christian exegetes urged, as many rabbis had, that the verse simply means that the splendor of the heavens stimulates human speech, in praise of the Creator. Others, however, proposed that the psalmist had set up a contrast between the "several Languages" of "divers Nations" and the "universal" language of the heavens, which "can speak to all people under them, and be clearly understood by all."⁴⁶ In view of a further potential in the root *qwm*, or *kav*, in verse 4, this latter position was made to dovetail with the idea that the heavens are a legible book.

The translation of the Hebrew as "line" in the Geneva and Authorized Versions owes a good deal to Calvin, whose commentary on Psalm 19 acknowledges that the term could refer to a building. Calvin preferred, however, to take the Hebrew as referring to a "line" of writing. The preference derives from the fact that the next verse goes on to discuss "speech." Calvin's reading yielded the idea that "Gods glorie is written owt in the heauens as in an open boke for all men to looke vppon" and was consistent with the idea which the opening verses begin to announce, that the heavens "haue giuen them a lowd voyce, which may come too the eares of all men." Thus, the poem was made to refer to a visible language that "speake[s] to men eyes." This writing is "open and easy too all men." In England the book of the creatures was now compared to "a Common-place book for all" and said to be rightly called "the *Shepherds Kalender*, and the *Plough-mans Alphabet*." It was "Gods *Primer*," meant "for all sorts of people."⁴⁷ Nonetheless, if the heavens were sometimes proclaimed by Calvin and others to be readily legible, it was not a simple matter to get the psalm itself to render up this declaration. Other commentators contrasted the heavens with the Bible and judged them to be much inferior.[48] Calvin himself produced a complicated commentary that ultimately took away most of the intelligibility that might have been ascribed to God's self-communication in nature.

Three other features of the opening lines elicited from Calvin's commentary raised, or evaded, questions that would prove of interest to Milton: the relation of "the heavens" to the rest of creation; the mixture of architectural and writerly metaphors; and the fact that, strictly speaking, there is no verbal basis in the Hebrew for the relative "where" inserted into modern translations of the third verse.[49]

Acknowledging that the Psalmist mentions only "the heauens," Calvin proposed that "it is not to bee doubted, but that vnder the part that is most noble . . . he betokeneth all the whole world, by the figure Synecdoche." The argument proceeds as follows: "Certesse, there is nothing so bace, or to be despysed, euen in the least od nookes of the earth, wherin there is not some mark of Gods myght and wisdome to bee seene. Howbeeit, forasmuch as there is a more expresse image of him engrauen in the heauens: Dauid chose them in especiaily [sic], as whole bryghtnesse myght direct vs to the serching of the whole world" (p. 75^r for 67^r). Milton, for his part, took this synecdochal reading for granted when, while offering evidence in *De Doctrina* for the existence of God, he cited the opening verse of the psalm along with other texts and urged that God "has left . . . many traces of his presence through the whole of nature" (*CPW*, VI, 130). Nonetheless, speaking to Adam in *Paradise Lost*, Raphael refers only to "heaven" when he encourages Adam to "read" the Book of God. That an educational sequence may be envisaged here is explained by Calvin's remark that "assoone as a man shall haue acknowledged God by beholding the heauen: he shall lerne to consider and to woonder at his wisdome and power euen in euery little plant" (p. 75^r, for 67^r). This is the sequence described by Adam as a lovely memory of what he did upon awakening into consciousness:

> Strait toward Heav'n my wondring Eyes I turnd,
> And gaz'd a while the ample Skie, till rais'd
> By quick instinctive motion up I sprung,
> As thitherward endevoring, and upright
> Stood on my feet; about me round I saw
> Hill, Dale, and shadie Woods, and sunnie Plaines,

And liquid Lapse of murmuring Streams; by these,
Creatures that livd, and movd, and walk'd, or flew,
Birds on the branches warbling; all things smil'd,
With fragrance and with joy my heart oreflow'd. (VIII, 257–66)

Going on then to "peruse" himself, Adam first addresses the sun, then the "Hills and Dales" and other "fair Creatures," only to infer immediately that all has derived from "some great Maker," whom he wishes to "know" and "adore."[50]

Psalm 19 does not explicitly enumerate the vegetative aspects of the creation but emphasizes objects said in Genesis to have been created on the first two days, the building of the heavens and the firmament. That the psalmist mixes writerly metaphors with architectural ones has already been intimated in the brief discussion of the Hebrew of verse 4, which even when it is translated as "line" may refer either to a line of writing or to a builder's plumb line. Calvin's commentary tends to reinscribe this blurring of metaphors, just as Raphael will in Book VIII of *Paradise Lost*. He refers to God as "the supreme Architect" and at the same time proposes that the world is "an open volume" for all to read. Yet Calvin actually offers a careful separation, one which stands behind Browne's distinction between the Book that God wrote Himself (through penmen) and "that universall and publik Manuscript, that lies expans'd unto the eyes of all," which was written by "his servant Nature." Calvin acknowledges that we know about "the tyme and maner of their creation" only from Scripture (p. 75^v, for 67^v) and concedes that God may "haue hild his peace" or have spoken "no woord at all" on the subject of creation. Although Calvin rejects the interpretation of the psalm whereby the heavens are said to stand for the apostles, the structure of his interpretation bears an important affinity to the older allegorical vein: for the heavens are said to be "teachers," who serve as a sort of substitute speaker for an otherwise silent Creator (p. 75^v, for 67^v).[51]

This conception of the physical world speaking up clearly for God seems to be undermined, however, by a striking feature of the psalm that many commentators may have glimpsed and sought to evade. Having announced in the opening lines that

The heavens declare the glory of God;
    and the firmament showeth his handiwork.
Day unto day uttereth speech,
    and night unto night showeth knowledge,

the next verse threatens to take it all back. Literally rendered, without the italicized words supplied in the Authorized Version, it says:

> no speech nor language,
>   their voice is not heard.

For centuries interpreters had debated whether this last verse meant to say that of course the heavens are literally mute but they function as eloquent speakers if one allows for a transfer from hearing to sight. Calvin acknowledged that this had been proferred as a possible interpretation. But he rejected it in favor of one that seems "contrarie," whereby precisely the heavenly writing announced in verse 4 does the work of declaring and proclaiming.

To guard against a reading whereby the Psalmist might be thought to assert that God's message goes unheeded because inherently it cannot be understood, modern translators regularly inserted a word or words that would sustain the excited and exalted tones of the opening verses. Calvin explains that the nature of the Hebrew language, being characteristically concise, warrants this sort of adaptation: "ofttymes somewhat is too bee supplyed: and specially it is a comon thing with the Hebrewes, to leaue out the relatyues" (p. 68^r). He goes on to insist that the heavens are universally eloquent and proposes that the psalmist contrasts their language with all human languages: "Dauid therfore by a couert comparison enlargeth the efficacie of this witnesse which the heauens beare to their maker: as if he shuld saye, although people differ among themselues in languages, yit the heauens haue a comon language to teach them all at once: and there is none other let, saue their owne dulnesse, but then euen they which be most straungers may profit as it were at the mouth of one teacher" (p. 68^r). In this way, sorting through "two interpretations in maner contrarie" (p. 75^v, for 67^v), the commentary manages to evade the interesting possibility that at verse 3 the psalm momentarily modulates into a lament that God's Word goes unheard because of qualities inherent in the cosmic language itself. Calvin's commentary on the Psalm, then, would protect it from interpretation along lines to be developed by scientific thinkers in the following century, who would propose that understanding the *liber naturae* requires specialized knowledge.

In the commentary on the latter verses of Psalm 19, Calvin insists that ignorance of God and failure to understand the divine language are purely a function of human depravity. Because of human sinfulness the Law has been given: "For although there remayne still in vs certein scrappes of our first creation: yet notwithstanding, bycause no part contineweth pure from defylinge and infection, the state of the sowle in such wyse appayred, differeth little from death. . . . And therfore, it is of necessitie, that GOD should succour vs by the remedie of his Lawe" (p. 77ᵛ, for 69ᵛ). Calvin's opinion, then, about the basis for the discontinuity beginning at verse 7 is that the two parts of the poem refer to two phases of history. Knowing that fallen humanity in its ignorance and stupidity has failed to read the "instructions ynow" that God has placed "in the Theatre of the world," Calvin says, the Psalmist "now . . . falleth in hand with the Jewes, to whom God hath bin made better knowen by his word" (p. 77ʳ, for 69ʳ).

In the pages that follow Calvin makes explicit his division of the history of reading the world into two discontinuous periods: original sin made the previously legible world-as-book seem unintelligible and necessitated the giving of God's second book, the Scriptures. This view parallels Calvin's assertion in his commentary on Genesis that the Bible provides fallen humanity with the spectacles that "not only make those things plain which would otherwise escape our notice, but almost compels us to behold them." Similarly in the *Institutes* Calvin insists that it would not even be "profitable for us to know that thyng which God himselfe to proue the modesty of our Faith, hathe of purpose willed to be hidden." Here the metaphor of the spectacles serves as a figure for the Scriptures as a belated gift to aid fallen humanity in reading the Book of the World:

> For as olde men, or people blinde, or they whose eyes are dim sighted, if you lay a fayre booke before them, though they perceiue that there is somewhat written therin, yet can they not read two wordes together: but being holpen with spectacles set betwene them and it, they begin to read distinctlie: so the Scripture gathering up together in our minds the knowledge of God, which otherwise is but confused, doth remoue the mist, and plainly shew us the true God. This therfore is a singuler gift, that to the instruction of his Church God useth not onely dum teachers, but also openeth his owne holy mouth: not onely publisheth that ther is some God to be worshipped, but also therwithal pronounceth that he himself is the same God.[52]

In the commentary on Psalm 19, Calvin returns often to the theme of the need for the Law. The psalm is said to contrast the Law with "the crooked ways wherin men entangle themselues by following their own wit" (p. 77ᵛ, for 69ᵛ). Even the saints, Calvin claims in his commentary on the "secret fawtes" of verse 12, get "besnareled in the snares of Sathan and perceiue not euen their grosse sinnes" (p. 71ᵛ). Moreover, the psalmist is said to acknowledge "that onlesse god help him, he must needes bee ouerwhelmed with the unmeasurable multitude and hougenesse of mischeeues"; from which it follows, Calvin adds, that "ther is no kynde of sin wherin Satan will not entangle vs" (p. 72ʳ). In this way Calvin's commentary on the psalm ultimately inducts the world-as-book topos into a dogmatic insistence on human depravity. Calvin presents the world as virtually unreadable except insofar as its very existence can be said to show up human ignorance, and he provides a theological rationale for a moralizing perspective that has often been assumed to have explanatory power with respect both to Milton's retelling of the story of Adam and Eve and to his depiction of the world-as-book.[53]

Difficulties in Reading the Book of the World

Paradise Lost not only allows that the world-as-book became more difficult to read after the Fall; it represents the world-as-book as having been already difficult to read before the Fall. This aspect of the poet's vision has been obscured for us by habits of thinking about Milton's redaction of the Fall narrative in terms provided by categories similar to those that have just been cited from works by Calvin. These categories sort oddly with Milton's treatment in his early writings of the notion that the world is like a text. In the 1630s Milton characteristically expressed views that were more appreciative of human capacities, and he reiterated these earlier views when he came to imagine paradise as a partly tangled text.

The terms provided in Book VIII of *Paradise Lost* for thinking about reading "the Book of God" are highly reminiscent of ones that may be found in the Seventh Prolusion (c. 1632), where Milton had been calling for intellectual labor in the face of "the world." In this work Milton sounded keenly optimistic about the readiness with which "Learning" can be "our guide and leader in the search after happiness." The perspective and tone of this passage anticipate those which are voiced by Raphael, and the issues raised here anticipate ones that are on the minds of Adam and Eve:

> God would indeed seem to have endowed us to no purpose, or even to our distress, with this soul which is capable and indeed insatiably desirous of the highest wisdom, if he had not intended us to strive with all our might toward the lofty understanding of those things, for which he had at our creation instilled so great a longing into the human mind. Survey from every angle the entire aspect of these things and you will perceive that the great Artificer of this

mighty fabric established it for His own glory. The more deeply we delve into the wondrous wisdom, the marvellous skill, and the astounding variety of its creation (which we cannot do without the aid of Learning), the greater grows the wonder and awe we feel for its Creator and the louder the praises we offer Him, which we believe and are fully persuaded that He delights to accept. Can we indeed believe, my hearers, that the vast spaces of boundless air are illuminated and adorned with everlasting lights, that these are endowed with such rapidity of motion and pass through such intricate revolutions, merely to serve as a lantern for base and slothful men, and to light the path of the idle and the sluggard here below? Do we perceive no purpose in the luxuriance of fruit and herb beyond the short-lived beauty of verdure? (trans. Phyllis B. Tillyard; *CPW*, I, 291–92)

The perspective and tone here are altogether different from what we find in the critical period when Milton began to think of the Bible as worthy of a comparable interpretive scrutiny. The unsympathetic reference to Arminius in *Areopagitica* (*CPW*, II, 519–20) alerts us to Milton's attempt in this period to frame arguments that would be acceptable to the Calvinist majority. It is not necessarily surprising therefore that in *Areopagitica* the effects of original sin are presented in the reference to Psyche's endless culling and that the difficulty of the interpretive task is emphasized. In the England of 1644, one might speak of the "mighty fabric" of the world as having been tattered. "[W]onder and awe" have been largely replaced by suspicion and repression, and "the luxuriance of fruit and herb" is easily taken as a sign that things are out of control. The "body" of "Truth" has been "hewd" and "scatter'd," and requires a "carefull search" and "gathering" that cannot be complete "till her Masters second comming" (II, 549). At such a moment, "all human learning and controversie in religious points" evinces the intermixture. "[Y]ea the Bible it selfe" is now said

> oftimes [to] relate . . . blasphemy not nicely, it describes the carnall sense of wicked men not unelegantly, it brings in holiest men passionately murmuring against providence through all the arguments of *Epicurus:* in other great disputes it answers dubiously and darkly to the common reader. (II, 517)

In short, *Areopagitica* (1644) incorporates the argument from the divorce pamphlets about the importance of acknowledging ambiguity in the Scriptures, and it extends that argument so that it applies to the Book of the fallen World as well. Milton no longer thinks of the Scriptures as "plain," and he posits a consistency in interpretive tasks of every sort, all of which are now said to require the kind of labor that before 1643 he had been reserving for interpreting secular books and *liber Naturæ*.

The continuity of Milton's argument in *Areopagitica* with Calvinist doctrine is most dramatically apparent in its ascription of the origin of interpretive complexities to the Fall. It was not unusual in seventeenth-century England that the sort of language used by Calvin to describe the fallen world—images of a labyrinth and crooked bypaths, talk about entanglement and carrying an immense load—would be put at the service of a strongly moralistic condemnation of human sinfulness and corruption. In fact, such language was frequently used in similar ways by divines, as Stanley Fish has emphasized. Clearly, it was available to poets. In "The Coronet" by Marvell, the speaker finds in the garland he seeks to weave "the Serpent . . . twining" and looks to Christ to "disintangle all his winding Snare." Similarly, in poems by George Herbert—"A Wreath," the two poems called "Jordan," and several others gathered in *The Temple*— "crooked winding wayes" are figured as morally degenerate and degenerating.[54] And of course before Marvell and Herbert and Milton used such imagery there had been Spenser, whose connection with Milton is often illustrated by way of *Areopagitica*.

The tendency to think of Milton as a moralizing poet has been reinforced by the widespread habit of citing passages from *Areopagitica*, which is manifestly concerned with books and reading, as a key with which to gloss *Paradise Lost*. This propensity is especially evident in the theory that "the reader" is not only the principal addressee of the poem but its subject, and that the humiliation of this reader is the poet's, or at least the poem's, principal goal. In the course of *Surprised by Sin* Fish cited *Areopagitica* several times, the first in an attempt to intimate that Milton read the Bible in the way Bunyan's burdened Christian does at the outset of *The Pilgrim's Progress*: "Books draw out what is in a man," Fish paraphrases a passage from *Areopagitica* accurately enough, and then goes on: "and Scripture, the best of books, searches out a man's corruption and reveals it to him." Applying this idea directly to the interpretation of *Paradise Lost*, Fish claims that Milton "would be derelict in his duty" if he allowed us to think that God is "loving." The harshness of Milton's God, indeed any distaste we feel for the "doctrine" of the poem, derives from our sinful "recalcitrance" (pp. 84–86). *Areopagitica* is later invoked to urge us to think that Milton dwelt on human sinfulness: "The inaccessibility of Paradise is more a question of psychology than geography. 'Assuredly we bring not innocence into the world, we bring impurity much rather.' . . . Fallen man's perceptual equipment . . . is his prison" (p. 103). Having been "[e]ndowed with 'minds that can wander beyond all limit and satiety' (*Areopagitica*), we come naturally to" raise impertinent "questions" about the Creator's designs, whereas "it is our duty, once they have arisen and shown themselves unanswerable except by blasphemies, to give them over and . . . [accept] on faith what we are unable to understand" (p. 245). From Fish's perspective, since the whole poem is deliberately designed to humiliate and chasten us, the advice offered by Raphael in the passage that stands as epigraph for this chapter is addressed above all to the fallen reader, who must be "lowly wise" and learn to eschew "vain curiosities." These include "ambiguity and metaphor," which are "the basis of all distortion." These "enemies live within" the reader and insure that he "is unable to limit his response to the literal signification of a word descriptive of paradise or its inhabitants" (p. 128). To encounter words like "wander" or "wanton," "disshevll'd" or "tangl'd" in the prelapsarian portions of the poem is to be "surprised by sin" and required to acknowledge one's own sinfulness and the depravity of human nature.

The section from *Areopagitica* most often cited by interpreters of *Paradise Lost* includes the famous reference to Guyon's journey "through the cave of Mammon, and the bowr of earthly blisse" (*CPW*, II, 516). It is not surprising therefore that Milton's conception of the fallen world is often compared to Spenser's. Maureen Quilligan, for instance, praises Milton's sophisticated adaptations of Spenserian language to depict that world. In her view, the choice posed for Adam and Eve before the Fall, though "momentous," is "sheer simplicity." By contrast, postlapsarian choices, which *Paradise Lost* is said to represent in language and imagery borrowed from *The Faerie Queene,* illustrate that Milton "replicates Spenser's methods of ensuring his reader's entanglement" (p. 75).

> Milton's landscapes, unlike Spenser's, are more clearly labeled good and evil— heaven is heaven, hell hell, and paradise, while it lasts, a good place. But the process of negotiating the journey through them is filled with as many pitfalls, for both reader and narrator, as any thicket in fairyland. Because we bring not innocence into the world but impurity much rather, the reader of *Paradise Lost* needs to be just as wary of his or her responses as Spenser's reader does. (pp. 77–78)

Focusing on the "reader and narrator," Quilligan posits an utter discontinuity (reminiscent of Johnson's remarks on the history of the language) between prelapsarian simplicity and postlapsarian complexity. Spenserian choice requires us to make our way through a "linguistically dense landscape" (p. 14). By contrast with Adam and Eve's "clearly labeled" choice in Eden, "Spenser's kind of choosing" is said to involve a "densely interwoven plurality of possibility" and to call for a "deliberative picking of [one's] way through a landscape which may be good, or may be evil" (p. 77). What this sharp contrast asks us to ignore, however, is that *Paradise Lost* does not represent such a landscape as coming into being only after the Fall. That is, as Raphael's comparison of the heavens to a book intimates, Milton had come to imagine that even before the Fall humankind had encountered a burden of interpretation. In describing the unfallen world Milton took up language that moralizing divines and some poets, including Spenser, had associated with human depravity, and invited readers to imagine a time when that language aptly described a complex world that could be understood in large part on the model of their experiences with books and reading.

The familiar language of moralists and the practice of several other poets notwithstanding, it ought not to be presupposed that when *Paradise Lost* deploys a language of tangles and thickets and wanton growth, its meaning must be understood only in conventional ways. To return for a moment to the semantic field that has given rise to the hypothesis that Adam and Eve are "always already" fallen, we may consider that in *Paradise Lost* there are numerous images of things that are said to be "thick": stars, bushes, woods, coverings, clouds, and so forth. Already in the prelapsarian section of the poem, these images carry a decided multivalence. Sometimes, particularly in descriptions of the stars (e.g., VII, 358; X, 411), "thickness" is a quality linked to beauty. Sometimes it suggests superabundance. This brings it into another rich semantic domain, one elaborated in Renaissance books of rhetoric, where *copia* is a veritable synonym for "eloquence." As Terence Cave has shown, "[a]lthough *copia rerum* and *copia verborum* are often referred to separately" in this literature, "their integration in an ideally abundant discourse is always recommended, as is the priority of *res*."[55] The priority appears, of course, in the idea that "the heavens declare the glory of God." It profoundly informs Milton's conception of the thick, dense natural world as a copious text:

> A Wilderness of sweets; for Nature here
> Wantond as in her prime, and plaid at will
> Her Virgin Fancies, pouring forth more sweet,
> Wilde above Rule or Art; enormous bliss. (V, 294–97)

Drawing on the conventions of classical rhetoric, Milton's representation of the unfallen world makes it like the Bible as Milton came to conceive it in

The Bookish Burden Before the Fall   221

his maturity: it is a "treasure-chest" or "store" from which the first human actors are able to draw for their nourishment and entertainment and delight. As if to renew by anticipation the injunction of the parable of the talents, when Raphael approaches, Adam counsels Eve to

> goe with speed,
> And what thy stores contain, bring forth and poure
> Abundance, fit to honour and receive
> Our Heav'nly stranger; well we may afford
> Our givers thir own gifts, and large bestow
> From large bestowd, where Nature multiplies
> Her fertil growth, and by disburd'ning grows
> More fruitful, which instructs us not to spare.   (V, 313–20)

In preparing the meal, Eve shows herself to be a consummate gatherer from a vast world condensed into near-by spaces:

> Whatever Earth all-bearing Mother yeilds
> In *India* East or West, or middle shoare
> In *Pontus* or the *Punic* Coast, or where
> *Alcinous* reign'd, fruit of all kindes, in coate,
> Rough, or smooth rin'd, or bearded husk, or shell
> She gathers, Tribute large, and on the board
> Heaps with unsparing hand; for drink the Grape
> She crushes, inoffensive moust, and meathes
> From many a berrie, and from sweet kernels prest
> She tempers dulcet creams, nor these to hold
> Wants her fit vessels pure, then strews the ground
> With Rose and Odours from the shrub unfum'd.   (V, 338–49)

Yet this dense cornucopia is not yet fully explored, nor fully known. Occasionally, a "thicket" is the locus of mysterious voices and presences. Attempting to enter paradise proper, Satan encounters the "entwin'd" thicket, where the "undergrowth / Of shrubs and tangling bushes had perplext / All path of Man or Beast" (IV, 174–77). Elsewhere, he supposes that he may find "Some wandring Spirit of Heav'n" couched in "thick shade" (IV, 531–32). This is consistent with what Adam and Eve have already discovered about the thicket that surrounds paradise proper, from which, as Adam says to Eve, they have "often . . . heard / Celestial voices"

(IV, 680–82). Occasionally, "thicknesss" suggests an almost wholly unattractive quality, as when Satan is compared to someone too long "pent" in a "populous City," "Where Houses thick and Sewers annoy the Aire" (IX, 445–46). Yet sometimes a thicket creates protection or even seems to make for impenetrability, implying however a need for defenses. It may also provide privacy, as in the roof of the "blissful Bower," which, as Milton revises Spenser, has been "fram'd" by God for "delightful use." It seems to be a desire for privacy that prompts Adam and Eve, after their original transgression, to hide themselves "among / The thickest Trees," where they nonetheless hear "the voice of God" (X, 101, 97).

The poet of *Paradise Lost* was under no obligation to play up a variety of senses of "thick," which hardly seem consistent or reconcilable or divisible into discontinuous prelapsarian and postlapsarian senses. Nor was there necessity to insist that the fertile garden of Eden was hedged about by "a steep wilderness, whose hairie sides / With thicket overgrown, [are] grottesque and wilde" (IV, 135–36). Doing so, Milton was not merely calling attention to a transgression by Satan, who leaped over a thick wall that "Access deni'd" (137). He was able also to suggest the likelihood that eventually unfallen humans were to cross the boundaries of paradise proper into an area still to be explored and made habitable, an area filled with places thus far unknown and, as Raphael observes, not "yet distinct by name" (VII, 536).[56] Later in the poem Michael proposes a basic continuity when he advises Adam,

> All th' Earth he gave thee to possess and rule,
> No despicable gift; surmise not then
> His presence to these narrow bounds confin'd
> Of Paradise or *Eden:* this had been
> Perhaps thy Capital Seate, from whence had spred
> All generations.   (XI, 339–44)

Milton thus invites readers to imagine that unfallen Adam and Eve and their descendents would be able to participate in the creation of a wider paradise wherein more "hands" would enjoy the process of untangling and of creating. Addressing Eve, Adam already envisages such an augmentation of pleasure. (Anticipation is of course part of their pleasure.)

> To morrow ere fresh Morning streak the East
> With first approach of light, we must be ris'n,

The Bookish Burden Before the Fall 223

> And at our pleasant labour, to reform
> Yon flourie Arbors, yonder Allies green,
> Our walk at noon, with branches overgrown,
> That mock our scant manuring, and require
> More hands then ours to lop thir wanton growth:
> Those Blossoms also, and those dropping Gumms,
> That lie bestrowne unsightly and unsmooth,
> Ask riddance, if we mean to tread with ease;
> Mean while, as Nature wills, Night bids us rest.   (IV, 623–33)

Milton's prelapsarian paradise, far from being a "perfect" world in the older sense of the term, complete in itself, is a realm in which humans are required to pick up "unsightly" objects strewn about here and there and to prune "overgrown" branches, if they mean to make themselves a suitable place of rest. For "where any row / Of Fruit-trees overwoodie reachd too farr / Thir pamperd boughes," they "needed hands to check / Fruitless imbraces" (V, 212–15). As Eve later attests, this paradise entails a set of meaning-making tasks already understood to be too large for their scanty hands. The very acts by which they tend the garden compound the complexity of the landscape:

> till more hands
> Aid us, the work under our labour grows,
> Luxurious by restraint; what we by day
> Lop overgrown, or prune, or prop, or bind,
> One night or two with wanton growth derides
> Tending to wilde.   (IX, 207–12)

This feature of paradise suggests that Adam and Eve are not only "authors to themselves" but editors of their work—and God's work. The acts of lopping and pruning, propping up and binding together (cf. the conference of places) are all of them analogous to activities well known to and often practiced with pleasure by mature writers. The need to manage a wonderfully "wilde" and "wanton growth" to which their own work contributes confers a sense of purpose upon Adam and Eve's existence and proves the source of their vocations. It motivates a desire for propagation, and that desire matches the first of God's commands, to be fruitful and multiply. Until they fall Adam and Eve look forward to sharing bounties that include a "Dignity" inherent in having their daily work. At the same time this paradise would cease to be paradise if there were not leisure: "Mean while, as Nature wills, Night bids us rest." The conversation that Adam and Eve have been experiencing, and the love-making and rest that they enjoy, all have their places in making up a grand harmonious daily symphony which Adam attempts to name and which Book IV celebrates. This conception of paradise as a process in which humans participate involves a delicate balancing act. Adam's straining to make his interpretation work at once shows him carrying out the most dignified of his appointed tasks and reveals the point where paradise is most vulnerable. That vulnerability is presented by the poet, interpreting Genesis by way of his knowledge of the whole Bible, as a constituent feature of paradise itself. In *Paradise Lost* it is a condition of possibility for meaningful interpretive labors, and therefore for the pleasures to be experienced in and through interpretive activity.

Tangles and Pleasures in the Landscape and in the Language

John Leonard's fine book on "naming" in *Paradise Lost* has renewed appreciation that Milton did not share the view that all language is arbitrarily established by custom and convention. Adam "had the wisdom giv'n him to know all creatures," Milton observed in *Tetrachordon*, "and to name them according to their properties" (*CPW*, II, 602). Adam "could not have given names to the animals in that extempore way," Milton later proposed in *De Doctrina*, "without very great intelligence" (*CPW*, VI, 324). Hence, the celebration in *Paradise Lost* of the "knowledg" with which "God endu'd / [His] sudden apprehension" (VIII, 353–54). Yet this does not mean that Milton was merely closing his or his readers' eyes to current developments and desperately clinging to outmoded views. In his view, human language, although tainted since the Fall, might still operate as a vehicle for joining humans and God, just as the Scriptures, though corrupted over the course of the history of their transmission, would nonetheless serve as the means for reconstructing the Word of God.[57]

In *Paradise Lost* Milton shows that he does not read Psalm 19 as a poem describing two discontinuous periods in human history, a time before the Fall when all was clear and simple and a time after the Fall when language became entangled and obscure. Comparing Psalm 19 and Genesis 1–3, Milton inferred that already before the Fall the Book of the World had been a site of interpretation and, in large part, a book that was difficult to read. In particular, Raphael's speech to Adam in Book VIII suggests that Milton understood the key phrase, "no speech, no language, their voice is not heard," in a way that leaves room to suppose, as Spenser had when he represented "antique" experience in *The Faerie Queene*, that the intelligibility of the material world is not purely a function of linguistic experience. The world-as-book is assumed in *Paradise Lost* to be intelligible in its own non-verbal terms before it is compared to a written book. Once the comparison is made, the world-as-book may be "read" as a source of both mathematical and linguistic communications, for many of which only a specialized training equips "readers" to understand. It is against the possibility that Adam may think that God requires such training of him personally and at his moment in history that Raphael assures him that "Heav'n / Is as the Book of God before thee set, / Wherein to read his wondrous Works, and learne / His Seasons, Hours, or Dayes, or Months, or Yeares." After giving this assurance, Raphael then proceeds to unsettle Adam's inchoate conceptions about the world by raising a series of questions about cosmology. These questions give way to advice that suggests that the time is not ripe to pursue them:

> Leave them to God above, him serve and feare;
> Of other Creatures, as him pleases best,
> Wherever plac't, let him dispose: joy thou
> In what he gives to thee, this Paradise
> And thy faire *Eve*; Heav'n is for thee too high
> To know what passes there; be lowlie wise:
> Think onely what concernes thee and thy being;
> Dream not of other Worlds, what Creatures there
> Live, in what state, condition or degree,
> Contented that thus farr hath been reveal'd
> Not of Earth onely but of highest Heav'n.   (VIII, 168–78)

"Thus farr": the speech is addressed not to the fallen reader, but to Adam, in his particular place and time. It is a "not unseasonable" place (201), from which he sees that there will be other times for him and for his progeny to encounter the considerable obscurity and many tangles that are already present in the unfallen world:

> How fully hast thou satisfi'd mee, pure
> Intelligence of Heav'n, Angel serene,
> And freed from intricacies, taught to live,

> The easiest way, nor with perplexing thoughts
> To interrupt the sweet of Life, from which
> God hath bid dwell farr off all anxious cares,
> And not molest us, unless we our selves
> Seek them with wandring thoughts, and notions vain.
> But apt the Mind or Fancie is to roave
> Uncheckt, and of her roaving is no end;
> Till warn'd, or by experience taught, she learne,
> That not to know at large of things remote
> From use, obscure and suttle, but to know
> That which before us lies in daily life,
> Is the prime Wisdom.   (VIII, 180–94)

The Fall, then, "interrupt[s] the sweet of Life." It hastens Adam and Eve's contact with "things . . . obscure and suttle." It increases the difficulty of interpretive labors immensely. It does not originate those difficulties.

Paradise Lost does not present the tangles of language as a result of the Fall any more than it presents the tangles of landscape as a postlapsarian condition. The Fall of Adam and Eve is shown to have greatly intensified an interpretive burden that was already there, and whether they fell or not humans would have had to deal with it in due season at the undefined borders of a garden paradise that was "tending to wilde."[58] Milton's poem does not represent prelapsarian experience simply as wholeness, postlapsarian as doubleness: doubleness and ambiguity are there for Adam and Eve to encounter from the beginning. They are a constituent of paradise, an aspect of its *copia* and an epitome of the distinctively human "place" which is Eden, a "Wilderness of sweets" offering "enormous bliss."

A Coda

If Milton accepted as an assumption that writing provides a model for creating meaning he may be thought merely a product of his moment in history. Insofar as he contributed to the establishment of this new assumption, however, he was expecting that readers who had made their way through the first ten books of his epic would be capable of rather considerable sophistication in reading the last books. For the ascription of priority to writing over all other possible realms of meaning, when it is tied to the idea that God is the "Author" of the universe and of history, promotes a conception of human life that allows little scope for human freedom and responsibility. The predestinarian framework of Protestant divinity posited divine foreknowledge of each individual's eternal destiny. This cardinal tenet — almost as inevitably as the divine prohibition of forbidden knowledge in the Genesis myth — stimulated curiosity. The fact that writing fixes language visibly in space suggested to many who were committed to live by "the Bible only" that God not only foresees the outcome of each human story but that all outcomes have already been scripted. Moreover, the twin claims that the Bible was a unique repository of saving truth and that its canon was closed seemed to confirm the surmise that each person's destiny had been determined in advance. Milton therefore risked a good deal when, in Books XI and XII, he depicted Adam viewing and hearing future events as if they were already fixed. It is importantly true that what Michael shows Adam is contingent on the first parents' decision to go ahead and begin human history. Yet the concreteness of future persons and events would seem to create a context that radically limits the degree to which any given human being might be thought to "author" the meaning of his or her own life-narrative.

The story of an original man and woman placed in a garden paradise and forbidden to eat from a tree of knowledge likely exercised the imaginations of seventeenth-century English Protestants, then, in historically specific ways. What was especially problematic in "experimental" religion, it will be recalled, was generated by the presupposition that one's faith might turn out to have been merely temporary. The problem was made the more urgent by popular insistence that the truly elect would make their calling and election sure by diligent searching of the Scriptures to find a personally appropriate "place." In the context of this problematic the last two books of *Paradise Lost* merit reconsideration, despite Stanley Fish's pre-emptive insinuation that attention to these books has been superfluous for more than twenty years.[59]

When Books XI and XII are seen in the context of seventeenth-century "experimentalist" advice about finding an assuring "place," they constitute an imaginative attempt to revise popular notions about what the Scriptures have to offer and how they are to be read. Set between the judgment of Adam and Eve and their banishment, these books concern a period about which the Bible itself is virtually silent. To fill in what happened Milton made a bold comparison of places, obliquely drawing not only on epic precedents that offered a vision of the future but also on a structural parallel that had been explicitly proposed in the medieval exegetical tradition. He revised that parallel in accord with what had become his habitual means of dealing with the parable of talents.

In the exegetical tradition, the banishment of Adam and Eve from the garden was sometimes compared to the casting out of the unprofitable servant at the end of Matthew's parable.[60] As Chapter Three has shown, for many centuries burying one's talent was read as a figure for failing to interpret the Scriptures and to multiply converts. Milton's extensive allusion to this text in *The Reason of Church Government,* where he imagines being called to account for having failed to use "those few talents which God . . . had lent" him (*CPW,* I, 804), rested upon this traditional line of interpretation. In Book X of *Paradise Lost,* after the Fall, he drew once again on the imagery of accountability that figures prominently in the parable, assimilating the task which the master enjoined upon his servants to the first commandment given to Adam and Eve, to "Increase and multiply" (730). Adam responds to his recollection of this command in terms closely analogous to those in which the unprofitable servant is thinking when he renders back the one talent he has hidden, protesting that he knew his master was "a hard man, reaping where [he had] not sown, and gathering where [he had] not strewed." Adam protests that he never asked for being, nor to be "promote[d]" from "darkness" (the unprofitable servant's ultimate "place") into the "delicious Garden":

> as my Will
> Concurd not to my being, it were but right
> And equal to reduce me to my dust,
> Desirous to resigne, and render back
> All I receav'd, unable to performe
> Thy terms too hard, by which I was to hold
> The good I sought not. (X, 746–52)

Nonetheless, if it is to be acknowledged that Milton exploited the possibility of comparing the parable of the talents with the story of the first parents, an obvious difficulty interposes itself. The conjunction of these texts made eating the forbidden fruit the functional equivalent of burying one's talent. Yet Adam and Eve live long before the Scriptures are written. Even Milton's version of the story, in which they are afforded a preview, makes no mention of Jesus' parables, and the vast majority of materials that will go into the Bible become available only after the Fall. This suggests that if Milton did draw on the parable of the talents, read as an injunction to interpret the Scriptures, to fill in events between the Fall and the banishment, then he asks his readers to think that something functionally equivalent to the Scriptures had already been part of Adam and Eve's experience in paradise. Moreover, the visions and narrations provided by Michael are thus implied to be as an aspect of the *restoration* of the conditions which make up paradise. An earlier section of this chapter has intimated that Milton made and invited just this sort of conference of biblical places and that in particular he drew on Psalm 19, interpreted as a poem about the relations between God's two books, to justify the inference that even in paradise Adam and Eve were living under an injunction to increase and multiply the knowledge of God's proliferating writing. From the outset the world was defined as a site of interpretive activity and Eden as a place of interpretive pleasures.

There are of course reasons for thinking that it does not matter that Adam and Eve do not have written canonical Scriptures. Georgia Christopher proposed, for instance, that, following Luther's understanding of the law and the gospel, Milton insured that the first parents had the essence of the Bible when he highlighted the importance of the *protevangelium*. This "text," which contains the gospel in miniature, is "opened" at a crucial moment in Book X, initiating the process of regeneration which then carries through the final books. Moreover, according to Marshall Grossman, the revelations provided by Raphael and by Michael serve a role analogous in the experience of Adam and Eve to what the Bible served for seventeenth-century Protestants: they provide normative paradigms in relation to which all human actions are to be understood, so that "an individual authors himself by acting out a story foreseen and revealed by God." In Grossman's view when Adam interprets the *protevangelium* in terms of God's mercy it is because he already knows the future proleptically via his access to the transcendental plot of God's providence.[61]

It is accurate to say that the sort of interpretive breakthrough reported in many spiritual autobiographies of the seventeenth century was delicately inscribed in *Paradise Lost*. After the Fall, in Book X, Adam seems suddenly to have a delayed insight of considerable power: in the midst of his despair he remembers the promise about "the seed of the woman" and applies it to the situation in which he and Eve find themselves. Subsequently, they develop new hopes in God's forgiveness and in the possibility that future events will transform the significance of their guilty action. To borrow the phrase singled out of the poem by Grossman, Adam and Eve recover their original God-given ability to be "authors to themselves." The significance of the moment in Book X when Adam remembers the promise was pointed out by Georgia Christopher, who proposed that Adam's interpretive insight was modeled on a paradigm whereby Bible readers would find personally appropriate texts that served as vehicles of grace. The relevance of this paradigm to the structure of *Paradise Lost* is, however, more thoroughgoing and much more troubled than its application to the moment when Adam remembers the words that will become the biblical *protevangelium*. As the presence of the phrase "authors to themselves" in the passage in which God predicts the fall of Adam and Eve might suggest, the concept of self-authorship in Milton's epic is not utterly benign.

By the seventeenth century, it was becoming evident that some cardinal assumptions of Luther and Tyndale made for serious difficulties: a person might be persuaded of his or her election, but what if one were really a reprobate destined, like Saul or Judas, eventually to fall away? Moreover, not every "case or state" found by introspective Bible-readers involved a happy "end." Calvin had foreseen the problems and warned against looking for biblical evidence that fixed the end of one's life-story in advance. He forbade a reader to pry into "the hidden secrets of the wisdome of God, and to pearce even to the hyest eternitie to understand what is determined of himself at the iudgement seat of God." One who should attempt this, according to Calvin, "wrappeth himselfe with innumerable snares."[62] Not all "Calvinists" followed Calvin's advice. Bunyan thought that his case most closely resembled that of Esau, who "found no place of repentance, though he sought it carefully with tears." The speaker at the beginning of Milton's sonnet, "When I consider how my light is spent," thought his case resembled that of the man who hid his talent and was cast into "utter darkness." After his fall, Adam in *Paradise Lost* is likewise in danger of thinking himself "cast out" and destined for damnation.

In the last two books of *Paradise Lost* Adam is educated to deal with the "horror of horrors" for readers who sought "experimental" knowledge in the Bible: the danger of apostasy. In the 1650s and 1660s introspective Bible-reading had begun to spill over into the writing of numerous diaries and conversion narratives, many of which explored in narrative terms the principal practical difficulty to which Calvin's theology gave rise, the problem of temporary faith. The ramifications of this problem have been explored in Chapter One, and briefly recapitulating, the problem was that it was possible to be deceived about one's faith, supposing oneself to be numbered among the elect when in reality one was a reprobate who would inevitably fall away. If you were to be damned anyway, why not, as Bunyan put it, take your fill of sinning? Against the horrifying surmise that one's "case" conformed to that of a reprobate like Cain or Esau, believers were counseled to read the Bible to find an assuring text that would motivate them to persevere. In accord with such advice, it seems, Michael is made to shape his materials in the light of a biblical "place" that will single out models of perseverance.

It has long been recognized that the last two books of *Paradise Lost* owe a very great deal to the eleventh chapter of the Epistle to the Hebrews. This section of the letter begins by defining faith as "the substance of things hoped for, the evidence of things not seen" (11: 1). It goes on to illustrate the workings of faith in a number of specific cases, in particular the very ones which Michael stresses. The principal focus of the Epistle is on the fact that Christ, "the author and finisher of *our* faith" (12: 2), has already completed his journey to the heavenly sanctuary, so that his followers have access now to God, but they must continue to labor and persevere through the long course of their lives. Abel, Enoch, Noah, Abraham, and the other "elders" enumerated in Hebrews — but not Adam, who is absent from the list — provided "ensambles" of those whose "case or state" had likewise reached a happy "end." For this reason, Hebrews had an especially great appeal in seventeenth-century England, what with many people running "through the professions" (as changing affiliations was called), and many fearing as they witnessed extensive apostacies among their neighbors that they themselves would fail to persevere. It is an index of the powerful hold that this way of thinking had that Hebrews is the biblical book to which Bunyan refers most often in his autobiography.[63]

At one point early on in *Grace Abounding*, Bunyan tells of an experience like that which in Milton's epic Michael provides for Adam. Soon after his conversion, he felt it necessary to "put [him]self upon the tryal," Bunyan says, "whether [he] had Faith or no," that is, whether he had the sort of "saving faith" that would enable him to persevere to the end. Although he did not know how to go about this, it turns out that he was directed by a text that imposed itself like a heavy "weight" upon his consciousness: "Look at the generations of old, and see, did ever any trust in God and were confounded?" And the idea then came upon him, "*Begin at the beginning of Genesis, and read to the end of the Revelations, and see if you can find that there was any that ever trusted in the Lord, and was Confounded*" (*GA*, p. 21). Bunyan did not begin at Genesis and search the Scriptures sequentially or systematically, however, to be certain that there was no damning counter-example: an instance of someone who had trusted and was nonetheless "cast out."

Instead, as he tells the story, he rummaged through the Bible for more than a year, and in vain, looking for a short-cut. He was trying to find the particular text which he thought he remembered hearing. Eventually, he discovered that the sentence came from one of the "Apocrypha-Books." This proved an occasion for a new way of thinking about how to interpret, the development of a conviction about what would be for him a personal rule of faith: he took such comfort as he could from the fact that this text seemed to be "the sum and substance of many of the promises" in the genuine Scriptures (*GA*, p. 22). Although abstracting a general drift from the Scriptures represented an advance over searching for talismanic "places," this comfort nonetheless proved quite scant. Almost immediately he was plunged into his obsessive anxiety that he had sinned irrevocably and that "the day of grace [was] past and gone." And before he learned to read more intelligently and responsibly he proceeded, for a number of years longer, to continue searching for a personally consoling text in one of the canonical books.

The final two books of *Paradise Lost* constitute an alternative version (first published within a year of Bunyan's) of "Grace Abounding to the Chief of Sinners." The first sinners in history have recently been converted from sin by "Prevenient Grace" (XI, 3). For his "sanctification," Adam needs to learn that it is not too late: his story is not over, its ending, although foreknown by God, is not thereby predetermined. Under the tutelage of Michael, who was sent that Adam may "beleeve, and be confirmd" (XI, 355), Adam searches the materials that will eventually be written down in the Scriptures, even before the events which they record and interpret ever happen. What Michael reveals about "future dayes" is foreknown, and will be added to Adam's experience so as to constitute the Word of God from the fourth chapter of "Genesis to the end of the Revelations." Adam's task consists in learning to "read" these materials in a manner that will provide him assurance of his salvation. In the course of his education Adam sees many examples of people who do not trust in God and are "confounded," that is, not only "put to shame" (*OED*, sense 3) but "brought to perdition" (sense 2); he learns too, as first he sees and later hears examples of "the one just man," that those who trust in God are not confounded. He learns it by way of making many errors, which Michael helps him to correct.[64] Like Cain and Nimrod and the Sons of God, but in a less serious because less permanent sense (which is the point), Adam in Books XI and XII is often "confounded," that is, (sense 4) "thrown into confusion of mind or feelings," so that he "loses for the moment his presence of mind, and discernment what to do."

The sorts of expectations brought by Bunyan and dozens of other "place"-seekers to the reading of the Bible provide a helpful horizon within which to appreciate how interpretation is represented as working in the last two books of *Paradise Lost*. Having experienced a spectacular "opening" when he remembered the promise, Adam, we may notice, keeps looking for similarly consoling epiphanies when Michael reveals what is to come. If his rehabilitation began when he applied the promise "experimentally," his faith is tested in the long series of visions and narratives about "the Race of time" (XII, 554). The revelations turn out mostly to concern terrible events — murders, treachery, and crimes of various sorts. Rather than fully to acknowledge these phenomena and his responsibility with respect to them, Adam tries repeatedly to get Michael to stop by proclaiming that his education is complete. Frequently he places an optimistic interpretation on what he sees or hears: "now first I finde / Mine eyes true op'ning, and my heart much eas'd" (XII, 273–74); "Now clear I understand" (XII, 376). Instead of producing the sense of an ending, however, Adam's declarations of "definitive understanding" repeatedly give way to disappointment, or at least to new opportunities for learning, as Michael is obliged to intervene and to correct his attempts to effect a premature resolution.[65] To some extent, however, Michael does accommodate Adam's weakness when he "intermix[es]" further evidences of the "Cov'nant in the womans seed renewd" (XI, 115–16). The cumulative effect on Adam is represented as chastening, but not debilitating. In his final speech he tells Michael that he will accept living with incomplete knowledge:

> How soon hath thy prediction, Seer blest,
> Measur'd this transient World, the Race of time,
> Till time stand fixt: beyond is all abyss,
> Eternitie, whose end no eye can reach.
> Greatly instructed I shall hence depart,
> Greatly in peace of thought, and have my fill
> Of knowledge, what this Vessel can containe.   (XII, 553–59)

To many readers' ears this may now sound as if Adam has at last accepted Raphael's advice to be "lowlie wise." Yet there is a significant difference between what Raphael had counseled about speculating on other worlds and what Adam claims here to have learned from a preview of the Scriptures.

When in the course of the discussion of cosmology in Book VIII, Raphael had counseled Adam to be "lowlie wise," there was something curiously literal about the word "lowlie." It was tied to explicit advice about avoiding speculation about the heavens:

> Dream not of other Worlds, what Creatures there
> Live, in what state, condition or degree,
> Contented that thus farr hath been reveal'd
> Not of Earth onely but of highest Heav'n.   (VIII, 175–79)

Nonetheless, the word "lowlie" is likely to have other associations for readers of the poem, ones that are not only less literal but also more demeaning. So habitual has the idea now become to think of Adam as a figure for Milton's "reader" that actual readers may ignore altogether the dramatic moment in history when this advice is tendered and instinctively suppose that Raphael is a spokesman for a narrator who seeks to teach his "reader" humility. Yet it needs to be recognized that Adam, besides being archetypal, is represented in *Paradise Lost* also as a concrete historical person, living long before the opportunities available to later historical figures, Galileo and the narrator and Milton's readers, who are able to explore the heavens with a telescope and to read the whole of the canonical Scriptures. For Adam to pre-empt the achievements of his successors might be ruinous both for his life and for theirs.[66] Raphael therefore advises that he work with what has "thus farr . . . been reveal'd."

Still, in view of the argument of this book, there are grounds for hearing in Raphael's words something like advice for Milton's readers. Acquaintance with popular reading habits of the period enables us to discern a genuine basis in this language for supposing that it gives advice about interpretation. The words "state" and "condition" were widely used by "experimentalist" divines to refer to election and reprobation, the twin "estates" or "conditions" that were thought to define the only possible categories into which any human story might be fitted. Against the background of the quest to make one's calling and election sure by finding one's "place," Raphael's advice to live only by the Book of the World sounds like an analogue to Protestant insistence upon "the Bible only." It also resonates with Calvin's much unheeded insistence that one ought not to try to find out what decision had been made about one's destiny at God's eternal judgment seat. John Hales, it may be recalled, argued specifically that the Holy Ghost does not provide "particular information for resolution in any doubtfull case," and he urged that difficult interpretive questions such as those concerning predestination be deferred indefinitely, lest people suffer from "the same disease that my first parents in Paradise had, a desire to knowe more then [we] need."[67]

The theme of Adam's final speech, then, articulates something that Milton's readers might learn by attending chiefly to the performance by the narrator, with whom they share a knowledge of biblical literature, in his work as an interpreter. Retelling the story from Genesis, the narrator has imposed limits analogous to the ones that Scripture imposes: neither the Bible nor *Paradise Lost* attempts to represent divine foreknowledge of the first parents' eventual fate. Whereas in Book III God had predicted the fall, in Books XI and XII Michael's revelation of "what shall come in future days" leaves the question of Adam and Eve's eternal destinies undecided. This is, in fact, one of the most important ways in which Milton makes Adam and Eve archetypal.[68] He puts them in fundamentally the same position as himself and his readers, who also do not know their eternal destiny. In taking "Mans First Disobedience" as his subject for *Paradise Lost*, Milton chose to set his story at a time before the eternal destiny of any human being was fixed. And in choosing Adam and Eve as his human subjects, he was able to imagine their story as truly open-ended, because on the question of their salvation or damnation, the Bible was inconclusive.[69]

In Genesis, God says to Adam concerning the tree of knowledge, "in the day thou eatest thereof thou shalt surely die" (Gen. 2: 17). Yet Adam and Eve do not die immediately when they eat the fruit; they are only driven out of the garden. The narrative does not confer closure on their stories. While it does say that Adam lived nine hundred and thirty years (Gen. 5: 5), it opens out into a history of their descendants. Subsequent legends would number Adam and Eve among the chosen souls delivered by Christ at the harrowing of hell. These stories did not constrain an interpreter committed to "the Bible only." Milton could therefore feel at once obliged and imaginatively free to treat the aftermath of the Fall inconclusively. Although he dramatized, as Genesis did not, the first stage of regeneration in the sinful pair with the descent of "Prevenient Grace," at the end of his poem the narrator sends them out into the fallen world chastened but hopeful, their eternal destinies, like the "World," still "before them . . . , and Providence thir guide." Adam, having been chastened by his recognition that he may err in the short run, and may perish in the long one, seems ready to leave the realms of the poem. There is no single text in the Scriptures which will reveal to him a predestined place in eternity, only the promise "Intermix[ed]" with the Law, which is to motivate him to strive to find a "Paradise within." By trusting in God Adam and Eve may achieve a "saving faith" that cannot be represented dramatically, since faith is "the evidence of things not seen" and their destiny does not yet "stand fixt," any more than Milton's own does, or that of any of his readers.

In this way *Paradise Lost* offers a practical interpretation of the most troubling crux in its biblical original. Milton interpreted the prohibition by judiciously choosing biblical texts outside Genesis with which to recast the story, and he made those interpretive choices with a view to getting readers to forebear making too much of any particular biblical place. In these ways, and others that have been examined in the course of this book, he regarded the Bible less as a stable frame of reference than as a starting point for a massive and potentially pleasurable project of interpretation. Assigning himself and his readers the task of constructing from the written Scriptures a Word of God that cannot be prematurely fixed was, after all, Milton's preeminent contribution to dissolving the characteristic Protestant problem of belatedness.

* * *

This book has located the most conspicuous discontinuity in Milton's career as an interpreter in the months after he had publicly declared his aspiration to be an interpreter. The relevant passage in *The Reason of Church Government* ostensibly emphasizes the writer's decision to write heroic poetry in English, but it includes an observation that seems to define what Milton took to be especially advantageous about his situation in history. Having announced his design "to fix all the industry and art [he] could unite to the adorning of [his] native tongue," Milton clarified his ambition:

> not to make verbal curiosities the end, that were a toylsom vanity, but to be an interpreter & relater of the best and sagest things among mine own Citizens throughout this Iland in the mother dialect. That what the greatest and choycest wits of *Athens, Rome,* or modern *Italy,* and those Hebrews of old did for their country, I in my proportion with this over and above of being a Christian, might doe for mine: not caring to be once nam'd abroad, though perhaps I could attaine to that, but content with these British Ilands as my world, whose fortune hath hitherto bin, that if the Athenians, as some say, made their small deeds great and renowned by their eloquent writers, England hath had her noble atchievments made small by the unskilfull handling of monks and mechanicks. (*CPW,* I, 811–12)

It is well known that by the time he came to write his epic Milton had abandoned the idea of writing on Arthur or Brutus or some manifestly

British subject. Yet given his eventual choice of subject matter the phrase "in my proportion with this over and above of being a Christian" suggests that he wrought continuity with other features of his youthful plan. What Milton may have meant by this phrase in 1642 must remain an object of speculation, although we may acknowledge that he himself went some distance toward delimiting its meaning. What should be clear, however, is that by writing his biblical poetry Milton defined in functional terms what he took to be advantageous for poetry about "being a Christian." That is, Milton was supremely conscious of his difference from poets who had been eloquent speakers for other historic groups. By contrast with pagan, Jewish, and papist poets, and even with biblical figures themselves, including Jesus and the biblical authors, he and his readers had access to the entire collection of biblical literature. And while there had no doubt been significant corruptions over the centuries in the "written Records pure" (*PL* XII, 513), they were much better equipped to reconstruct the Word of God than were the "monks," for whom the Scriptures had been locked up, and the "mechanicks," whose "openings" frequently served to show up their own ignorance and egocentricity.

By contrast with other possible Protestant poems retelling the story of Adam and Eve, *Paradise Lost* allows considerable importance to the Book of Nature. It does this not in spite of the poet's commitment to "the Bible only" but because of the way in which he had come to understand the contours of that commitment. Milton's mature understanding of the Bible as a book marked by many tangles and obscurities involved looking both inside and outside the exegetical tradition to find models for imagining that interpretive complexity was an aspect of the original creation. Whereas the Protestant moralizing tradition had posited that difficulties in reading the Book of the World were introduced through human sinfulness, an emerging scientific perspective offered the possibility that the Book of Nature had always entailed interpretive difficulties which required specialized training and knowledge. In composing his heroic poem, Milton allotted considerable scope to this understanding of the world-as-book and showed that before the Fall readers of this book were implicated in its complex language as a climactic feature of the creation. Adam and Eve are God's "Master work" (VII, 505) above all in the sense that they are interpreters. As signs and sign-makers, they are themselves dense with significance and with possibility. At the same time they are the opposite of the detached observers of the emerging experimental philosophy with its heuristic framework that had begun to define "nature" precisely over against human knowers.

In *Paradise Lost* then Milton took what seemed a simple story from the best known of books, the better to emphasize that what constitutes the real advantage of "being a Christian" has to do with interpreting.[70] The "over and above" is not conceived in terms whereby Scripture makes available a definitive eschatological perspective from which all events may be fully understood by proleptic retrospection. Rather the advantages consist in having access to the whole of biblical literature and in the benefits that can be derived from two foundational interpretive principles announced at the start of the collection. These criteria are figured in God's original commands, the one positive, the other negative. The command to be fruitful and multiply is seen to apply to the handling of Scriptural places, which require to be compared with one another and to be made to reveal more than the "penmen" could have known when they first wrote them down. For this work of comparison Milton found inspiration not only in the place about Mary treasuring things in her heart but more especially in the parable of the talents, which had long been interpreted as concerning the opportunities of interpreters to disseminate the Word.

In addition, however, to the positive criterion for interpretive labor found in these and other biblical places, Milton's mature hermeneutics entailed a potentially decisive negative criterion. Made most explicit in the chapter on the Son of God in his theological treatise, this criterion — that readers must learn how not to pry further than was meant — appears in subtler and no less powerful ways in the poet's abstemious treatment of Jesus' "sonship" throughout *Paradise Regained,* in his respect for the ambiguity surrounding the tragic hero's "rouzing motions" in *Samson Agonistes,* and in his interpretation of the prohibition in *Paradise Lost.* This negative criterion recognizes one sort of priority in the act of interpretation at the same time that it posits another sort in the written text of Scripture, to which the interpreter remains answerable. Sometimes relating "the best and sagest things" entails forbearing to speak further.

Appendix:
The Parable of the Talents (Matthew 25: 14–30)
The Authorized Version (King James Bible)

[14] For *the kingdom of heaven* is as a man traveling into a far country, *who* called his own servants, and delivered unto them his goods. [15] And unto one he gave five talents, to another two, and to another one; to every man according to his several ability; and straightway took his journey. [16] Then he that had received the five talents went and traded with the same, and made *them* other five talents. [17] And likewise he that *had received* two, he also gained other two. [18] But he that had received one went and digged in the earth, and hid his lord's money. [19] After a long time the lord of those servants cometh, and reckoneth with them. [20] And so he that had received five talents came and brought other five talents, saying, Lord, thou deliveredst unto me five talents: behold, I have gained beside them five talents more. [21] His lord said unto him, Well done, *thou* good and faithful servant: thou hast been faithful over a few things, I will make thee ruler over many things: enter thou into the joy of thy lord. [22] He also that had received two talents came and said, Lord, thou deliveredst unto me two talents: behold, I have gained two other talents beside them. [23] His lord said unto him, Well done, good and faithful servant; thou hast been faithful over a few things, I will make thee ruler over many things: enter thou into the joy of thy Lord. [24] Then he which had received the one talent came and said, Lord, I knew thee that thou art a hard man, reaping where thou hast not sown, and gathering where thou hast not strewed: [25] And I was afraid, and went and hid thy talent in the earth: lo, *there* thou hast *that is* thine. [26] His lord answered and said unto him, *Thou* wicked and slothful servant, thou knewest that I reap where I sowed not, and gather where I have not strewed: [27] Thou oughtest therefore to have put my money to the exchangers, and *then* at my coming I should have received mine own with usury. [28] Take therefore the talent from him, and give *it* unto him which hath ten talents. [29] For unto every one that hath shall be given, and he shall have abundance: but from him that hath not shall be taken away even that which he hath. [30] And cast ye the unprofitable servant into outer darkness: there shall be weeping and gnashing of teeth.

Notes

Preface

1. "A prologe shewinge the vse of the scripture," in *William Tyndale's Five Books of Moses Called the Pentateuch*, ed. J. I. Mombert (1884; rpt. Carbondale: Southern Illinois University Press, 1967), pp. 12, 10 respectively.
2. The best account of reading for "experimental knowledge" remains Geoffrey Nuttall's *The Holy Spirit in Puritan Faith and Experience* (1946; rpt. Chicago: University of Chicago Press, 1991).
3. Among the most prominent studies of Milton in this vein, see Robert L. Entzminger, *Divine Word: Milton and the Redemption of Language* (Pittsburgh: Duquesne University Press, 1985) and especially Georgia B. Christopher, *Milton and the Science of the Saints* (Princeton, NJ: Princeton University Press, 1982). For a more "ecumenical" approach, see Michael Lieb, *Poetics of the Holy: A Reading of Paradise Lost* (Chapel Hill: University of North Carolina Press, 1981). For a judicious characterization of how the liberal humanist picture of Milton rendered his religious vision harmless, see Margarita Stocker, *Paradise Lost* (Atlantic Highlands, NJ: Humanities Press International, 1988), pp. 14–20.
4. *GA*, p. 43, where Bunyan is quoting Heb. 12: 16–17. I laid some groundwork for the present book in an earlier study of seventeenth-century searches for a "place": see "Bunyan's Scriptural Acts," in *Bunyan in Our Time*, ed. Robert G. Collmer (Kent, OH: Kent State University Press, 1989), pp. 61–92, 205–9.
5. Robert Darnton, "Toward a History of Reading," *Princeton Alumni Weekly* 87 (8 April 1987), pp. 20, 24. Christopher Hill's book of 1977, *Milton and the English Revolution* (rpt. New York: Viking, 1978), represents an important turning point in its self-conscious attempt to place Milton in relation to contemporary English radicals.
6. Georgia B. Christopher, "The Verbal Gate to Paradise: Adam's 'Literary Experience' in Book X of *Paradise Lost*," *PMLA* 90 (1975): 69–77. The passages from Tyndale cited above were called to my attention in this article; see pp. 72–73.
7. Marshall Grossman, *"Authors to Themselves": Milton and the Revelation of History* (Cambridge: Cambridge University Press, 1987); quoted here from pp. 2 and ix.
8. Owen C. Watkins, *The Puritan Experience* (London: Routledge & Kegan Paul, 1972); Charles Lloyd Cohen, *God's Caress: The Psychology of Puritan Religious Experience* (New York: Oxford University Press, 1986).
9. For a fine study of the extraordinary range and diversity of uses to which biblical language was put in this era, see Nigel Smith, *Perfection Proclaimed: Language and Literature in English Radical Religion 1640–1660* (Oxford: Clarendon Press,

1989). On Bible-reading in seventeenth-century New England, see David D. Hall, *Worlds of Wonder, Days of Judgment: Popular Religious Belief in Early New England* (New York: Knopf, 1989), chapter 1.

10. For helpful introductions, see Mary Ann Radzinowicz, "How Milton Read the Bible: The Case of *Paradise Regained*," in *The Cambridge Companion to Milton*, ed. Dennis Danielson (Cambridge: Cambridge University Press, 1989), pp. 207–23, and Barbara K. Lewalski, "Milton, the Bible, and Human Experience," *Topoi* 7 (1988): 221–29.

Increasingly, studies of Milton have been showing how fruitful it can be to view his work as interventions in interpretive disputes. For a particularly successful example, see Mary Nyquist, "Textual Overlapping and Dalila's Harlot-lap," in *Literary Theory/Renaissance Texts*, ed. Patricia Parker and David Quint (Baltimore: Johns Hopkins University Press, 1986), pp. 341–72. See also her "Reading the Fall: Discourse and Drama in *Paradise Lost*," *English Literary Renaissance* 14 (1984): 199–229; Regina M. Schwartz, *Remembering and Repeating: Biblical Creation in Paradise Lost* (Cambridge: Cambridge University Press, 1988); James Grantham Turner, *One Flesh: Paradisal Marriage and Sexual Relations in the Age of Milton* (Oxford: Clarendon Press, 1987); Philip J. Gallagher, *Milton, the Bible, and Misogyny*, ed. Eugene R. Cunnar and Gail L. Mortimer (Columbia: University of Missouri Press, 1990). Mary Ann Radzinowicz's *Milton's Epics and the Book of Psalms* (Princeton, NJ: Princeton University Press, 1989) is also relevant here, as is her earlier book, *Toward Samson Agonistes: The Growth of Milton's Mind* (Princeton, NJ: Princeton University Press, 1978). In *Interpreting Samson Agonistes* (Princeton, NJ: Princeton University Press, 1986), Joseph Wittreich considers Milton's poem in the context of the long history of the story of Samson. It is curious, and disappointing, that the Introduction to *Milton and Scriptural Tradition: The Bible into Poetry* (ed. James H. Sims and Leland Ryken [Columbia: University of Missouri Press, 1984]), has little to say about Milton's own work as an interpreter.

11. For the history of dividing the Bible into verses, see Lewis Lupton, *A History of the Geneva Bible*, vol. 3: *Truth* (London: Olive Tree, 1971), pp. 75–76. For a perceptive study of biblical marginalia, see William W. E. Slights, "'Marginall Notes that spoile the Text': Scriptural Annotation in the English Renaissance," *Huntington Library Quarterly* 55 (1992): 255–78. Cf. also Richard W. F. Kroll, *The Material Word: Literate Culture in the Restoration and Early Eighteenth Century* (Baltimore: Johns Hopkins University Press, 1991), especially chapter 7.

12. "An Essay For the understanding of St. Paul's Epistles," in *The Works of John Locke*, 3 vols. (London, 1714), 3: 103–4. I was led to Locke's posthumously published "Essay" (1707) by Richard Kroll's article, "*Mise-en-Page*, Biblical Criticism, and Inference During the Restoration," *Studies in Eighteenth-Century Culture*, ed. O. M. Brack, Jr., vol. 16 (Madison: University of Wisconsin Press, 1986): 3–40.

13. Arthur Barker, *Milton and the Puritan Dilemma 1641–1660* (Toronto: University of Toronto Press, 1942), p. 72; Stanley E. Fish, "Re-Covering Meaning: Intention and Interpretation in Milton's *Doctrine and Discipline of Divorce*," a paper read at the annual convention of the Modern Language Association, San Francisco, December, 1987; "Wanting a Supplement: The Question of Interpretation in Milton's Early Prose," in *Politics, Poetics, and Hermeneutics in Milton's Prose*, ed. David

Loewenstein and James Grantham Turner (Cambridge: Cambridge University Press, 1990), pp. 41–68, especially pp. 56–58.

14. Jason P. Rosenblatt, "Milton's Chief Rabbi," *Milton Studies XXIV*, ed. James D. Simmonds (Pittsburgh: University of Pittsburgh Press, 1989), pp. 43–71.

15. See my article, "Tracing a Genealogy of 'Talent': The Descent of Matthew 25: 14–30 into Contemporary Philanthropical Discourse," in *Wealth in Western Thought: The Case For and Against Riches*, ed. Paul G. Schervish (Westport, CT: Greenwood Press, 1994).

16. John Peter Rumrich, "Uninventing Milton," *Modern Philology* 87 (1988–89): 249–65.

Chapter One

1. "Preface to Latin Writings," trans. Lewis W. Spitz, Sr., in *Luther's Works*, vol. 34: *Career of the Reformer IV*, ed. Lewis W. Spitz (Philadelphia: Muhlenberg Press, 1960), pp. 336–37. (The biblical quotations here are from Spitz's translation of Luther.) For a discussion of this account in relation to Milton's poetry, see Georgia B. Christopher, *Milton and the Science of the Saints* (Princeton, NJ: Princeton University Press, 1982), pp. 168–74.

2. Paul de Man, "The Return to Philology," in *The Resistance to Theory*, Theory and History of Literature 33 (Minneapolis: University of Minnesota Press, 1986), p. 24.

3. See Paul Delany, *British Autobiography in the Seventeenth Century* (London: Routledge and Kegan Paul; New York: Columbia University Press, 1969), pp. 27–39.

4. Quoted here from Edmund Bunny's "correction" of *A Booke of Christian exercise appertaining to Resolution* (1584; London, 1585), p. 175. Subsequent references to page numbers may be found in the text.

5. Anne Ferry, *The "Inward" Language: Sonnets of Wyatt, Sidney, Shakespeare, Donne* (Chicago: University of Chicago Press, 1983).

6. William Watts, "To the devout Reader," *Saint Augustines Confessions translated; and With some marginall notes illustrated* (London, 1631), n. p. Cf. *The Confessions of the Incomparable Doctovr S. Avgvstine*, [trans. Sir Tobie Matthew] ([St. Omer's], 1620). Another Protestant translation, by T. R. and E. M., appeared in 1650 as *S. Augustine's Confessions: With the Continuation of his Life*; it was reprinted in 1679. See Ferry, *The "Inward" Language*, pp. 38–39.

7. Stephen Brinkley (alias James Sancer) had Englished the work of the Spanish Jesuit Gaspar Loarte (Paris, 1579), and Parsons expanded it under the title *The First Booke of the Christian Exercise, appertayning to resolution* ([Rouen?], 1582).

8. These "Confessions" were published by the Bermuda Historical Society under an altered title, *The Journal of Richard Norwood, Surveyor of Bermuda* (New York: Scholars' Facsimiles & Reprints for Bermuda Historical Monuments Trust, 1945); see pp. 81–84. See *The Autobiography of Richard Baxter*, abridged by J. M. Lloyd Thomas, ed. N. H. Keeble (London: Dent; Totowa, NJ: Rowman & Littlefield, 1974), p. 7.

9. Bunny, *A Booke of Christian Exercise*, pp. 174–76. Bunny's text of the quotation from Augustine follows very closely what had appeared in Parsons's version. I have expanded abbreviations in the quotation.

10. See Joseph Anthony Mazzeo, "St. Augustine's Rhetoric of Silence," *Journal of the History of Ideas* 23 (1962): 175–96. For commentary on this episode, see Pierre Courcelle, "Source Chrétienne et allusions païennes de l'épisode du 'Tolle, lege,'" *Revue d'Histoire et de Philosophie Religieuses* 32 (1952): 171–200.

11. Bunny, p. 175. Abbreviations have been expanded and italics (in which the entire passage is printed) removed.

12. John Boys, *An Exposition of the Dominical Epistles and Gospels vsed in our English Liturgie . . . The Spring-part from the first in Lent to Whitsunday* (London, 1610), pp. 33–34 (italics have been omitted); William Perkins, *Works*, 3 vols. (London, 1612), 1: 583.

13. "Aprologue shewinge the vse of the scripture," in *William Tyndale's Five Books of Moses, Called the Pentateuch*, ed. J. I. Mombert (1884; rpt. Carbondale: Southern Illinois University Press, 1967), pp. 10n., 12, 11 respectively. Abbreviations are expanded.

14. Richard Sibbes, *The Brvised Reed and Smoaking Flax*, 5th ed. (London, 1635), pp. 119, 304–6; William Ames, *The Svbstance of Christian Religion* (London, 1659), p. 56. On the popularity of Matt. 11: 28–30, see Owen C. Watkins, *The Puritan Experience* (London: Routledge & Kegan Paul, 1972), p. 41; Nigel Smith, *Perfection Proclaimed: Language and Literature in English Radical Religion 1640–1660* (Oxford: Clarendon Press, 1989), pp. 34, 43; Patricia Caldwell, *The Puritan Conversion Narrative: The Beginnings of American Expression* (Cambridge: Cambridge University Press, 1983), pp. 20–21.

15. See, for example, Jane Turner, *Choice Experiences* (London, 1653), pp. 49–61; Anne Venn, *A Wise Virgins Lamp* (London, 1658), p. 24. Cf. John Morgan, *Godly Learning: Puritan Attitudes Towards Reason, Learning, and Education, 1560–1640* (Cambridge: Cambridge University Press, 1986), pp. 30–31. For a study of some literary implications of a "rhetoric" about election in the late sixteenth century, see Martha Tuck Rozett, *The Doctrine of Election and the Emergence of Elizabethan Tragedy* (Princeton, NJ: Princeton University Press, 1984).

16. The title of Perkins's work is quoted here from the 1608 edition; Samuel Hieron (d. 1617), *The Triall of Adoption* (1632), in *Works*, 2 vols. (London, 1635), 1: 327 [a misprint for 311]. See also Richard Hooker, "A Learned and Comfortable Sermon of the Certaintie and Perpetuitie of Faith in the Elect," in *Tractates and Sermons*, Vol. V of *The Folger Library Edition of the Works of Richard Hooker*, ed. Laetitia Yeandle and Egil Grislis (Cambridge, MA: Belknap Press of Harvard University Press, 1990), pp. 69–82; cf. John E. Booty, Introduction to Vol. IV (1982), xxvii–xxviii.

On faith and assurance, see Tony Lane, "The Quest for the Historical Calvin," *Evangelical Quarterly* 55 (1983): 105. For a list of the casuistical writers whom Robert Burton regarded as "excellent," see *The Anatomy of Melancholy*, ed. A. R. Shilleto, with an Introduction by A. H. Bullen, 3 vols. (1893; London: G. Bell & Sons, 1923), 3: 468. (Here and elsewhere reference to the *Anatomy* will include Partition, Section, Member, and Subsection numbers, as follows: III, IV, II, VI.)

17. See R. T. Kendall, *Calvin and English Calvinism to 1649* (Oxford: Oxford University Press, 1979), pp. 67–76. See in particular the popular treatise by John Rogers of Dedham, *The Doctrine of Faith* (London, 1627); it was dedicated to delivering readers from the "dangerous and deadly" implications of the ease with which one might deceive oneself in this matter. On temporary faith, see esp. pp. 7–8, 319 ff. The thirteenth and twenty-fifth chapters of Matthew provided useful texts for illustrating the theory.

18. *The Life of Mr Robert Blair, Minister of St Andrews, Containing His Autobiography, from 1593 to 1636*, ed. Thomas M'Crie (Edinburgh: Wodrow Society, 1848), pp. 22, 33. The experiences to which Blair was referring in the passages cited here occurred about 1622.

19. This hallowed verse appeared as the epigraph on the title pages of two of Perkins's most popular works, *A Case of Conscience, the greatest that euer was*, and the treatise in which he lays the theoretical groundwork for the advice, *A Treatise Tending vnto a Declaration*. See Kendall, p. 8.

20. Shakespeare's *Twelfth Night* shows that in the period when Perkins's writings were becoming widely popular, seeking a "place" in a text had already become an object of ridicule. Malvolio, who is said to be "a kind of puritan," shows how an obscure text may be applied "feelingly" to his own "case." Even before he chances upon a (forged) letter that makes him promises and offers him comfort, he has been intent on being the object of good "fortune." Shakespeare represents him, in other words, as an interested reader of a particular sort. As a "place-seeker," he is a ridiculous instance of the person who seeks to be assured by a text of the happy outcome of his life's story. The analogy on which the humor turns depends in some measure on the accidents of usage whereby the word "place" in sixteenth- and seventeenth-century English bore several distinct but potentially related senses. The sense which the steward himself appropriates as he imagines how he will act once he is promoted to "Count Malvolio" refers to an "office, employment, [or] situation" (*OED*, sense 14). Yet a "place" was also a "particular part, page, or other point in a book or writing" (sense 7), and in a casual vein the forerunner of the still current sense of the "place" that a reader can lose by becoming distracted. More richly, "place" was the English equivalent of the Latin *locus* and Greek *topos*, and "the places" referred to "common places or heads of Inuention." Metaphorically, the "places" were often conceived as "storehouses," containers from which materials could be drawn out for rhetorical uses. (See below, Chapter Five.) Mediating among these senses of "place" may have been other senses: "The space which one person occupies by usage, allotment, or right," as in having a "place" at table (sense 13), or a "proper, appropriate, or natural place (for the person or thing in question to occupy)" (sense 12). All these senses were available in Elizabethan times, and they all remained current through the seventeenth century as many earnest Bible-readers sought scriptural "places" to assure themselves of a "place" among the elect.

21. See Christopher Hill, *The Experience of Defeat: Milton and Some Contemporaries* (New York: Elisabeth Sifton Books, Viking, 1984), pp. 294–96; and *The World Turned Upside Down: Radical Ideas During the English Revolution* (1972; rpt. Harmondsworth: Penguin, 1975), pp. 342–43. A balanced estimate of the anxieties prevalent in English society at mid-century may be found in J. C. Davis, *Fear, Myth,*

and History: The Ranters and the Historians (Cambridge: Cambridge University Press, 1986), pp. 98–99. See also Keith W. F. Stavely, "Roger Williams: Bible Politics and Bible Art," *Prose Studies* 14 (1991): 82–83; Bunyan, *GA,* p. 31.

22. For Elizabeth Chambers's account, see John Rogers, *Ohel or Beth-shemesh, A Tabernacle for the Sun* (London, 1653), p. 407. For E. C. and D. R., see *Spirituall Experiences, of Sundry Beleevers,* 2d impression enlarged (London, 1651 [actually, 1652 or 1653]), pp. 27, 113–14; *A Few Sighs from Hell, or The Groans of a damned Soul* (1658), ed. T. L. Underwood, in Vol. I of *The Miscellaneous Works of John Bunyan,* gen. ed. Roger Sharrock (Oxford: Clarendon Press, 1980), p. 378.

23. See Francis Roberts, "An Introductory Advertisement to the Reader," *Clavis Bibliorum, The Key of The Bible, Unlocking the Richest Treasury of the Holy Scriptures,* 2 vols. (2d ed., London, 1649), 1: 22–29 (the "Advertisement" is paginated separately); Lewis Bayly, *The Practice of Pietie,* 7th ed. (London, 1616), pp. 245–46.

24. The quotations from "The H. Scriptures II" and "The Bunch of Grapes" (below) are taken from *The Works of George Herbert,* ed. F. E. Hutchinson (Oxford: Clarendon Press, 1941), pp. 58 and 128 respectively. For a discussion of Herbert and experimental religion, see Richard Strier, *Love Known: Theology and Experience in George Herbert's Poetry* (Chicago: University of Chicago Press, 1983), pp. 143–73.

25. Herbert, *Works,* pp. 228–29.

26. See Morgan, *Godly Learning,* p. 58.

27. In New England, these terms remained in use well into the eighteenth century, especially during the Great Awakening.

28. Roberts, "Advertisement," 1: 38.

29. I[ohn] P[reston], *An Elegant and Lively Description of Spirituall Life and Death,* a sermon preached on 9 Nov. 1623 (London, 1633), pp. 153, 159. For the classic study of "experimental" religious practices, see Geoffrey F. Nuttall, *The Holy Spirit in Puritan Faith and Experience* (1946; rpt. Chicago: University of Chicago Press, 1991). For the currency of the word in the first two-thirds of the seventeenth century, see the *OED;* note esp. "experimental," I, 2a; cf. 2c, and the entries on "experimental religion" and "experimental divinity." On Reformed religious experience as a "literary" experience, see Christopher, *Milton and the Science of the Saints,* pp. 3–14.

30. *Memoirs of Master John Shawe . . . Written by himself in the year 1663–64,* ed. J. R. Boyle (Hull: Peck & Son, 1882), p. 77; Venn, *A Wise Virgins Lamp,* p. 53.

31. On the conventions of typological symbolism, see Barbara Kiefer Lewalski, *Protestant Poetics and the Seventeenth-Century Religious Lyric* (Princeton, NJ: Princeton University Press, 1979), chap. 4. For further bibliography, see Mason I. Lowance, Jr., *The Language of Canaan: Metaphor and Symbol in New England from the Puritans to the Transcendentalists* (Cambridge, MA: Harvard University Press, 1980), p. 318. Edward W. Tayler provides a shrewd analysis of typological symbolism in *Milton's Poetry: Its Development in Time* (Pittsburgh: Duquesne University Press, 1979), pp. 22ff. For the extensive use of this sort of reading among the seventeenth-century Dutch, see Simon Schama, *The Embarrassment of Riches: An Interpretation of Dutch Culture in the Golden Age* (Berkeley and Los Angeles: University of California Press, 1988), pp. 93–125.

32. Va[vasor] Powel, "To the sober and spirituall Readers of this Booke,"

Spirituall Experiences, A2ʳ; A2ᵛ; William Bridge, *Scripture-Light the Most Sure Light* (London, 1656), pp. 52–53.

33. Burton, *Anatomy,* 3: 479–80; III, IV, II, VI.

34. Bunyan, *Miscellaneous Works,* 1: 359.

35. Burton, *Anatomy,* 3: 456; III, IV, II, III; Bunyan, *Miscellaneous Works,* 1: 359; cf. p. 353.

36. Peter J. Carlton, "Bunyan: Language, Convention, Authority," *ELH* 51 (1984): 19, 20, 22–23, 28. The use of the passive voice, it should be emphasized, had good biblical precedents; many biblical writers used it to suggest God's responsibility for events in the world.

37. Augustine, *Confessions,* IV, iii, 5. Trans. Tobie Matthew, p. 133.

38. For Augustine's discussion of pagan *sortes,* see *Patrologiae Latina,* ed. J.-P. Migne (Paris, 1841), 33: 222; Sir Philip Sidney, *An Apology for Poetry, or The Defence of Poesy,* ed. Geoffrey Shepherd (1965; Manchester: Manchester University Press; New York: Barnes & Noble, 1973), p. 98; Reginald Scot, *The discoverie of witchcraft* ([London], 1584), XI, x, pp. 197–98; cited here from the edition published at London, 1665, pp. 110–11.

39. For an account of Charles I's use of the *sortes,* see the "Diary of Dr. Edward Lake," in *The Camden Miscellany,* Vol. I (Camden Society, 1847), pp. 25–26: the entry for 29 Jan. 1677/78. Cf. the entry on "Divination" by E. P. Graham in *The Catholic Encyclopedia,* 15 vols. (New York: Encyclopedia Press, 1909), 5: 48–51, and the discussion by Charles Lloyd Cohen, in *God's Caress: The Psychology of Puritan Religious Experience* (New York: Oxford University Press, 1986), pp. 88–89. For an example of opening the Bible at random in seventeenth-century New England, see David D. Hall, *Worlds of Wonder, Days of Judgment: Popular Religious Belief in Early New England* (New York: Knopf, 1989), p. 26.

40. See Keith Thomas, *Religion and the Decline of Magic* (New York: Charles Scribner's Sons, 1971), pp. 118ff., 214–15. Thomas's citation of William Bridge in his discussion of bibliomancy is, however, quite inappropriate. In *Scripture-Light the Most Sure* (1656), Bridge did suggest, as Thomas has it, that "there was no telling when God might 'please to open a place of Scripture to the Soul'" (see p. 25). But the context of the remark is Bridge's discussion of mistaken impressions, and Bridge's work is aimed at setting out sensible rules for interpretation, especially for those who feel themselves trapped "in a dark place" (p. 10). For the story of Joan Drake, see William Turner, *A Compleat History of the Most Remarkable Providences, Both of Judgment and Mercy, Which Have Hapned in This Present Age* (London, 1697), p. 123. For a late seventeenth-century description of *sortes,* see John Aubrey, *Remaines of Gentilisme and Judaisme* (1688), ed. James Britten (London: Stachell, Peyton, 1881), pp. 90–92.

41. Bunyan, *Miscellaneous Works,* 1: 358.

42. John Bunyan, *The Life and Death of Mr. Badman,* ed. James F. Forrest and Roger Sharrock (Oxford: Clarendon Press, 1988), pp. 127–28. The idea that interpreters often treated the Bible as a "Nose of Wax" was proverbial; cf. Bridge, p. 55. On the damaging results of introspective reading, see the narratives in *Spirituall Experiences,* especially p. 88. For a richly perceptive and sympathetic treatment of the conversion literature written before 1640, see Cohen, *God's Caress.*

43. George Wither, "Of Despaire," in *Abvses Stript, and Whipt: or Satyricall*

Essayes, 2 vols. (London, 1622), Book 1: satyr 11; rpt. in *Juvenilia* (Menston, England: A Scolar Press facsimile, 1970), p. 119.

44. *A Relation of the Fearfvl Estate of Francis Spira, In the Year 1548*, compiled by Natth[aniel] Bacon (London, 1649), p. 68. (The original of the passage quoted here appears entirely in italic type.) On the popularity of the tale, see Hall, *Worlds of Wonder*, pp. 132–35 et passim.

45. See Burton, *Anatomy*, 3: 466; III, IV, II, VI; Bunyan, *GA*, pp. 45, 49–50, 55; Baird Tipson, "A Dark Side of Seventeenth-Century English Protestantism: The Sin Against the Holy Spirit," *Harvard Theological Review* 77 (1984): 301; see 301–30. Other places that refer to the sin against the Holy Ghost are Mark 3: 28–30 and Luke 12: 10. With these passages Calvin associated Heb. 6: 4–6 and 10: 26–29, which concern apostacy from the faith. Milton discusses these places in *De Doctrina Christiana* (*CPW*, VI, 295–96, 509).

46. John Hales, *A Sermon Preached At St Maries in Oxford Vpon Tvesday in Easter VVeake, 1617* (Oxford, 1617), pp. 23, 25, 39.

47. *A Commentarie of Master Doctor Martin Lvther vpon the Epistle of S. Pavl to the Galathians*, [trans. Thomas Vautrollier?] (1575; London, 1644), fol. 114^v. Compare the gloss on Matt. 11: 28–29 (where the "burden" or "yoak" is said to be "doctrine") by J. H. [John Hieron?], in *The Way to Salvation* (London, 1668), p. 449.

Chapter Two

1. Studies of Milton's "vocation" that are, respectively, unusually explicit and particularly influential include John Spencer Hill, *John Milton Poet, Priest and Prophet: A Study of Divine Vocation in Milton's Poetry and Prose* (London: Macmillan; Totowa, NJ: Rowman and Littlefield, 1979), chaps. 1–2, and Douglas Bush, *John Milton: A Sketch of His Life and Writings* (New York: Macmillan; London: Collier-Macmillan, 1964), pp. 45–47. The seminal treatment of the subject by William Haller appears in Chap. VIII ("Church-Outed by the Prelates") of the oft-reprinted *The Rise of Puritanism* (1938; rpt. New York: Harper Torchbooks, 1957); for the quoted phrases, see pp. 296, 297, 322, 310, and 289–90 respectively. The extent to which this interpretation of Milton's "vocation" is now well established may be seen (*inter alia*) in William Riley Parker's discussion of Sonnet 19 as "On serving God, or his neglected poetic faculty," in *Milton: A Biography*, 2 vols. (Oxford: Clarendon Press, 1968), 1: 469 ff., and in the thoughtful essay on "Talents" contributed by Michael Lieb to *A Milton Encyclopedia*, gen. ed. William B. Hunter, Jr., 9 vols. (Lewisburg, PA: Bucknell University Press, 1978–83), 8: 48–51. William Kerrigan discusses "the financial metaphors of Christianity" in relation to Milton's personal psychology in *The Sacred Complex: On the Psychogenesis of Paradise Lost* (Cambridge, MA: Harvard University Press, 1983), pp. 44–46.

2. John Donne, Sermon on 1 Timothy 1: 15, in *The Sermons of John Donne*, ed. George R. Potter and Evelyn M. Simpson, 10 vols. (Berkeley: University of California Press, 1953–62), 1: 318.

3. Because the more literal translation in *Works* (VIII, 67) makes such un-

wieldy English, I have cited instead the translation adapted from Robert Fellowes, in *John Milton: Prose Selections,* ed. Merritt Y. Hughes (New York: Odyssey, 1947), pp. 334–35.

4. See *GA*, p. 65. For Milton's interest in the passage, see Parker, 1: 389. Cf. also Gary A. Stringer, "Milton's 'Thorn in the Flesh': Pauline Didacticism in Sonnet XIX," *Milton Studies X,* ed. James D. Simmonds (Pittsburgh: University of Pittsburgh Press, 1977), pp. 141–54.

5. Marshall Grossman, *"Authors to Themselves": Milton and the Revelation of History* (Cambridge: Cambridge University Press, 1987), chap. 8.

6. For a helpful discussion of how "a fantasized futurity . . . demand[s] a present account" here, see Jonathan Goldberg, "Dating Milton," in *Soliciting Interpretation: Literary Theory and Seventeenth-Century English Poetry,* ed. Elizabeth D. Harvey and Katharine Eisaman Maus (Chicago: University of Chicago Press, 1990), pp. 207–12.

7. But see Dixon Fiske, "Milton in the Middle of Life: Sonnet XIX," *ELH* 41 (1974): 37–49. John F. Huntley, who recognizes that the speaker in the sonnet hears in the parable "a very terrifying" threat and proposes that "Milton dissociates himself from the third servant," takes an unwarranted further step when he claims that "Milton identifies himself with the first two servants." See "The Ecology and Anatomy of Criticism: Milton's Sonnet 19 and the Bee Simile in 'Paradise Lost,' I.768–76," *Journal of Aesthetics and Art Criticism* 24 (1965–66): 383–91, viz. 387.

8. For a fine discussion of this subject, see Arthur Barker, *Milton and the Puritan Dilemma 1641–1660* (Toronto: University of Toronto Press, 1942), chaps. XVI and XVII.

9. Various attempts by C. A. Patrides, J. H. Adamson, and William B. Hunter to reclaim Milton for orthodoxy are gathered in *Bright Essence: Studies in Milton's Theology* (Salt Lake City: University of Utah Press, 1971).

10. See *Canones et Decreta Concilii Tridentini,* Sessio VI, caput ix. Cf. Howard Schultz, *Milton and Forbidden Knowledge* (New York: Modern Language Association, 1955), pp. 127–28. Schultz's discussion of Milton's relation to seventeenth-century religious developments, including sectarianism and radicalism, remains helpful.

11. See Margo Swiss, "Crisis of Conscience: A Theological Context for Milton's 'How Soon Hath Time,'" *Milton Quarterly* 20 (1986): 98–103. Although Swiss has illuminated the poem by setting it in this context, she proceeds as if its autobiographical significance were made thereby transparent.

12. For a recent interpretation of the "contest" between these two parables in Milton's writing, see John Guillory, "The Father's House: *Samson Agonistes* in Its Historical Moment," in *Re-membering Milton: Essays on the Texts and Traditions,* ed. Mary Nyquist and Margaret W. Ferguson (New York: Methuen, 1987), pp. 156–59. Guillory also offers a sustained discussion of Milton's "calling."

13. See George Herbert, as cited above in Chapter One, p. 15.

14. Parker proposed Cyriak Skinner (1: xiii–xv, 2: 677–78), Helen Darbishire John Phillips. See *The Early Lives of Milton,* ed. Darbishire (London: Constable, 1932), pp. xiv–xxvii. Cf. Edward S. Parsons, "The Authorship of the Anonymous Life of Milton," *PMLA* 50 (1935): 1057–64.

15. "The Life of Mr. John Milton," in *The Early Lives*, p. 22. Subsequent references appear within parentheses in the text.

16. See Charles Cotton's commendatory verses of 1672/3, printed in the fourth edition of Izaak Walton's *Lives of Dr. John Donne, Sir Henry Wotton, Mr. Richard Hooker, Mr. George Herbert* (London, 1675), n. p. (The poem is printed in italic type.)

17. See the marginal commentary on Matt. 25: 14–30, in *The Geneva Bible: A facsimile of the 1560 edition*, with an introduction by Lloyd E. Berry (Madison: University of Wisconsin Press, 1969). The condemnation of "idlenes" appears in marginalia on the corresponding parable in Luke's gospel (19: 12–27), to which the commentary on Matthew refers.

18. This remained the case even in the 7th ed. of Phillips's *New World of Words: or Universal English Dictionary* (London, 1720), as it had been in lists of "hard words" in the sixteenth century. See, for example, Thomas Elyot, *Dictionary* (1538; rpt. Menston, England: Scolar Press, 1970).

19. Cf. also Prolusion III: "useless and barren controversies and bickerings lack all power to affect the emotions [*ingenio*] in any way whatever" (*CPW*, I, 244).

20. Quoted from *The Latin Poems of John Milton*, ed. Walter MacKellar, Cornell Studies in English XV (New Haven, CT: Yale University Press for Cornell University, 1930).

21. Robert A. Greene, "Whichcote, Wilkins, 'Ingenuity,' and the Reasonableness of Christianity," *Journal of the History of Ideas* 42 (1981): 227–52. For a late seventeenth-century appropriation of the term to support women's capacity for a life of study, see *Triumphs of Female Wit, In Some Pindarick Odes. Or, the Emulation. Together with an Answer to an Objector against Female Ingenuity, and Capacity of Learning* (London, 1683).

22. For a Catholic criticism of this Protestant proof-text, see S[ylvester] N[orris], *An Antidote or Soveraigne Remedie Against the Pestiferovs Writings of All English Sectaries* ([St. Omers], 1615), p. 25. Erasmus gave a characteristically unpolemical gloss, in *The First Tome or Volume of the Paraphrase of Erasmus upon the Newe Testament* (1548); see the Facsimile Reproduction with an Introduction by John N. Wall, Jr. (Delmar, NY: Scholars' Facsimiles & Reprints, 1975), ad loc.

23. *The Commentaries of M. Iohn Calvin vpon the Actes of the Apostles*, trans. Christopher Fetherstone (London, 1585), p. 414; *The Geneva Bible*, ad loc.

24. See Greene's fine study, especially pp. 238, 244. Greene cites Jackson's *Third Booke of Commentaries Vpon the Apostles Creede* (London, 1614), p. 233. See also Poole's *Synopsis Criticorum Aliorumque S. Scripturae Interpretum*, 4, i (London, 1674).

25. *Commentaries . . . vpon the Actes*, pp. 414–15.

26. I[ohn] P[reston], *An Elegant and Lively Description of Spirituall Life and Death* [a sermon preached on 9 Nov. 1623] (London, 1633), pp. 168–69, 176–77.

27. *Annotations Upon the Holy Bible. Being a Continuation of Mr. Pool's Work by Certain Judicious and Learned Divines*, 2 vols. (London, 1683–85), 2 (1685): ad loc.

28. *CPW*, VII, 243. Cf. pp. 87–88, below.

29. On "*the necessity and use of humane industry for attaining vnto the faith*," see Thomas Iackson, *Ivstifying Faith* (London, 1615), p. A3^r, describing Section III of

the work; cf. also Section I, chap. 6. Cf. Richard Hooker: "by longe experience we have found ytt trew, as many as have entered there names in the mysticall *booke of Lyfe, eos maximum laborem suscipere,* they have taken upon them a labersome, a toylefull, a painefull proffession"; quoted from "A Learned and Comfortable Sermon of the Certaintie and Perpetuitie of Faith in the Elect," in *Tractates and Sermons,* Vol. V of *The Folger Library Edition of the Works of Richard Hooker,* ed. Laetitia Yeandle and Egil Grislis (Cambridge, MA: Belknap Press of Harvard University Press, 1990), p. 81.

30. Christopher Grose, "'Unweapon'd Creature in the Word': A Revision in Milton's Letter to a Friend," *English Language Notes* 21 (1983–84): 29–34. I follow Grose's emendation ("word") of the text in *CPW,* I, 319, which prints "world." To these two passages can be added one from the opening pages of *Tetrachordon,* where Milton presents his work as a response to those who wished to see the argument of his first divorce tract *"furder . . . labour'd in the Scriptures"* (*CPW,* II, 582).

31. See John Aubrey, "Minutes of the Life of Mr John Milton," in *The Early Lives of Milton,* ed. Darbishire, p. 10. Cf. Kerrigan, pp. 48–49.

32. *The Miscellanies; or Stromata* in *The Writings of Clement of Alexandria,* trans. William Wilson, Vol. IV of *Ante-Nicene Christian Library: Translations of the Writings of the Fathers Down to A. D. 325,* ed. Alexander Roberts and James Donaldson (Edinburgh: T. & T. Clark, 1880), pp. 350–51; Caesarius of Arles, Sermon 230, in *Sermons,* 3 vols., trans. Mary Magdeleine Mueller (Washington, DC: Catholic University of America Press, 1956–73), 3 (1973): 182–83; Origen, Homily XIII on Exodus, in *Homilies on Genesis and Exodus,* trans. Ronald E. Heine (Washington, DC: Catholic University of America Press, 1982), p. 376.

33. Athanasius, Letter XLIX (to Dracontius, c. 354–55), in *Select Works and Letters,* Vol. IV of *A Select Library of Nicene and Post-Nicene Fathers of the Christian Church,* ed. Philip Schaff and Henry Wace, 2nd ser. (New York: Christian Literature, 1892), p. 558; Augustine, Sermon LXXXVII, "Sermons on Selected Lessons of the New Testament," trans. R. G. MacMullen, in Vol. VI of *A Select Library of the Nicene and Post-Nicene Fathers of the Christian Church,* ed. Philip Schaff (Grand Rapids, MI: Wm. B. Eerdmans, 1979), pp. 522–23; Sermon XLIV, p. 406.

34. [Pseudo-]Bede, *In Matthaei Evangelium Expositio,* in *Patrologiæ cursus completus, series Latina,* ed. J.-P. Migne, 92: 108; Hugh of St. Victor, *Allegoriæ in Evangelia,* in *Patrologiae Latina,* 175: 800.

35. John Chrysostom, *Homilies on the Gospel of Matthew,* trans. George Prevost, Vol. X of *A Select Library of the Nicene and Post-Nicene Fathers of the Christian Church,* ed. Philip Schaff (rpt. Grand Rapids, MI: Wm. B. Eerdmans, 1956), p. 472; Homily X in *On the Incomprehensible Nature of God,* trans. Paul W. Harkins (Washington, DC: Catholic University of America Press, 1984), pp. 245–46. On the similarity between Milton's interpretation of the parable in the letter of 1633 and Chrysostom's interpretation, see Grose, p. 34.

36. See the intelligently assembled compendium by Stephen L. Wailes, *Medieval Allegories of Jesus' Parables* (Berkeley: University of California Press, 1987), pp. 184–94, especially p. 189. One work that made the interpretations of the Fathers and schoolmen available in seventeenth-century England was John Mayer's book on "hard places," *A Treasvry of Ecclesiasticall Expositions, vpon the difficult and doubtfull*

places of the Scriptures, Collected out of the best esteemed Interpreters, both auncient and moderne (London, 1622); see pp. 290–95 on Matthew 25: 14.

37. Gregory the Great, *Forty Gospel Homilies*, trans. David Hurst (Kalamazoo, MI: Cistercian Publications, 1990), pp. 130, 132; Wailes, p. 194.

Chapter Three

1. Milton's silence about precedents in Luther and other reformed writers for his stance in face of "tradition" suggests that while he felt no anxiety of influence with respect to the biblical writers, the precursors with whom he struggled were other interpreters. Cf. the studies by Harold Bloom beginning with *The Anxiety of Influence: A Theory of Poetry* (New York: Oxford University Press, 1973).

2. See Maurice Kelley, Introduction, *The Complete Prose Works of John Milton*, Vol. VI: *Christian Doctrine* (New Haven, CT: Yale University Press, 1973), pp. 15–22. Kelley has speculated that Milton went through three phases en route to the composition of his theological treatise: (1) his youthful studies, when he was compiling the Theological Index for his Commonplace Book and gathering scriptural passages under headings; (2) ca. 1645–1655, when, according to his nephew, he compiled "A perfect System of Divinity" and read widely in orthodox theological treatises, to his dissatisfaction; and (3) from 1655 onward, when he was developing his own highly heterodox views in earnest. Characteristically, Kelley emphasizes Milton's heterodoxy. William B. Hunter's attempt, in "The Provenance of the *Christian Doctrine*" (*Studies in English Literature* 32 [1991]: 129–42), to discredit Milton's authorship of *De Doctrina Christiana* is unconvincing; see the remarks by Barbara K. Lewalski and John T. Shawcross in the same issue, pp. 143–62.

3. Mary Thomas Crane, *Framing Authority: Sayings, Self, and Society in Sixteenth-Century England* (Princeton, NJ: Princeton University Press, 1993), chap. 1. The terms "cultural code" and "*doxa*" are inflected in Crane's study in ways that are familiar to readers of Michel Foucault's *The Order of Things: An Archaeology of the Human Sciences* (1966; New York: Vintage, 1973), pp. xx–xxi, and Roland Barthes's *S/Z*, trans. Richard Miller (New York: Hill and Wang, 1974), pp. 97–98.

4. Kelley's notes on the passage point out, however, precedents for Milton's use of the phrase "the analogy of faith." The biblical allusion seems to have been missed by Michael Bauman in his otherwise highly useful *Scripture Index to John Milton's De doctrina christiana* (Binghampton, NY: Medieval & Renaissance Texts & Studies, 1989), p. 123. According to Bauman's list, Rom. 12: 6 is never quoted as such anywhere in Milton's treatise. To appreciate how conventional was Milton's list of requisites for proper interpretation, see William Whitaker, *A Disputation on Holy Scripture, Against the Papists, Especially Bellarmine and Stapleton*, trans. William Fitzgerald (Cambridge: Cambridge University Press, 1849; rpt. New York: Johnson Reprint Corp., 1968), Question V: Concerning the Interpretation of Scripture, pp. 466–73. (The Latin *Disputatio* was published at Cambridge, 1588.)

5. On Milton's increasing willingness to rest content with the words of Scripture, see H. R. MacCallum, "Milton and Figurative Interpretation of the Bible," *University of Toronto Quarterly* 31 (1961–62): 397–415.

6. Arthur Barker, *Milton and the Puritan Dilemma, 1641–1660* (Toronto: University of Toronto Press, 1942); see above, Preface, p. xiv.

7. Milton's continued emphasis on his mental labors and his claim that such labor suits his natural ability show up in a number of ways in the divorce tracts. They are epitomized, however, in this generalization from *Tetrachordon* contrasting the "ease" with which God "executes" divine "exploits" and the difficulties of human labor: "no worthy enterprise can be don by us without continuall plodding and wearisomnes to our faint and sensitive abilities" (*CPW*, II, 597). Cf. also II, 489–90.

8. See the excellent discussion by John R. Knott, Jr., in *The Sword of the Spirit: Puritan Responses to the Bible* (Chicago: University of Chicago Press, 1980), chap. 5. Cf. Stanley E. Fish, "Reason in *The Reason of Church Government*," in *Self-Consuming Artifacts: The Experience of Seventeenth-Century Literature* (Berkeley and Los Angeles: University of California Press, 1972), pp. 265–302. It should be noted, however, that in *Of Prelatical Episcopacy* Milton did design to "club quotations" with his opponents.

9. That the first months of Milton's married life proved an enormous shock was elaborated in considerable detail by Denis Saurat, in *Milton, Man and Thinker* (1925; rev. ed. London: Dent, 1944), pp. 41–59. For a more recent discussion that discerns Milton's "rage" in the divorce tracts, see James Grantham Turner, *One Flesh: Paradisal Marriage and Sexual Relations in the Age of Milton* (Oxford: Clarendon Press, 1987), pp. 213–15, 228–29.

10. See Amy R. McCready, "Milton's Casuistry: The Case of *The Doctrine and Discipline of Divorce*," *Journal of Medieval and Renaissance Studies* 22 (1992): 393–428.

11. It is significant that in this treatise Milton explicitly cites Perkins as an authority (*CPW*, II, 341). See also *Tetrachordon*, where Milton speaks of having "leave to breake the intolerable yoake of a never well joyn'd wedlocke for the removing of our heaviest afflictions" (II, 637). In making out his argument Milton takes for granted the virtual powerlessness of women. His personal bias seems to have kept him from noticing that biblical literature does not unequivocally support his perspective. In Mark's gospel (10: 12), for instance, Jesus's saying about divorce is framed in a way that envisages a woman's ability to initiate divorce proceedings. This gospel has traditionally been associated with readers at Rome; on Milton's thinking with respect to Roman marriage laws, see Turner, pp. 220–22.

12. Understanding quite well that biblical categories shaped Milton's desires, Stanley Fish has claimed that Milton's idea of Christian liberty entailed being "given over to the even stricter rules" of "an *internalized* law" that Christ set up when he demanded that his followers "'should be more perfect than those who were under the law'" of Moses. (For the phrase that Fish quotes from Milton, cf. *CPW*, VI, 535. Fish cites Sumner's translation here.) See "Unger and Milton," in *Doing What Comes Naturally: Change, Rhetoric, and the Practice of Theory in Literary and Legal Studies* (Durham, NC: Duke University Press, 1989), pp. 400–401. This quoting is highly selective. It is also misleading. Fish says nothing of Milton's own attempt, in *The Doctrine and Discipline of Divorce*, to disallow the implications that Fish asks us to draw: "The Gospel indeed exhorts to highest perfection; but bears with weakest infirmity more then the Law. . . . [S]ay they, there is a greater portion of spirit powr'd upon the Gospel which requires perfecter obedience. But that consequence

is deceavable; for it is the Law that is the exacter of our obedience ev'n under the Gospel; how can it then exact concerning divorce, that which it never exacted before? The Gospel is a covnant reveling grace, not commanding a new morality, but assuring justification by faith only" (1643 ed.; *CPW,* II, 302–3; cf. 1644 ed., 304–5). A. S. P. Woodhouse's account of Milton's views on the relations between Law and Gospel remains valuable: see "Milton, Puritanism, and Liberty," *University of Toronto Quarterly* 4 (1934–35): 483–513.

13. See Barker, pp. 320–21. The phrase "matter of compulsion" is adapted from Sumner's translation, *Works,* XVI, 153.

14. See Nigel Smith, "*Areopagitica*: Voicing Contexts, 1643–5," in *Politics, Poetics, and Hermeneutics in Milton's Prose,* ed. David Loewenstein and James Grantham Turner (Cambridge: Cambridge University Press, 1990), pp. 103–22.

15. R. Kenneth Kirby, "Milton's Biblical Hermeneutics in *The Doctrine and Discipline of Divorce,*" *Milton's Quarterly* 18 (1984): 116–25, especially 121. Kirby refers frequently to Milton's use of the analogy of faith, and his references show that he confuses this interpretive criterion with the conference of places. For the provocative proposal that in *De Doctrina* Milton placed "his own system of divinity in the authorized position, and turn[ed] the Bible into a gloss—on Milton," see Regina M. Schwartz, "Citation, authority, and *De Doctrina Christiana,*" in *Politics, Poetics, and Hermeneutics,* p. 228. For a more reliable account of Milton's hermeneutics, see Knott, pp. 115–16.

16. See John Halkett, *Milton and the Idea of Matrimony: A Study of the Divorce Tracts and Paradise Lost* (New Haven, CT: Yale University Press, 1970), p. 139.

17. For the idea that Milton understood that every rule provides a "test of the interpreter," see Lana Cable, "Coupling Logic and Milton's Doctrine of Divorce," *Milton Studies XV,* ed. James D. Simmonds (Pittsburgh: University of Pittsburgh Press, 1981), pp. 143–59, especially p. 153; on the popular reception of Milton's divorce tracts, see Christopher Hill, *Milton and the English Revolution* (1977; New York: Viking, 1978), pp. 130–35.

18. Two variorum commentaries published in Latin after the Restoration gathered up views that had been widely disseminated by sixteenth- and seventeenth-century biblical scholars; and they thus provide evidence of the availability of this view. See *Criticorum Sacrorum,* [ed. John Pearson], 8 vols. (1660; new ed., Amsterdam, 1698), 6: columns 659–90; Matthew Poole, *Synopsis Criticorvm,* 4 (London, 1694): columns 442–48, especially 446–47. The idea that men were abusing the text of Deut. 24: 1 out of "Cruelty to [their] Wives" was explicit in the vernacular variorum published by Poole's successors; see *Annotations upon the Holy Bible,* 2 vols. (London, 1683–85), 2 (1685): at Matt. 19: 3 and 8. Milton's argument for divorce in *De Doctrina Christiana* suggests his familiarity with, but not his support for, the idea that Moses and Christ were concerned about the vulnerable situation of women in their societies; see *CPW,* VI, 368–81. In *A Paraphrase and Annotations Upon all the Books of the New Testament,* Henry Hammond interpreted Matt. 19: 7–9 in a way designed to exclude just the sort of interpretation that Milton had proposed in the divorce tracts; see 2d ed. (London, 1659), p. 93.

19. Augustine, Preface to *De Doctrina Christiana,* trans. J. F. Shaw, in Vol. II of *A Select Library of Nicene and Post-Nicene Fathers of the Christian Church,* ed. Philip Schaff (New York: Charles Scribner's Sons, 1887), pp. 520–21.

20. Edward Phillips, "The Life of Mr. John Milton" (1674), in *The Early Lives of Milton*, ed. Helen Darbishire (London: Constable, 1932), p. 66.

21. For a useful survey of developments in the age of sacred philology, see George Newton Conklin, *Biblical Criticism and Heresy in Milton* (New York: King's Crown Press of Columbia University Press, 1949), chaps. I–II. To appreciate that much of Milton's knowledge of Hebrew sources was derivative, see Jason P. Rosenblatt's study of how John Selden's work mediated to Milton the learning of the rabbis: "Milton's Chief Rabbi," *Milton Studies XXIV*, ed. James D. Simmonds (Pittsburgh: University of Pittsburgh Press, 1989), pp. 43–71.

22. This has been newly and richly elaborated by Joan S. Bennett, in *Reviving Liberty: Radical Christian Humanism in Milton's Great Poems* (Cambridge, MA: Harvard University Press, 1989).

23. On Milton's new insistence on reading to discern God's "intention" in Scripture, see Stanley Fish, "Wanting a supplement: the question of interpretation in Milton's early prose," in *Politics, Poetics, and Hermeneutics*, pp. 41–68.

24. See above, Chapter One, pp. 2–3.

25. See Augustine, *Confessions*, III, v; VI, iii.

26. Thomas Gataker, *De Novi Instrumenti Stylo Dissertatio* (1648); on the debate, see Conklin, p. 21. On the ways in which these title pages also suggest Milton's relation to the rabbinical scholarship mediated to him by Selden, see Rosenblatt, "Milton's Chief Rabbi," pp. 57–62.

27. See Mary Ann Radzinowicz, *Toward Samson Agonistes: The Growth of Milton's Mind* (Princeton, NJ: Princeton University Press, 1978), p. 280.

28. On the distinctiveness of Milton's conception that the *adiaphora* may not be legislated, see Bernard J. Verkamp, *The Indifferent Mean: Adiaphorism in the English Reformation to 1554* (Athens: Ohio University Press; Detroit: Wayne State University Press, 1977), p. 132; Theodore L. Huguelet, "The Rule of Charity in Milton's Divorce Tracts," *Milton Studies VI*, ed. James D. Simmonds (Pittsburgh: University of Pittsburgh Press, 1975), pp. 199–214.

29. The story of Master Jenney and Mistris Attaway was reported by Thomas Edwards in *The Third Part of Gangraena* (London, 1646), pp. 26–27. For its connection to Milton's reputation, see Hill, *Milton and the English Revolution*, pp. 131–32. For an important caution, see Joseph Wittreich, *Feminist Milton* (Ithaca, NY: Cornell University Press, 1987), pp. 138–44.

30. Quoted from *CPW*, II, 103. See H. D. McDonald, *Ideas of Revelation: An Historical Study A.D. 1700 to A.D. 1860* (London: Macmillan, 1959), p. 202. (McDonald mistakenly refers to "Henry" Palmer, but his account is otherwise accurate.)

31. For the prevailing view, see Matthew Henry, *Exposition of the Old and New Testament*; cited by McDonald, p. 201. Others of Milton's affinities with John Goodwin are remarked by Barker, pp. 310–13 et passim. See also Bennett, *Reviving Liberty*, pp. 219–20.

32. In *An Antidote or Soveraigne Remedie Against the Pestiferovs Writings of All English Sectaries* ([St. Omer's], 1615), the Jesuit Sylvester Norris observed that "*Arius* likewise boasted of the patronage of *Scripture*, yea of the collation of places, our *Sectaries* chiefest refuge" (p. 9).

33. Joseph Caryl, *An Exposition with Practicall Observations Vpon the three first Chapters of the Booke of Iob* (London, 1643), p. 4.

34. A representative list of criteria for interpretation in which the "analogy of faith" appears in the final position can be found in one of the treatises on which Milton's *De Doctrina* is known to have been modeled: see Johannes Wollebius, *Compendivm Theologiæ Christianæ* (Amsterdam, 1633); translated by Alexander Ross as *The Abridgment of Christian Divinitie* (London, 1650), p. 10. Two nineteenth-century scholars provided brief and useful accounts of "the analogy of faith." See Charles Augustus Briggs, *Biblical Study: Its Principles, Methods and History* (New York: Charles Scribner's Sons, 1883), pp. 331–41; Frederic W. Farrar, *History of Interpretation* (New York: Dutton, 1886), pp. 332–33, 365. The more recent work by Battista Mondin, *The Principle of Analogy in Protestant and Catholic Theology* (The Hague: Martinus Nijhoff, 1963), although it treats Karl Barth's revival of a doctrine of "the analogy of faith" in our century, virtually ignores the cardinal importance of this principle in Protestant scholasticism.

In *Toward Samson Agonistes,* Radzinowicz has observed that the "concept of 'the analogy of faith' is crucial to understanding Milton's way of reading Scripture" (p. 279). Her discussion of how Milton compared and put together various scriptural texts (pp. 280–82) is excellent. She has not treated, however, the relation of the analogy of faith to tradition, and she has little to say about how Milton came to develop his distinctive understanding of this concept. The importance of the analogy of faith was glimpsed by U. Milo Kaufmann, whose account of it in *The Pilgrim's Progress and Traditions in Puritan Meditation* (New Haven, CT: Yale University Press, 1966), pp. 106–17, is quite unsatisfactory. Kaufmann erases significant differences in how the principle was invoked by different interpreters in different historical contexts. He presents, for instance, the views of Perkins and of John Owen as if they belong to a unified field of "Puritan hermeneutics," which served to uncover the timeless unity of the Word and to generate a coherent and static body of Puritan "doctrine."

35. See above, Chapter One, p. 3. Cf. Karl Barth: "This *analogia fidei* is . . . the point of the remarkable passages in Paul in which man's knowledge of God is inverted into man's being known by God." See *The Doctrine of the Word of God,* Vol. I of *Church Dogmatics,* trans. G. W. Bromiley, 2nd ed. (Edinburgh: T. & T. Clark, 1975), p. 244. Cf. Gal. 4: 8–9. Significantly, Calvin did not invoke the analogy of faith as an exegetical principle. See John H. Leith, "John Calvin—Theologian of the Bible," *Interpretation* 25 (1971): 329–44.

36. Whitaker, pp. 493, 471, 472 respectively. For Augustine's principle of explaining the hard places in terms of the plain, see his *De Doctrina Christiana,* Book II, chaps. 6 and 9; Book III, chap. 26. For a helpful exposition of another late sixteenth-century model for interpretation, which advocated "consensus as a meaningful route to the discovery of truth," see Egil Grislis, "The Hermeneutical Problem in Richard Hooker," in *Studies in Richard Hooker: Essays Preliminary to an Edition of His Works,* ed. W. Speed Hill (Cleveland: Press of Case Western Reserve University, 1972), pp. 159–206.

37. Whitaker, p. 472. To the idea already found in Whitaker that the analogy of faith was "a certaine *abridgement* or *summe* of the Scriptures," William Perkins added, citing 2 Tim. 1: 13, that appeal to this criterion entailed "charity or loue, which is explicated in the tenne Commaundements." See *The Arte of Prophecying,* in *Workes,* 2 vols. (London, 1613), 2: 651–52.

38. *The Sermons of John Donne,* ed. George R. Potter and Evelyn M. Simpson, 10 vols. (Berkeley: University of California Press, 1953–62), 2: 72; 4: 218–19; 2: 204. For less conservative homage to this interpretive principle, see the work of the Independent preacher, William Bridge, *Scripture-Light a Most Sure Light* (London, 1656), pp. 50–52.

39. See *The Creeds of Christendom, with a History and Critical Notes,* ed. Philip Schaff, 4th ed., 3 vols. (1877; rpt. Grand Rapids, MI: Baker Book House, 1977), 3: 606; H[enry] Hammond, *A Paraphrase and Annotations Upon all the Books of the New Testament,* 2d ed. enlarged (London, 1659), p. 1.

40. Jeremy Taylor, "The Minister's Duty in Life and Doctrine," *The Whole Works,* ed. Reginald Heber, 15 vols. (London: Ogle, Duncan, 1822), 6: 518, 519.

41. Grotius, in his *Annotationes* of 1641, made exactly this correlation, glossing the unequal distribution of talents to each man *secumdum propriam virtutem,* with Paul's principle of prophesying according to the proportion of one's faith. Grotius's annotation was included in *Criticorum Sacrorum,* Vol. VI (1660; Amsterdam, 1698), "Annotata ad . . . Matthæum," col. 852. See also Iohn Boys, *An Exposition of the Dominical Epistles and Gospels, vsed in our English Liturgie* (the Winter part) (London, 1611), p. 134.

42. The phrase "proportion of faith" translates the Greek κατὰ τὴν ἀναλογίαν τῆς πίστεως, which the Vulgate had rendered as *secundum rationem fidei.*

43. Taylor, *The Second Part of the Dissuasive from Popery,* in *The Whole Works,* 10: 416–17. Seventeenth-century English Protestants typically traced the analogy of faith as an interpretive principle to Augustine (*De utilitate credendi,* 5).

44. Taylor, 6: 520, 521; Thomas Edwards, *Antapologia: Or, A Full Answer to the Apologeticall Narration* (London, 1644), pp. 67–73; John Owen, ΣΥΝΕΣΙΣ ΠΝΕΥ-ΜΑΤΙΚΗ. *The Causes, Ways, and Means of Understanding the Mind of God as Revealed in His Word, with Assurance Therein* (1678), in *The Works of John Owen,* ed. William H. Goold, 16 vols. (1850–53; rpt. Edinburgh: Banner of Truth Trust, 1967), 4: 215–16, 227.

45. Acts 17: 11 appeared as the epigraph on the title page of Stephen Nye's *Brief History of the Unitarians Called also Socinians* and in the same capacity for the collection of Unitarian tracts called *The Faith of One God, Who is only the Father* (London, 1691), in which the 2d ed. of Nye's work was reprinted. The Preface for *The Faith of One God* declares on the basis of Acts 17: 11 that Paul "has thereby given to all free Inquirers, the Character of *Noble,* and pronounced all others to be base, ungenerous, ignoble vile" (p. 4). Cf. [Abraham Underwood], *The Protestants Plea for a Socinian: Justifying His Doctrine from being opposite to Scripture or Church-Authority* (London, 1686), pp. 1–4. See also [William Sherlock], *The Protestant Resolution of Faith* (London, 1683), pp. 13–14, 19–20, 22–23.

46. [Anne Docwra], *An Epistle of Love and Good Advice To my Old Friends & Fellow-Sufferers in the Late Times, the Old Royalists and their Posterity* ([London?], 1683), pp. 4, 7.

47. For a ready application of the Derridean doctrine of the supplement to Milton's case, see Fish, "Wanting a supplement."

48. William Shullenberger, "Linguistic and Poetic Theory in Milton's *De Doctrina Christiana,*" *English Language Notes* 19 (1981–82): 262–78, especially 277–78. The metaphor of the body was already prominent in one of Milton's principal

models, William Ames's *Medvlla Theologica*, translated into English as *The Marrow of Sacred Divinity, Drawne out of the holy Scriptures* (London, 1642).

49. Shullenberger, p. 270. Fear of transferring the techniques of secular reading to Bible reading was voiced, *inter alia*, by William Pemble, who condemned as "Prophane" "collecting" texts that "pleaseth [the] fancy" like so many "flowres of Rhetorick" to be "scattered" again as a "garnish" for a writer's own "discourse." See *Vindiciæ Gratiæ. A Plea for Grace* (Oxford, 1659), p. 9.

50. On nervousness in the face of *copia* and "authentic discourse" in this period, see Terence Cave, *The Cornucopian Text: Problems of Writing in the French Renaissance* (Oxford: Clarendon Press; New York: Oxford University Press, 1979). On differing "gifts," see the foundational treatise by Rudolph Agricola, in the translation by J. R. McNally, "Rudolph Agricola's *De Inventione Dialectica Libri Tres*: A Translation of Selected Chapters," *Speech Monographs* 34 (1967): 375; cited by Crane, p. 19.

51. Prolusion III, "Against Scholastic Philosophy," *Works*, XII, 158–59; *CPW*, I, 240–41.

Chapter Four

1. See Jonathan Goldberg, "Dating Milton," in *Soliciting Interpretation: Literary Theory and Seventeenth-Century English Poetry*, ed. Elizabeth D. Harvey and Katharine Eisaman Maus (Chicago: University of Chicago Press, 1990), pp. 199–220.

2. In addition to the pieces of biographical criticism cited in Chapter Two, see William McCarthy, "The Continuity of Milton's Sonnets," *PMLA* 92 (1977): 96–109. The relation of Sonnets 7 and 19 to puritan diaries has been observed by Jerome Mazzaro, "Gaining Authority: John Milton at Sonnets," *Essays in Literature* 15 (1988): 3–4, 8.

3. On Milton's relation to Protestant casuistry, see Camille Wells Slights, *The Casuistical Tradition in Shakespeare, Donne, Herbert, and Milton* (Princeton, NJ: Princeton University Press, 1981), chap. 6.

4. Perkins, *The Combat betweene Christ and the Deuill displayed*, 2nd ed. (London, 1606), p. 16. Christopher Hill has proposed this exegetical treatment of the temptations in the wilderness as a source for *Paradise Regained*; see *Milton and the English Revolution* (1977; New York: Viking, 1978), p. 427n.

5. *A Treatise of Callings*, in *The Works of William Perkins newly corrected according to his own copies* (Cambridge, 1605), p. 937.

6. Perkins, *Works*, p. 937; abbreviations have been expanded.

7. John Wollebius, *The Abridgment of Christian Divinitie*, trans. Alexander Ross (London, 1650), pp. 198–99; Hugo Grotius, *His Most Choice Discovrses*, trans. Cl. Barksdale, 3d ed. (London, 1658), pp. 112–13; John Gardner, "To the Reader," in J[ane] Turner's *Choice Experiences* (London, 1653), n. p.; [Mary Mersen], *This Treatise Proving Three Worlds/Foundations Mentioned in Scripture* (London, 1696), pp. 303 ff., 314, 426–44. Cf. also the *Journal of Richard Norwood, Surveyor of Bermuda* (New York: Scholars' Facsimiles & Reprints for Bermuda Historical Monuments Trust, 1945), pp. 66–67, 72, 80–85, 91.

8. Thomas Newton, ed., *The Poetical Works of John Milton. With Notes of*

various Authors, 3 vols. (London, 1761), 3: 531n. It should be noted that other seventeenth-century poets had referred the parable to their own situations in self-deprecating fashion. See George Wither, *Hallelujah, Or Britain's Second Remembrancer* (1641) (London: John Russell Smith, 1857), p. xxx; Henry Vaughan, *The Works of Henry Vaughan*, ed. L. C. Martin, 2d ed. (Oxford: Clarendon Press, 1957), p. 392; *All The Workes of John Taylor the Water Poet* (1630; rpt. London: Scolar Press, 1977), p. A3.

9. William Riley Parker, *Milton: A Biography*, 2 vols. (Oxford: Clarendon Press, 1968), 1: 470.

10. *The Poetical Works of Robert Herrick*, ed. L. C. Martin (Oxford: Clarendon Press, 1956), p. 289.

11. *Dictionary of the English Language*; "On the Death of Dr. Robert Levet" (1783), in *The Yale Edition of the Works of Samuel Johnson, Vol. VI: Poems*, ed. E. L. McAdam, Jr., with George Milne (New Haven, CT: Yale University Press, 1964), lines 25–28.

12. See Charles L. Cohen, "The Saints Zealous in Love and Labor: The Puritan Psychology of Work," *Harvard Theological Review* 76 (1983): 455–80. A revised form of this essay appears in *God's Caress: The Psychology of Puritan Religious Experience* (New York: Oxford University Press, 1986).

13. Joel F. Wilcox, "'Spending the Light': Milton and Homer's Light of Hope," *Milton Quarterly* 18 (1984): 77–78.

14. See the striking letter of 26 April 1814 to Joseph Cottle, *Unpublished Letters of Samuel Taylor Coleridge*, ed. Earl Leslie Griggs, 2 vols. (London: Constable, 1932), 2: 107.

15. Parker, 1: 469–71. See also Antony Easthope, "Towards the autonomous subject in poetry: Milton's 'On His Blindness,'" in *Post-Structuralist Readings of English Poetry*, ed. Richard Machin and Christopher Norris (Cambridge: Cambridge University Press, 1987), pp. 122–33.

16. Christopher Hill, *The Experience of Defeat: Milton and Some Contemporaries* (New York: Elisabeth Sifton Books; Viking, 1984).

17. Ur. Quarles, address to the "Courteous Reader," in *The Complete Works in Prose and Verse of Francis Quarles*, ed. Alexander B. Grosart, Chertsey Worthies' Library, 3 vols. ([Printed privately in England], 1880–81; rpt. New York: AMS Press, 1967), 1: 102. Quotations from Quarles are from this edition and are referred to by volume and page number.

18. See *A Meditation of a Penitent Sinner*, appended to *Sermons of John Calvin* (London, 1560). The poems are available in a transcription by Roland Greene from the Women Writers Project at Brown University.

19. In his article on "Talents" for the *Milton Encyclopedia*, Michael Lieb opens up the possibility of setting a certain distance between the speaker of the octave and the poet; he also suggests that the poem be seen chiefly in didactic terms. Beyond this, Gary A. Stringer has shown that the poem has a narrative and dramatic structure and that Milton's craft has imparted to the sonnet form a distinctively Pauline teaching. See Lieb, in *A Milton Encyclopedia*, 8 vols. (Lewisburg, PA: Bucknell University Press, 1978–83), 8 (1980): 48–51; Stringer, "Milton's 'Thorn in the Flesh': Pauline Didacticism in *Sonnet XIX*," *Milton Studies X*, ed. James D. Simmonds (Pittsburgh: University of Pittsburgh Press, 1977), pp. 141–54.

20. Mary Ann Radzinowicz points out a number of similarities and differences between this figure and Samson in *Toward Samson Agonistes: The Growth of Milton's Mind* (Princeton, NJ: Princeton University Press, 1978), pp. 141–42. The word "vtter" appears in the Geneva Bible, "outer" in the Authorized Version. The two words seem to be etymologically related and they were pronounced alike. See Anne Ferry, *The "Inward" Language: Sonnets of Wyatt, Sidney, Shakespeare, Donne* (Chicago: University of Chicago Press, 1983), p. 63. On the relevance of various biblical passages to the sonnet and on the "misapplication" of the parable of the talents, see Anna K. Nardo, *Milton's Sonnets and the Ideal Community* (Lincoln: University of Nebraska Press, 1979), pp. 145–51.

21. See H[enry] Jessey, *A Storehouse of Provision* (London, 1650), p. 67. The "puritan psychology of work" has been helpfully described by Cohen (*God's Caress*, pp. 111–33).

22. See *The Sermons of John Donne*, ed. George R. Potter and Evelyn M. Simpson, 10 vols. (Berkeley: University of California Press, 1953–62), 10: 85. Cf. Jeanne M. Shami, "Donne on Discretion," *ELH* 47 (1980): 48–66.

23. The popular view against which I am arguing has been made explicit by Ann Gossman and George W. Whiting. They maintain that "Talent, of course, means the poetic gift" and that the poem does not concern "salvation or damnation." See "Milton's First Sonnet on His Blindness," *Review of English Studies* ns 12 (1961): 364–70, viz. 365.

24. See *Spirituall Experiences of sundry Beleevers*, 2nd impression enlarged (London, 1651 [an error for 1652 or 1653]), pp. 160–91, especially 170–71, 173. The image of burying the talent in a napkin involved a conflation of Luke 19: 20 and Matt. 25: 25 that was quite common.

25. Jeremy Taylor, *Ductor Dubitantium, or The Rule of Conscience* (London, 1660), Book 2, chap. 3, rule 2, p. 395.

26. "A Further Testimony to Truth, Revived Out of the Ruins of the Apostacy," in *The Works of Isaac Pennington, A Minister of the Gospel in the Society of Friends*, 4th ed. (Philadelphia, 1863), 4: 29–31.

27. John Calvin, *The Institution of Christian Religion*, trans. Thomas Norton (London, 1599), III.xxiv.4. Cf. David J. Aitken, "Milton's Use of 'Stand' and the Doctrine of Perseverance," *English Language Notes* 19 (1981–82): 233–36.

28. M. S. Berkowitz has pointed out that in a sermon of 28 February 1644, before the Commons, Milton's former tutor invoked Matthew's parable "to suggest that patience is a sort of talent whose exercise will cause it to multiply, whereas in Milton the parable forms part of the speaker's complaint." See "Thomas Young's 'Hopes Encouragement' and Milton's 'Sonnet XIX,'" *Milton Quarterly* 16 (1982): 94–97, viz. 95. My argument suggests, however, that Milton's treatment of patience may be more continuous with the view expressed by Young than Berkowitz thinks.

29. *A Variorum Commentary on the Poems of John Milton*, Vol. II, Part 2: *The Minor Poems*, ed. A. S. P. Woodhouse and Douglas Bush (New York: Columbia University Press, 1972), p. 469. Cf. Parker, 2: 1043.

30. Many passages are potentially relevant, including Ps. 27: 14; Ps. 37: 7; Dan. 7: 10; Isa. 8: 17; 50: 10; Lam. 3: 25–26. Robert Reiter has suggested to me the relevance of a passage to which modern commentators do not so routinely refer:

"Draw not nigh hither: put off thy shoes from off thy feet; for the place whereon thou standest *is* holy ground" (Exod. 3: 5).

31. For an especially thoughtful discussion of the popular uses of Matt. 11: 28, see Cohen, *God's Caress*, pp. 196–99.

32. "Bent" was the standard term in puritan vocabulary for what the Spirit of God altered at one's conversion: unregenerate humanity lacked "the capacity and mental stamina necessary to perform righteous deeds continuously." Only after conversion did one have the "ability to do the Lord's bidding." See Cohen, "The Saints Zealous in Love and Labor," p. 456.

33. *Shakespeare's Sonnets*, edited with analytic commentary by Stephen Booth (New Haven, CT: Yale University Press, 1977), p. 243; Ferry, chap. 4.

34. Ferry has shown that, in the poem where Booth uncovered "two paradoxically compatible alternatives" (Sonnet 62), Shakespeare assimilates into himself the judges that Astrophil had found in an external body, "greatest companie." See *The "Inward" Language*, pp. 198–200, 202.

35. See the fine discussion of this "capping sonnet" by Radzinowicz, *Towards Samson Agonistes*, p. 133. The religious tradition has been studied by William L. Stull in "Sonnets Courtly and Christian," *University of Hartford Studies in Literature* 15–16 (1983–84): 1–15. For a treatment of Milton's various handlings of the sonnet conventions relating to God and to a mistress, see Kay Stanton, "From 'Jove' to 'Task-Master': The Transformation from Pagan to Christian Diety in Milton's Sonnets 1–7," in the same issue, 67–79.

36. Josephus, *Antiquities* II, ix, 6: #230; quoted by Raymond E. Brown, *The Birth of the Messiah: A Commentary on the Infancy Narratives in Matthew and Luke* (Garden City, NY: Doubleday, 1977), p. 495.

37. See *Synopsis Criticorum*, ed. Matthew Poole, 4 vols. in 5 (London: 1669–1676), I (1669): on Exod. I: 11–14.

38. John Lightfoot, *The Harmony, Chronicle and Order of the Old Testament* (London, 1647), p. 44.

39. See William Kerrigan, *The Sacred Complex: On the Psychogenesis of Paradise Lost* (Cambridge, MA: Harvard University Press, 1983), pp. 170–81, 190–92.

40. Lancelot Andrewes, *A Pattern of Catechisticall Doctrine* (London, 1630), pp. 327–28.

41. The sonnet is quoted here from Shakespeare's *Poems* (London, 1640), p. [A6ᵛ], which follows closely the text of 1609. For another discussion of these two "When I consider . . ." sonnets, see Jonathan Goldberg, *Voice/Terminal/Echo: Postmodernism and English Renaissance Texts* (London: Methuen, 1986), pp. 129–32.

42. Quoted from *The Works of George Herbert*, ed. F. E. Hutchinson (Oxford: Clarendon, 1941), p. 143. Easthope (p. 131) suggests a contrast between Milton's sonnet and "The Holdfaste."

Chapter Five

1. Hugh MacCallum, "*Samson Agonistes*: The Deliverer as Judge," *Milton Studies XXIII*, ed. James D. Simmonds (Pittsburgh: University of Pittsburgh Press, 1988), pp. 260, 264, 265.

2. See my article, "Milton's Strange Pantheon: The Apparent Tritheism of the *De Doctrina Christiana*," *Heythrop Journal* 16 (1975): 129–48. Cf. Regina M. Schwartz, "Citation, Authority, and *De Doctrina Christiana*," in *Politics, poetics, and hermeneutics in Milton's prose*, ed. David Loewenstein and James Grantham Turner (Cambridge: Cambridge University Press, 1990), pp. 239–40.

3. Among the passages which helped to confirm Milton in the belief that the Scriptures bear witness to a prior and unwritten Word of God that is not exhausted were the opening verses of the Gospel of Luke (where the evangelist spoke of his having followed closely the narratives of previous writers, of having consulted eyewitnesses, and then of having sought to write a truly orderly account), and the seventh chapter of First Corinthians (where Paul distinguished between the Lord's teachings and his own attempts to apply them under altered circumstances); cf. *CPW*, II, 338–39.

4. See Elizabeth Marie Pope, *Paradise Regained: The Tradition and the Poem* (1947; New York: Russell & Russell, 1962), pp. 20–21.

5. *Reliquiæ Baxterianæ: Or, Mr. Richard Baxter's Narrative of The most Memorable Passages of his Life and Times*, ed. Matthew Sylvester (London, 1696), p. 7.

6. For a summary account of Marian doctrine in the early Reformation period, see Hilda Graef, *Mary: A History of Doctrine and Devotion*, 2 vols. (New York: Sheed & Ward, 1965), 2: 1–16, 62–67. The most telling reference to Mariolatry in Milton's prose appears almost as an obiter dictum in the course of an attempt to discredit the authority of Irenaeus in *Of Prelatical Episcopacy*; see *CPW*, I, 642.

7. Carolyn H. Smith has observed that there are no precedents in the apocrypha, the mystery cycles, standard Renaissance commentaries, or the poems of Vida and Fletcher, for the emotional struggles that Milton gives to Mary after the baptism of Jesus; see "The Virgin Mary in *Paradise Regained*," *South Atlantic Quarterly* 71 (1972): 557.

8. See Maurice Vlober, *La Vie de Marie Mère de Dieu* (Paris: Librairie Bloud et Gay, 1949), p. 209; Louis Réau, *Iconographie de l'art chrétien*, 3 vols. (Paris: Presses Universitaires de France, 1955–59), 2, ii (1957): 284–85. For Mary as the *sedes sapientiae*, see Gertrud Schiller, *Iconography of Christian Art*, trans. Janet Seligman, 2 vols. (1966; 1st American edition: Greenwich, CT: New York Graphic Society, 1971), 1: 23–25. For resistance to the idea of Mary as Jesus' teacher, see Mrs. [Anna] Jameson, *Legends of the Madonna as Represented in the Fine Arts*, corrected and enlarged ed. (Boston: Houghton, Mifflin, n. d.), pp. 405–6. Cf. John Sparrow's discussion of Botticelli's *Madonna of the Magnificat*, in *Visible Words: A Study of Inscriptions in and as Books and Works of Art* (Cambridge: Cambridge University Press, 1969), pp. 53–57.

9. See Réau, 2, ii: 180. In the English liturgy the passage from Isaiah was read as the Epistle on the Feast of the Annunciation, while Luke 1: 26 ff. was read as the Gospel. Iohn Boys, in *An Exposition of the Festivall Epistles and Gospels, vsed in our English Liturgie*, the 2nd Part, (London, 1614), commented that "This Epistle then is all one with the Gospell, *Esay* and *Gabriel* are messengers of the same errand; for that which *Esay* speakes of *Mary*, *Gabriel* speakes vnto *Mary*" (p. 48).

10. *A Codly [i.e., Godly] Form of Hovseholde Gouernement: for the ordering of priuate Families according to Gods word*, gathered by R[obert] C[awdry] (London,

1598), p. 39. On the religious upbringing of children, see Lawrence Stone, *The Family, Sex and Marriage in England 1500–1800* (New York: Harper & Row, 1977), pp. 139–42 and passim.

11. *The Rev. Oliver Heywood, B.A., 1630–1702: His Autobiographies, Diaries, Anecdote and Event Books*, ed. J. Horsfall Turner (Brighouse, England: A. B. Bayes, 1881–85), 1 (1882): 42, 48, 51; cited by Margaret Spufford, "First steps in literacy: the reading and writing experiences of the humblest seventeenth-century spiritual autobiographers," *Social History*, 4, no. 3 (1979): 435. For a treatment of women thinking biblically, see Elaine V. Beilin, *Redeeming Eve: Women Writers of the English Renaissance* (Princeton, NJ: Princeton University Press, 1987), pp. 46–47, 51. See also Anna Maria à Schurman, *The Learned Maid, Or, Whether a Maid May Be a Scholar? A Logick Exercise* (London, 1659), p. 3; cf. pp. 30–31. (This work was translated from the author's Latin.)

12. To appreciate how much traditional material concerning Mary the author of *Paradise Regained* ignores and omits, one may compare Julia Kristeva's reflections on the history of Marian devotion in "Héréthique de l'amour," *Tel Quel* 74 (Winter, 1977): 30–49. The essay has been translated by León S. Roudiez and appears in *The Kristeva Reader*, ed. Toril Moi (New York: Columbia University Press, 1986) under the title "Stabat Mater," pp. 160–86. See also the history of medieval Marian devotion sketched by Clarissa W. Atkinson, in *The Oldest Vocation: Christian Motherhood in the Middle Ages* (Ithaca, NY: Cornell University Press, 1991), chap. 4.

13. Calvin commented, e.g., that we would know nothing about the episode with the twelve-year-old in the Temple, "but that Mary kept it layde vppe in her heart, that afterwardes she might bring the same from thence with other treasures for the common vse of the godly"; see *A Harmonie Vpon the Three Euangelistes Matthewe, Marke, and Luke*, trans. E[usebius] P[agit] (London, 1610), p. 103.

14. On "puritan" objections to the Magnificat, see Herbert Mortimer Luckock, *Studies in the History of the Book of Common Prayer*, 2nd ed. (London: Rivingtons, 1882), p. 84; see Boys, *An Exposition of Al the Principal Scriptvres Vsed in our English Liturgie* (London, 1610), pp. 56, 57, 61, 62. On Mary as a prophet, see, e.g., William Perkins, *A Reformed Catholike*, in *Workes*, 2 vols. (London, 1612), 1: 601. For Milton's definition of a prophet, see *CPW*, VI, 572.

15. Edward Phillips, *Theatrum Poetarum, or a compleat Collection of the Poets, Especially The most Eminent, of all Ages* (London, 1675), p. 243. Another writer who considered the implications of Mary's poem was John Trapp; he associated Christ and Mary as readers with the Bereans of Acts 17. Mary, he reports, "spent a third part of her time in reading the Scriptures. Sure it is, shee was excellently well versed in them, as appeares in her Song." See *Theologia Theologiae, the True Treasure; Or A Treasury of holy Truths, touching Gods Word, and God the Word* (London, 1641), p. 303. On Milton's association of creative activity with female figures, see William Kerrigan, "The Riddle of *Paradise Regained*," in *Poetic Prophecy in Western Literature*, ed. Jan Wojcik and Raymond-Jean Frontain (Rutherford, NJ: Fairleigh Dickinson University Press, 1984), pp. 73–74.

16. Boys, *An Exposition of the Dominical Epistles and Gospels vsed in our English Liturgie . . . The Spring-part from the first in Lent to Whitsunday* (London, 1610), pp. 33–34. See also William Whitaker, *A Disputation on Holy Scripture, Against the*

Papists, Especially Bellarmine and Stapleton, trans. William Fitzgerald (Cambridge: Cambridge University Press, 1849; rpt. New York: Johnson Reprint Corp., 1968), Question VI: Concerning the Perfection of Scripture, Against Human Traditions, pp. 502, 538–39. (The Latin *Disputatio* was published at Cambridge, 1588.)

17. Perkins, *A Reformed Catholike,* in *Workes,* 1: 580–81, 583. See above, Chapter Three, pp. 76–83.

18. Boys, *An Exposition of the Dominical Epistles and Gospels, vsed in our English Liturgie . . . The Winter Part* (London, 1611), pp. 133–34, 146. Iohn Preston, *The Nevv Covenant, or The Saints Portion,* 2d ed. (London, 1629), p. 600. For the quotation from Milton I have cited Charles Sumner's translation (rather than Carey's), because it better suggests the sense of Milton's Latin. See *Works,* XIV, 8–9.

19. Of course long before Milton many writers and painters had effected a fusion of the accounts by Matthew and Luke. But in the time-scheme of Milton's poem, Mary is using words and phrases — and Jesus is remembering them — some years before Matthew and Luke will set them down in the Scriptures.

20. See, e.g., John Diodati, *Pious and Learned Annotations Upon the Holy Bible,* 3d ed. (London, 1651), at Luke 2: 19.

21. *The Book of Common Prayer 1559,* ed. John E. Booty (Charlottesville: Published for The Folger Shakespeare Library by University Press of Virginia, 1976), p. 248. This prayer dates to the Prayerbook of 1549; see Frederick Armitage, *A History of the Collects* (London: Weare, n.d.). On the use of phrases such as "the closet of the heart" and its characteristic connection with one's "treasure," see Anne Ferry, *The "Inward" Language: Sonnets of Wyatt, Sidney, Shakespeare, Donne* (Chicago: University of Chicago Press, 1983), pp. 48–55.

22. Eusebius Pagit, *The Historie of the Bible, Briefly Collected by way of Question and Answer* (London, 1613).

23. See *Mary in the New Testament,* ed. Raymond E. Brown et al. (Philadelphia: Fortress, 1978), p. 149. Cf. Joseph A. Fitzmyer's commentary in the Anchor Bible, *The Gospel According to Luke (I–IX)* (Garden City, NY: Doubleday, 1981), p. 413. Calvin emphasized Mary's exemplary activities of collecting and combining in his commentary on Luke 2: 19: "*Symballein* doth else signifie to conferre, as to make vp one perfect body, by gathering all thinges together, which agreed amongst themselues to prooue the glory of Christe" (*Harmonie,* p. 77).

24. See Brown, *Mary,* pp. 149–50. Cf. W. C. van Unnik, "Die rechte Bedeutung des Wortes treffen, Lukas 2,19," in *Verbum: Essays on Some Aspects of the Religious Function of Words: Festschrift for H. W. Obbink,* ed. T. P. van Baaren et al. (Utrecht: Kemink, 1964), pp. 129–47.

25. I owe this point to a suggestion by Geoffrey Nuttall.

26. Cf. the excellent commentary by Sanford Budick, *The Dividing Muse: Images of Sacred Disjunction in Milton's Poetry* (New Haven, CT: Yale University Press, 1985), pp. 128–29.

27. See Anne Ferry's discussion of "places" in sixteenth-century rhetorical theory, in *The Art of Naming* (Chicago: University of Chicago Press, 1988), pp. 90–96. Cf. Mary Thomas Crane, *Framing Authority: Sayings, Self, and Society in Sixteenth-Century England* (Princeton, NJ: Princeton University Press, 1993), chap. 1.

28. Thomas Wilson, *The Rule of Reason Conteinyng the Arte of Logique* (1551),

ed. Richard S. Sprague (Northridge, CA: San Fernando Valley State College, 1972), p. 89; Raphe Lever, *The Arte of Reason, rightly termed Witcraft, teaching a perfect way to argue and dispute* (London, 1573), pp. 7ff.; Robert Cawdray, *A Treasvrie or Store-hovse of Similes* (London, 1600; facsimile ed., New York: Da Capo, 1971), p. 853; Henry Jessey, *A Storehovse of Provision* (London, 1650), p. A2^r. On commonplace books as storehouses, see Sister Joan Marie Lechner, *Renaissance Concepts of the Commonplaces* (New York: Pageant, 1962), pp. 147–51.

29. Cf. also John Spencer, ΚΑΙΝΑ ΚΑΙ ΠΑΛΑΙΑ. *Things New and Old. Or, A Storehouse of Similies, Sentences, Allegories, . . . Collected and observed from the Writings and Sayings of the Learned in all Ages to this present* (London, 1658).

30. See Laurie Zwicky, "Kairos in *Paradise Regained*: The Divine Plan," *ELH* 31 (1964): 271–77.

31. See Dayton Haskin, "*Samson Agonistes* on the Stage at Yale," *Milton Quarterly* 19 (1985): 48–53.

32. The word "business" appears nowhere else in the Authorized Version of the gospels. For representative seventeenth-century commentary on this passage, see H[enry] Hammond, *A Paraphrase and Annotations Upon All the Books of the New Testament*, 2d ed. (London, 1659), pp. 194, 196; cf. also *Annotations upon the Holy Bible*, compiled by successors to Matthew Poole (Vol. 2 [1685]), where there is also a gloss on the seeming rebuke to Mary.

33. Stanley Fish, "Spectacle and Evidence in *Samson Agonistes*," *Critical Inquiry* 15 (1989): 556–86.

34. John Guillory, "The Father's House: *Samson Agonistes* in Its Historical Moment," in *Re-membering Milton: Essays on the Texts and Traditions*, ed. Mary Nyquist and Margaret W. Ferguson (New York: Methuen, 1987), p. 158.

35. In a paper presented at the annual convention of the Modern Language Association in New York, 1992, "*Paradise Regained* and Puritan Social Theology," Jodi Mikalachki developed Milton's suggestion that the Son imbibes oral culture from his mother's breasts.

Chapter Six

1. Stanley Fish, "Spectacle and Evidence in *Samson Agonistes*," *Critical Inquiry* 15 (1989): 556–86.

2. The phrase "hermeneutic combat" derives from Mary Ann Radzinowicz, "*Paradise Regained* as Hermeneutic Combat," *University of Hartford Studies in Literature* 15–16 (1983–84): 99–107. The longer quotation comes from Emory Elliott, "Milton's Biblical Style in *Paradise Regained*," *Milton Studies VI*, ed. James D. Simmonds (Pittsburgh: University of Pittsburgh Press, 1975), pp. 227–41, viz. 236. See also, as representative examples, Louis L. Martz, "*Paradise Regained*: The Meditative Combat," *ELH* 27 (1960): 223–47; revised in *Milton: Poet of Exile*, 2d ed. (New Haven, CT: Yale University Press, 1986), pp. 247–71; Roger H. Sundell, "The Narrator as Interpreter in *Paradise Regained*," *Milton Studies II*, ed. James D. Simmonds (Pittsburgh: University of Pittsburgh Press, 1970), pp. 83–101; Georgia B. Christopher, *Milton and the Science of the Saints* (Princeton, NJ: Princeton

University Press, 1982), chap. 7; and Ashraf H. A. Rushdy, "Of *Paradise Regained:* The Interpretation of Career," *Milton Studies XXIV,* ed. James D. Simmonds (Pittsburgh: University of Pittsburgh Press, 1989), pp. 253–75. For a challenge to the prestige in which interpretive criticism has been held in our time, see Barbara Hernstein Smith, *Contingencies of Value: Alternative Perspectives for Critical Theory* (Cambridge, MA: Harvard University Press, 1988), chaps. 2–3.

3. For a standard account of the relation of Milton's narrative to Luke and the synoptic gospels, see Elizabeth Marie Pope, *Paradise Regained: The Tradition and the Poem* (1947; New York: Russell & Russell, 1962), chap. 1. For Job as generic model, see Barbara Kiefer Lewalski, *Milton's Brief Epic: The Genre, Meaning, and Art of "Paradise Regained"* (Providence, RI: Brown University Press; London: Methuen, 1966), Part I. The importance of the Fourth Gospel was pointed out by Ira Clark, "*Paradise Regained* and the Gospel according to John," *Modern Philology* 71 (1973–74): 1–15; it has been further explored by Stella P. Revard, "The Gospel of John and *Paradise Regained:* Jesus as 'True Light,'" in *Milton and Scriptural Tradition: The Bible into Poetry,* ed. James H. Sims and Leland Ryken (Columbia: University of Missouri Press, 1984), pp. 142–59. The importance of the Pauline letters and of Revelation has been richly demonstrated by Elliott, pp. 227–41; of Hebrews, by Sanford Budick, *The Dividing Muse: Images of Sacred Disjunction in Milton's Poetry* (New Haven, CT: Yale University Press, 1985), pp. 54–56, 122–48. The centrality of certain Psalms is explored by Mary Ann Radzinowicz, *Milton's Epics and the Book of Psalms* (Princeton, NJ: Princeton University Press, 1989).

4. The quoted phrases are from Arnold Stein's treatment of the hero's classical learning in *Heroic Knowledge: An Interpretation of Paradise Regained and Samson Agonistes* (1957; Hamden, CT: Archon, 1965), p. 111. For the classic study of the poem as meditation, see Martz, "*Paradise Regained*: The Meditative Combat"; on other biblical epics of the period, see Burton O. Kurth, *Milton and Christian Heroism: Biblical Epic Themes and Forms in Seventeenth-Century England* (1959; Hamden, CT: Archon, 1966); see especially pp. 107–8; cf. Lewalski, *Milton's Brief Epic,* pp. 68–101.

5. Matt. 19: 1–12; Luke 20: 19–26. Frank Kermode has pointed out that Luke explicitly ends his account of what happened in the wilderness (4: 13) with the remark that Satan departed until an opportune time to renew his temptations. Thus Luke planted a narrative seed that bears fruit when, Satan-like, the Pharisees devise ways to tempt Jesus. See *The Art of Telling: Essays on Fiction* (Cambridge, MA: Harvard University Press, 1983), pp. 186, 188.

6. For a fine exposition of *philosophia Christi,* see John W. O'Malley, "Grammar and rhetoric in the *pietas* of Erasmus," *Journal of Medieval and Renaissance Studies* 18 (1988): 81–98. For Milton's interest in the Pauline basis of this commonplace, see Timothy J. O'Keeffe, *Milton and the Pauline Tradition: A Study of Theme and Symbolism* (Washington, DC: University Press of America, 1982), chap. 5. See also Kermode, *The Art of Telling,* p. 193.

7. E. M. W. Tillyard, *Milton,* rev. ed. (New York: Barnes & Noble, 1967), p. 262; Douglas Bush, *The Renaissance and English Humanism* (Toronto: University of Toronto Press, 1939), p. 125.

8. Malcolm Kelsall, "The Historicity of *Paradise Regained,*" *Milton Studies*

XII, ed. James D. Simmonds (Pittsburgh: University of Pittsburgh Press, 1979), pp. 235–51. On the possibility that Milton thought that the historical Jesus was bilingual and had more Greek learning than the evangelists explicitly indicated, see Donald Swanson, "Milton's Scholarly Jesus in *Paradise Regained*," *Cithara* 27, 2 (1988): 3–10.

9. In *Paradise Lost and the Rhetoric of Literary Forms* (Princeton, NJ: Princeton University Press, 1985), Barbara Kiefer Lewalski frequently emphasizes that, by setting his poem at the beginning of history, Milton was able to create the fiction that various characters were creating the prototypes for one or other literary genre. For attention to the term "prevention," see Jonathan Goldberg, "Dating Milton," in *Soliciting Interpretation: Literary Theory and Seventeenth-Century English Poetry*, ed. Elizabeth D. Harvey and Katharine Eisaman Maus (Chicago: University of Chicago Press, 1990), pp. 207–10.

10. Cf. Werner Jaeger, *Early Christianity and Greek Paideia* (Cambridge, MA: Belknap Press of Harvard University Press, 1961), pp. 11–12.

11. Eusebius, *Demonstration of the Gospel*, 3.6.8, in *Patrologiæ cursus completus*, series *Græca*, ed. J.-P. Migne 22 (Paris, 1857): 225. See also James Shiel, *Greek Thought and the Rise of Christianity* (London: Longmans; New York: Barnes & Noble, 1968), pp. 1–3.

12. For an exposition of the differences among Jesus's acquired knowledge, his infused knowledge, and his beatific knowledge, see the article by J. J Walsh, "Jesus Christ (II)," in *The New Catholic Encyclopedia* (New York: McGraw-Hill, 1967), 7: 924–26.

13. See Jaroslav Pelikan, *The Emergence of the Catholic Tradition (100–600)* (Chicago: University of Chicago Press, 1971), pp. 143–46. On the meeting of Greek and Hebrew traditions before New Testament times, see Elias J. Bickerman, *The Jews in the Greek Age* (Cambridge, MA: Harvard University Press, 1988), especially chap. 13.

14. Although the idea that Paul had a conversion remains common, even many Protestants now recognize that Luther interpreted the story from Acts in terms that made it more readily compatible with the Pauline theology he was seeking to apply against the papal church. See Krister Stendahl, *Paul Among Jews and Gentiles and Other Essays* (Philadelphia: Fortress, 1976). On the Protestant paradigm of salvation, see Barbara Kiefer Lewalski, *Protestant Poetics and the Seventeenth-Century Religious Lyric* (Princeton, NJ: Princeton University Press, 1979), pp. 13–27.

15. See William Perkins, *The Combat Between Christ and the Devill displayed*, 2d ed. (London, 1606), p. 9; cf. p. 11.

16. See Robert E. Reiter, "On Biblical Typology and the Interpretation of Literature," *College English* 30 (1968–69): 562–71. See also the discussion of Milton's use of Ephesians 6: 10–14 by Neil Forsyth in "Having Done All to Stand: Biblical and Classical Allusion in *Paradise Regained*," *Milton Studies XXI*, ed. James D. Simmonds (Pittsburgh: University of Pittsburgh Press, 1986), pp. 202–3.

17. Tillyard, *Milton*, p. 258; Perkins, *Combat*, pp. 7, 13. See Kermode's summary (in *The Art of Telling*, pp. 189–91) of Origen's influential use of Hebrews to interpret Jesus's victory in the wilderness as a prelude to the Passion and Resurrection.

18. John M. Steadman, *Milton and the Renaissance Hero* (Oxford: Clarendon Press, 1967), pp. vi, 40.

19. William Riley Parker describes Milton's habit of connecting his blindness with Paul's "weakness," in *Milton: A Biography,* 2 vols. (Oxford: Clarendon Press, 1968), 1: 389. On the view that Paul's "thorn in the flesh" may have been "some severe form of ophthalmia," an interpretation which seems to have originated after Milton's time, see Philip Edgcumbe Hughes, *Paul's Second Epistle to the Corinthians* (Grand Rapids, MI: Eerdmans, 1962), p. 444.

20. *A Commentarie of Master Doctor Martin Lvther vpon the Epistle of S. Pavl to the Galathians* (1575; London, 1644), Fol. 169^v. Cf. Rom. 7: 7–25.

21. Cf. Marshall Grossman, *"Authors to Themselves": Milton and the Revelation of History* (Cambridge: Cambridge University Press, 1987), pp. 70–76.

22. Richard Capel, *Tentations: Their Nature/Danger/Cure,* 2d ed. (London, 1635), pp. 14–15, 12.

23. *Commentarie vpon Galathians,* Fol. 262^r, Fol. 39^r.

24. *Commentarie vpon Galathians,* Fol. 177^r, preface, "TO ALL AFFLICTED CONSCIENCES," Fol. A3^v.

25. *Commentarie vpon Galathians,* Fol. 176^v. For a rich discussion of how Luther developed the Pauline doctrine into a general principle of legalism, see Krister Stendahl, "The Apostle Paul and the Introspective Conscience of the West," in *Paul Among Jews and Gentiles,* pp. 78–96.

26. Stanley Fish, "Question and Answer in *Samson Agonistes,*" *Critical Quarterly* 11 (1969): 237–64.

27. Even critics who acknowledge "ambiguity" in *Samson Agonistes* often seek to clear it away. For a recent claim that a "historical" approach can do just that, see Christopher Hill, "*Samson Agonistes* Again," *Literature and History* 2d series 1 (1990): 24–39. The best study of the historical setting of Milton's poem is by Hugh MacCallum, in "*Samson Agonistes*: The Deliverer as Judge," *Milton Studies XXIII,* ed. James D. Simmonds (Pittsburgh: University of Pittsburgh Press, 1988), pp. 259–90. For seventeenth-century controversy, see Joseph Wittreich, *Interpreting Samson Agonistes* (Princeton, NJ: Princeton University Press, 1986), chap. 4.

28. On the propensity of Hebrew narrative towards indeterminacy, see Robert Alter, *The Art of Biblical Narrative* (New York: Basic Books, 1981), p. 126 and passim. In *Interpreting Samson Agonistes,* Alter's approach is frequently cited by Wittreich, who attempts to put it at the service of his thesis that Milton presents a decidedly "unregenerate" Samson. For affinities with *Hamlet,* see Marshall Grossman, "Writing the Inside Out: Shakespeare, Milton and the Supplement of Publication," a paper presented to the Renaissance Society of America, Harvard University, April 1989. The really notable exception to what has been almost a conspiracy *against* silence is Anne Ferry's observation that Milton "might have chosen rather to present Samson's sin exclusively as a violation of his vow of abstinence, a sexual lapse, a vicious susceptibility to touch, to feeling, to physical ease and delight. Or he could have made Samson's lapse seem primarily a kind of forgetfulness or triviality, or a failure to act, or prideful self-assertiveness." Yet "Milton gives almost as much emphasis [to secrecy] as to [Samson's] blindness." See "Samson's 'Fort of Silence,'"

in *Milton and the Miltonic Dryden* (Cambridge, MA: Harvard University Press, 1968), pp. 127–77; quoted from p. 158. MacCallum has called attention again to the secrecy motif, pp. 270 ff.

29. For the view that *Samson* bears structural affinities to the Book of Revelation, see Joseph Anthony Wittreich, Jr., *Visionary Poetics: Milton's Tradition and His Legacy* (San Marino, CA: Huntington Library, 1979), pp. 193, 210–11. The most powerful argument for *Samson* as the culmination of Milton's development has been made by Mary Ann Radzinowicz, *Toward Samson Agonistes: The Growth of Milton's Mind* (Princeton, NJ: Princeton University Press, 1978). On the joint publication, see John T. Shawcross, "The Genres of *Paradise Regain'd* and *Samson Agonistes*: The Wisdom of Their Joint Publication," *Milton Studies XVII: Composite Orders: The Genres of Milton's Last Poems*, ed. Richard S. Ide and Joseph Wittreich (Pittsburgh: University of Pittsburgh Press, 1983), pp. 225–48. Shawcross has consistently argued for an early date for the composition of *Samson*; Radzinowicz, in Appendix E of *Toward Samson* (pp. 387–407), makes out the case for the late date. For the currently standard ideas about the working of typological symbolism in seventeenth-century England, see Lewalski, *Protestant Poetics*, chap. 4. The seminal study with respect to Milton's poem is by F. Michael Krouse, *Milton's Samson and the Christian Tradition* (Princeton, NJ: Princeton University Press for University of Cincinnati, 1949); for the idea of *homo victor*, see pp. 132–33. Various deficiencies of Krouse's study are amply reviewed by Wittreich, *Interpreting Samson Agonistes*, pp. 19–23.

30. See Grossman, "Writing the Inside Out."

31. For Bunyan, see Brainerd P. Stranahan, "Bunyan and the Epistle to the Hebrews: His Source for the Idea of Pilgrimage in *The Pilgrim's Progress*," *Studies in Philology* 79 (1982): 279–96. For accounts that raise good questions about the idea that Milton's Samson should be included among the elected "children of God," see Irene Samuel, "*Samson Agonistes* as Tragedy," in *Calm of Mind: Tercentenary Essays on "Paradise Regained" and "Samson Agonistes" in Honor of John S. Diekhoff*, ed. Joseph Anthony Wittreich, Jr. (Cleveland: Press of Case Western Reserve University, 1971), pp. 235–57; John T. Shawcross, "Irony as Tragic Effect: *Samson Agonistes* and the Tragedy of Hope," in *Calm of Mind*, pp. 289–306. Wittreich's *Interpreting Samson Agonistes* attempts to make the case that already in the seventeenth century Samson's "elect" status was considered questionable.

32. The idea that Samson is a "puritan saint" has been developed by Georgia B. Christopher, *Milton and the Science of the Saints* (Princeton, NJ: Princeton University Press, 1982), pp. 226–28. Lewalski provides a lucid map of the "Protestant paradigm" in the first chapter of *Protestant Poetics*.

33. John Guillory was of course not the first reader to judge that the parable has considerable explanatory power in relation to *Samson*. A representative attempt to explicate the poem in relation to "When I consider . . ." has been formulated by Lawrence W. Hyman: "[Samson] knows that even if the one talent lodged in him is useless, he must still serve God. But it goes against the very core of his being to stand and wait." See *The Quarrel Within: Art and Morality in Milton's Poetry* (Port Washington, NY: Kennikat Press, 1972), p. 109. Cf. also John C. Ulreich, Jr., "'This Great Deliverer': *Samson Agonistes* as Parable," *Milton Quarterly* 13 (1979): 79–84.

34. See Radzinowicz, pp. 188–226, 368–82; MacCallum, pp. 265–66. See also Radzinowicz, "'In those days there was no king in Israel': Milton's Politics and Biblical Narrative," *Yearbook of English Studies* 21 (1991): 242–52.

35. For Samson as a hero of faith, see William Perkins, *The Works of that Famous and Worthy Minister of Christ*, 3 vols. (London, 1612), 1: 751–52; cited by Guillory, who provides a brilliant discussion of these matters, pp. 152–53. There are ways, however, in which Samson may be said to resemble a suffering servant. See William G. Madsen, "From Shadowy Types to Truth," in *The Lyric and Dramatic Milton: Selected Papers from the English Institute*, ed. Joseph H. Summers (New York: Columbia University Press, 1965), pp. 111–13.

36. See the comments on Matt. 13: 12, by the Westminster Divines, *Annotations upon All the Books of the Old and New Testament* (London, 1645); by John Diodati, *Pious and Learned Annotations upon the Holy Bible*, 3d ed. (London, 1651); by Edward Leigh, *Annotations upon all the New Testament Philologicall and Theological* (London, 1650). That the explicitly "experimentalist" view was still current well after *Samson* was published and was brought to bear at these places is evident from the commentary brought out by the successors to Matthew Poole, *Annotations*, 2 (1685): at Matt. 13: 12.

37. See Laurie Zwicky, "Kairos in *Paradise Regained:* The Divine Plan," *ELH* 31 (1964): 271–77; A. B. Chambers, "The Double Time Scheme in *Paradise Regained*," *Milton Studies VII: "Eyes Fast Fixt": Current Perspectives in Milton Methodology*, ed. Albert C. Labriola and Michael Lieb (Pittsburgh: University of Pittsburgh Press, 1975), pp. 189–205. For a more general study, see Mother M. Christopher Pecheux, "Milton and Kairos," *Milton Studies XII*, ed. James D. Simmonds (Pittsburgh: University of Pittsburgh Press, 1979), pp. 197–211.

38. Frank Kermode, *The Genesis of Secrecy: On the Interpretation of Narrative* (Cambridge, MA: Harvard University Press, 1979), p. 45. The Westminster Divines, for instance, gloss Jesus's saying about teaching in parables with reference to the doctrine of double predestination: to understand the teaching is itself evidence of election. Kermode by the way is frequently cited by Wittreich, in *Interpreting Samson Agonistes*, usually in an attempt to bolster the thesis that Milton's Samson is a negative moral exemplum.

39. See *Annotations upon All the Books of the Old and New Testament* (1645), gloss on Matt. 13: 11: "The gift of understanding heavenly things to their good, is given to the faithfull, the rest know not these things, or know them not to their good. This difference comes onely from Gods free grace." Cf. Leigh, *Annotations*, at Mark 4: 11.

40. See Diodati, *Pious and Learned Annotations*, at Matt. 13: 11–12.

41. H[enry] Hammond, *A Paraphrase and Annotations Upon All The Books of the New Testament*, 2d ed. (London, 1659), p. 148. The comment appears at Mark 4: 22, cross-referenced with Matt. 10: 26.

42. William Wrede, *The Messianic Secret in the Gospels*, trans. J. C. G. Grieg (Cambridge: James Clarke; Greenwood, SC: Attic, 1971).

43. *Annotations upon the Holy Bible*, 2 (1685): at Matt. 16: 20.

44. See, e.g., *Annotations upon all the Books of the Old and New Testament*

(1645), at Matt. 9: 30, 16: 20, Luke 9: 21; Leigh, at Matt. 8: 4, 16: 20, Mark 1: 34; Diodati, at Mark 1: 45; *Annotations upon the Holy Bible*, 2 (1685): at Matt. 9: 30–31.

45. Hammond, pp. 43–44.

46. William Kerrigan, "The Irrational Coherence of *Samson Agonistes*," *Milton Studies XXII*, ed. James D. Simmonds (Pittsburgh: University of Pittsburgh Press, 1987), pp. 217–32.

47. Kerrigan ("Irrational Coherence," pp. 227–31) sees the revised choice as a decision to lose again the spiritual "virginity" which Samson has regained. For speculations about the workings of a "compulsion to repeat," see Guillory, pp. 160 ff.

48. This former way of reading would be consistent with the argument advanced by Camille Wells Slights that Milton's poem illustrates the classic workings of a "case of conscience." See *The Casuistical Tradition in Shakespeare, Donne, Herbert, and Milton* (Princeton, NJ: Princeton University Press, 1981), pp. 268 ff., especially p. 284. The latter way of reading is the great theme of Wittreich's *Interpreting Samson Agonistes*. Wittreich reads "of my own accord" as setting up a contrast with something like "by the power of God." Repeatedly, he adduces this phrase as evidence for his thesis that Milton's Samson is unregenerated.

49. See also Isa. 1: 21–26; Jer. 2: 2; Hos. 1–3; Ezek. 23. The potential relevance of Hosea has been observed by John C. Ulreich, Jr., "'Incident to All Our Sex': The Tragedy of Dalila," in *Milton and the Idea of Woman*, ed. Julia M. Walker (Urbana: University of Illinois Press, 1988), pp. 185–210, viz. 210n.

50. E.g., Isa. 50: 1; Jer. 3: 1–12.

Chapter Seven

1. For a rich account of the *topos* of Scriptural obscurity as it had been disseminated through Augustine's *De doctrina christiana*, see Terence Cave, *The Cornucopian Text: Problems of Writing in the French Renaissance* (Oxford: Clarendon Press; New York: Oxford University Press, 1979), pp. 80 ff.

2. For an exemplary study of the history of Gen. 1: 28, see Jeremy Cohen, *"Be Fertile and Increase, Fill the Earth and Master It": The Ancient and Medieval Career of a Biblical Text* (Ithaca, NY: Cornell University Press, 1989). In his materialist and Marxist interpretation of *Paradise Lost,* Christopher Kendrick loses an astonishing opportunity to broaden his analysis when he ignores the presence of God's original command to "be fruitful and multiply." Kendrick claims that the poem involves an "ethic of permission" and a "dominant" "ethic of prohibition" but no positive "injunction." See *Milton: A Study in Ideology and Form* (New York: Methuen, 1986), viz. pp. 199, 208.

3. For a particularly extensive treatment of differences between prelapsarian and postlapsarian experience in the poem, see Kathleen M. Swaim, *Before and After the Fall: Contrasting Modes in Paradise Lost* (Amherst: University of Massachusetts Press, 1986). The first chapter contains a representative appeal to *Areopagitica* to gloss Milton's handling of the Fall in the epic (pp. 21–23). For a shrewd critique of

this practice, see John S. Tanner, *Anxiety in Eden: A Kierkegaardian Reading of Paradise Lost* (New York: Oxford University Press, 1992), pp. 80–81.

4. Jacques Derrida, "Plato's Pharmacy," *Dissemination*, trans. Barbara Johnson (Chicago: University of Chicago Press, 1981). The quotations are, respectively, from pp. 149, 97, 99, and 127.

5. For a helpful discussion of this passage, see Philip J. Gallagher, *Milton, the Bible, and Misogyny*, ed. Eugene R. Cunnar and Gail L. Mortimer (Columbia: University of Missouri Press, 1990), pp. 17–26.

6. Regina M. Schwartz, *Remembering and Repeating: Biblical Creation in Paradise Lost* (Cambridge: Cambridge University Press, 1988), p. 65.

7. For "mazie error," see the discussion by Arnold Stein, *Answerable Style: Essays on Paradise Lost* (Minneapolis: University of Minnesota Press, 1953), pp. 66–67. For "lapse," "luxuriant" and "luxurious," and "wanton," see Christopher Ricks, *Milton's Grand Style* (Oxford: Clarendon Press, 1963), pp. 111–12. The common interpretation by which the first parents are claimed to be "fallen before the Fall" has been classically formulated by A. J. A. Waldock, in *Paradise Lost and Its Critics* (Cambridge: Cambridge University Press, 1947). For a history and critique of this interpretation, see Tanner, chap. 2.

8. Stanley Eugene Fish, *Surprised by Sin: The Reader in Paradise Lost* (London: Macmillan; New York: St. Martin's Press, 1967), p. ix. (Fish's quotation is from Richard Bernard.) J. Hillis Miller, "How Deconstruction Works," (1986), rpt. in *Theory Now and Then* (Hemel Hempstead: Harvester Wheatsheaf; Durham, NC: Duke University Press, 1991), pp. 293–94.

9. Victoria Kahn, "Allegory and the Sublime in *Paradise Lost*," in *John Milton*, ed. Annabel Patterson (London: Longman, 1992), pp. 185–201; quoted here from pp. 185, 194, and 197. Tanner's *Anxiety in Eden* borrows the Kierkegaardian category of *angst* to offer "a philosophically sophisticated explanation of free yet motivated action" before the Fall (20), and thus proposes an even more elaborate account of prelapsarian agency.

10. Samuel Johnson, Preface, *A Dictionary of the English Language* (London, 1755; rpt. London: Times Books, 1979), n. p.

11. Cf. Johnson's charge that the "plan of *Paradise Lost* has this inconvenience, that it comprises neither human actions nor human manners. The man and woman who act and suffer are in a state which no other man or woman can ever know." See *The Lives of the Poets: Selections*, ed. Warren Fleischauer (Chicago: Henry Regenery, 1964), p. 26. For an especially illuminating study of Johnson on Milton, see Stephen Fix, "Johnson and the 'Duty' of Reading *Paradise Lost*," *ELH* 52 (1985): 649–71.

12. Derrida, pp. 142 ff.

13. Ernst Robert Curtius, *European Literature and the Latin Middle Ages*, trans. Willard R. Trask (1948; New York: Pantheon, 1953), chap. 16; see especially p. 321.

14. Sir Thomas Browne, *Religio Medici*, sect. 16, in *Religio Medici and Other Works*, ed. L. C. Martin (Oxford: Clarendon Press, 1964), p. 15.

15. Milton's relation to the "new science" has not received serious reconsideration in nearly forty years, since the appearance of Kester Svendsen's *Milton and Science* (Cambridge, MA: Harvard University Press, 1956). Recently, a revaluation

has begun in work by Stephen M. Fallon, in particular, *Milton Among the Philosophers: Poetry and Materialism in Seventeenth-Century England* (Ithaca, NY: Cornell University Press, 1991). Fallon's interest in Milton's monism involves ontological issues. A treatment of allied epistemological issues, and a thoroughgoing reconsideration of Milton's relation to the new science, will be found in Karen Edwards's important study, *Reading the Book of the World in "Paradise Lost"* (forthcoming).

16. Michel Foucault, *The Order of Things: An Archaeology of the Human Sciences* (1966; New York: Vintage, 1973), p. 38.

17. John Leonard, *Naming in Paradise: Milton and the Language of Adam and Eve* (Oxford: Clarendon Press, 1990), pp. 35, 34.

18. See, for Satan, II, 381, 864; VI, 262; X, 236, 356; for Adam and Eve, III, 122; IV, 635. For a study of some uses of the word "author" in the poem, see Marshall Grossman, *"Authors to Themselves": Milton and the Revelation of History* (Cambridge: Cambridge University Press, 1987), pp. 1–5. See also: Keith W. F. Stavely, "Satan and Arminianism in *Paradise Lost*," *Milton Studies XXV*, ed. James D. Simmonds (Pittsburgh: University of Pittsburgh Press, 1990), pp. 125–39.

19. Anne Ferry, *The Art of Naming* (Chicago: University of Chicago Press, 1988), pp. xvii–xviii.

20. On relations between Spenser and Milton, see especially Maureen Quilligan, *Milton's Spenser: The Politics of Reading* (Ithaca, NY: Cornell University Press, 1983), and John Guillory, *Poetic Authority: Spenser, Milton, and Literary History* (New York: Columbia University Press, 1983). When *Milton's Spenser* is quoted later in this chapter, relevant page numbers are given in parentheses in the text.

21. Grossman, pp. 1–2.

22. *The Art of Naming*, p. 15.

23. This claim has been made by Herbert Marks, "The Blotted Book," in *Remembering Milton: Essays on the Texts and Traditions*, ed. Mary Nyquist and Margaret W. Ferguson (New York: Methuen, 1987), pp. 211–33; see in particular pp. 214–15, 229. The starting point for Marks's study is the passage cited below, *PL* I, 361–63.

24. See Leonard (pp. 69 ff.), who reviews and criticizes comments on this passage by Milton's early editors and beautifully relates the passage to the issue of naming.

25. On the rich, energetic nature of this universe, see Leonard, pp. 258–59.

26. Keith W. F. Stavely, *Puritan Legacies: Paradise Lost and the New England Tradition, 1630–1890* (Ithaca, NY: Cornell University Press, 1987), p. 28; Jacques Derrida, "Living On: Border Lines," trans. James Hulbert, in *Deconstruction and Criticism*, by Harold Bloom et al. (New York: Seabury, 1979), pp. 83–85.

27. See Anne Ferry, *Milton's Epic Voice: The Narrator in Paradise Lost* (1963; rpt. with a new preface, Chicago: University of Chicago Press, 1983), pp. 70–73.

28. See Edwards, chap. 1, and also her "Prospectus" for the book.

29. The work of critics who associate Galileo with Satan (Neil Harris, Roy Flannagan) has been reviewed and criticized by Julia M. Walker, in "Milton and Galileo: The Art of Intellectual Canonization," *Milton Studies XXV*, ed. James D. Simmonds (Pittsburgh: University of Pittsburgh Press, 1990), pp. 109–23. Work

on Milton and Galileo in the 1920s and 1930s (e.g., by Allan H. Gilbert and Marjorie Nicolson) was usefully summarized and criticized by Grant McColley in "The Astronomy of *Paradise Lost*," *Studies in Philology* 34 (1937): 209–47.

30. Judith Scherer Herz, "'For whom this glorious sight?': Dante, Milton, and the Galileo Question," in *Milton in Italy: Contexts Images Contradictions*, ed. Mario A. Di Cesare (Binghamton, NY: Medieval & Renaissance Texts & Studies, 1991), pp. 147–57. Cf. Harold Bloom, *A Map of Misreading* (New York: Oxford University Press, 1975), pp. 130–33.

31. Amy Boesky, "On Sunspots: Galileo, Milton and *Paradise Lost*," a paper presented at the annual convention of the Modern Language Association, New York, 30 December 1992. Donald Friedman, "Galileo and the Art of Seeing," *Milton in Italy*, pp. 159–74, viz. p. 171. The translation is by Stillman Drake, in his *Discoveries and Opinions of Galileo* (Garden City, NY: Anchor Books, 1957), pp. 237–38. I have given slightly more of the passage than Friedman himself quotes. This passage is also cited by Margreta de Grazia, "The Secularization of Language in the Seventeenth Century," *Journal of the History of Ideas* 41 (1980): 319–29, viz. p. 320. In the paragraph that follows I am indebted to this valuable article.

32. Thomas Sprat, *The History of the Royal-Society of London For the Improving of Natural Knowledge* (London, 1667), pp. 112–13; John Locke, Letter to Molyneux (26 Dec. 1692); cited by Hans Aarsleff, "Leibniz on Locke on Language," *American Philosophical Quarterly* 1 (1964): 166; Locke, *An Essay Concerning Human Understanding*, ed. Peter H. Nidditch (Oxford: Clarendon Press, 1975), Book 4, Chap. 3, Section 30; p. 561.

33. Edwards, chap. 1.

34. *The Psalms of Sir Philip Sidney and the Countess of Pembroke*, ed. J. C. A. Rathmell, the Stuart Editions (New York: New York University Press, 1963), p. 39.

35. Mary Ann Radzinowicz, *Milton's Epics and the Book of Psalms* (Princeton, NJ: Princeton University Press, 1989), pp. ix and 6 respectively; for that history, see her *Toward Samson Agonistes: The Growth of Milton's Mind* (Princeton, NJ: Princeton University Press, 1978), pp. 188–226. Psalm 19 is one of eight psalms which Professor Radzinowicz has shown to have been "of particular interest to Milton"; see *Milton's Epics*, pp. 207–9. Another helpful treatment of some ways in which the Psalms underpin *Paradise Lost* may be found in Schwartz's *Remembering and Repeating*, especially chap. 3.

36. John Hollander, *The Figure of Echo: A Mode of Allusion in Milton and After* (Berkeley and Los Angeles: University of California Press, 1981), pp. 37–41. Cf. Thomas Newton, ed., *"Paradise Lost": A Poem in Twelve Books. The Author John Milton. A New Edition with Notes of Various Editors*, 2 vols. (London, 1749), 1: 321–22.

37. Henry Ainsworth, for instance, defined *torah* as "*doctrine*, and an *orderly-disposition* of the same." He acknowledged that while the word "is most comonly ascribed, to the precepts given by Moses," it refers also to "the history of Genesis" and sometimes even to the books of the prophets and to the Psalms themselves (abbreviations expanded). See *Annotations upon the Book of Psalms*, 2d ed. ([London], 1617), at Ps. 19: 8.

38. For the rabbinic interpretations, see *Tehillim: A New Translation with*

Commentary Anthologized from Talmudic, Midrashic and Rabbinic Sources, ed. and trans. Avrohom Chaim Feuer, 2d ed. (Brooklyn: Mesorah Publications, 1979), pp. 239–51, especially p. 249n.

39. Louis L. Martz, "Trials of Faith," in *Milton: Poet of Exile* (1980; 2nd ed., New Haven, CT: Yale University Press, 1986), pp. 181, 179.

40. See Fish, *Surprised by Sin*, pp. 286–331.

41. Addison, *Spectator*, No. 369; cited by Martz, p. 328; for the critique of style, see pp. 183–84; for the quotation from Dryden, p. 170.

42. See R. Gerald Hobbs, "*Hebraica Veritas* and *Traditio Apostolica*: Saint Paul and the Interpretation of the Psalms in the Sixteenth Century," in *The Bible in the Sixteenth Century*, ed. David C. Steinmetz (Durham, NC: Duke University Press, 1990), pp. 94–97.

43. For Ibn Ezra and the rabbis, see *Tehillim*, pp. 240–41; for Luther and his Christian predecessors, see Scott H. Hendrix, *Ecclesia in Via: Ecclesiological Developments in the Medieval Psalms Exegesis and the Dictata Super Psalterium (1513–1515) of Martin Luther* (Leiden: Brill, 1974). Cf. Augustine, *Enarrationes in Psalmos*, Corpus Christianorum, Series Latina, vols. 38–40 (Turnholt: Typographi Brepols Editores Pontificii, 1956), 38: 102–13; cf. Peter Lombard, *Commentarium in Psalmos, Patrologiæ cursus completus, series Latina*, ed. J.-P. Migne, 191 (Paris, 1879): 205–16 (for Peter, as for Augustine, the Psalm was numbered as 18); *Luther's Works*, Vol. 12: *Selected Psalms I*, ed. Jaroslav Pelikan (St. Louis, MO: Concordia, 1955), pp. 139–44.

The triumphalist uses to which the familiar Christian reading might be put by western Europeans are evident in the 1516 Polyglot Psalter, where a note on Psalm 19 gives a sketch of the life of Columbus and his discovery of America. See *Psalterium, Hebreum, Grecum, Arabicum, & Chaldeum, cum tribus latinis interpretationibus & glossis* (1516).

44. Obadiah Sedgwick, *Anatomy of Secret Sins* (London, 1660), pp. 2–3.

45. *The Geneva Bible: A facsimile of the 1560 edition*, with an introduction by Lloyd E. Berry (Madison: University of Wisconsin Press, 1969), 238^v.

46. This line of interpretation is found in *Annotations upon the Holy Bible*, 2 vols. (London, 1683–85), 1 (1683): at Ps. 19: 3.

47. Iohn Calvin, *The Psalmes of David and Others*, trans. Arthur Golding ([London], 1571), p. 68^r. The pagination in the section on Ps. 19 is highly irregular. Hereafter, where two page numbers are given, the first refers to the erroneous page number actually printed and the second to what the page number should be. The relevant Hebrew word from verse 4 is transliterated as *Caua* in Golding's translation. For the metaphors common in England, see *An Exposition of the Proper Psalmes Vsed in ovr English Litvrgie*, in *The Workes of Iohn Boys* (London, 1622), pp. 791–92.

48. John Pearson's *Criticorum Sacrorum* incorporates a common view, expressed by Sixtinus Amana, whereby the Book of Nature is said to be imperfect and unable to provide saving knowledge. Cf. also Boys.

49. A fourth feature of Calvin's commentary might have interested Milton: his insistence that the psalmist does not teach "the secrets of Astrologie too the rude and unlerned" or dispute "captiously among [natural] Philosophers concerning the full going about of the Sonne" (p. 68^v). This point about the absence of what we

would now call scientific discourse is made, however, almost in passing and does not constitute a principal feature of the commentary.

50. For a discussion of the *scala naturæ* in relation to *Paradise Lost*, see William G. Madsen, *From Shadowy Types to Truth: Studies in Milton's Symbolism* (New Haven, CT: Yale University Press, 1968), pp. 113–24; on the world as book, see pp. 124–44.

51. Cf. Geneva Bible, 238ᵛ: "The heauens are a scholemaster to all nations [abbreviations expanded], be they neuer so barbarous." Elsewhere, Calvin introduces a third metaphor, one which has less footing in the Hebrew. The heavens are compared to a mirror that reflects "the glorie of God." Since the mirror had been used frequently as a metaphor for the Scriptures, on the principle that two things equal to a third are equal to each other, Calvin's use of it here may have facilitated the transition to seeing the first part of the poem as a meditation on the Book of Creation.

52. John Calvin, *Commentaries on the First Book of Moses Called Genesis*, trans. John King (1847; rpt. Grand Rapids, MI: Baker Book House, 1981), p. 62; *The Institution of Christian Religion*, trans. Thomas Norton (London, 1574), I, xiv, i (Fol. 40ʳ) and I, vi, i (Fol. 11ʳ). Here and in some quotations from translations of Calvin's work abbreviations have been expanded.

53. The key biblical place for Calvin, and for many who likewise relied on "the Bible only," was Rom. 1: 20: "For the invisible things of [God] from the creation of the world are clearly seen, being understood by the things that are made, *even* his eternal power and Godhead; so that they are without excuse." Cf. *Annotations upon the Holy Bible*, 1 (1683): at Ps. 19: 7.

54. *The Poems and Letters of Andrew Marvell*, ed. H. M. Margoliouth, 3d ed., Vol. 1: *Poems*, rev. by Pierre Legouis with the collaboration of E. E. Duncan-Jones (Oxford: Clarendon Press, 1971), pp. 14–15; *The Works of George Herbert*, ed. F. E. Hutchinson (Oxford: Clarendon Press, 1941), p. 185.

55. Cave, chap. 1; quoted here from p. 6.

56. Leonard (pp. 274 ff.) discusses some ambiguities in the surrounding passage, especially as they were treated by eighteenth-century editors.

57. The argument is made out in detail by Leonard, who has gathered these three quotations as the starting point for his book (p. 1). Cf. also William Shullenberger, "Linguistic and Poetic Theory in Milton's *De Doctrina Christiana*," *English Language Notes* 19 (1981–82): 262–78.

58. See Boyd M. Berry, *Process of Speech: Puritan Religious Writing & Paradise Lost* (Baltimore: Johns Hopkins University Press, 1976), especially chap. 17.

59. For a summary of how this reading came to be established, and for an attempt to curtail further discussion of the subject, see Stanley Fish, "Transmuting the Lump: *Paradise Lost*, 1942–1979," in *Doing What Comes Naturally: Change, Rhetoric, and the Practice of Theory in Literary and Legal Studies* (Durham, NC: Duke University Press, 1989), pp. 247–93. In this article Fish seeks to close down further discussion of the subject by declaring its superfluity in advance of its appearance.

Books XI and XII are now routinely said to depict the "education" of Adam, and that education, which is tailored to a figure who is manifestly lacking in experience, seems generally to be understood to provide a normative perspective from which to read the whole of *Paradise Lost*. It is now widely taken for granted that Adam is a figure for "the reader," who is the object of a moral education at the hands of Milton's narrator. For more than a generation *Paradise Lost* has been widely read as Fish insisted on reading it in *Surprised by Sin*, as a didactic and moralistic poem that exposes human depravity. Whether readers now characteristically think of "Milton" as John Peter Rumrich claims, that is, as "a knuckle-rapping, peremptory prig—a teacher who already knows the truth of things, humiliates and berates his charges for their errors, and requires conformity to his authoritative understanding," it is probably true that "students" who have been required to read *Paradise Lost* as a canonical work by a patriarchal author continue to "hear Milton's epic narrator as a censorious preacher." See "Uninventing Milton," *Modern Philology* 87 (1989–90): 249–65; quoted here from p. 259.

60. See Ambrose, "The Prayer of Job and David" (c. 387–89), in *Seven Exegetical Works*, trans. Michael P. McHugh (Washington, DC: Catholic University of America Press, 1972), pp. 417–18.

61. Grossman, p. 5; see also pp. 157–61. For Georgia Christopher's contribution, see above, Preface, p. xi.

62. *Institution*, trans. Norton, III.xxiv.4; Fol. 299^v.

63. See the discussion of Hebrews 11 by Barbara Kiefer Lewalski, "Structure and the Symbolism of Vision in Michael's Prophecy, *Paradise Lost*, Books XI–XII," *Philological Quarterly* 42 (1963): 25–35. On perseverance, see R. T. Kendall, *Calvin and English Calvinism to 1649* (Oxford: Oxford University Press, 1979), especially pp. 67–76. On the importance of Hebrews for Bunyan, see Brainerd P. Stranahan, "Bunyan and the Epistle to the Hebrews: His Source for the Idea of Pilgrimage in *The Pilgrim's Progress*," *Studies in Philology* 79 (1982): 279–96.

64. On Adam's need for correction, see Dennis Burden, *The Logical Epic: A Study of the Argument of Paradise Lost* (Cambridge, MA: Harvard University Press, 1967), pp. 192 ff. That the Adam of Books XI and XII was progressing toward what Milton in *De Doctrina Christiana* called the second stage of regeneration, "saving faith," is explained by Lewalski, "Structure and Symbolism," p. 30.

65. See Regina Schwartz, "From Shadowy Types to Shadowy Types: The Unendings of *Paradise Lost*," *Milton Studies XXIV*, ed. James D. Simmonds (Pittsburgh: University of Pittsburgh Press, 1989), pp. 123–39, viz. p. 124.

66. See the shrewd commentary by Schwartz, who proposes that "The temptation is for Adam to . . . 'know' his future, rather than to determine it. . . . The temptation is to believe that the sum of wisdom can be gained from reading—or seeing and hearing—the story Michael unfolds, and that wisdom can be thus summarized" ("From Shadowy Types," p. 134).

67. See above, Chapter One, p. 24.

68. Cf. Burden's remark, apropos of Adam's learning about human sinfulness, that "Milton presents an Adam not merely archetypal but also typical" (p. 188). In Book III, God contrasts man's situation—after the fall he will again be offered grace—with that of the fallen angels. He does not say whether man will accept it, nor does He specify which particular persons will be saved (see especially lines 130ff.). See also Schwartz, "From Shadowy Types," p. 129.

69. In this section I refer chiefly to the experience of Adam in accord with the

handling of these matters in Books XI and XII. Although Eve is asleep, she is supposed to be learning the same lessons that Adam is being taught. But the tone of her final speech (XII, 610ff.) is more hopeful than that of Adam's, and her hopes are more firmly grounded.

70. For a helpful treatment of the mutual relations between text and interpretation in Milton's hermeneutics, see J. F. Worthen, "On the Matter of the Text," *University of Toronto Quarterly* 60 (1990–91): 337–53.

Bibliography

This bibliography lists items actually cited in the text and notes of *Milton's Burden of Interpretation*. It does not, however, provide a comprehensive list of works cited. I have omitted from the bibliography (but not from the index) some items referred to in the notes that bear a relatively slight relation to the principal concerns of the book. My assumption is that readers encountering these references in the notes will already have there the relevant bibliographical data if, for reasons I cannot anticipate, they wish to consult these items. My hope is that, by eliminating some references here, I enable readers who skim the bibliography to gain from it a more nearly accurate picture of the sorts of discourses this book seeks to engage.

For books published before 1900, only places and dates of publication are given; names of publishers are omitted.

Ainsworth, Henry. *Annotations upon the Book of Psalms.* 2d ed. [London], 1617.
Aitken, David J. "Milton's Use of 'Stand' and the Doctrine of Perseverance." *English Language Notes* 19 (1981–82): 233–36.
Alter, Robert. *The Art of Biblical Narrative.* New York: Basic Books, 1981.
Ambrose. *Seven Exegetical Works.* Trans. Michael P. McHugh. Washington, DC: Catholic University of America Press, 1972.
Ames, William. *Medvlla Theologica.* Translated as *The Marrow of Sacred Divinity, Drawne out of the holy Scriptures.* London, 1642.
———. *The Svbstance of Christian Religion.* London, 1659.
Andrewes, Lancelot. *A Pattern of Catechisticall Doctrine.* London, 1630.
Annotations Upon the Holy Bible. Being a Continuation of Mr. Pool's Work by Certain Judicious and Learned Divines. 2 vols. London, 1683–85.
Annotations upon All the Books of the Old and New Testament. London, 1645.
Armitage, Frederick. *A History of the Collects.* London: Weare, n.d.
Athanasius. Letter XLIX (to Dracontius, c. 354–55). In *Select Writings and Letters.* Ed. Archibald Robertson. Vol. 4 of *A Select Library of Nicene and Post-Nicene Fathers of the Christian Church.* Ed. Philip Schaff and Henry Wace. 2d ser. 1892. Reprint, Grand Rapids, MI: Wm. B. Eerdmans, 1953.
Atkinson, Clarissa W. *The Oldest Vocation: Christian Motherhood in the Middle Ages.* Ithaca, NY: Cornell University Press, 1991.
Aubrey, John. "Minutes of the Life of Mr John Milton." In *The Early Lives of Milton.* Ed. Helen Darbishire. London: Constable, 1932.
———. *Remaines of Gentilisme and Judaisme* (1688). Ed. James Britten. London, 1881.
Augustine. *The Confessions of the Incomparable Doctovr S. Avgvstine.* [Trans. Sir Tobie Matthew]. [St. Omer's], 1620.

———. *De Doctrina Christiana.* Trans. J. F. Shaw. In Vol. 2 of *A Select Library of the Nicene and Post-Nicene Fathers of the Christian Church.* Ed. Philip Schaff. 1887. Reprint, Grand Rapids, MI: Wm. B. Eerdmans, 1956.

———. *Enarrationes in Psalmos.* Corpus Christianorum, Series Latina, 38–40. Turnholt: Typographi Brepols Editores Pontificii, 1956.

———. *Saint Augustines Confessions translated; and With some marginall notes illustrated.* Trans. William Watts. London, 1631.

———. *S. Augustine's Confessions: With the Continuation of his Life.* Trans. T. R. and E. M. London, 1650.

———. "Sermons on Selected Lessons of the New Testament." Trans. R. G. MacMullen. In Vol. 6 of *A Select Library of the Nicene and Post-Nicene Fathers of the Christian Church.* Ed. Philip Schaff. 1887. Reprint, Grand Rapids, MI: Wm. B. Eerdmans, 1956.

à Schurman, Anna Maria. *The Learned Maid, Or, Whether a Maid May Be a Scholar? A Logick Exercise.* London, 1659.

Barker, Arthur. *Milton and the Puritan Dilemma 1641–1660.* Toronto: University of Toronto Press, 1942.

Barth, Karl. *The Doctrine of the Word of God,* Vol. 1 of *Church Dogmatics.* Trans. G. W. Bromiley. 2nd ed. Edinburgh: T. & T. Clark, 1975.

Barthes, Roland. *S/Z.* Trans. Richard Miller. New York: Hill and Wang, 1974.

Bauman, Michael. *Scripture Index to John Milton's De doctrina christiana.* Binghampton, N.Y.: Medieval & Renaissance Texts & Studies, 1989.

Baxter, Richard. *Reliquiæ Baxterianæ: Or, Mr. Richard Baxter's Narrative of The most Memorable Passages of his Life and Times.* Ed. Matthew Sylvester. London, 1696.

Bayly, Lewis. *The Practice of Pietie.* 7th ed. London, 1616.

Beilin, Elaine V. *Redeeming Eve: Women Writers of the English Renaissance.* Princeton, NJ: Princeton University Press, 1987.

Bennett, Joan S. *Reviving Liberty: Radical Christian Humanism in Milton's Great Poems.* Cambridge, MA: Harvard University Press, 1989.

Berkowitz, M. S. "Thomas Young's 'Hopes Encouragement' and Milton's 'Sonnet XIX.'" *Milton Quarterly* 16 (1982): 94–97.

Berry, Boyd M. *Process of Speech: Puritan Religious Writing & Paradise Lost.* Baltimore: Johns Hopkins University Press, 1976.

Bickerman, Elias J. *The Jews in the Greek Age.* Cambridge, MA: Harvard University Press, 1988.

Blair, Robert. *The Life of Mr Robert Blair, Minister of St Andrews, Containing His Autobiography, from 1593 to 1636.* Ed. Thomas M'Crie. Edinburgh, 1848.

Bloom, Harold. *A Map of Misreading.* New York: Oxford University Press, 1975.

———. *The Anxiety of Influence: A Theory of Poetry.* New York: Oxford University Press, 1973.

Boesky, Amy. "On Sunspots: Galileo, Milton and *Paradise Lost.*" A paper presented at the annual convention of the Modern Language Association, New York, December 1992.

The Book of Common Prayer 1559. Ed. John E. Booty. Charlottesville: Published for the Folger Shakespeare Library by the University Press of Virginia, 1976.

Booth, Stephen, ed. *Shakespeare's Sonnets.* New Haven, CT: Yale University Press, 1977.

Boys, John. *An Exposition of Al the Principal Scriptvres Vsed in our English Liturgie.* London, 1610.
——. *An Exposition of the Dominical Epistles and Gospels vsed in our English Liturgie . . . The Spring-part from the first in Lent to Whitsunday.* London, 1610.
——. *An Exposition of the Dominical Epistles and Gospels, vsed in our English Liturgie . . . The Winter Part.* London, 1611.
——. *An Exposition of the Festivall Epistles and Gospels, vsed in our English Liturgie.* 2nd Part. London, 1614.
——. *An Exposition of the Proper Psalmes Vsed in ovr English Litvrgie.* In *Workes.* London, 1622.
Bridge, William. *Scripture-Light a Most Sure Light.* London, 1656.
Briggs, Charles Augustus. *Biblical Study: Its Principles, Methods and History.* New York, 1883.
Brown, Raymond E. *The Birth of the Messiah: A Commentary on the Infancy Narratives in Matthew and Luke.* Garden City, NY: Doubleday, 1977.
Browne, Sir Thomas. *Religio Medici and Other Works.* Ed. L. C. Martin. Oxford: Clarendon Press, 1964.
Budick, Sanford. *The Dividing Muse: Images of Sacred Disjunction in Milton's Poetry.* New Haven, CT: Yale University Press, 1985.
Bunny, Edmund. *A Booke of Christian exercise appertaining to Resolution.* 1584. London, 1585.
Bunyan, John. *A Few Sighs from Hell, or The Groans of a damned Soul.* Ed. T. L. Underwood. In Vol. 1 of *The Miscellaneous Works of John Bunyan.* Gen. ed. Roger Sharrock. Oxford: Clarendon Press, 1980.
——. *Grace Abounding to the Chief of Sinners.* Ed. Roger Sharrock. Oxford: Clarendon Press, 1962.
——. *The Life and Death of Mr. Badman.* Ed. James F. Forrest and Roger Sharrock. Oxford: Clarendon Press, 1988.
——. *The Pilgrim's Progress from This World to That Which Is to Come.* Ed. James Blanton Wharey. Rev. by Roger Sharrock. Oxford: Clarendon Press, 1960.
Burden, Dennis. *The Logical Epic: A Study of the Argument of Paradise Lost.* Cambridge, MA: Harvard University Press, 1967.
Burton, Robert. *The Anatomy of Melancholy.* Ed. A. R. Shilleto, with an Introduction by A. H. Bullen. 3 vols. 1893. London: G. Bell & Sons, 1923.
Bush, Douglas. *John Milton: A Sketch of His Life and Writings.* New York: Macmillan; London: Collier-Macmillan, 1964.
——. *The Renaissance and English Humanism.* Toronto: University of Toronto Press, 1939.
Cable, Lana. "Coupling Logic and Milton's Doctrine of Divorce." *Milton Studies XV.* Ed. James D. Simmonds. Pittsburgh: University of Pittsburgh Press, 1981. Pp. 143–59.
Caesarius of Arles. *Sermons.* 3 vols. Trans. Mary Magdeleine Mueller. Washington, DC: Catholic University of America Press, 1956–73.
Caldwell, Patricia. *The Puritan Conversion Narrative: The Beginnings of American Expression.* Cambridge: Cambridge University Press, 1983.
Calvin, John. *The Commentaries of M. Iohn Calvin vpon the Actes of the Apostles.* Trans. Christopher Fetherstone. London, 1585.

——. *Commentaries on the First Book of Moses Called Genesis*. Trans. John King. 1847. Reprint, Grand Rapids, MI: Baker Book House, 1981.
——. *A Harmonie Vpon the Three Euangelistes Matthewe, Marke, and Luke*. Trans. E[usebius] P[agit]. London, 1610.
——. *The Institution of Christian Religion*. Trans. Thomas Norton. London, 1574.
——. *The Psalmes of David and Others*. Trans. Arthur Golding. [London], 1571.
Capel, Richard. *Tentations: Their Nature/Danger/Cure*. 2d ed. London, 1635.
Carlton, Peter J. "Bunyan: Language, Convention, Authority." *ELH* 51 (1984): 17–32.
Caryl, Joseph. *An Exposition with Practicall Observations Vpon the three first Chapters of the Booke of Iob*. London, 1643.
Cave, Terence. *The Cornucopian Text: Problems of Writing in the French Renaissance*. Oxford: Clarendon Press; New York: Oxford University Press, 1979.
Cawdray, Robert. *A Treasvrie or Store-hovse of Similes*. 1600. Facsimile reprint, New York: Da Capo, 1971.
C[awdry], R[obert]. *A Codly [i.e., Godly] Form of Hovseholde Gouernement: for the ordering of priuate Families according to Gods word*. London, 1598.
Chambers, A. B. "The Double Time Scheme in *Paradise Regained*." *Milton Studies VII: "Eyes Fast Fixt": Current Perspectives in Milton Methodology*. Ed. Albert C. Labriola and Michael Lieb. Pittsburgh: University of Pittsburgh Press, 1975. Pp. 189–205.
Christopher, Georgia B. *Milton and the Science of the Saints*. Princeton, NJ: Princeton University Press, 1982.
——. "The Verbal Gate to Paradise: Adam's 'Literary Experience' in Book X of *Paradise Lost*." *PMLA* 90 (1975): 69–77.
Chrysostom, John. *Homilies on the Gospel of Matthew*. Trans. George Prevost. Vol. 10 of *A Select Library of the Nicene and Post-Nicene Fathers of the Christian Church*. Ed. Philip Schaff. 1888. Reprint, Grand Rapids, MI: Wm. B. Eerdmans, 1956.
——. *On the Incomprehensible Nature of God*. Trans. Paul W. Harkins. Washington, DC: Catholic University of America Press, 1984.
Clark, Ira. "*Paradise Regained* and the Gospel according to John." *Modern Philology* 71 (1973–74): 1–15.
Clement of Alexandria. *The Miscellanies; or Stromata*. In *The Writings of Clement of Alexandria*. Trans. William Wilson. Vol. 2 of *The Ante-Nicene Christian Library: Translations of the Writings of the Fathers Down to A. D. 325*. Ed. Alexander Roberts and James Donaldson. 1880. Reprint, Grand Rapids, MI: Wm. B. Eerdmans, 1962.
Cohen, Charles L. *God's Caress: The Psychology of Puritan Religious Experience*. New York: Oxford University Press, 1986.
——. "The Saints Zealous in Love and Labor: The Puritan Psychology of Work." *Harvard Theological Review* 76 (1983): 455–80.
Cohen, Jeremy. *"Be Fertile and Increase, Fill the Earth and Master It": The Ancient and Medieval Career of a Biblical Text*. Ithaca, NY: Cornell University Press, 1989.
Coleridge, Samuel Taylor. *Unpublished Letters of Samuel Taylor Coleridge*. Ed. Earl Leslie Griggs. 2 vols. London: Constable, 1932.
Conklin, George Newton. *Biblical Criticism and Heresy in Milton*. New York: King's Crown Press of Columbia University Press, 1949.

Cotton, Charles. Commendatory verses. In *Lives of Dr. John Donne, Sir Henry Wotton, Mr. Richard Hooker, Mr. George Herbert.* By Izaak Walton. London, 1675.
Courcelle, Pierre. "Source Chrétienne et allusions païennes de l'episode du 'Tolle, lege.'" *Revue d'Histoire et de Philosophie Religieuses* 32 (1952): 171–200.
Crane, Mary Thomas. *Framing Authority: Sayings, Self, and Society in Sixteenth-Century England.* Princeton, NJ: Princeton University Press, 1993.
The Creeds of Christendom, with a History and Critical Notes. Ed. Philip Schaff. 4th ed. 3 vols. 1877. Reprint, Grand Rapids, MI: Baker Book House, 1977.
Criticorum Sacrorum. [Ed. John Pearson]. 8 vols. 1660. New ed., Amsterdam, 1698.
Curtius, Ernst Robert. *European Literature and the Latin Middle Ages.* Trans. Willard R. Trask. 1948. Reprint, New York: Pantheon, 1953.
Darbishire, Helen, ed. *The Early Lives of Milton.* London: Constable, 1932.
Darnton, Robert. "Toward a History of Reading." *Princeton Alumni Weekly* 87 (8 April 1987): 19–24, 32.
Davis, J. C. *Fear, Myth, and History: The Ranters and the Historians.* Cambridge: Cambridge University Press, 1986.
de Grazia, Margreta. "The Secularization of Language in the Seventeenth Century." *Journal of the History of Ideas* 41 (1980): 319–29.
de Man, Paul. *The Resistance to Theory.* Theory and History of Literature 33. Minneapolis: University of Minnesota Press, 1986.
Delany, Paul. *British Autobiography in the Seventeenth Century.* London, Routledge and Kegan Paul; New York: Columbia University Press, 1969.
Derrida, Jacques. *Dissemination.* Trans. Barbara Johnson. Chicago: University of Chicago Press, 1981.
———. "Living On: Border Lines." Trans. James Hulbert. In *Deconstruction and Criticism*, by Harold Bloom et al. New York: Seabury, 1979. Pp. 75–176.
Diodati, John. *Pious and Learned Annotations upon the Holy Bible.* 3d ed. London, 1651.
[Docwra, Anne]. *An Epistle of Love and Good Advice To my Old Friends & Fellow-Sufferers in the Late Times, the Old Royalists and their Posterity.* [London?], 1683.
Donne, John. *The Sermons of John Donne.* Ed. George R. Potter and Evelyn M. Simpson. 10 vols. Berkeley: University of California Press, 1953–62.
Easthope, Antony. "Towards the Autonomous Subject in Poetry: Milton's 'On His Blindness.'" In *Post-Structuralist Readings of English Poetry.* Ed. Richard Machin and Christopher Norris. Cambridge: Cambridge University Press, 1987. Pp. 122–33.
Edwards, Karen. "Reading the Book of the World in 'Paradise Lost.'" Unpublished manuscript.
Edwards, Thomas. *Antapologia: Or, A Full Answer to the Apologeticall Narration.* London, 1644.
———. *The Third Part of Gangraena.* London, 1646.
Elliott, Emory. "Milton's Biblical Style in *Paradise Regained.*" *Milton Studies VI.* Ed. James D. Simmonds. Pittsburgh: University of Pittsburgh Press, 1975. Pp. 227–41.
Elyot, Thomas. *Dictionary.* 1538. Reprint, Menston, England: Scolar Press, 1970.
Entzminger, Robert L. *Divine Word: Milton and the Redemption of Language.* Pittsburgh: Duquesne University Press, 1985.

Erasmus, Desiderius. *The First Tome or Volume of the Paraphrase of Erasmus upon the Newe Testament* (1548). Facsimile Reproduction with an Introduction by John N. Wall, Jr. Delmar, NY: Scholars' Facsimiles & Reprints, 1975.

Eusebius. *Demonstrationis Evangelicæ*. In Vol. 22 of *Patrologiæ cursus completus, series Græca*. Ed. J.-P. Migne. Paris, 1857.

Fallon, Stephen M. *Milton Among the Philosophers: Poetry and Materialism in Seventeenth-Century England*. Ithaca, NY: Cornell University Press, 1991.

Farrar, Frederic W. *History of Interpretation*. New York, 1886.

Ferry, Anne. *The Art of Naming*. Chicago: University of Chicago Press, 1988.

———. *The "Inward" Language: Sonnets of Wyatt, Sidney, Shakespeare, Donne*. Chicago: University of Chicago Press, 1983.

———. *Milton and the Miltonic Dryden*. Cambridge, MA: Harvard University Press, 1968.

———. *Milton's Epic Voice: The Narrator in Paradise Lost*. 1963. Reprint with a new preface, Chicago: University of Chicago Press, 1983.

Fish, Stanley E. *Doing What Comes Naturally: Change, Rhetoric, and the Practice of Theory in Literary and Legal Studies*. Durham, NC: Duke University Press, 1989.

———. "Question and Answer in *Samson Agonistes*." *Critical Quarterly* 11 (1969): 237–64.

———. "Reason in *The Reason of Church Government*." In his *Self-Consuming Artifacts: The Experience of Seventeenth-Century Literature*. Berkeley and Los Angeles: University of California Press, 1972. Pp. 265–302.

———. "Re-Covering Meaning: Intention and Interpretation in Milton's *Doctrine and Discipline of Divorce*." A paper read at the annual convention of the Modern Language Association, San Francisco, December, 1987.

———. "Spectacle and Evidence in *Samson Agonistes*." *Critical Inquiry* 15 (1989): 556–86.

———. *Surprised by Sin: The Reader in Paradise Lost*. London: Macmillan; New York: St. Martin's Press, 1967.

———. "Wanting a Supplement: The Question of Interpretation in Milton's Early Prose." In *Politics, Poetics, and Hermeneutics in Milton's Prose*. Ed. David Loewenstein and James Grantham Turner. Cambridge: Cambridge University Press, 1990. Pp. 41–68.

Fiske, Dixon. "Milton in the Middle of Life: Sonnet XIX." *ELH* 41 (1974): 37–49.

Fitzmeyer, Joseph A., ed. *The Gospel According to Luke (I–IX)*. The Anchor Bible. Garden City, NY: Doubleday, 1981.

Fix, Stephen. "Johnson and the 'Duty' of Reading *Paradise Lost*." *ELH* 52 (1985): 649–71.

Forsyth, Neil. "Having Done All to Stand: Biblical and Classical Allusion in *Paradise Regained*." *Milton Studies XXI*. Ed. James D. Simmonds. Pittsburgh: University of Pittsburgh Press, 1986. Pp. 199–214.

Foucault, Michel. *The Order of Things: An Archaeology of the Human Sciences*. 1966. Reprint, New York: Vintage, 1973.

Friedman, Donald. "Galileo and the Art of Seeing." In *Milton in Italy: Contexts Images Contradictions*. Ed. Mario A. Di Cesare. Binghamton, NY: Medieval & Renaissance Texts & Studies, 1991. Pp. 159–74.

Galilei, Galileo. *Discoveries and Opinions of Galileo*. Trans. Stillman Drake. Garden City, NY: Anchor Books, 1957.
Gallagher, Philip J. *Milton, the Bible, and Misogyny*. Ed. Eugene R. Cunnar and Gail L. Mortimer. Columbia: University of Missouri Press, 1990.
Gardner, John. "To the Reader." In *Choice Experiences*. By J[ane] Turner. London, 1653.
Gataker, Thomas. *De Novi Instrumenti Stylo Dissertatio*. [place?], 1648.
The Geneva Bible: A facsimile of the 1560 edition. Introduction by Lloyd E. Berry. Madison: University of Wisconsin Press, 1969.
Goldberg, Jonathan. "Dating Milton." In *Soliciting Interpretation: Literary Theory and Seventeenth-Century English Poetry*. Ed. Elizabeth D. Harvey and Katharine Eisaman Maus. Chicago: University of Chicago Press, 1990. Pp. 199–220.
———. *Voice/Terminal/Echo: Postmodernism and English Renaissance Texts*. London: Methuen, 1986.
Gossman, Ann, and George W. Whiting. "Milton's First Sonnet on His Blindness." *Review of English Studies* ns 12 (1961): 364–70.
Graef, Hilda. *Mary: A History of Doctrine and Devotion*. 2 vols. New York: Sheed & Ward, 1965.
Graham, E. P. "Divination." In *The Catholic Encyclopedia*. 15 vols. New York: Encyclopedia Press, 1909. 5: 48–51.
Greene, Robert A. "Whichcote, Wilkins, 'Ingenuity,' and the Reasonableness of Christianity." *Journal of the History of Ideas* 42 (1981): 227–52.
Gregory the Great. *Forty Gospel Homilies*. Trans. David Hurst. Kalamazoo, MI: Cistercian Publications, 1990.
Grislis, Egil. "The Hermeneutical Problem in Richard Hooker." In *Studies in Richard Hooker: Essays Preliminary to an Edition of His Works*. Ed. W. Speed Hill. Cleveland: Press of Case Western Reserve University, 1972. Pp. 159–206.
Grose, Christopher. "'Unweapon'd Creature in the Word': A Revision in Milton's Letter to a Friend." *English Language Notes* 21 (1983–84): 29–34.
Grossman, Marshall. *"Authors to Themselves": Milton and the Revelation of History*. Cambridge: Cambridge University Press, 1987.
———. "Writing the Inside Out: Shakespeare, Milton and the Supplement of Publication." A paper presented to the Renaissance Society of America, Harvard University, April 1989.
Grotius, Hugo. *His Most Choice Discovrses*. Trans. Cl. Barksdale. 3d ed. London, 1658.
Guillory, John. "The Father's House: *Samson Agonistes* in Its Historical Moment." In *Re-membering Milton: Essays on the Texts and Traditions*. Ed. Mary Nyquist and Margaret W. Ferguson. New York: Methuen, 1987. Pp. 148–76.
———. *Poetic Authority: Spenser, Milton, and Literary History*. New York: Columbia University Press, 1983.
Hales, John. *A Sermon Preached At St Maries in Oxford Vpon Tvesday in Easter VVeake, 1617*. Oxford, 1617.
Halkett, John. *Milton and the Idea of Matrimony: A Study of the Divorce Tracts and Paradise Lost*. New Haven, CT: Yale University Press, 1970.
Hall, David D. *Worlds of Wonder, Days of Judgment: Popular Religious Belief in Early New England*. New York: Knopf, 1989.

Haller, William. *The Rise of Puritanism.* 1938. Reprint, New York: Harper Torchbooks, 1957.
Hammond, H[enry]. *A Paraphrase and Annotations Upon All the Books of the New Testament.* 2d ed. London, 1659.
Haskin, Dayton. "Bunyan's Scriptural Acts." In *Bunyan in Our Time.* Ed. Robert G. Collmer. Kent, OH: Kent State University Press, 1989. Pp. 61–92.
———. "Milton's Strange Pantheon: The Apparent Tritheism of the *De Doctrina Christiana.*" *Heythrop Journal* 16 (1975): 129–48.
———. "*Samson Agonistes* on the Stage at Yale." *Milton Quarterly* 19 (1985): 48–53.
———. "Tracing a Genealogy of 'Talent': The Descent of Matthew 25: 14–30 into Contemporary Philanthropical Discourse." In *Wealth in Western Thought: The Case For and Against Riches.* Ed. Paul G. Schervish. Westport, CT: Greenwood Press, 1994.
Hendrix, Scott H. *Ecclesia in Via: Ecclesiological Developments in the Medieval Psalms Exegesis and the Dictata Super Psalterium (1513–1515) of Martin Luther.* Leiden: Brill, 1974.
Herbert, George. *The Works of George Herbert.* Ed. F. E. Hutchinson. Oxford: Clarendon Press, 1941.
Herrick, Robert. *The Poetical Works of Robert Herrick.* Ed. L. C. Martin. Oxford: Clarendon Press, 1956.
Herz, Judith Scherer. "'For whom this glorious sight?': Dante, Milton, and the Galileo Question." In *Milton in Italy: Contexts Images Contradictions.* Ed. Mario A. Di Cesare. Binghamton, NY: Medieval & Renaissance Texts & Studies, 1991. Pp. 147–57.
Heywood, Oliver. *The Rev. Oliver Heywood, B.A., 1630–1702: His Autobiographies, Diaries, Anecdote and Event Books.* Ed. J. Horsfall Turner. Brighouse, 1881–85.
Hieron, Samuel. *The Triall of Adoption* (1632). In *Works.* 2 vols. London, 1635.
Hill, Christopher. *The Experience of Defeat: Milton and Some Contemporaries.* New York: Elisabeth Sifton Books; Viking, 1984.
———. *Milton and the English Revolution.* 1977. Reprint, New York: Viking, 1978.
———. "*Samson Agonistes* Again." *Literature and History* 2d series 1 (1990): 24–39.
———. *The World Turned Upside Down: Radical Ideas During the English Revolution.* 1972. Reprint, Harmondsworth: Penguin, 1975.
Hill, John Spencer. *John Milton Poet, Priest and Prophet: A Study of Divine Vocation in Milton's Poetry and Prose.* London: Macmillan; Totowa, NJ: Rowman and Littlefield, 1979.
Hobbs, R. Gerald. "*Hebraica Veritas* and *Traditio Apostolica*: Saint Paul and the Interpretation of the Psalms in the Sixteenth Century." In *The Bible in the Sixteenth Century.* Ed. David C. Steinmetz. Durham, NC: Duke University Press, 1990. Pp. 83–99.
Hollander, John. *The Figure of Echo: A Mode of Allusion in Milton and After.* Berkeley and Los Angeles: University of California Press, 1981.
The Holy Bible. Authorized [King James] Version. 1611.
Hooker, Richard. *Tractates and Sermons,* Vol. 5 of *The Folger Library Edition of the Works of Richard Hooker.* Ed. Laetitia Yeandle and Egil Grislis. Cambridge, MA: Belknap Press of Harvard University Press, 1990.

Hughes, Philip Edgcumbe. *Paul's Second Epistle to the Corinthians*. Grand Rapids, MI: Eerdmans, 1962.
Huguelet, Theodore L. "The Rule of Charity in Milton's Divorce Tracts." *Milton Studies VI*. Ed. James D. Simmonds. Pittsburgh: University of Pittsburgh Press, 1975. Pp. 199–214.
Hunter, William B. "The Provenance of the *Christian Doctrine*." *Studies in English Literature* 32 (1992): 129–42; 163–66.
Hunter, William B., C. A. Patrides, and J[ack] H. Adamson. *Bright Essence: Studies in Milton's Theology*. Salt Lake City: University of Utah Press, 1971.
Huntley, John F. "The Ecology and Anatomy of Criticism: Milton's Sonnet 19 and the Bee Simile in 'Paradise Lost,' I.768–76." *Journal of Aesthetics and Art Criticism* 24 (1965–66): 383–91.
Hyman, Lawrence W. *The Quarrel Within: Art and Morality in Milton's Poetry*. Port Washington, NY: Kennikat Press, 1972.
Jackson, Thomas. *Ivstifying Faith*. London, 1615.
———. *Third Booke of Commentaries Vpon the Apostles Creede*. London, 1614.
Jaeger, Werner. *Early Christianity and Greek Paideia*. Cambridge, MA: Belknap Press of Harvard University Press, 1961.
Jameson, Mrs. [Anna]. *Legends of the Madonna as Represented in the Fine Arts*. Corrected and enlarged ed. Boston: Houghton, Mifflin, n.d.
Jessey, H[enry]. *A Storehouse of Provision*. London, 1650.
Johnson, Samuel. *A Dictionary of the English Language*. 1755. Facsimile reprint, London: Times Books, 1979.
———. *The Lives of the Poets: Selections*. Ed. Warren Fleischauer. Chicago: Henry Regenery, 1964.
———. "On the Death of Dr. Robert Levet" (1783). In *The Yale Edition of the Works of Samuel Johnson*, Vol. 6: *Poems*. Ed. E. L. McAdam, Jr., with George Milne. New Haven, CT: Yale University Press, 1964.
Kahn, Victoria. "Allegory and the Sublime in *Paradise Lost*." In *John Milton*. Ed. Annabel Patterson. London: Longman, 1992. Pp. 185–201.
Kaufmann, U. Milo. *The Pilgrim's Progress and Traditions in Puritan Meditation*. New Haven, CT: Yale University Press, 1966.
Kelsall, Malcolm. "The Historicity of *Paradise Regained*." *Milton Studies XII*. Ed. James D. Simmonds. Pittsburgh: University of Pittsburgh Press, 1979. Pp. 235–51.
Kendall, R. T. *Calvin and English Calvinism to 1649*. Oxford: Oxford University Press, 1979.
Kendrick, Christopher. *Milton: A Study in Ideology and Form*. New York: Methuen, 1986.
Kermode, Frank. *The Art of Telling: Essays on Fiction*. Cambridge, MA: Harvard University Press, 1983.
———. *The Genesis of Secrecy: On the Interpretation of Narrative*. Cambridge, MA: Harvard University Press, 1979.
Kerrigan, William. "The Irrational Coherence of *Samson Agonistes*." *Milton Studies XXII*. Ed. James D. Simmonds. Pittsburgh: University of Pittsburgh Press, 1987. Pp. 217–32.

———. "The Riddle of *Paradise Regained*." In *Poetic Prophecy in Western Literature*. Ed. Jan Wojcik and Raymond-Jean Frontain. Rutherford, NJ: Fairleigh Dickinson University Press, 1984. Pp. 64–80.

———. *The Sacred Complex: On the Psychogenesis of Paradise Lost*. Cambridge, MA: Harvard University Press, 1983.

Kirby, R. Kenneth. "Milton's Biblical Hermeneutics in *The Doctrine and Discipline of Divorce*." *Milton Quarterly* 18 (1984): 116–25.

Knott, John R., Jr. *The Sword of the Spirit: Puritan Responses to the Bible*. Chicago: University of Chicago Press, 1980.

Kristeva, Julia. "Stabat Mater." Trans. León S. Roudiez. In *The Kristeva Reader*. Ed. Toril Moi. New York: Columbia University Press, 1986. Pp. 160–86.

Kroll, Richard W. F. *The Material Word: Literate Culture in the Restoration and Early Eighteenth Century*. Baltimore: Johns Hopkins University Press, 1991.

———. "*Mise-en-Page*, Biblical Criticism, and Inference During the Restoration." *Studies in Eighteenth-Century Culture*. Ed. O. M. Brack, Jr. Madison: University of Wisconsin Press, 1986. 16: 3–40.

Krouse, F. Michael. *Milton's Samson and the Christian Tradition*. Princeton, NJ: Princeton University Press for University of Cincinnati, 1949.

Kurth, Burton O. *Milton and Christian Heroism: Biblical Epic Themes and Forms in Seventeenth-Century England*. 1959. Reprint, Hamden, CT: Archon, 1966.

Lane, Tony. "The Quest for the Historical Calvin." *Evangelical Quarterly* 55 (1983): 95–113.

Lechner, Sister Joan Marie. *Renaissance Concepts of the Commonplaces*. New York: Pageant, 1962.

Leigh, Edward. *Annotations upon all the New Testament Philologicall and Theological*. London, 1650.

Leith, John H. "John Calvin—Theologian of the Bible." *Interpretation* 25 (1971): 329–44.

Leonard, John. *Naming in Paradise: Milton and the Language of Adam and Eve*. Oxford: Clarendon Press, 1990.

Lever, Raphe. *The Arte of Reason, rightly termed Witcraft, teaching a perfect way to argue and dispute*. London, 1573.

Lewalski, Barbara Kiefer. "Forum: Milton's *Christian Doctrine*." *Studies in English Literature* 32 (1992): 143–54.

———. "Milton, the Bible, and Human Experience." *Topoi* 7 (1988): 221–29.

———. *Milton's Brief Epic: The Genre, Meaning, and Art of "Paradise Regained"*. Providence, RI: Brown University Press; London: Methuen, 1966.

———. *Paradise Lost and the Rhetoric of Literary Forms*. Princeton, NJ: Princeton University Press, 1985.

———. *Protestant Poetics and the Seventeenth-Century Religious Lyric*. Princeton, NJ: Princeton University Press, 1979.

———. "Structure and the Symbolism of Vision in Michael's Prophecy, *Paradise Lost*, Books XI–XII." *Philological Quarterly* 42 (1963): 25–35.

Lieb, Michael. *Poetics of the Holy: A Reading of Paradise Lost*. Chapel Hill: University of North Carolina Press, 1981.

———. "Talents." In *A Milton Encyclopedia*. 9 vols. Ed. William B. Hunter et al. Lewisburg, PA: Bucknell University Press, 1978–83. 8 (1980): 48–51.

Lightfoot, John. *The Harmony, Chronicle and Order of the Old Testament*. London, 1647.
Locke, Anne. *A Meditation of a Penitent Sinner*, appended to *Sermons of John Calvin*. London, 1560.
Locke, John. *An Essay Concerning Human Understanding*. Ed. Peter H. Nidditch. Oxford: Clarendon Press, 1975.
———. "An Essay For the Understanding of St. Paul's Epistles." In Vol. 3 of *The Works of John Locke*. 3 vols. London, 1714.
Lombard, Peter. *Commentarium in Psalmos*. In Vol. 191 of *Patrologiæ cursus completus, series Latina*. Ed. J.-P. Migne. Paris, 1879.
Lowance, Mason I., Jr. *The Language of Canaan: Metaphor and Symbol in New England from the Puritans to the Transcendentalists*. Cambridge, MA: Harvard University Press, 1980.
Luckock, Herbert Mortimer. *Studies in the History of the Book of Common Prayer*. 2nd ed. London, 1882.
Lupton, Lewis. *A History of the Geneva Bible*, Vol. 3: *Truth*. London: Olive Tree, 1971.
Luther, Martin. *A Commentarie of Master Doctor Martin Lvther vpon the Epistle of S. Pavl to the Galathians*. [Trans. Thomas Vautrollier?]. 1575. London, 1644.
———. "Preface to Latin Writings." In *Career of the Reformer IV*, Vol. 34 of *Luther's Works*. Ed. and trans. Lewis W. Spitz, Sr. Philadelphia: Muhlenberg Press, 1960.
———. *Selected Psalms I*. Ed. Jaroslav Pelikan. Vol. 12 of *Luther's Works*. St. Louis, MO: Concordia, 1955.
MacCallum, H. R. "Milton and Figurative Interpretation of the Bible." *University of Toronto Quarterly* 31 (1961–62): 397–415.
MacCallum, Hugh. "*Samson Agonistes*: The Deliverer as Judge." *Milton Studies XXIII*. Ed. James D. Simmonds. Pittsburgh: University of Pittsburgh Press, 1988. Pp. 259–90.
Madsen, William G. "From Shadowy Types to Truth." In *The Lyric and Dramatic Milton: Selected Papers from the English Institute*. Ed. Joseph H. Summers. New York: Columbia University Press, 1965. Pp. 95–114.
———. *From Shadowy Types to Truth: Studies in Milton's Symbolism*. New Haven, CT: Yale University Press, 1968.
Marks, Herbert. "The Blotted Book." In *Re-membering Milton: Essays on the Texts and Traditions*. Ed. Mary Nyquist and Margaret W. Ferguson. New York: Methuen, 1987. Pp. 211–33.
Martz, Louis L. *Milton: Poet of Exile*. 1980. 2nd ed., New Haven, CT: Yale University Press, 1986.
Marvell, Andrew. *The Poems and Letters of Andrew Marvell*. Ed. H. M. Margoliouth. 3d ed. Vol. 1: *Poems*. Rev. by Pierre Legouis with the collaboration of E. E. Duncan-Jones. Oxford: Clarendon Press, 1971.
Mary in the New Testament. Ed. Raymond E. Brown et al. Philadelphia: Fortress Press, 1978.
Mayer, John. *A Treasvry of Ecclesiasticall Expositions, vpon the difficult and doubtfull places of the Scriptures, Collected out of the best esteemed Interpreters, both auncient and moderne*. London, 1622.

Mazzaro, Jerome. "Gaining Authority: John Milton at Sonnets." *Essays in Literature* 15 (1988): 3–12.
Mazzeo, Joseph Anthony. "St. Augustine's Rhetoric of Silence." *Journal of the History of Ideas* 23 (1962): 175–96.
McCarthy, William. "The Continuity of Milton's Sonnets." *PMLA* 92 (1977): 96–109.
McColley, Grant. "The Astronomy of *Paradise Lost*." *Studies in Philology* 34 (1937): 209–47.
McCready, Amy R. "Milton's Casuistry: The Case of *The Doctrine and Discipline of Divorce*." *Journal of Medieval and Renaissance Studies* 22 (1992): 393–428.
McDonald, H. D. *Ideas of Revelation: An Historical Study A.D. 1700 to A.D. 1860.* London: Macmillan; New York: St. Martin's Press, 1959.
[Mersen, Mary]. *This Treatise Proving Three Worlds/Foundations Mentioned in Scripture.* London, 1696.
Mikalachki, Jodi. "*Paradise Regained* and Puritan Social Theology." A paper presented at the annual convention of the Modern Language Association, New York, December, 1992.
Miller, J. Hillis. *Theory Now and Then.* Hemel Hempstead: Harvester Wheatsheaf; Durham, NC: Duke University Press, 1991.
Milton, John. *Complete Prose Works of John Milton.* Ed. Don M. Wolfe et al. 8 vols. New Haven, CT: Yale University Press, 1953–82.
———. *John Milton: Prose Selections.* Ed. Merritt Y. Hughes. New York: Odyssey Press, 1947.
———. *The Latin Poems of John Milton.* Ed. Walter MacKellar. Cornell Studies in English 15. New Haven, CT: Yale University Press, for Cornell University, 1930.
———. *The Works of John Milton.* Gen. ed. Frank Allen Patterson. 18 vols. New York: Columbia University Press, 1931–38.
Morgan, John. *Godly Learning: Puritan Attitudes towards Reason, Learning, and Education, 1560–1640.* Cambridge: Cambridge University Press, 1986.
Nardo, Anna K. *Milton's Sonnets and the Ideal Community.* Lincoln: University of Nebraska Press, 1979.
Newton, Thomas, ed. *"Paradise Lost": A Poem in Twelve Books. The Author John Milton. A New Edition with Notes of Various Editors.* 2 vols. London, 1749.
———. *The Poetical Works of John Milton. With Notes of various Authors.* 3 vols. London, 1761.
N[orris], S[ylvester]. *An Antidote or Soveraigne Remedie Against the Pestiferovs Writings of All English Sectaries.* [St. Omer's], 1615.
Norwood, Richard. *Journal of Richard Norwood, Surveyor of Bermuda.* New York: Scholars' Facsimiles & Reprints for Bermuda Historical Monuments Trust, 1945.
Nuttall, Geoffrey F. *The Holy Spirit in Puritan Faith and Experience.* 1946. Reprint, Chicago: University of Chicago Press, 1991.
Nye, Stephen. *Brief History of the Unitarians Called also Socinians.* In *The Faith of One God, Who is only the Father.* London, 1691.
Nyquist, Mary. "Reading the Fall: Discourse and Drama in *Paradise Lost*." *English Literary Renaissance* 14 (1984): 199–229.

———. "Textual Overlapping and Dalila's Harlot-lap." In *Literary Theory/ Renaissance Texts*. Ed. Patricia Parker and David Quint. Baltimore: Johns Hopkins University Press, 1986. Pp. 341–72.
O'Keeffe, Timothy J. *Milton and the Pauline Tradition: A Study of Theme and Symbolism*. Washington, DC: University Press of America, 1982.
O'Malley, John W. "Grammar and Rhetoric in the *pietas* of Erasmus." *Journal of Medieval and Renaissance Studies* 18 (1988): 81–98.
Origen. *Homilies on Genesis and Exodus*. Trans. Ronald E. Heine. Washington, DC: Catholic University of America Press, 1982.
Owen, John. ΣΥΝΕΣΙΣ ΠΝΕΥΜΑΤΙΚΗ. *The Causes, Ways, and Means of Understanding the Mind of God as Revealed in His Word, with Assurance Therein* (1678). In Vol. 4 of *The Works of John Owen*. Ed. William H. Goold. 16 vols. 1850–53. Reprint, Edinburgh: Banner of Truth Trust, 1967.
The Oxford English Dictionary. 2d ed. Oxford: Clarendon Press, 1989.
Pagit, Eusebius. *The Historie of the Bible, Briefly Collected by way of Question and Answer*. London, 1613.
Parker, William Riley. *Milton: A Biography*. 2 vols. Oxford: Clarendon Press, 1968.
Parsons, Edward S. "The Authorship of the Anonymous Life of Milton." *PMLA* 50 (1935): 1057–64.
Parsons, Robert. *The First Booke of the Christian Exercise, appertayning to resolution*. [Rouen?], 1582.
Pecheux, Mother M. Christopher. "Milton and Kairos." *Milton Studies XII*. Ed. James D. Simmonds. Pittsburgh: University of Pittsburgh Press, 1979. Pp. 197–211.
Pelikan, Jaroslav. *The Emergence of the Catholic Tradition (100–600)*. Chicago: University of Chicago Press, 1971.
Pemble, William. *Vindiciæ Gratiæ. A Plea for Grace*. Oxford, 1659.
Pennington, Isaac. "A Further Testimony to Truth, Revived Out of the Ruins of the Apostacy." In *The Works of Isaac Pennington, A Minister of the Gospel in the Society of Friends*. 4th ed. Philadelphia, 1863.
Perkins, William. *A Treatise of the Vocations*. In *The Works of William Perkins newly corrected according to his own copies*. Cambridge, 1605.
———. *The Combat betweene Christ and the Deuill displayed*. 2nd ed. London, 1606.
———. *The Works of that Famous and Worthy Minister of Christ*. 3 vols. London, 1612.
Phillips, Edward. "The Life of Mr. John Milton" (1674). In *The Early Lives of Milton*. Ed. Helen Darbishire. London: Constable, 1932.
———. *New World of Words: or Universal English Dictionary*. 7th ed. London, 1720.
———. *Theatrum Poetarum, or a compleat Collection of the Poets, Especially The most Eminent, of all Ages*. London, 1675.
Pope, Elizabeth Marie. *Paradise Regained: The Tradition and the Poem*. 1947. Reprint, New York: Russell & Russell, 1962.
Powel, Va[vasor]. "To the sober and spirituall Readers of this Booke." In *Spirituall Experiences of sundry Beleevers*. 2nd impression enlarged. London, 1651 [an error for 1652 or 1653].
P[reston], I[ohn]. *An Elegant and Lively Description of Spirituall Life and Death*. London, 1633.

Preston, Iohn. *The Nevv Covenant, or The Saints Portion*. 2d ed. London, 1629.
Psalterium, Hebreum, Grecum, Arabicum, & Chaldeum, cum tribus latinis interpretationibus & glossis. [Place?], 1516.
[Pseudo-]Bede. *In Matthaei Evangelium Expositio*. In Vol. 92 of *Patrologiæ cursus completus, series Latina*. Ed. J.-P. Migne. Paris, 1862.
Quarles, Ur. Address to the Reader. In Vol. 1 of *The Complete Works in Prose and Verse of Francis Quarles*. Ed. Alexander B. Grosart. Chertsey Worthies' Library. 3 vols. [Printed privately in England], 1880–81. Reprint, New York: AMS Press, 1967.
Quilligan, Maureen. *Milton's Spenser: The Politics of Reading*. Ithaca, NY: Cornell University Press, 1983.
Radzinowicz, Mary Ann. "How Milton Read the Bible: The Case of *Paradise Regained*." In *The Cambridge Companion to Milton*. Ed. Dennis Danielson. Cambridge: Cambridge University Press, 1989. Pp. 207–23.
———. " 'In those days there was no king in Israel': Milton's Politics and Biblical Narrative." *Yearbook of English Studies* 21 (1991): 242–52.
———. *Milton's Epics and the Book of Psalms*. Princeton, NJ: Princeton University Press, 1989.
———. "*Paradise Regained* as Hermeneutic Combat." *University of Hartford Studies in Literature* 15–16 (1983–84): 99–107.
———. *Toward Samson Agonistes: The Growth of Milton's Mind*. Princeton, NJ: Princeton University Press, 1978.
Reiter, Robert E. "On Biblical Typology and the Interpretation of Literature." *College English* 30 (1968–69): 562–71.
Relation of the Fearfvl Estate of Francis Spira, In the Year 1548. Compiled by Natth[aniel] Bacon. London, 1649.
Revard, Stella P. "The Gospel of John and *Paradise Regained*: Jesus as 'True Light.'" In *Milton and Scriptural Tradition: The Bible into Poetry*. Ed. James H. Sims and Leland Ryken. Columbia: University of Missouri Press, 1984. Pp. 142–59.
Réau, Louis. *Iconographie de l'art chrétien*. 3 vols. Paris: Presses Universitaires de France, 1955–59.
Ricks, Christopher. *Milton's Grand Style*. Oxford: Clarendon Press, 1963.
Roberts, Francis. *Clavis Bibliorum, The Key of The Bible, Unlocking the Richest Treasury of the Holy Scriptures*. 2 vols. 2d ed. London, 1649.
Rogers, John, of Dedham. *The Doctrine of Faith*. London, 1627.
Rogers, John. *Ohel or Beth-shemesh, A Tabernacle for the Sun*. London, 1653.
Rosenblatt, Jason P. "Milton's Chief Rabbi." *Milton Studies XXIV*. Ed. James D. Simmonds. Pittsburgh: University of Pittsburgh Press, 1989. Pp. 43–71.
Rozett, Martha Tuck. *The Doctrine of Election and the Emergence of Elizabethan Tragedy*. Princeton, NJ: Princeton University Press, 1984.
Rumrich, John Peter. "Uninventing Milton." *Modern Philology* 87 (1989–90): 249–65.
Rushdy, Ashraf H. A. "Of *Paradise Regained*: The Interpretation of Career." *Milton Studies XXIV*. Ed. James D. Simmonds. Pittsburgh: University of Pittsburgh Press, 1989. Pp. 253–75.
Samuel, Irene. "*Samson Agonistes* as Tragedy." In *Calm of Mind: Tercentenary Essays on*

"Paradise Regained" and "Samson Agonistes" in Honor of John S. Diekhoff. Ed. Joseph Anthony Wittreich, Jr. Cleveland: Press of Case Western Reserve University, 1971. Pp. 235–57.
Saurat, Denis. *Milton, Man and Thinker*. 1925. Rev. ed. London: Dent, 1944.
Schama, Simon. *The Embarrassment of Riches: An Interpretation of Dutch Culture in the Golden Age*. Berkeley and Los Angeles: University of California Press, 1988.
Schiller, Gertrud. *Iconography of Christian Art*. Trans. Janet Seligman. 2 vols. 1966. 1st American edition: Greenwich, CT: New York Graphic Society, 1971.
Schultz, Howard. *Milton and Forbidden Knowledge*. New York: Modern Language Association, 1955.
Schwartz, Regina M. "Citation, Authority, and *De Doctrina Christiana*." In *Politics, Poetics, and Hermeneutics in Milton's Prose*. Ed. David Loewenstein and James Grantham Turner. Cambridge: Cambridge University Press, 1990. Pp. 227–40.
———. "From Shadowy Types to Shadowy Types: The Unendings of *Paradise Lost*." *Milton Studies XXIV*. Ed. James D. Simmonds. Pittsburgh: University of Pittsburgh Press, 1989. Pp. 123–39.
———. *Remembering and Repeating: Biblical Creation in Paradise Lost*. Cambridge: Cambridge University Press, 1988. Reprint, with a new preface, Chicago: University of Chicago Press, 1993.
Scot, Reginald. *The discoverie of witchcraft*. 1584. Reprint, London, 1665.
Sedgwick, Obadiah. *Anatomy of Secret Sins*. London, 1660.
Shakespeare, William. *Poems*. London, 1640.
Shami, Jeanne M. "Donne on Discretion." *ELH* 47 (1980): 48–66.
Shawcross, John T. "Forum: Milton's *Christian Doctrine*." *Studies in English Literature* 32 (1992): 155–62.
———. "The Genres of *Paradise Regain'd* and *Samson Agonistes*: The Wisdom of Their Joint Publication." *Milton Studies XVII: Composite Orders: The Genres of Milton's Last Poems*. Ed. Richard S. Ide and Joseph Wittreich. Pittsburgh: University of Pittsburgh Press, 1983. Pp. 225–48.
———. "Irony as Tragic Effect: *Samson Agonistes* and the Tragedy of Hope." In *Calm of Mind: Tercentenary Essays on "Paradise Regained" and "Samson Agonistes" in Honor of John S. Diekhoff*. Ed. Joseph Anthony Wittreich, Jr. Cleveland: Press of Case Western Reserve University, 1971. Pp. 289–306.
Shawe, John. *Memoirs of Master John Shawe . . . Written by himself in the year 1663–64*. Ed. J. R. Boyle. Hull, 1882.
[Sherlock, William]. *The Protestant Resolution of Faith*. London, 1683.
Shiel, James. *Greek Thought and the Rise of Christianity*. London: Longmans; New York: Barnes & Noble, 1968.
Shullenberger, William. "Linguistic and Poetic Theory in Milton's *De Doctrina Christiana*." *English Language Notes* 19 (1981–82): 262–78.
Sibbes, Richard. *The Brvised Reed and Smoaking Flax*. 5th ed. London, 1635.
Sidney, Sir Philip. *An Apology for Poetry, or The Defence of Poesy*. Ed. Geoffrey Shepherd. 1965. Reprint, Manchester: Manchester University Press; New York: Barnes & Noble, 1973.
Sidney, Sir Philip, and the Countess of Pembroke. *The Psalms of Sir Philip Sidney and*

the Countess of Pembroke. Ed. J. C. A. Rathmell. New York: New York University Press, 1963.
Sims, James H. and Leland Ryken, eds. *Milton and Scriptural Tradition: The Bible into Poetry*. Columbia: University of Missouri Press, 1984.
Slights, Camille Wells. *The Casuistical Tradition in Shakespeare, Donne, Herbert, and Milton*. Princeton, NJ: Princeton University Press, 1981.
Slights, William W. E. "'Marginall Notes that spoile the Text': Scriptural Annotation in the English Renaissance." *Huntington Library Quarterly* 55 (1992): 255–78.
Smith, Barbara Hernstein. *Contingencies of Value: Alternative Perspectives for Critical Theory*. Cambridge, MA: Harvard University Press, 1988.
Smith, Carolyn H. "The Virgin Mary in *Paradise Regained*." *South Atlantic Quarterly* 71 (1972): 557–64.
Smith, Nigel. "*Areopagitica*: Voicing Contexts, 1643–5." In *Politics, Poetics, and Hermeneutics in Milton's Prose*. Ed. David Loewenstein and James Grantham Turner. Cambridge: Cambridge University Press, 1990. Pp. 103–22.
———. *Perfection Proclaimed: Language and Literature in English Radical Religion, 1640–1660*. Oxford: Clarendon Press, 1989.
Sparrow, John. *Visible Words: A Study of Inscriptions in and as Books and Works of Art*. Cambridge: Cambridge University Press, 1969.
Spencer, John. ΚΑΙΝΑ ΚΑΙ ΠΑΛΑΙΑ. *Things New and Old. Or, A Storehouse of Similies, Sentences, Allegories, . . . Collected and observed from the Writings and Sayings of the Learned in all Ages to this present*. London, 1658.
Spirituall Experiences of sundry Beleevers. 2nd impression enlarged. London, 1651 [an error for 1652 or 1653].
Sprat, Thomas. *The History of the Royal-Society of London For the Improving of Natural Knowledge*. London, 1667.
Spufford, Margaret. "First Steps in Literacy: The Reading and Writing Experiences of the Humblest Seventeenth-Century Spiritual Autobiographers." *Social History* 4, no. 3 (October 1979): 407–35.
Stanton, Kay. "From 'Jove' to 'Task-Master': The Transformation from Pagan to Christian Diety in Milton's Sonnets 1–7." *University of Hartford Studies in Literature* 15–16 (1983–84): 67–79.
Stavely, Keith W. F. *Puritan Legacies: Paradise Lost and the New England Tradition, 1630–1890*. Ithaca, NY: Cornell University Press, 1987.
———. "Roger Williams: Bible Politics and Bible Art." *Prose Studies* 14 (1991): 76–91.
———. "Satan and Arminianism in *Paradise Lost*." *Milton Studies XXV*. Ed. James D. Simmonds. Pittsburgh: University of Pittsburgh Press, 1990. Pp. 125–39.
Steadman, John M. *Milton and the Renaissance Hero*. Oxford: Clarendon Press, 1967.
Stein, Arnold. *Answerable Style: Essays on Paradise Lost*. Minneapolis: University of Minnesota Press, 1953.
———. *Heroic Knowledge: An Interpretation of Paradise Regained and Samson Agonistes*. 1957. Reprint, Hamden, CT: Archon, 1965.
Stendahl, Krister. *Paul Among Jews and Gentiles and Other Essays*. Philadelphia: Fortress Press, 1976.

Stocker, Margarita. *Paradise Lost*. Atlantic Highlands, NJ: Humanities Press International, 1988.
Stone, Lawrence. *The Family, Sex and Marriage in England 1500–1800*. New York: Harper & Row, 1977.
Stranahan, Brainerd P. "Bunyan and the Epistle to the Hebrews: His Source for the Idea of Pilgrimage in *The Pilgrim's Progress*." *Studies in Philology* 79 (1982): 279–96.
Strier, Richard. *Love Known: Theology and Experience in George Herbert's Poetry*. Chicago: University of Chicago Press, 1983.
Stringer, Gary A. "Milton's 'Thorn in the Flesh': Pauline Didacticism in Sonnet XIX." *Milton Studies X*. Ed. James D. Simmonds. Pittsburgh: University of Pittsburgh Press, 1977. Pp. 141–54.
Stull, William L. "Sonnets Courtly and Christian." *University of Hartford Studies in Literature* 15–16 (1983–84): 1–15.
Sundell, Roger H. "The Narrator as Interpreter in *Paradise Regained*." *Milton Studies II*. Ed. James D. Simmonds. Pittsburgh: University of Pittsburgh Press, 1970. Pp. 83–101.
Svendsen, Kester. *Milton and Science*. Cambridge, MA: Harvard University Press, 1956.
Swaim, Kathleen M. *Before and After the Fall: Contrasting Modes in Paradise Lost*. Amherst: University of Massachusetts Press, 1986.
Swanson, Donald. "Milton's Scholarly Jesus in *Paradise Regained*." *Cithara* 27, no. 2 (May 1988): 3–10.
Swiss, Margo. "Crisis of Conscience: A Theological Context for Milton's 'How Soon Hath Time.'" *Milton Quarterly* 20 (1986): 98–103.
Synopsis Criticorum Aliorumque S. Scripturae Interpretum. Ed. Matthew Poole. 4 vols. in 5. London: 1669–1676.
Tanner, John S. *Anxiety in Eden: A Kierkegaardian Reading of Paradise Lost*. New York: Oxford University Press, 1992.
Tayler, Edward W. *Milton's Poetry: Its Development in Time*. Pittsburgh: Duquesne University Press, 1979.
Taylor, Jeremy. *Ductor Dubitantium, or The Rule of Conscience*. London, 1660.
———. *The Whole Works of Jeremy Taylor*. Ed. Reginald Heber. 15 vols. London: Ogle, Duncan, 1822.
Taylor, John. *All The Workes of John Taylor the Water Poet*. 1630. Reprint, London: Scolar Press, 1977.
Tehillim: A New Translation with Commentary Anthologized from Talmudic, Midrashic and Rabbinic Sources. Ed. and trans. Avrohom Chaim Feuer. 2d ed. Brooklyn: Mesorah Publications, 1979.
Thomas, Keith. *Religion and the Decline of Magic*. New York: Charles Scribner's Sons, 1971.
Tillyard, E. M. W. *Milton*. Rev. ed. New York: Barnes & Noble, 1967.
Tipson, Baird. "A Dark Side of Seventeenth-Century English Protestantism: The Sin Against the Holy Spirit." *Harvard Theological Review* 77 (1984): 301–30.
Trapp, John. *Theologia Theologiae, the True Treasure; Or A Treasury of holy Truths, touching Gods Word, and God the Word*. London, 1641.

Triumphs of Female Wit, In Some Pindaric Odes. Or, the Emulation. Together with an Answer to an Objector against Female Ingenuity, and Capacity of Learning. London, 1683.
Turner, James Grantham. *One Flesh: Paradisal Marriage and Sexual Relations in the Age of Milton.* Oxford: Clarendon Press, 1987.
Turner, Jane. *Choice Experiences.* London, 1653.
Turner, William. *A Compleat History of the Most Remarkable Providences, Both of Judgment and Mercy, Which Have Hapned in This Present Age.* London, 1697.
Tyndale, William. *William Tyndale's Five Books of Moses, Called the Pentateuch.* Ed. J. I. Mombert. 1884. Reprint, Carbondale: Southern Illinois University Press, 1967.
Ulreich, John C., Jr. "'Incident to All Our Sex': The Tragedy of Dalila." In *Milton and the Idea of Woman.* Ed. Julia M. Walker. Urbana: University of Illinois Press, 1988. Pp. 185–210.
——. "'This Great Deliverer': *Samson Agonistes* as Parable." *Milton Quarterly* 13 (1979): 79–84.
[Underwood, Abraham]. *The Protestants Plea for a Socinian: Justifying His Doctrine from being opposite to Scripture or Church-Authority.* London, 1686.
van Unnik, W. C. "Die rechte Bedeutung des Wortes treffen, Lukas 2,19." In *Verbum: Essays on Some Aspects of the Religious Function of Words: Festschrift for H. W. Obbink.* Ed. T. P. van Baaren et al. Utrecht: Kemink, 1964. Pp. 129–47.
A Variorum Commentary on the Poems of John Milton, Vol. 2, Part 2: *The Minor Poems.* Ed. A. S. P. Woodhouse and Douglas Bush. New York: Columbia University Press, 1972.
Vaughan, Henry. *The Works of Henry Vaughan.* Ed. L. C. Martin. 2d ed. Oxford: Clarendon Press, 1957.
Venn, Anne. *A Wise Virgins Lamp.* London, 1658.
Verkamp, Bernard J. *The Indifferent Mean: Adiaphorism in the English Reformation to 1554.* Athens, OH: Ohio University Press; Detroit, MI: Wayne State University Press, 1977.
Vlober, Maurice. *La Vie de Marie Mère de Dieu.* Paris: Librairie Bloud et Gay, 1949.
Wailes, Stephen L. *Medieval Allegories of Jesus' Parables.* Berkeley: University of California Press, 1987.
Waldock, A. J. A. *Paradise Lost and Its Critics.* Cambridge: Cambridge University Press, 1947.
Walker, Julia M. "Milton and Galileo: The Art of Intellectual Canonization." *Milton Studies XXV.* Ed. James D. Simmonds. Pittsburgh: University of Pittsburgh Press, 1990. Pp. 109–23.
Walsh, J. J. "Jesus Christ (II)." In *The New Catholic Encyclopedia.* New York: McGraw-Hill, 1967. 7: 924–26.
Watkins, Owen C. *The Puritan Experience.* London: Routledge & Kegan Paul, 1972.
Watts, William. "To the devout Reader." In *Saint Augustines Confessions translated; and With some marginall notes illustrated.* London, 1631.
Whitaker, William. *A Disputation on Holy Scripture, Against the Papists, Especially Bellarmine and Stapleton.* Trans. William Fitzgerald. 1849. Reprint, New York: Johnson Reprint Corp., 1968.

Wilcox, Joel F. "'Spending the Light': Milton and Homer's Light of Hope." *Milton Quarterly* 18 (1984): 77–78.
Wilson, Thomas. *The Rule of Reason Conteinyng the Arte of Logique*. Ed. Richard S. Sprague. Northridge, CA: San Fernando Valley State College, 1972.
Wither, George. *Abvses Stript, and Whipt: or Satyricall Essayes*. 2 vols. London, 1622. Reprinted in *Juvenilia*. Menston, England: A Scolar Press facsimile, 1970.
——. *Hallelujah, Or Britain's Second Remembrancer*. 1641. Reprint, London: John Russell Smith, 1857.
Wittreich, Joseph. *Feminist Milton*. Ithaca, NY: Cornell University Press, 1987.
——. *Interpreting Samson Agonistes*. Princeton, NJ: Princeton University Press, 1986.
——. *Visionary Poetics: Milton's Tradition and His Legacy*. San Marino, CA: Huntington Library, 1979.
Wollebius, Johannes. *Compendivm Theologiæ Christianæ*. Amsterdam, 1633. Translated by Alexander Ross as *The Abridgment of Christian Divinitie*. London, 1650.
Woodhouse, A. S. P. "Milton, Puritanism, and Liberty." *University of Toronto Quarterly* 4 (1934–35): 483–513.
Worthen, J. F. "On the Matter of the Text." *University of Toronto Quarterly* 60 (1990–91): 337–53.
Wrede, William. *The Messianic Secret in the Gospels*. Trans. J. C. G. Grieg. Cambridge: James Clarke; Greenwood, SC: Attic, 1971.
Zwicky, Laurie. "Kairos in *Paradise Regained*: The Divine Plan." *ELH* 31 (1964): 271–77.

Index of Biblical Places

OLD TESTAMENT

Genesis
  chaps. 1–3 (creation), 189, 192, 202, 204, 213, 224
  1: 1 (the beginning), 151, 231
  1: 28 (be fruitful), xvii, 238, 271 n.2
  2: 16–17 (the prohibition), xvii, 188–89, 227, 234–36, 238, 271 n.2
  3: 15 (the *protevangelium*), 229–30
  3: 23–24 (exile from Eden), 228
  5: 5 (Adam's age), 235
  16: 1 (Sarah's barrenness), 138
  21: 8 (Isaac's growth), 113
  32: 24–32 (Jacob's wrestling), 139

Exodus
  1: 11–14 (taskmasters), 261 n.37
  2: 11 (Moses' maturity), 113
  3: 5 (the place is holy ground), 260–61 n.30
  chap. 5 (the Israelites' burdens), 68, 111–12, 114
  15: 20–21 (Miriam's song), 128

Deuteronomy
  4: 2 (no addition to God's words), 129, 152
  11: 18–21 (lay up God's words), 118, 133
  24: 1 (bill of divorce), 46, 64, 65, 254 n.18

Judges
  5: 1–31 (Deborah's song), 128
  chap. 13 (Samson's mother), 138–39, 168
  13: 2 (barrenness of Manoah's wife), 139
  13: 5 (no razor on Samson's head), 139
  13: 8 (how to raise Samson), 139
  13: 24–25 (Samson's growth), 113, 139–40
  16: 31 (Samson's burial place), 141
  19: 2 (concubine plays whore), 69

1 Samuel
  1: 5 (Hannah's barrenness), 138
  2: 1–10 (Hannah's song), 128
  2: 20–26 (Samuel's growth), 113

Job
  as a generic model for *Paradise Regained*, 148, 266 n.3
  chaps. 1–2 (Satan and the Lord), 114
  42: 7 (the Lord's anger against Job's friends), 75

Psalms
  as sources for *Paradise Regained*, 148, 266 n.3
  as sources for *Samson Agonistes*, 165
  in the preaching of John Donne, 78
  1: 2 (meditate on the Law day and night), 19
  Psalm 19, 202–16, 229, 274 nn. 35, 37, 274–75 n.38, 275 nn.43–48, 275–76 n.49, 276 nn. 51, 53
  27: 14 (wait on the Lord), 260 n.30
  37: 7 (wait patiently), 260 n.30
  Psalm 114 (paraphrased by Milton), 151
  Psalm 148 (song of creation), 205

Proverbs
  chap. 2 (laying up wisdom), 68
  3: 11–12 (Lord chastens those he loves), 114
  4: 26 (ponder the path), 133
  5: 6 (lest thou ponder), 133
  5: 21 (the Lord ponders all goings), 133
  21: 2 (the Lord ponders hearts), 134
  24: 12 (pondering the heart), 124

Isaiah
  1: 21–26 (the faithful city has become a harlot), 271 n.49
  6: 9–10 (see and not perceive, hear and not understand), 174
  7: 14 (virgin shall conceive), 125, 262 n.9
  8: 17 (I will wait upon the Lord), 260 n.30
  29: 14 (worldly wisdom perishes), 157
  50: 1 (Israel's bill of divorce), 271 n.50

300 Index of Biblical Places

50: 10 (who walketh in darkness?), 260 n.30
chap. 53 (the suffering servant), 167

Jeremiah
2: 2 (former espousal of Jerusalem and the Lord), 271 n.49
3: 1–12 (Israel called back after divorce), 271 n.50

Lamentations
3: 25–26 (the Lord is good unto them that wait), 260 n.30

Ezekiel
chap. 16 (Israel as harlot), 180
chap. 23 (Samaria and Jerusalem as harlots), 271 n.49

Daniel
7: 10 (thousand thousands ministered unto him), 260 n.30

Hosea
chaps. 1–3 (Israel turned harlot), 271 n.49

Habakkuk
2: 4 (the just shall live by faith), 1

NEW TESTAMENT

Matthew
chaps. 1–2 (birth of Jesus), 131
1: 18–25 (Joseph's view of Jesus' birth), 128
2: 1 (wise men from the East), 127
2: 13–15 (descent into Egypt), 150
4: 1–11 (temptations in wilderness), 129
chaps. 5–7 (Sermon on the Mount), 65
5: 16 (let your light shine), 102
5: 31–32 (divorce), xiv, 57, 59, 68, 71
7: 13–14 (the straight gate), 20
7: 21–23 (saying, "Lord, Lord"), 12, 20
8: 4 (Jesus prohibits publishing), 270–71 n.44
8: 20 (no place for Son of man), 124
9: 30 (Jesus prohibits publishing), 270–71 n.44
10: 26 (nothing covered, that shall not be revealed), 175, 270 n.41
11: 28–30 (the light burden), 7, 10, 13–14, 32, 62, 100–101, 108, 248 n.47, 261 n.31
12: 31–32 (sin against the Holy Ghost), 24
12: 36–37 (account on judgment day), 32
chap. 13 (parables and secrecy), 171, 245 n.17
13: 3–23 (parable of the sower), 11, 12, 20, 171
13: 11 (mysteries of the kingdom), 171, 270 nn.39–40
13: 12 (to one that hath shall be given), 171, 270 nn. 36, 40
13: 13–17 (teaching in parables), 171, 174
13: 35 (secret things), 171
13: 52 (the scribe brings out old and new), 73, 137, 146, 171
16: 13–20 (Peter's confession of faith), 175–76, 270 n.43, 270–71 n.44
17: 1–13 (the Transfiguration), 177
19: 3–12 (divorce), xiv, 57, 59, 71, 150, 254 n.18, 266 n.5
19: 21 (go and sell all that thou hast), 5
20: 1–16 (laborers in vineyard), 19, 20, 37, 169, 249 n.12
20: 16 (many are called, few chosen), 20
21: 9 (Hosanna to the Son of David), 17
22: 14 (few chosen), 19, 20
22: 15–22 (rendering to Caesar), 150
23: 4 (heavy burdens), 62
chap. 25 (ten virgins, talents, last judgment), 106–7, 245 n.17
25: 1–13 (parable of ten virgins), 51, 106
25: 14–30 (parable of talents), viii, xiii, xv, 11, 28, 29–53, 55, 57–58, 63, 81, 86, 89–90, 91, 93, 95–117, 129–30, 145, 165–73, 228–29, 238, 239, 249 n.12, 250 n.17
25: 15 (according to several ability), 37, 41, 85, 90, 116, 257 n.41
25: 25 (hiding the talent), 260 n.24
25: 26 (the slothful servant), 66–67, 103, 228
25: 28–29 (to one that hath shall be given), 170
25: 30 (outer darkness), 228, 260 n.20. See Gen. 3: 23–24
25: 31–46 (final judgment), 106–7

Mark
1: 34 (Jesus disallows devils to speak), 270–71 n.44
1: 40–45 (cure of leper), 173–74, 270–71 n.44

Index of Biblical Places   301

3: 28–30 (sin against the Holy Ghost), 248 n.45
4: 11–12 (teaching in parables), 174, 270 n.39
4: 22 (nothing hid, which shall not be manifested), 270 n.41
7: 36 (publishing the secret), 173–74
10: 11–12 (divorce), xiv, 253 n.11
10: 21 (Go and sell all that thou hast), 5
12: 13–17 (rendering to Caesar), 150

Luke
chaps. 1–2 (infancy narratives), 128, 131, 140
1: 1–4 (eyewitnesses as sources), 128, 131, 262 n.3
1: 7 (Elizabeth's barrenness), 138
1: 26–38 (the Annunciation), 262 n.9
1: 29 (Mary troubled), 128
1: 38 (handmaid of the Lord), 128
1: 46–55 (the Magnificat), 124, 128, 134
1: 80 (John's growth), 113
2: 7 (laying Jesus in a manger), 127
2: 19 (Mary pondered), 132–33, 136, 142, 145–46, 238, 264 nn.23–24
2: 40 (Jesus' growth), 113
2: 41–52 (Jesus at age twelve), 141, 159
2: 49 (the Father's business), 135, 141–42, 159, 265 n.32
2: 51 (Mary kept sayings), 45, 130, 132–33, 136, 142, 145–46, 238, 263 n.13
2: 52 (Jesus' growth), 113, 152–53
4: 1–13 (temptations in wilderness), 148, 155, 266 nn. 3, 5
4: 16–21 (Jesus applies the Scriptures), 137
8: 15 (fruit from the word), 136
9: 21 (Jesus prohibits publishing), 270–71 n.44
10: 42 (one thing necessary), 93
12: 2 (nothing covered, that shall not be revealed), 175
12: 10 (the sin against the Holy Ghost), 248 n.45
12: 32 (fear not, little flock), 20
12: 34 (heart and treasure), 136
15: 11–32 (prodigal son), 169–70
16: 18 (divorce), xiv
17: 34 (one received, the other left), 20
19: 11–27 (parable of pounds), 47, 63, 104, 107, 166, 177, 250 n.17, 260 n.24
20: 19–26 (rendering to Caesar), 150, 266 n.5

John
Fourth Gospel as "inspiration" for *Paradise Regained*, 148, 266 n.3
1: 1–3 (the beginning), 151
2: 1–11 (wedding at Cana), 137
2: 16 (temple as the Father's house), 144, 165, 170
2: 19–22 (temple as Jesus' body), 144
4: 22 (worshiping what is not known), 121
5: 39 (search the scriptures), 154
9: 4 (labor while light), 49
chap. 17 (Jesus' farewell discourse), 14

Acts of the Apostles
implications for church history and church government, 82, 153–54
chaps. 9, 22, and 26 (conversion of St. Paul), 3, 154, 267 n.14
17: 11 (the Bereans), 43–45, 60, 82, 84, 133, 154, 257 n.45, 263 n.15
17: 12 (many believed), 45
17: 16–34 (Paul in Athens), 151–52
17: 28 (Paul quotes Greek poetry), 152
22: 3 (Paul's rabbinic learning), 154
26: 4–5 (Paul's life as a Pharisee), 154

Romans
1: 17 (the just shall live by faith), 1, 50, 77
1: 20 (from the creation are clearly seen), 276 n.53
2: 29 (the inward Jew), 160
4: 2 (Abraham not justified by works), 77
5: 12–21 (Adam/Christ typology), 155–56, 163–64
chap. 8 (consolations of predestination), 14, 169
8: 28 (all works for good), 16
8: 30 (predestined and chosen), 20
9: 18 (mercy on whom He will), 20
10: 18 (quoting Ps. 19), 210
12: 6 (analogy of faith), xv, 7, 56, 77, 78, 80–81, 252 n.4, 257 nn.41–42
13: 13 (not in rioting and drunkenness), 4–7, 13

1 Corinthians
read in light of Romans and Galatians, 160–61
chap. 7 (Paul's applications of Jesus' teachings), 262 n.3

1: 23–27 (intellectual weakness), 156–57
2: 1–5 (weakness as lack of eloquence), 157
10: 1–13 (interpretation of temptations), 156
10: 12 (take heed lest he fall), 20
13: 7 (charity believeth all things), 72

2 Corinthians
4: 7–10 (temptation as crucifixion), 156
12: 2–21 (thorn in the flesh), 157
12: 9 (sufficient grace; perfect in weakness), 32
13: 5 ("examine yourselves"), 12

Galatians
chaps. 1–2 (Paul's autobiography), 3
1: 14 (Paul's zeal for Jewish tradition), 154
1: 17 (Paul's journey to Arabia), 155
4: 13–15 (Paul's physical affliction), 157
6: 4–5 (every man shall bear his own burden), 88

Ephesians
6: 10–14 (the armor of God), 267 n.16

Philippians
2: 12 (salvation in fear and trembling), 20
3: 4–6 (Paul as Hebrew of Hebrews), 154

Colossians
2: 8 (warning against philosophy), 152

1 Thessalonians
5: 17 (pray continually), 18

1 Timothy
1: 14–15 (grace abounding to the chief of sinners), 31, 248 n.2

2 Timothy
1: 13 (hold fast the form), 256 n.37
3: 15 (knowing Scriptures from childhood), 125

Hebrews
as source for *Paradise Regained,* 148, 266 n.3
4: 15 (Jesus in all points tempted), 149, 155, 267 n.17
6: 4–6 (impossible to renew), 12, 248 n.45
10: 26–29 (apostasy), 248 n.45
chap. 11 as source for *Pilgrim's Progress, Paradise Lost,* 164, 231, 269 n.31, 277 n.63
11: 1 (faith and things not seen), 231
11: 32 (Samson as hero of faith), 164–65, 167
11: 39–40 (good reports through faith), 165
12: 2 (Jesus as author of faith), 231
12: 6–7 (temptations as chastening), 155
12: 16–17 (case of Esau), xi, xiii, 25, 32, 33, 105, 230, 241 n.4

James
2: 21 (justification by works), 77

2 Peter
1: 5–8 (add to your faith), 36
1: 10 (make your calling sure), 12, 36, 154
1: 9–11 (advice for perseverance), 35

Revelation
as source for *Paradise Regained,* 148, 266 n.3
structural affinities with *Samson Agonistes,* 269 n.29
11: 3 (two witnesses), 17
22: 21 (end of Christian Bible), 231–32

General Index

Aarsleff, Hans, "Leibniz on Locke on Language," 274 n.32
Abel, 165, 231
Abraham, 77, 151, 231
Accedence, 40
Adamson, J. H., *Bright Essence*, 249 n.9
Addison, Joseph, *Spectator*, 208, 275 n.41
adiaphora ("things indifferent"), 72, 81, 255 n.28
Agricola, Rudolph. *See* Rudolph Agricola
Ainsworth, Henry, *Annotations upon the Book of Psalms*, 274 n.37
Aitken, David J., "Milton's Use of 'Stand,'" 260 n.27
Ajax, 97
Alter, Robert, *The Art of Biblical Narrative*, 268 n.28
Amana, Sixtinus, 275 n.48
Ambrose, St., 5–6; "The Prayer of Job and David," 277 n.60
Ames, William, 9, 21; *Medvlla Theologica*, 257–58 n.48; *Svbstance of Christian Religion*, 10, 244 n.14
Amos, 75
analogia entis ("analogy of being"), 80–81
analogia fidei. *See* analogy of faith
analogia scripturæ, 81
analogies, 1, 70, 77, 80, 174
analogy of Evangelick doctrine, 64, 70, 71
analogy of faith, 70, 71–76, 252 n.4, 257 nn.41–42; defined, 7, 56, 71–72, 78, 79–81, 256 n.37; as an interpretive criterion, xv, 54, 76–83, 119, 129, 130, 184, 187, 254 n.15, 256 n.34, 257 nn. 38, 43; Milton's redefinition of, 57–58, 76, 84–86; reinterpreted by Karl Barth, 256 n.35. *See also* Rom. 12: 6 in Index of Biblical Places
analogy of received doctrine, 79
Andrew (brother of Simon), 135
Andrewes, Lancelot, *A Pattern of Catechisticall Doctrine*, 115, 261 n.40

Animadversions, 43, 52
Anna (mother of Mary), 129
Annotations Upon the Holy Bible. Being a Continuation of Mr. Pool's Work, 250 n.27, 254 n.18, 265 n.32, 270 n.36, 270–71 n.44, 275 n.46, 276 n.53
Anthony, St., 4–7
Apologeticall Narration, The, 82
Apology Against a Pamphlet, An, 30, 49, 52
Areopagitica, 43, 48, 64, 84, 85, 120, 147, 160, 184, 185–86, 188–89, 217–19, 271 n.3
Aristotle, 80
Arius, 255 n.32
Arminianism, 21, 35
Armitage, Frederick, *A History of the Collects*, 264 n.21
Arthur (King), 236–37
à Schurman, Anna Maria, *The Learned Maid*, 125–26, 263 n.11
Athanasius, Letter XLIX, 50, 51, 251 n.33
Atkinson, Clarissa W., *The Oldest Vocation*, 263 n.12
Attaway, Mrs., 73, 255 n.29
Aubrey, John, "Minutes of the Life of Mr John Milton," 251 n.31; *Remaines of Gentilisme and Judaisme*, 247 n.40
auditing motif, 92, 110–17
Augustine, 3–7, 10, 13, 27, 54, 69, 70–71, 72, 78, 82, 94, 210, 247 n.38; *Confessions*, 3–7, 21, 31, 243 n.6, 247 n.37, 255 n.25; *De Doctrina Christiana*, 66–67, 77, 254 n.19, 256 n.36, 271 n.1; *De utilitate credendi*, 257 n.43; *Enarrationes in Psalmos*, 275 n.43; Sermon LXXXVII, 50, 51, 251 n.33; *The Spirit and Letter*, 3

Bacon, Francis, 199, 201
Barker, Arthur, *Milton and the Puritan Dilemma*, xiv, 242 n.13, 249 n.8, 253 n.6, 254 n.13, 255 n.31
Barth, Karl, 256 nn.34–35

General Index

Bauman, Michael, *Scripture Index to . . . De doctrina christiana*, 252 n.4
Baxter, Richard, 6; *Reliquiæ Baxterianæ*, 4, 123, 243 n.8, 262 n.5
Bayly, Lewis, *The Practise of Pietie*, 27, 246 n.23
Bede (pseudo-), 51, 251 n.34
Beilin, Elaine V., *Redeeming Eve*, 263 n.11
Bellarmine, Robert Cardinal, 74
Bennett, Joan S., *Reviving Liberty*, 255 nn. 22, 31
Bereans, 43, 60, 82–90, 133. *See also* Acts 17: 11 in Index of Biblical Places
Berkowitz, M. S. "Thomas Young's 'Hopes Encouragement,'" 260 n.28
Bernard, Richard, 272 n.8
Berry, Boyd M., *Process of Speech*, 276 n.58
Beza, Theodore, 10
Biblia Polyglotta (1653–57), xv
bibliomancy, 21–22
Bickerman, Elias J., *The Jews in the Greek Age*, 267 n.13
Blair, Robert, *Life*, 11–12, 245 n.18
Bloom, Harold, *The Anxiety of Influence*, 252 n.1, 274 n.30
Boesky, Amy, "On Sunspots: Galileo, Milton, and *Paradise Lost*," 200, 274 n.31
Book of Common Prayer, The, 264 n.21
Book of Nature, 186–87, 190–93, 197, 201, 205, 217, 237, 275 n.48
Booth, Stephen, ed., *Shakespeare's Sonnets*, 110, 261 nn.33–34
Booty, John E., 244 n.16
Botticelli, *Madonna of the Magnificat*, 262 n.8
Boys, John, *An Exposition of Al the Principal Scriptvres*, 129, 130, 263 n.14; *An Exposition of the Festivall Epistles and Gospels. . . . the 2d Part*, 262 n.9; *An Exposition of the Dominical Epistles and Gospels . . . Springpart*, 244 n.12, 263 n.16; *An Exposition of the Dominical Epistles and Gospels . . . Winterpart*, 257 n.41, 264 n.18; *An Exposition of the Proper Psalmes*, 275 nn.47–48
Brettergh, Mrs. Katherine, 14
Bridge, William, *Scripture-Light a Most Sure Light*, 17, 247 n.32, 246–47 nn. 40, 42, 257 n.38
Briggs, Charles Augustus, *Biblical Study*, 256 n.34
Brinkley, Stephen, 243 n.7

Brown, Raymond E., *The Birth of the Messiah*, 261 n.36; ed., *Mary in the New Testament*, 264 nn.23–24
Browne, Sir Thomas, *Religio Medici*, 191, 199, 202, 213, 272 n.14
Brutus, 236–37
Budick, Sanford, *The Dividing Muse*, 264 n.26, 266 n.3
Bunny, Edmund, 4; Bunny's *Resolution*, 4–7; *Book of Christian exercise*, 243 n.4, 244 nn. 9, 11
Bunyan, John, x–xi, xiii, 13, 25–28, 34, 41; *A Few Sighs from Hell*, 22, 246 n.22; *Grace Abounding*, x–xi, xxi, 20–21, 25, 27, 29–31, 100, 104–5, 123, 154–55, 158, 230–33, 241 n.4, 246 n.21, 248 n.45, 249 n.4; *The Life and Death of Mr. Badman*, 23, 247 n.42; *Miscellaneous Works*, 247 nn. 34–35, 41; *Pilgrim's Progress*, xxii, 1, 13, 23, 25–27, 100, 102, 112, 124, 164, 218, 269 n.31, 277 n.63
Burden, Dennis, *The Logical Epic*, 277 nn. 64, 68
Burton, Robert, *Anatomy of Melancholy*, 18–20, 22, 23, 244 n.16, 247 nn. 33, 35, 248 n.45
Bush, Douglas, *John Milton*, 248 n.1; *The Renaissance and English Humanism*, 151, 266 n.7

C., E. (spiritual autobiographer), 13, 246 n.22
Cable, Lana, "Coupling Logic," 254 n.17
Caesarius of Arles, Sermon 230, 50, 251 n.32
Cain, 24, 231, 232
Caldwell, Patricia, *The Puritan Conversion Narrative*, 244 n.14
Calvin, John, ix, 8, 218, 234, 248 n.45, 256 n.35, 259 n.18; commentary on Psalm 19, 203, 205, 211–16; *Commentaries . . . vpon the Acts*, 250 nn. 23, 25; *Commentaries on . . . Genesis*, 276 n.52; *Harmonie Vpon the Three Euangelistes, A*, 263 n.13, 264 n.23; *Institutes*, 8–9, 12, 24, 43–44, 105–6, 174–75, 215, 230, 260 n.27, 276 n.52, 277 n.62; *The Psalmes of David*, 275 n.47, 275–76 n.49, 276 nn. 51, 53
Capel, Richard, *Tentations*, 158–59, 268 n.22
Carey, John, 42, 56, 86–87, 120, 264 n.18
Carlton, Peter, "Bunyan: Language, Convention, Authority," 20–21, 247 n.36

Caryl, Joseph, 75; *An Exposition . . . Vpon . . . Iob*, 75–76, 255 n.33
casuistry, 92, 249 n.11, 253 n.10, 258 n.3
Cave, Terence, *The Cornucopian Text*, 220, 258 n.50, 271 n.1, 276 n.55
Cawdray, Robert, *A Treasvrie or Store-hovse*, 137, 265 n.28
Cawdry, Robert, *A Godly [sic] Form of Hovseholde Gouernment*, 125, 262–63 n.10
Chambers, A. B., "The Double Time Scheme in *Paradise Regained*," 270 n.37
Chambers, Elizabeth, 13, 246 n.22
Charles I (King), 22, 247 n.39
Christopher, Georgia B., *Milton and the Science of the Saints*, 241 n.3, 243 n.1, 246 n.29, 265–66 n.2, 269 n.32; "The Verbal Gate to Paradise," xi, 229–30, 241 n.6, 277 n.61
Christ's College, Cambridge, 9, 16
Chrysostom, John. *See* John Chrysostom
Cicero, 160
Clark, Ira, "*Paradise Regained* and the Gospel According to John," 266 n.3
Clement of Alexandria, 82; *Miscellanies*, 50, 251 n.32
Cohen, Charles Lloyd, *God's Caress*, xii, 241 n.8, 247 nn. 39, 42, 259 n.12, 260 n.21, 261 n.31; "The Saints Zealous in Love and Labor," 259 n.12, 261 n.32
Cohen, Jeremy, "Be Fertile and Increase," 271 n.2
Colasterion, 45–47, 65, 75
Coleridge, Samuel Taylor, *Unpublished Letters*, 98, 259 n.14
collation. *See* conference of places
Columbus, Christopher, 275 n.43
Commonplace Book (Milton's), 88, 91
comparing places. *See* conference of places
conference of places, 15, 75, 77, 129, 164, 171, 264 n.23; criticized, 75–76, 255 n.33, 258 n.49; enlisted by Milton, 37–38, 47, 55, 64, 70, 71, 86–87, 121–22, 128–38, 148, 159, 177, 182, 184, 204, 227–28, 238, 254 n.15; used by Arius, 255 n.32
Conklin, George Newton, *Biblical Criticism and Heresy*, 255 nn. 21, 26
contrapasso, 36
conversion narratives, x, xii, 3, 9–10, 31–32, 115, 154, 229, 244 n.14
Cotton, Charles, 39, 250 n.16
Courcelle, Pierre, "Source . . . du 'Tolle, lege,'" 244 n.10

Crane, Mary Thomas, *Framing Authority*, 55–56, 252 n.3, 258 n.50, 264 n.27
Crashaw, Richard, 191
Creeds of Christendom, The, 257 n.39
Critici sacri (or *Criticorum Sacrorum*), xv, 254 n.18, 257 n.41, 275 n.48
Curtius, E. R., *European Literature and the Latin Middle Ages*, 190–91, 272 n.13
Cyriak, this three years day these eys, 101

Dalila, 124, 145, 172, 178–81
Dante, 36
Darbishire, Helen, *The Early Lives of Milton*, 249 n.14
Darnton, Robert, "Toward a History of Reading," xi, 241 n.5
David, 155; as putative author of psalms, 19, 165, 211, 212, 214
Davis, J. C., *Fear, Myth, and History*, 245–46 n.21
Deborah, 128
débordement, 198
De Doctrina Christiana (Milton's), 47, 53, 63, 66, 76, 136, 152, 191, 253 n.12, 264 n.18, 276 n.57; citation of Psalm 19, 212; dates of composition, 91, 252 n.2; its self-presentation, 32, 48, 54, 73, 84–90, 130, 137, 254 n.15, 257–58 n.48; on Adam's naming of the animals, 224; on apostacy, 248 n.45; on assurance, 10, 35; on criteria for interpretation, 56, 118–21, 184, 256 n.34; on divorce, 74, 254 n.18; on martyrdom, 176; on predestination, 35–36, 93–94, 171; on saving faith, 107–8, 277 n.64; on temporary faith, 94; revisions in the ms., 57
Defensio Secunda, xiv, 31, 32, 41, 248–49 n.3
de Grazia, Margreta, "The Secularization of Language in the Seventeenth Century," 274 n.31
Delany, Paul, *British Autobiography in the Seventeenth Century*, 243 n.3
de Man, Paul, "The Return to Philology," 243 n.2
Dent, Arthur, *The Plaine Mans Path-way*, 27
Derrida, Jacques, 187, 190, 257 n.47; *Dissemination*, 186, 272 nn. 4, 12; "Living On: Border Lines," 198, 273 n.26
Descartes, René, 201
Diodati, Charles, 42

Diodati, John, *Pious and Learned Annotations,* 264 n.20, 270 nn. 36, 40, 270–71 n.44
disclaiming locutions, 20–21, 123
divination, 21–22, 247 nn.38–40
divorce, xiv, 55, 57, 59–76, 253 n.11, 254 nn.15–18
Doctrine and Discipline of Divorce, The, xiv, 45, 46, 47, 58, 59–76, 181, 183–84, 195, 253–54 nn.10–12; 2d edition, 66, 253–54 n.12; title pages, 73–76
Docwra, Anne, *An Epistle of Love,* 83, 257 n.46
Donne, John, 39, 191; *Sermons,* 30–31, 34, 78–79, 102, 104, 248 n.2, 257 n.38, 260 n.22
Drake, Mrs. Joan, 22, 247 n.40
Dryden, John, 186; preface to *Religio Laici,* 208, 275 n.41

Easthope, Antony, "Towards the autonomous subject in poetry," 259 n.15, 261 n.42
Edwards, Karen, "Reading the Book of the World," 199, 203, 272–73 n.15, 273 n.28, 274 n.33
Edwards, Thomas, *Antapologia,* 257 n.44; *The Third Part of Gangraena,* 82, 255 n.29
Elegia prima, 42
Elegia quinta, 42
Elegia tertia, 42
Elizabeth (cousin of Mary), 138, 140
Elliott, Emory, "Milton's Biblical Style in *Paradise Regained,*" 265 n.2, 266 n.3
Elyot, Thomas, *Dictionary,* 250 n.18
Enoch, 231
Entzminger, Robert L., *Divine Word: Milton and the Redemption of Language,* 241 n.3
Epicureanism, 152, 217
Erasmus, 72, 150, 266 n.6; *Paraphrase . . . upon the New Testament,* 250 n.22
Esau, xi, 25, 32, 33, 105, 230–31
Esay. *See* Isaiah
Eusebius, *Demonstration of the Gospel,* 267 n.11
"experimental" divinity, 12, 61, 227, 230, 246 n.29; as represented in *Paradise Lost,* 233
"experimental" knowledge, ix, 15–24, 36, 87, 92, 210–11, 246 nn. 27, 29; contrasted with "historical" knowledge, 16
"experimental" reading. *See* introspective reading

Faith of One God, The, 257 n.45
Fallon, Stephen M., *Milton Among the Philosophers,* 272–73 n.15
Farrar, Frederic W., *History of Interpretation,* 256 n.34
Fellowes, Robert, 41, 248–49 n.3
Fenner, Dudley, *The Artes of Logike and Rhetorike,* 56
Ferry, Anne, xi, 4; *The Art of Naming,* 193–95, 264 n.27, 273 nn. 19, 22; *The "Inward" Language,* 110, 243 nn.5–6, 260 n.20, 261 nn.33–34, 264 n.21; *Milton and the Miltonic Dryden,* 268–69 n.28; *Milton's Epic Voice,* 273 n.27
Fish, Stanley, 144–45, 147–48, 162–63; "Question and Answer in *Samson Agonistes,*" 268 n.26; "Reason in *The Reason of Church Government,*" 253 n.8; "Re-Covering Meaning: Intention and Interpretation in Milton's *Doctrine and Discipline of Divorce,*" xv, 242 n.13; "Spectacle and Evidence in *Samson Agonistes,*" 265 n.33, 265 n.1; *Surprised by Sin,* 188, 208, 218–19, 272 n.8, 275 n.40, 276–77 n.59; "Transmuting the Lump: *Paradise Lost,*" 227, 276–77 n.59; "Unger and Milton," 253–54 n.12; "Wanting a Supplement: The Question of Interpretation in Milton's Early Prose," xv, 242–43 n.13, 255 n.23, 257 n.47
Fiske, Dixon, "Milton in the Middle of Life," 249 n.7
Fitzmeyer, Joseph A., *Anchor Bible* commentary on Luke, 264 n.23
Fix, Stephen, "Johnson and the 'Duty' of Reading," 272 n.11
Flannagan, Roy, 273–74 n.29
Fletcher, Giles, *Christs Victorie, and Triumph,* 262 n.7
Forsyth, Neil, "Having Done All to Stand," 267 n.16
Foucault, Michel, xvii; *The Order of Things,* 189–93, 196, 205, 252 n.3, 273 n.16
framing, 55–56, 85, 162
Friedman, Donald, "Galileo and the Art of Seeing," 200, 274 n.31

Gabriel, 125, 131–32, 155, 195, 262 n.9
Galileo, 200, 234, 273–74 n.29; *The Assayer,* 200–201, 274 n.31; *Letters on Sunspots,* 200

Gallagher, Philip J., *Milton, the Bible, and Misogyny*, 242 n.10, 272 n.5
Gardner, John, introducing Jane Turner's *Choice Experiences*, 94, 258 n.7
Gataker, Thomas, *De Novi Instrumenti Stylo Dissertatio*, 71, 255 n.26
gathering, xiv–xv, 55–56, 72, 84–85, 130, 162, 182, 184
Geneva Bible, xxi, 37, 40, 43–44, 81, 143–44, 151, 166, 211, 242 n.11, 250 n.23, 275 n.45, 276 n.51
Gilbert, Allan H., 273–74 n.29
Goldberg, Jonathan, "Dating Milton," 249 n.6, 258 n.1, 267 n.9; *Voice/Terminal/Echo*, 261 n.41
Goodwin, John, *The Divine Authority of Scripture*, 75, 255 n.31
Gossman, Ann, "Milton's First Sonnet on His Blindness," 260 n.23
Graef, Hilda, *Mary: A History*, 262 n.6
Graham, E. P., "Divination," 247 n.39
Greenblatt, Stephen, xi
Greene, Robert A., "Whichcote, Wilkins, 'Ingenuity,'" 43–44, 250 nn. 21, 24
Greene, Roland, 259 n.18
Gregory the Great, *Forty Gospel Homilies*, 51–52, 252 n.37
Grislis, Egil, "The Hermeneutical Problem in Richard Hooker," 256 n.36
Grose, Christopher, "A Revision in Milton's Letter to a Friend," 49, 251 nn. 30, 35
Grossman, Marshall, *"Authors to Themselves,"* xi–xii, 32, 194, 229–30, 241 n.7, 249 n.5, 268 n.21, 273 nn. 18, 21; 277 n.61; "Writing the Inside Out: Shakespeare, Milton, and the Supplement of Publication," 268 n.28, 269 n.30
Grotius, Hugo, *Annotationes*, 257 n.41; *His Most Choice Discourses*, 94, 258 n.7
Guillory, John, "The Father's House," 145, 167, 169–70, 249 n.12, 265 n.34, 269 n.33, 270 n.35, 271 n.47; *Poetic Authority*, 273 n.20
Guyon, 219

Hales, John, "Abvses of obscure and difficult places," 24, 234–35, 248 n.46
Halkett, John, *Milton and the Idea of Matrimony*, 254 n.16
Hall, David D., *Worlds of Wonder . . . Popular Religious Belief in Early New England*, 242 n.9, 247 n.39, 248 n.44

Hall, Joseph, 52
Haller, William, *The Rise of Puritanism*, 29–32, 50, 248 n.1
Hammond, Henry, 175, 177; *A Paraphrase and Annotations Upon . . . the New Testament*, 79, 254 n.18, 257 n.39, 265 n.32, 270 n.41, 271 n.45
Hannah, 128, 138
Harapha, 167, 173, 178
Harris, Neil, 273–74 n.29
harrowing of hell, 235
Haskin, Dayton, "Bunyan's Scriptural Acts," 241 n.4; "Milton's Strange Pantheon: The Apparent Tritheism of De Doctrina Christiana," 262 n.2; "*Samson Agonistes* on the Stage," 265 n.31; "Tracing a Genealogy of 'Talent,'" 243 n.15
Hebraisms, in Greek Scripture, 68–71
Hendrix, Scott H., *Ecclesia in Via*, 275 n.43
Henry, Mathew, *Exposition of the Old and New Testament*, 255 n.31
Heraclitus, 152
Herbert, George, 14, 39, 111, 191, 246 nn.24–25; "The Bunch of Grapes," 18, 246 n.24; "The Collar," 107; *The Country Parson*, 15, 38, 249 n.13; "The Holdfaste," 116, 261 n.42; "The H. Scriptures," 14–15, 246 n.24; "Jordan," 107, 218; *The Temple*, 100, 218; "A Wreath," 218, 276 n.54
Hercules, 47, 48, 84
Herrick, Robert, *Poetical Works*, 95–96, 259 n.10
Herz, Judith Scherer, "Dante, Milton, and the Galileo Question," 200, 274 n.30
Heywood, Oliver, *Autobiographies, Diaries*, 125, 263 n.11
Hieron, John, *The Way to Salvation*, 248 n.47
Hieron, Samuel, *The Triall of Adoption*, 244 n.16
Hill, Christopher, *The Experience of Defeat*, 99, 245 n.21, 259 n.16; *Milton and the English Revolution*, 241 n.5, 254 n.17, 255 n.29, 258 n.4; "*Samson Agonistes* Again," 268 n.27; *The World Turned Upside Down*, 245 n.21
Hill, John Spencer, *John Milton Poet, Priest and Prophet*, 248 n.1
Hobbes, R. Gerald, "The Interpretation of the Psalms in the Sixteenth Century," 275 n.42
Holland, John, 14

Hollander, John, *The Figure of Echo*, 205, 274 n.36
Homer, 21; *Iliad*, 97, 259 n.13
Hooker, Richard, 39; "A Learned . . . Sermon of the Certaintie and Perpetuitie of Faith," 244 n.16, 251 n.29
How soon hath time, xvi, 30, 36, 68, 92, 110–15, 249 n.11, 258 n.2, 261 n.35
Hughes, Philip Edgcumbe, *Paul's Second Epistle to the Corinthians*, 268 n.19
Hugh of St. Victor, 51, 251 n.34
Huguelet, Theodore, "The Rule of Charity in Milton's Divorce Tracts," 72–73, 255 n.28
Hunter, William B., *Bright Essence*, 249 n.9; "The Provenance of the *Christian Doctrine*," 252 n.2
Huntley, John F., "The Ecology and Anatomy of Criticism: Milton's Sonnet 19," 249 n.7
Hus, John, 72
Hyman, Lawrence W., *The Quarrel Within*, 269 n.33

Ibn Ezra, 210, 275 n.43
ingenium, 41–42, 53
ingenuity, 42–44, 59, 73
introspective reading, ix, 8, 13–24, 210–11
Isaac, 113
Isaiah (Esay), 75, 262 n.9. *See also* Index of Biblical Places
Italian sonnets (Milton's), 111

Jackson, Thomas, *Jvstifying Faith*, 250–51 n.29; *Third Booke of Commentaries*, 44, 250 n.24
Jacob, 94, 139
Jaeger, Werner, *Early Christianity and Greek Paideia*, 267 n.10
Jameson, Mrs. Anna, *Legends of the Madonna*, 262 n.8
Jenny, William, 73, 255 n.29
Jeremiah, 172
Jessey, Henry, *A Storehouse of Provision*, 102, 137, 260 n.21, 265 n.28
Joachim (father of Mary), 129
Job, 31, 75–76, 114, 151
John Chrysostom, *Homilies on . . . Matthew*, 51, 251 n.35; *On the Incomprehensible Nature of God*, 51, 251 n.35
John the Baptist, 113

Johnson, Samuel, 96–98, 186, 189; *Dictionary*, 96–97, 219, 259 n.11, 272 n.10; *Lives of the Poets*, 272 n.11; "On the Death of Dr. Robert Levet," 96, 259 n.11
Jonas, 155
Jonson, Ben, 95–96
Joseph (husband of Mary), 125, 128
Josephus, *Antiquities*, 113, 125, 261 n.36
Judas, 24
Judgement of Martin Bucer, 60, 65, 69

K., M. (autobiographer), 104–5, 169
Kahn, Victoria, "Allegory and the Sublime in *Paradise Lost*," 188, 272 n.9
kairos, 137, 173, 265 n.30, 270 n.37
Kaufmann, U. Milo, *The Pilgrim's Progress and Traditions in Puritan Meditation*, 256 n.34
Kelley, Maurice, Introduction to Milton's *Christian Doctrine*, 252 nn.2, 4
Kelsall, Malcolm, "The Historicity of *Paradise Regained*," 266–67 n.8
Kendall, R. T., *Calvin and English Calvinism*, 245 n.17, 277 n.63
Kendrick, Christopher, *Milton: A Study in Ideology and Form*, 271 n.2
Kepler, Johannes, 201
Kermode, Frank, *The Art of Telling*, 266 nn.5–6, 267 n.17; *The Genesis of Secrecy*, 174–75, 270 n.38
Kerrigan, William, "The Irrational Coherence of *Samson Agonistes*," 178, 271 nn.46–47; *The Sacred Complex*, 49, 114, 248 n.1, 261 n.39; "The Riddle of *Paradise Regained*," 263 n.15
Kierkegaard, Søren, 272 n.9
Kilby, Richard, *Burthen of a Loaden Conscience*, 25; *Hallelv-iah*, 25
Kirby, R. Kenneth, "Milton's Biblical Hermeneutics in *The Doctrine and Discipline of Divorce*," 254 n.15
Knott, John R., Jr., *The Sword of the Spirit*, 253 n.8, 254 n.15
Kristeva, Julia, "Stabat Mater," 263 n.12
Kroll, Richard W. F., *The Material Word*, 242 n.11; "*Mise-en-Page*, Biblical Criticism and Inference," 242 n.12
Krouse, F. Michael, *Milton's Samson and the Christian Tradition*, 269 n.29
Kurth, Burton O., *Milton and Christian Heroism*, 266 n.4

Lake, Edward, "Diary," 247 n.39
Lane, Tony, "The Quest for the Historical Calvin," 244 n.16
Latin Poems of John Milton, The, 250 n.20
Laud, William, 22
Lechner, Sister Joan Marie, *Renaissance Concepts of the Commonplaces,* 265 n.28
Legislative style, the, 208
Leigh, Edward, *Annotations upon All the New Testament,* 270 nn.36–37, 270–71 n.44
Leith, John H., "John Calvin—Theologian of the Bible," 256 n.35
Leonard, John, *Naming in Paradise,* 224, 273 nn. 17, 24–25; 276 nn. 56–57
"letter to an unknown friend" (by Milton, c. 1633), 30, 36–37, 40, 49, 110, 251 nn. 30, 35
Lever, Raphe, *The Arte of Reason,* 136, 265 n.28
Levet, Dr. Robert, 96
Lewalski, Barbara K., *Milton's Brief Epic,* 266 nn.3–4; "Forum: Milton's *Christian Doctrine,*" 252 n.2; "Milton, the Bible, and Human Experience," 242 n.10; *Paradise Lost and the Rhetoric of Literary Forms,* 267 n.9; *Protestant Poetics,* 246 n.31, 267 n.14, 269 nn. 29, 32; "Structure and the Symbolism of Vision in Michael's Prophecy," 277 nn.63–64
Lieb, Michael, *Poetics of the Holy,* 241 n.3; "Talents," 248 n.1, 259 n.19
"Life of Mr. John Milton, The" (anonymous), 38–40, 250 n.15
Lightfoot, John, xv; *The Harmony . . . of the Old Testament,* 114, 261 n.38
Loarte, Gaspar, 243 n.7
Locke, Anne, 100, 259 n.18
Locke, John, *An Essay Concerning Human Understanding,* 274 n.32; "Essay for the understanding of St. Paul's Epistles," xiii–xiv, 242 n.12; Letter to Molyneux, 201, 274 n.32
Logica (Milton), 40
Lombard, Peter, *Commentarium in Pslamos,* 275 n.43
Lowance, Mason I., Jr., *The Language of Canaan,* 246 n.31
Luckock, Herbert Mortimer, *Studies in . . . the Book of Common Prayer,* 263 n.14
Lupton, Lewis, *History of the Geneva Bible,* 242 n.11

Luther, Martin, ix, 1–3, 7–8, 10, 26–27, 41, 50, 54, 78, 115, 123, 154, 210, 229–30, 252 n.1, 267 n.14, 275 n.43; *Commentarie vpon Galathians,* 32, 157–60, 248 n.47, 268 nn. 20, 23–25; *Lectures on Romans,* 77; Preface to the Latin Writings, 1–3, 243 n.1
Lycidas, 29, 116, 153

MacCallum, Hugh, "Milton and Figurative Interpretation of the Bible," 252 n.5; "*Samson Agonistes*: The Deliverer as Judge," 119, 165–66, 261 n.1, 268 n.27, 268–69 n.28, 270 n.34
Madsen, William G., "From Shadowy Types to Truth" (article), 270 n.35; *From Shadowy Types to Truth* (book), 276 n.50
Magnificat, the, 124, 128, 134, 262 n.8, 263 nn.14–15
Mahomet, 13
Malvolio, 245 n.20
Mammon, in *Faerie Queene,* 219
Manoa (in *Samson Agonistes*), 118, 138–46, 165, 168–70, 178, 181
Manoah (in Judges), 138–39, 141
Manoah's wife. *See* mother of Samson
Mariolatry, Milton's attitude toward, 262 n.6
Marks, Herbert, "The Blotted Book," 273 n.23
Martz, Louis L., *Milton: Poet of Exile,* 208, 265 n.2, 275 nn. 39, 41; "*Paradise Regained*: The Meditative Combat," 265 n.2, 266 n.4
Marvell, Andrew, "The Coronet," 218, 276 n.54
Mary (mother of Jesus), 118, 121–38, 140, 142–46, 148, 238, 262 nn. 3, 6–9, 263 n.12, 264 nn. 19, 23, 265 n.32; as a prophet, 263 n.14; as *sedes sapientiae,* 262 n.8
Masque, A ("Comus"), 46
Matthew, Sir Tobie, 4, 243 n.6, 247 n.37
Mayer, John, *Treasvry of Ecclesiasticall Expositions,* 251–52 n.36
Mazzaro, Jerome, "Gaining Authority: John Milton at Sonnets," 258 n.2
Mazzeo, Joseph Anthony, "St. Augustine's Rhetoric of Silence," 244 n.10
McCarthy, William, "The Continuity of Milton's Sonnets," 258 n.2
McColley, Grant, "The Astronomy of *Paradise Lost,*" 273–74 n.29

McCready, Amy R., "Milton's casuistry," 253 n.10
McDonald, H. D., *Ideas of Revelation*, 255 nn.30–31
Mersen, Mary, *This Treatise Proving Three Worlds*, 94, 258 n.7
Michael, 184–85, 207–209, 227, 231–33, 235, 277 nn. 63, 66
Midgely, Mr., 13–14
Mikalachki, Jodi, "*Paradise Regained* and Puritan Social Theology," 265 n.35
Miller, J. Hillis, "How Deconstruction Works," 188, 272 n.8
Milton, John, senior, 44
Miriam, 128
Mondin, Battista, *The Principle of Analogy*, 256 n.34
Morgan, John, *Godly Learning*, 244 n.15, 246 n.26
Moses, 65, 75, 76, 113, 129, 155, 160, 165, 253 n.12
mother of Samson, 138–42, 168
Muggleton, Lodowick, 17
murmuring, 18, 102–3, 109, 135–36

Nardo, Anna K., *Milton's Sonnets and the Ideal Community*, 260 n.20
Naylor, James, 17
Newton, Thomas, ed., *Paradise Lost*, 274 n.36; *The Poetical Works of John Milton*, 91, 95–96, 98–103, 258–59 n.8
Nicolson, Marjorie, 273–74 n.29
Nimrod, 232
Noah, 231
Norris, Sylvester, *An Antidote or Soveraigne Remedie Against . . . Sectaries*, 250 n.22, 255 n.32
North, Helen, 41
Norwood, Richard, *Confessions*, 4–5, 9–10, 20, 243 n.8, 258 n.7
Nuttall, Geoffrey, 264 n.25; *The Holy Spirit in Puritan Faith and Experience*, 241 n.2, 246 n.29
Nye, Stephen, *Brief History of the Unitarians*, 257 n.45
Nyquist, Mary, "Reading the Fall," 242 n.10; "Textual Overlapping and Dalila's Harlot-lap," 242 n.10

O., A. (autobiographer), 23
Of Prelatical Episcopacy, 253 n.8, 262 n.6
Of Reformation, 58, 183
O'Keeffe, Timothy J., *Milton and the Pauline Tradition*, 266 n.6
O'Malley, John W., "Grammar and rhetoric in the *pietas* of Erasmus," 266 n.6
"openings," xi, xii
ordo salutis, 9–10, 35
Origen, 267 n.17; Homily XIII on Exodus, 50, 251 n.32
Osiris, 84
Owen, John, 256 n.34; *The Causes, Ways, and Means of Understanding the Mind of God*, 82, 257 n.44

Pagit, Eusebius, *The Historie of the Bible*, 118, 133, 264 n.22
Palmer, Herbert, 74, 255 n.30
parable of the talents. *See* Matt. 25: 14–30 in Index of Biblical Places
Paradise Lost, xi, xii, xvi, xvii, 36, 40, 57, 95, 98, 151, 158, 164, 182, 183–238, 271–72 n.3, 272 nn. 6–9, 11; 273 nn. 17–18, 20–21, 23–28; 273–74 n.29; 274 nn. 30–31, 33, 35–36; 275 nn.39–41; 276 nn. 50, 56–58; 276–77 n.59; 277 nn. 61, 63–66, 68; 277–78 n.69
Paradise Regained, xvi, xvii, 40, 57, 118–19, 121–38, 142–46, 147–62, 168, 173, 182, 183, 238, 258 n.4, 263 n.12, 265 nn. 30, 35, 265–66 n.2, 266 nn.3–4, 266–67 n.8, 267 nn. 8, 16; 270 n.37; temptation of learning, 148–53
Paraphrase on Psalm 114, 151
Parker, William Riley, *Milton: A Biography*, 95, 98–99, 248 n.1, 249 nn. 4, 14; 259 nn. 9, 15; 260 n.29, 268 n.19
Parsons, Edward S., "The Authorship of the Anonymous Life of Milton," 249 n.14
Parsons, Robert, *The First Booke of the Christian Exercise*, 4–7, 244 n.9
passive righteousness, doctrine of, 2, 21, 50
Patrides, C. A., *Bright Essence*, 249 n.9
Paul, St., 1–5, 12, 13, 18, 26–27, 43–44, 54, 72, 75, 82, 88, 148, 165, 177, 210; as an interpreter of Psalms, 275 n.42; as a model for Milton's Son of God, 153–62; conversion of, 267 n.14
Pearson, John, ed., *Criticorum Sacrorum*, 275 n.48
Pecheux, Mother M. Christopher, "Milton and Kairos," 270 n.37

Pelikan, Jaroslav, *The Emergence of the Catholic Tradition,* 267 n.13
Pemble, William, *Vindiciæ Gratiæ,* 258 n.49
Pennington, Isaac, "A Further Testimony to Truth," 105, 260 n.26
Perkins, William, 6–12, 19–20, 25, 35, 61, 245 n.20, 253 n.11; *The Arte of Prophecying,* 256 n.37; *A Case of Conscience,* 245 n.19; *The Combat betweene Christ and the Deuill,* 93, 154–56, 258 n.4, 267 nn. 15, 17; *A Golden Chain,* 9, 24; *A Reformed Catholike,* 129, 263 n.14, 264 n.17; *A Treatise of Callings,* 93, 166, 258 nn.5–6; *A Treatise of Conscience,* 61; *A Treatise Tending unto a Declaration,* 11, 244 n.16, 245 n.19; treatment of analogy of faith, 256 nn. 34, 37; *Works,* 244 n.12, 270 n.35
Phillips, Edward, "The Life of Mr. John Milton," 67, 255 n.20; *New World of Words,* 41, 128, 250 n.18; *Theatrum Poetarum,* 263 n.15
Phillips, John, 249 n.14
philology, 2, 67–71, 97–98, 243 n.2
places, x, xiii–xvii, 1–28, 104, 117, 146, 166, 181–82, 202, 227, 232, 247 n.40; "hard places," 251–52 n.36, 256 n.36; in *De Doctrina Christiana,* 89; variety of its senses, 245 n.20, 264 n.27. *See also* conference of places and Index of Biblical Places
Plato, 80, 150, 152; *Phaedrus,* 186
Poems of Mr. John Milton, 36, 47, 111
Polyglot Psalter, 275 n.43
Poole, Matthew, *Synopsis Criticorum,* 250 n.24, 254 n.18, 261 n.37
Pope, Elizabeth Marie, *Paradise Regained: The Tradition and the Poem,* 262 n.4, 266 n.3
portion (mental labor as Milton's), 47–49, 53
Powell, Mary, 31, 40, 55, 67, 253 n.9
Powell, Vavasor, 17, 246–47 n.32
Preston, John, *An Elegant and Lively Description,* 16, 44–45, 130, 246 n.29, 250 n.26; *The Nevv Covenant,* 264 n.18
prohibition, the, 187, 188–89, 228, 236, 238
Prolusion III, 250 n.19, 258 n.51
Prolusion VII, 216–17
prophesying, xii, 22, 71; Milton's definition, 263 n.14
Protestants and Protestantism, xii, 3, 119; doctrine, x, 21, 56, 78, 159–62; etymology, 88; hermeneutics, x, 2, 68, 71–83, 148, 256 n.34; poetics, ix–x; scholasticism, 48, 79, 256 n.34; spirituality, 4–7, 10–13, 24; tradition, 2, 82, 129–31, 154
protevangelium, 229–30
Psyche, 185, 188, 217
puritan autobiographies. *See* conversion narratives

Quakers, xi
Quarles, Francis, *Judgement and Mercie,* 99–101, 109, 113, 191, 259 n.17
Quilligan, Maureen, *Milton's Spenser,* 219–20, 273 n.20

R., D. (spiritual autobiographer), 13, 246 n.22
Rabelais, François, 34, 85
Radak, 207
Radzinowicz, Mary Ann, "How Milton read the Bible," 242 n.10; *Milton's Epics and the Book of Psalms,* 165, 204, 242 n.10, 266 n.3, 274 n.35; "Milton's Politics and Biblical Narrative," 270 n.34; "*Paradise Regained* as Hermeneutic Combat," 265 n.2; *Toward Samson Agonistes,* 204, 242 n.10, 255 n.27, 256 n.34, 260 n.20, 261 n.35, 269 n.29, 270 n.34, 274 n.35
Ramistic method, 72–73
Ranters, 245–46 n.21
Raphael, 184–86, 190, 194, 195, 197–99, 201–203, 208–209, 212, 213, 216, 219–22, 224–25, 229, 233–34
reading, discontinuities in Milton's reading, xv–xvi, 54–90; how conceived in *The Faerie Queene,* 193–94; how depicted in *Paradise Lost,* xvii, 192–204; popular habits, xi–xiii, 15; silent reading, 5–6. *See also entries for* introspective reading, typological symbolism and reading
Reason of Church Government, The, 40, 228, 236–37; allusion to parable of talents, 30, 33, 64, 171–72, 228; ideas about interpretation, xiv, 50, 52–54, 58–59, 236–37; ideas about personal accountability, 31–34, 36–47, 93, 107, 109; treatment of mental labor, 47–49, 53
Réau, Louis, *Iconographie de l'art chrétien,* 262 nn.8–9
Reeve, John, 17
regula fidei (Tertullian), 71, 80. *Cf.* analogy of faith

Reiter, Robert, 260–61 n.30; "On Biblical Typology and the Interpretation of Literature," 267 n.16
Revard, Stella P., "The Gospel of John and *Paradise Regained*," 266 n.3
Ricks, Christopher, *Milton's Grand Style*, 272 n.7
Roberts, Francis, *Clavis Bibliorum*, 13–14, 16, 246 nn. 23, 27
Rogers, John, of Dedham, *The Doctrine of Faith*, 245 n.17
Rogers, John, *Ohel or Beth-shemesh*, 246 n.22
Rosenblatt, Jason, "Milton's Chief Rabbi," xv, 243 n.14, 255 nn. 21, 26
Royal Society, the, 201
Rozett, Martha Tuck, *The Doctrine of Election and the Emergence of Elizabethan Tragedy*, 244 n.15
Rudolph Agricola, *De Inventione*, 258 n.50
Rule of Charity, The, 70, 71–76, 256 n.37
Rumrich, John Peter, "Uninventing Milton," xvi, 243 n.16, 276–77 n.59
Rushdy, Ashraf H. A., "Of *Paradise Regained*: The Interpretation of Career," 265–66 n.2
Ryken, Leland, ed., *Milton and Scriptural Tradition*, 242 n.10

Samson Agonistes, xvi, xvii, 40, 57, 102, 118–19, 122–24, 138–46, 147–48, 152, 162–82, 183, 238, 265 nn. 31, 33–34; 265 n.1, 268 nn.26–27, 268–69 n.28, 269 nn. 29, 31–33; 271 nn.46–48
Samson (in Judges), 113
Samuel, 75, 113
Samuel, Irene, "*Samson Agonistes* as Tragedy," 269 n.31
Sancer, James, 243 n.7
Sarah, 138
Saurat, Denis, *Milton, Man and Thinker*, 253 n.9
Schama, Simon, *The Embarrassment of Riches*, 246 n.31
Schiller, Gertrud, *Iconography of Christian Art*, 262 n.8
Schultz, Howard, *Milton and Forbidden Knowledge*, 249 n.10
Schwartz, Regina M., "Citation, Authority, and *De Doctrina Christiana*," 254 n.15, 262 n.2; "From Shadowy Types to Shadowy Types," 277 nn. 65–66, 68; *Remembering and Repeating*, 187, 242 n.10, 272 n.6, 274 n.35
Scot, Reginald, *The discoverie of witchcraft*, 21–22, 247 n.38
Sedgwick, Obadiah, *Anatomy of Secret Sins*, 210–11, 275 n.44
Selden, John, xv, 255 nn. 21, 26
Seneca, 151
Shakespeare, William, 110–17; *Hamlet*, 163, 268 n.28; *Sonnets*, 261 nn.33–34; Sonnet 15, 115–17, 261 n.41; *Twelfth Night*, 245 n.20
Shami, Jeanne M., "Donne on Discretion," 260 n.22
Shawcross, John T., 42; "Forum: Milton's *Christian Doctrine*," 252 n.2; "The Genres of *Paradise Regain'd* and *Samson Agonistes*," 269 n.29; "Irony as Tragic Effect," 269 n.31
Shawe, John, *Memoirs*, 16, 246 n.30
Sherlock, William, *The Protestant Resolution of Faith*, 83, 257 n.45
Shiel, James, *Greek Thought and the Rise of Christianity*, 267 n.11
Shullenberger, William, "Linguistic and Poetic Theory in Milton's *De Doctrina Christiana*," 84–85, 257–58 nn.48–49, 276 n.57
Sibbes, Richard, *The Brvised Reed*, 10, 244 n.14
Sidney, Mary, Countess of Pembroke, *Psalms*, 204, 274 n.34
Sidney, Sir Philip, *Apologie for Poetrie*, 22, 247 n.38; *Astrophil and Stella*, 107, 110–12, 115–16; *Psalms*, 204, 274 n.34
Simon (Peter, brother of Andrew), 135, 175
Sims, James H., ed., *Milton and Scriptural Tradition*, 242 n.10
Slights, Camille Wells, *The Casuistical Tradition*, 258 n.3, 271 n.48
Slights, William W. E., "Scriptural Annotation in the English Renaissance," 242 n.11
Skinner, Cyriak, 101, 249 n.14
Smith, Barbara Hernstein, *Contingencies of Value*, 266 n.2
Smith, Carolyn H., "The Virgin Mary in *Paradise Regained*," 262 n.7
Smith, Nigel, "*Areopagitica*: Voicing Contexts," 254 n.14; *Perfection Proclaimed: Language and Literature in English Radical Religion*, 241–42 n.9, 244 n.14
Socinianism. See Unitarianism

General Index   313

Socrates, 151, 152, 190
Solomon, 68
Sonnets (Milton's). *See* first lines for individual poems
sortes. *See* divination
Sparrow, John, *Visible Words*, 262 n.8
Spencer, John, *Things New and Old*, 265 n.29
Spenser, Edmund, *The Faerie Queene*, 193–95, 218–20, 225, 273 nn.19–20
Spira, Francis, *Relation of the Fearfvl Estate*, 23–24, 248 n.44
spiritual autobiographies. *See* conversion narratives
Spirituall Experiences of Sundry Beleevers, 246 n.22, 247 n.42, 260 n.24
Sprat, Thomas, *The History of the Royal-Society*, 274 n.32
Spufford, Margaret, "First steps in literacy," 263 n.11
Stanton, Kay, "From 'Jove' to 'Taskmaster': The Transformation from Pagan to Christian Deity in Milton's Sonnets," 261 n.35
Stavely, Keith W. F., *Puritan Legacies*, 198, 273 n.26; "Roger Williams: Bible Politics and Bible Art," 246 n.21; "Satan and Arminianism in *Paradise Lost*," 273 n.18
Steadman, John, *Milton and the Renaissance Hero*, 156, 268 n.18
Stein, Arnold, *Answerable Style*, 272 n.7; *Heroic Knowledge*, 266 n.4
Stendahl, Krister, *Paul Among Jews and Gentiles*, 267 n.14, 268 n.25
Stocker, Margarita, *Paradise Lost*, 241 n.3
Stoicism, 152
Stone, Lawrence, *The Family, Sex, and Marriage*, 262–63 n.10
storehouse, 15, 85, 130, 136–38, 142–46, 162, 182, 221, 245 n.20, 265 nn.28–29
Stranahan, Brainerd P., "Bunyan and the Epistle to the Hebrews," 269 n.31, 277 n.63
Strier, Richard, *Love Known*, 246 n.24
Stringer, Gary A., "Milton's 'Thorn in the Flesh,'" 249 n.4, 259 n.19
Stull, William L., "Sonnets Courtly and Christian," 261 n.35
Sumner, Charles, translator of *De Doctrina Christiana*, 86–87, 120, 253–54 nn.12–13, 264 n.18
Sundell, Roger H., "The Narrator as Interpreter in *Paradise Regained*," 265 n.2

Svendsen, Kester *Milton and Science*, 200, 272–73 n.15
Swaim, Kathleen M., *Before and After the Fall*, 271 n.3
Swanson, Donald, "Milton's Scholarly Jesus in *Paradise Regained*," 267 n.8
Swiss, Margo, "Crisis of Conscience: A Theological Context for Milton's 'How Soon Hath Time,'" 249 n.11
Synopsis Criticorum. *See* Poole, Matthew

talent, xvi, 30, 86, 91–92, 95, 116, 170, 259 n.19. *See also* Matt. 25: 14–30 in Index of Biblical Places
Tanner, John S., *Anxiety in Eden*, 271–72 n.3, 272 n.9
Tayler, Edward W., *Milton's Poetry*, 246 n.31
Taylor, Jeremy, *Dissuasive from Popery*, 79–82, 257 nn. 40, 43–44; *Ductor Dubitantium*, 104–5, 260 n.25
Taylor, John, the water poet, *All the Workes*, 259 n.8
temporary faith, doctrine of, 11–13, 19–20, 92–95, 108, 168, 181, 227, 230–31, 245 n.17
Tertullian, 71, 80, 82, 153
Tetrachordon, 43, 45–47, 65, 68, 70, 71, 184, 186, 224, 251 n.30, 253 nn. 7, 11
Thomas Aquinas, 72
Thomas, Keith, *Religion and the Decline of Magic*, 247 n.40
Tillyard, E. M. W., *Milton*, 150–51, 156, 266 n.7, 267 n.17
Tipson, Baird, "A Dark Side of Seventeenth-Century English Protestantism," 24, 248 n.45
tolle, lege (Augustine's *Confessions*), 5, 13, 244 n.10
Torah, 206–207, 274 n.37
Trapp, John, *Theologia Theologiae*, 263 n.15
Treatise of Civil Power, A, 43, 45, 87
Trent, Council of, 76, 249 n.10
Trinity ms., 110
Triumphs of Female Wit, 250 n.21
Turner, James Grantham, *One Flesh: Paradisal Marriage and Sexual Relations in the Age of Milton*, 242 n.10, 253 nn. 9, 11
Turner, Jane, *Choice Experiences*, 94, 244 n.15, 258 n.7
Turner, William, *A Compleat History of the Most Remarkable Providences*, 247 n.40

Tyndale, William, xvi, 8, 230; prologue to the *Five Books of Moses*, ix, 241 nn. 1, 6; 244 n.13
typological symbolism and reading, 17, 155–56, 162–65, 168, 177–78, 182

Ulreich, John C., Jr., "*Samson Agonistes* as Parable," 269 n.33; "The Tragedy of Dalila," 271 n.49
Underwood, Abraham, *The Protestants Plea for the Socinian*, 257 n.45
Unitarianism, 82–83, 88, 257 n.45

van Unnik, W. C., "Die rechte Bedeutung des Wortes treffen, Lukas 2, 19," 264 n.24
Variorum Commentary on the Poems of John Milton, A, 107, 260 n.29
Vaughan, Henry, 191; *Works*, 259 n.8
Venn, Anne, *A Wise Virgins Lamp*, 16, 244 n.15, 246 n.30
Verkamp, Bernard J., *The Indifferent Mean: Adiaphorism in the English Reformation*, 255 n.28
Vida, Marcus Hieronymus, *Christiad*, 262 n.7
Virgil, 21
Vlober, Maurice, *La Vie de Marie*, 262 n.8

Wailes, Stephen L., *Medieval Allegories of Jesus' Parables*, 251 n.36
Waldock, A. J. A., *Paradise Lost and Its Critics*, 272 n.7
Walker, Julia M., "Milton and Galileo," 273–74 n.29
Waller, William, 22
Walsh, J. J., "Jesus Christ," 267 n.12
Walton, Izaak, *Lives*, 39, 250 n.16
Watkins, Owen, *The Puritan Experience*, xii, 241 n.8, 244 n.14
Watts, William, "To the devout Reader," 4, 243 n.6
weakness, as a Pauline theme, 156–62; how understood by Luther, 157–59; redefined by Milton, 159–62
Weber, Max, 145, 169
Westminster Confession, The, 79

Westminster Divines, *Annotations upon All the Books of the Old and New Testament*, 270 n.36, 270 nn.38–39, 270–71 n.44
When I consider how my light is spent, viii, ix, xvi, 30, 40, 41, 94–95, 118, 248 n.1, 249 n.4, 249 n.7, 258 n.2, 259 nn. 15, 19; 260 n.28, 261 n.41; date, 91–92, 258 n.1
Whitaker, William, *A Disputation on Holy Scripture*, 74, 77–78, 82, 252 n.4, 256 nn.36–37, 263–64 n.16
Whiting, George W., "Milton's First Sonnet on His Blindness," 260 n.23
Wilcox, Joel F., "'Spending the Light': Milton and Homer's Light of Hope," 259 n.13
Wilson, Thomas, *The Arte of Logique*, 136; *The Rule of Reason*, 56, 264–65 n.28
Wither, George, *Abvses Stript, and Whipt*, 23, 247–48 n.43; *Hallelujah, or Britain's Second Remembrancer*, 259 n.8
Wittreich, Joseph A., *Feminist Milton*, 255 n.29; *Interpreting Samson Agonistes*, 242 n.10, 268 nn.27–28, 269 nn. 29, 31; 270 n.38, 271 n.48; *Visionary Poetics*, 269 n.29
Wollebius, Johannes, *Abridgment of Christian Divinitie*, 94, 256 n.34, 258 n.7; *Compendivm*, 256 n.34
Woodhouse, A. S. P., "Milton, Puritanism, and Liberty," 253–54 n.12
world-as-book topos, the, 186, 190–91, 199, 201, 203, 215–16; in *Paradise Lost*, 224–25, 234, 237, 276 n.50
Worthen, J. F., "On the Matter of the Text," 278 n.70
Wotton, Henry, 39
Wrede, Wilhelm, *The Messianic Secret*, 175–76, 270 n.42

Xenophon, 160

Young, Thomas, 260 n.28

Zwicky, Laurie, "Kairos in *Paradise Regained*," 265 n.30, 270 n.37
Zwingli, Ulrich, 10

This book has been set in Carter & Cone Galliard. Galliard was designed for Mergenthaler in 1978 by Matthew Carter. Galliard retains many of the features of a sixteenth-century typeface cut by Robert Granjon but has some modifications that give it a more contemporary look.

Printed on acid-free paper.

DATE DUE			